Employee Share S

Employee Share Schemes

Sixth Edition

Mark Ife LLB MJur
Partner, Herbert Smith Freehills LLP

Bloomsbury Professional

Bloomsbury Professional Ltd, Maxwelton House, 41–43 Boltro Road, Haywards Heath, West Sussex, RH16 1BJ

© Bloomsbury Professional Limited 2014

Bloomsbury Professional is an imprint of Bloomsbury Publishing Plc

A CIP Catalogue record for this book is available from the British Library.

ISBN 978 1 78043 231 1

Typeset by Phoenix Photosetting, Chatham, Kent
Printed and bound by CPI Group (UK) Ltd, Croydon, CR0 4YY

Preface

Employee Share Schemes is designed to offer practical guidance on the implementation and operation of the most common employees' share schemes which are offered by companies to their employees. It includes, in particular, guidance on the impact that events such as grants, exercises, takeovers, share capital variations and cessations of employment have on the operation of those schemes and is written, therefore, with the needs in mind of human resource executives, company secretaries and finance executives as well as consultants and other advisers on employees' share schemes.

This sixth edition includes all legislative changes through to the Finance Act 2014. It builds upon the previous editions authored by my former colleague, Colin Chamberlain, who was able to lend over 30 years' experience to the text.

I would like to thank our many clients who have provided the opportunity to work on their employees' share schemes and so develop, with their input, my understanding of the practical issues with which they deal on a day-to-day basis.

Thanks are also due to my very talented colleagues who have helped with their time and expertise in the preparation of this edition, and in particular to Bradley Richardson and Niall Crean for their assistance with updating the model plan rules.

Mark Ife
Herbert Smith Freehills LLP
Exchange House
Primrose Street
London EC2A 2EG
Tel: 020 7374 8000
Email: mark.ife@hsf.com

August 2014

Contents

Contents

Table of Cases

T

W

Table of Statutes

[*References are to paragraph number and appendices*]

Table of Statutory Instruments

[References are to paragraph number and appendices]

Table of EC and International Legislation

[References are to paragraph number and appendices]

Abbreviations and References

ABI	=	Association of British Insurers, the investment affairs division of which has been merged with the IMA
ABI Guidelines	=	The ABI Guidelines on employees' share schemes (as described in Chapter 3)
AIM	=	Alternative Investment Market
CA 2006	=	Companies Act 2006
CGT	=	Capital Gains Tax
CSOP	=	Company Share Option Plan, satisfying the conditions of ITEPA 2003, Sch 4
CTA 2009	=	Corporation Tax Act 2009
CTA 2010	=	Corporation Tax Act 2010
DTR	=	Disclosure and Transparency Rules
EBT	=	Employee Benefit Trust
EMI	=	Enterprise Management Incentive, satisfying the conditions of ITEPA 2003, Sch 5
ESSA 2002	=	Employee Share Schemes Act 2002
FA	=	Finance Act
FRS	=	Financial Reporting Standards
FSMA 2000	=	Financial Services and Markets Act 2000
HMRC	=	Her Majesty's Revenue and Customs
IASB	=	International Accounting Standards Board
ICTA 1988	=	Income and Corporation Taxes Act 1988
IFRS	=	International Financial Reporting Standards
IHTA 1984	=	Inheritance Tax Act 1984
ITA 2007	=	Income Tax Act 2007
ITEPA 2003	=	Income Tax (Earnings and Pensions) Act 2003
ITTOIA 2005	=	Income Tax (Trading and Other Income) Act 2005
Listing Rules (LR)	=	The Listing Rules published by the UKLA
LTIP	=	Long Term Incentive Plan (as described in Chapter 7)
Model Code	=	Model Code on Directors' Dealings in Securities contained in Chapter 9 of the Listing Rules
NAPF	=	National Association of Pension Funds
NASDAQ	=	National Association of Securities Dealers Automated Quotations
NICs	=	National Insurance Contributions
NISA	=	New Individual Savings Account
PDMR	=	Person Discharging Managerial Responsibilities
PSP	=	Performance Share Plan

Remuneration Committee	=	The committee of directors established by most listed companies comprising mostly non-executive directors which is authorised to consider directors' remuneration
RIS	=	Regulatory Information Service
s	=	Section
SAYE	=	Save As You Earn (as described in Chapter 12), satisfying the conditions of ITEPA 2003, Sch 3
Sch	=	Schedule
Share Incentive Plan	=	SIP (see SIP below)
SIP	=	Share Incentive Plan (as described in Chapters 8 to 11), satisfying the conditions of ITEPA 2003, Sch 2
SIPP	=	Self Invested Personal Pension Plan
STC	=	Simon's Tax Cases
TA 1988	=	Income and Corporation Taxes Act 1988
TCGA 1992	=	Taxation of Chargeable Gains Act 1992
TUPE	=	Transfer of Undertakings (Protection of Employment) Regulations (SI 2006/246)
UKLA	=	United Kingdom Listing Authority which at present is the Financial Conduct Authority

Chapter 1

Introduction

1.1   Significant amendments to the way in which employee share plans are now established and operate have been introduced under the 2013 and 2014 Finance Acts to reflect the outcome of the tax simplification project undertaken by the Office of Tax Simplification, which has reported both on 'approved' share plans, and also unapproved arrangements. One of the most significant changes for companies operating approved plans came into effect from 6 April 2014, after which date HMRC will no longer formally approve Share Incentive Plans (SIPs), Save-As-You-Earn (SAYE) option plans and Company Share Option Plans (CSOPs) before they can be operated. Instead, the tax beneficial status of such plans will, from 6 April 2014, depend on the company establishing and operating the plan 'self-certifying' compliance with the relevant legislation. Whether these changes will, in fact, simplify the operation of tax-advantaged plans is yet to be seen.

1.2   These recent changes, coupled with a long-awaited increase in the contribution limits under SIPs and SAYE option plans, have been the most significant since the introduction of the Income Tax (Earnings and Pensions) Act 2003 (ITEPA 2003), as amended almost immediately by the Finance Act 2003 (FA 2003), which rewrote the tax legislation relating to the acquisition of employee shares.

1.3   The Corporation Tax Act 2009 (CTA 2009) rewrote the provisions originally introduced in FA 2003, Sch 23 relating to the statutory corporation tax deduction which gives tax relief to employing companies in respect of employee share acquisitions. The original legislation was introduced to preclude a deduction for the cost of providing shares under any other arrangements, except Share Incentive Plans (SIPs), and so replaced the 'common law' tax symmetry arrangements. Further amendments have been made under FA 2014 to extend the availability of the statutory corporation tax deduction following a takeover of the relevant company and also to provide relief to companies who benefit from work undertaken by individuals employed overseas.

1.4   The CTA 2009 also includes the provisions relating to tax deductions for contributions into Employee Benefit Trusts (EBTs), which are restricted to those cases where the statutory corporation tax deduction is not available and the contributions can be directly linked to payments and transfers out of a trust which are subject to income tax and national insurance contributions. This, and the anti-avoidance provisions in ITEPA 2003, Pt 7, Chs 3A and 3B (which replaced the former dependent subsidiary legislation) were intended to deny tax relief to a number of tax avoidance remuneration arrangements which used EBTs. Notwithstanding these provisions, HMRC were concerned that EBTs were continuing to be used in connection with tax avoidance arrangements and, in 2011 introduced the wide-ranging 'disguised remuneration' legislation which now forms ITEPA 2003, Pt 7A. As a result of the legislation being widely drafted, it has significantly restricted the way in which EBTs may now be operated in connection with employee share plans.

1.5   Awards which give a right to acquire shares, including traditional 'share options', are taxable under the 'securities options' legislation in ITEPA 2003, Pt 7, Ch 5, whilst the legislation in relation to the taxation of 'restricted securities' can be found in ITEPA 2003, Pt 7, Ch 2, and, in particular, restricted securities which are subject to risk of forfeiture. These provisions also entitle the employee and employer to elect jointly to be taxed in full at the time of acquisition, irrespective of the restrictions which apply. Otherwise, income tax may apply when restrictions are lifted (including where the securities cease to be subject to risk of forfeiture), or are sold. FA 2014 introduces further measures to simplify the taxation on a 'roll-over' where restricted securities held by an employee are exchanged for other restricted securities.

1.6   HMRC continues to focus on the taxation of internationally mobile employees to ensure that the exchequer does not lose out on revenue, but that the employee is treated fairly and does not suffer an undue tax burden. FA 2014 includes a rewrite of the legislation relating to the taxation of employment-related securities and securities options granted to internationally mobile employees.

1.7   The tax-advantaged (previously, HMRC-approved) share schemes continue to be popular, and it is anticipated that both the number of employees participating in SIPs and SAYEs, and the level at which those employees participate, will grow following the introduction of the enhanced contribution limits. The Government continues to believe that productivity will be increased by encouraging employee participation, which is evidenced by their commitment to public sector 'mutualisations' and, in the private sector, through such increased participation in employee share plans. As interest rates remain low many employees have turned to equity ownership through their employers' share plans as an alternative savings structure, and this has contributed to the increased uptake of SAYE offers. Very few companies have ceased to operate share schemes, and deferred bonus arrangements into shares have become expected in both listed companies and in large financial institutions subject to various European Directives requiring equity deferral.

Chapter 2

Types of Scheme Available

INTRODUCTION

2.1   There are many types of employees' share schemes, ranging from those where the employee pays the full value for the shares to those where they receive free shares. In between these extremes are various arrangements under which payment is deferred in some way, for example, share option schemes and partly-paid share schemes. Partly-paid share schemes are not common because they involve an annual liability to income tax – on the unpaid part of the subscription price under the Income Tax (Earnings and Pensions) Act 2003 (ITEPA 2003), Pt 7, Ch 3C – even though the employee is not usually in a position to realise any shares in order to pay the tax.

2.2   It is possible to classify schemes as being 'discretionary' (generally speaking, adopted for senior executives and other key employees) or as 'all-employee' schemes. Discretionary schemes for senior executives and other key employees usually involve substantial numbers of shares and confer no tax advantages. Schemes for all employees usually involve smaller parcels of shares and, if structured to meet the legislative criteria, can confer tax advantages. There are, however, no set rules as to the types of arrangement which can be used on an all employee basis, and there are examples of companies introducing market value options or restricted share awards for all employees.

DISCRETIONARY SCHEMES

Share option schemes

2.3   For many years the most common type of share scheme was the discretionary share option scheme under which the company grants a right to buy shares at the market price at the date of grant, exercisable for a set period (usually between three and ten years) after the date of grant, provided the optionholder remains in employment (see Chapter 5). Former employees are normally allowed to buy the shares within a limited period of leaving employment, even if this is before the third anniversary of grant. There is usually also a right of exercise on a takeover of the company.

2.4   The optionholder, therefore, has a right to buy shares at a fixed price. If the shares increase in value, he will wish to exercise the option and realise the accrued gain. If the shares do not increase in value, he will not exercise the option, but he will not be out of pocket since the option will have been granted for nil, or only nominal, consideration. The incentive therefore, is to achieve the greatest possible increase in the share price by the date of exercise.

2.5   Discretionary share option schemes are usually established in two parts: a tax-advantaged part which satisfies the conditions under ITEPA 2003, Pt 7, Ch 8 and Sch 4 (and therefore attracts the income tax and National Insurance reliefs available on options over shares worth up to £30,000 for each participant) and a non-tax advantaged part (which provides for options to be granted in excess of this limit, and which will be subject to income tax and, generally, National Insurance contributions) – see Chapter 5. Any employer's Class I National Insurance contributions arising on option gains may be passed on to the employee (see **5.17–5.22** below).

2.6   Discretionary share options granted by a listed company to its directors and senior executives will invariably be subject to performance targets as a condition of exercise (see **5.97–5.106**). Discretionary share options granted by private companies often do not impose such targets.

2.7   For many years, discretionary share option schemes were usually operated using unissued shares. For various reasons, many public as well as private companies now choose to use existing shares which will normally be held by an Employee Benefit Trust (EBT) until transferred to the optionholder on exercise of the option (see **16.6** below).

Bridging and deferred finance arrangements

2.8   Where a large number of share options are to be exercised, employees will not usually have the financial resources to finance the exercise of their options without selling at least some of their shares. Employees may approach their bank to arrange bridging finance, but banks are often reluctant to make loans on competitive terms where they cannot obtain security over the shares, especially as option rights are usually non-transferable.

2.9   Many companies have, therefore, established arrangements under which the company's broker, or some other financial institution, will provide finance to enable optionholders to exercise their options out of the proceeds of a sale of all, or part, of the shares arising on exercise of the option. Originally this involved the broker advancing the exercise monies by way of bridging finance, but more recently the arrangement has taken the form of an undertaking by the broker (or the optionholder, if the arrangements are entered into directly between the company and the optionholder) to pay the subscription monies out of the proceeds of sale. The broker may require the company to ensure that any share certificates are held as security for the loan until it is repaid. Such arrangements will usually enable an employee to split his holding with any spouse or civil partner before sale so as to take advantage of the spouse or civil partner's annual capital gains tax exemption.

Similar arrangements are popular on a takeover, where the company will agree with the optionholder to receive the consideration due under the offer and will deduct the exercise price from this amount. In these circumstances the company would not need to use its broker or other financial institution.

Long Term Incentive Plans

2.10   Long Term Incentive Plans (LTIPs) are now more popular than discretionary share option schemes amongst larger companies (see Chapter 7), particularly in the UK. LTIPs can take various forms as follows:

(a)   performance share awards – awards of free shares which vest to the extent set performance targets are achieved after three or more years;

(b)   restricted shares – shares in which the employee acquires a beneficial interest (subject to a risk of forfeiture or some other factor which reduces their initial market value); and

(c)   convertible shares – shares in which the employee acquires a beneficial interest and which are convertible into other (usually more valuable) shares.

Similar to LTIPs are deferred share awards which take the form either of an award of shares (structured in the same way as an LTIP) in lieu of a portion of the participant's annual bonus, or of an acquisition of shares with a portion of the participant's annual bonus, which are released after a specified period into the name of the participant, provided he has not left employment. Some deferred share schemes also provide for matching share awards – an award of additional free shares often made if deferred shares are held for a specified period and further performance conditions have been met.

2.11   Performance share awards (the traditional version of the LTIP – often referred to as a Performance Share Plan (PSP)) focus management's attention on the achievement of the company's objectives, which under most schemes usually boils down to achieving relative levels of performance compared to a peer group of other companies in the same business sector, or achieving a chosen benchmark such as an index of total shareholder return or earnings per share. Remuneration committees of listed companies have largely responded to the calls of institutional investors to ensure that shares are only released under schemes where the company has outperformed at least median performance in the sector. Annual allocations of the larger listed companies did not originally exceed shares worth 100 per cent of the participant's annual rate of salary, but schemes are now established to allow for much higher multiples of salary, although the actual award levels may be much lower than the maximum allowed.

2.12   Deferred share awards are usually established as an incentive to the executive to remain with the company. Most deferred share awards involve the participant forfeiting his rights to the shares if he leaves early, and will often involve the employee being required to acquire shares out of his annual cash bonus. Where the employee has been required to purchase shares, if those shares are left with the trustee of an EBT for a period of, usually, three years, then the participant may be entitled to an award of matching shares (see **2.13** below).

2.13   Matching share awards involve awards of additional free shares to match deferred shares which have been held for the required period under the provisions of the deferred share scheme. Under pressure from shareholder bodies, the release of the matching shares will normally be subject to the achievement of a performance target over the period of deferral.

2.14   Restricted shares and convertible shares both involve the participant acquiring the beneficial interest in the shares from the outset. Most listed companies prefer incentive schemes which involve performance share awards or options, so restricted and convertible shares schemes are relatively unusual amongst such companies. Performance share awards have sometimes been structured as forfeitable free shares taxed under the restricted shares regime, although the FA 2008 changes to the capital gains tax regime have largely removed the advantages of this approach. However, private equity companies and other non-listed companies may establish restricted and convertible share schemes in appropriate circumstances.

2.15   LTIPs do not attract any reliefs from income tax or National Insurance contributions (NICs). Although the provisions for passing the employer's Class 1 NICs on to employees by agreement or election under the provisions of the Social Security Contributions and Benefits Act 1992, Sch 1, paras 3A(2) or 3B(1) were originally limited to 'securities options' subject to income tax under ITEPA 2003, Pt 7, Ch 5 (see **7.3**(b) below), the provisions were extended to restricted securities and convertible securities in 2004 pursuant to the NIC and Statutory Payments Act 2004.

2.16   Many LTIPs were originally established using only existing shares delivered to participants at vesting by an EBT. However, most LTIPs will now be established to also allow for the use of newly subscribed shares and treasury shares.

2.17   Since the publication of the Greenbury Report in 1995, institutional investors have given widespread encouragement to this type of scheme in public companies, culminating in the approval given in the Combined Code (now the UK Corporate Governance Code). Whilst many large companies operate LTIPs in one form or another, most smaller companies still prefer share options, and even many larger companies which operate LTIPs for directors and key employees, believe that share options are more appropriate for the layers of management below the main board.

Enterprise Management Incentives (EMIs)

2.18   Enterprise Management Incentives (EMIs) were introduced in the Finance Act 2000 to provide tax incentives for share options worth up to

£250,000 at the date of grant (this limit was increased to £120,000 from the original £100,000 in 2008, and to the present level in 2012) to employees in high-risk trading companies with significant growth potential. Income tax and NICs relief is provided at exercise (at least to the extent of gains in excess of the market value of the shares at the date of grant), and gains may, depending on the length of time between the grant of the option and the sale of shares, qualify for capital gains tax Entrepreneurs' Relief (see Chapter 6).

Phantom share schemes

2.19   Phantom share schemes are a form of cash bonus scheme made to look like a share scheme. Such schemes will usually be established by a company which is not in a position to establish a share scheme, perhaps because it is a subsidiary of a non-listed company which does not allow minority interests to arise, or as a result of local tax or securities law requirements in a jurisdiction in which the company wishes to extend its existing employee share schemes. Very few listed companies have established phantom share schemes because of the uncapped liability on the company to pay cash. Most companies prefer share schemes for the hedge provided on the increase in the share price, although this hedge can often be replicated for a phantom share scheme by funding an EBT to acquire shares to mirror the phantom awards.

SCHEMES FOR ALL EMPLOYEES

Share option schemes

2.20   A few companies have granted discretionary share options on an 'all-employee' basis, although in most cases, such an approach has not been maintained for long, usually because such schemes use shares at a far greater rate than other types of all-employee share scheme, or are not seen to provide the same benefits as a conventional savings-related share option scheme. To the extent options are to be granted at a price equivalent to the market value over shares valued at no more than £30,000 then the options may be granted with income tax and National Insurance relief.

Share Incentive Plan (SIP)

2.21   The Finance Act 2000 introduced the Share Incentive Plan (SIP), which involves three types of share allocation as follows:

(a)   partnership shares – employees may buy shares worth up to £1,800 per tax year (increased from the original £1,500 from 6 April 2014) out of their pre-tax income. The income tax and National Insurance relief given to employees in respect of their expenditure is generally lost if the shares are sold within five years of acquisition;

(b)   free shares – employees may receive free shares worth up to £3,600 per tax year (increased from the original £3,000 from 6 April 2014) with income tax relief if the shares are retained in trust for five years. This type of allocation must be made on broadly similar terms to all eligible employees on various bases of allocation: equal numbers of shares, pro-rata salary or pro-rata length of service. Allocations can also be made on the basis of pre-allocation performance conditions of the employment unit involved. Allocations may also be subject to restrictions, including forfeiture provisions; and

(c)   matching shares – employees may also receive additional free shares to match any partnership shares they have bought. Matching shares are limited to no more than two free matching shares for each partnership share acquired (effectively a limit of £3,600 per tax year) with income tax and National Insurance relief where shares are held in trust for five years.

According to HMRC statistics, over 500 companies operate a SIP. The average amount contributed by employees acquiring partnership shares is about £81 per month, with over 80 per cent of companies operating a SIP offering such partnership shares to their employees.

Savings-related share option schemes

2.22   Savings-related share option (or 'sharesave') schemes (see Chapter 12) are linked to certified contractual savings schemes under ITTOIA 2005, s 703. Such savings arrangements, which provide for participants to save up to £500 per month (increased from £250 per month from 6 April 2014), can only be offered by building societies, banks or European financial institutions. The maximum value of shares, which may be acquired after five years on savings of £500 a month at their original market value, is £37,750 (on the basis of the five-year savings bonus rate, payable at the end of the contractual savings period, applicable from 28 July 2014).

2.23   These schemes are popular for a number of reasons:

(a)   options may be granted at a discount of up to 20 per cent to market value at the date of grant;

(b)   there is no obligation on optionholders to acquire the shares, so they will only do so if a gain has accrued; and

(c)   any price discount on grant, gains on exercise, or bonus payable under the savings contract, are normally tax free.

2.24   Annually, around 400,000 employees in the UK are granted options under this type of scheme, meaning that between 1 and 2 million employees may be participating at any one time. The average amount saved is about £105 per month.

Discounted share schemes

2.25   Discounted share purchase arrangements are popular with non-UK companies, particularly as a result of the beneficial tax regime which may be available for local employees. Such arrangements do not, however, provide tax advantages for UK employees and the discount will either be taxable as a benefit on acquisition, or the shares subject to the restricted securities regime of ITEPA 2003, Pt 7, Ch 2.

Sponsored individual savings accounts (ISAs)

2.26   Some companies sponsor individual savings account managers to provide plans using only the shares of the sponsoring company. Such arrangements may be attractive to employees particularly as shares emerging from a SIP or savings-related share option scheme (but not a discretionary share option scheme) may be transferred into the plan directly (see Chapter 17).

OTHER ARRANGEMENTS

Share purchase schemes

2.27   Some companies, usually private companies, allow employees to subscribe or purchase shares at the market price. In private companies, existing shareholders often have pre-emption rights over shares which are to be transferred, but to encourage wider employee share ownership, the articles of association might provide for an EBT to have a right of pre-emption so that the trust can distribute the shares amongst employees. Alternatively, the shares may be offered through trustees to employees on regular 'offer' days without any prior pre-emption rights.

2.28   The company may provide financial assistance both to trustees, in order to buy shares from employees, and to employees, to buy shares from the trustees. Such financial assistance will be lawful for a private company, but in relation to public company shares will only be lawful if given in the best interests of the company for the purposes of an employees' share scheme (Companies Act 2006 (CA 2006), s 682(2)(b)). In addition, where the assistance is given by a public company, should net assets be reduced to a material extent, the financial assistance must be given out of distributable profits (CA 2006, s 682(1)(b)). However, companies offering financing arrangements for the acquisition of shares may need to consider whether authorisation from the FCA to provide consumer credit is necessary and whether such arrangements may be taxable as a beneficial loan under ITEPA 2003, Pt 3, Ch 7.

Partly-paid share schemes

2.29   The benefit of any interest-free loan by the company to employees will be subject to income tax on the value of the notional interest foregone. Similarly, where shares are acquired on partly-paid terms, they will be treated as if acquired with a loan equal to the unpaid amount and income tax will be payable on the value of the notional interest foregone under ITEPA 2003, Pt 7, Ch 3C. Partly-paid share schemes are, therefore, regarded as generally unattractive because the tax under ITEPA 2003, Pt 7, Ch 3C is payable before the shares can be realised to provide the amount of tax due.

Subsidiary company schemes

2.30   Schemes to acquire shares in a subsidiary company, whether share option schemes or other types of scheme, are relatively uncommon. This is partly due to the attitude of institutional investor bodies, which are hostile to such schemes in public companies, and partly because of the absence of any market in the shares of a subsidiary (usually only the holding company will be prepared to acquire the shares).

Chapter 3

The ABI/IMA and Other Institutional Investor Guidelines

INTRODUCTION

3.1   A company with listed shares, or whose shares are traded on the Alternative Investment Market (AIM), and any private company with significant institutional shareholdings (such as a management buy-out vehicle) needs to take note of the guidelines on employees' share schemes published by certain bodies representing institutional investors in order to ensure institutional support for any share scheme proposals.

3.2   Essentially, institutional investors are concerned to see some link between the size of the reward contemplated under any LTIP or share option scheme and the type and nature of the performance targets to be satisfied. Institutional investors expect to see challenging and stretching performance targets.

CURRENT GUIDELINES

3.3   The Association of British Insurers (ABI) has for many years operated a monitoring service in which it reports to institutional investors on directors' remuneration issues arising out of circulars and other information provided by listed companies to their shareholders. With effect from 30 June 2014, the investment affairs division of the ABI was merged with the Investment Management Association (IMA), the trade body representing the UK asset management industry. The IMS, which will be renamed The Investment Association from early 2015, will now be responsible for the ABI's monitoring service and, consequently, its guidelines on remuneration and share plans. Many institutional investors, and other organisations, such as Institutional Shareholder Services (ISS) and Pensions Investment Research Consultants (PIRC), also publish their own guidelines or proffer views on the appropriate design of directors' share schemes and performance targets.

3.4   The current guidelines on employees' share schemes now form part of a more general Principles of Remuneration and the current version (November 2013), can be found at www.ivis.co.uk/media/5887/ABI-Principles-of-Remuneration-2013-final.pdf.

3.5   The National Association of Pension Funds (NAPF) published guidelines on share schemes for many years but no longer does so, although it publishes general guidelines on corporate governance, including remuneration, and generally recommends adherence to the IMA's guidance.

HISTORICAL DEVELOPMENT OF THE ABI GUIDELINES

3.6   The earliest ABI Guidelines were published nearly 50 years ago and contained just three recommendations, all in relation to share option schemes:

(a)   only full-time employees should participate;

(b)   a limit on the number of shares which may be made available under share option schemes of five per cent of share capital over any period of ten years; and

(c)   no option could be granted over shares at a price which was less than the market value of those shares.

3.7   The spread of profit-sharing schemes in the 1970s using shares instead of cash led to the introduction of a limit on the number of new shares which could be made available each year of one per cent of share capital.

3.8   An overall scheme limit of ten per cent of share capital in ten years was put forward as a response to the growing number of all-employee share schemes in the late 1970s.

3.9   Performance targets in executive share option schemes first appeared in the ABI Guidelines in 1987 when companies were recommended to grant options exercisable upon the achievement of a real growth in earnings per share over a three-year period. This requirement was often disregarded but the requirement to impose performance conditions is now one of the key elements in the design of executive share schemes, a requirement which has grown in importance with the requirements for disclosure provided for in the regulations relating to directors' remuneration reports.

SUMMARY OF CURRENT ABI (IMA) GUIDELINES

Aims and principles

3.10   Although the ABI's investment affairs division has been merged with the IMA, the current guidelines on remuneration were those last published by the ABI in November 2013. Until new guidelines are published, it is likely that companies, advisors and shareholders will continue to refer to 'the ABI Guidelines' rather than 'the IMA Guidelines' or 'the Investment Association Guidelines', and so this term has been continued to be used in this book.
The ABI Guidelines set out the broad objectives which institutional investors wish to see achieved, as follows:

(a)   remuneration structures should be appropriate for the specific business, and efficient and cost-effective in delivering its longer-term strategy; they should not be complex; and should have a long-term focus;

(b)   executive share incentive schemes should be regularly reviewed by remuneration committees to ensure their effectiveness and there should be shareholder approval of the schemes by means of a separate binding resolution;

(c)   there should be a link between remuneration and performance;

(d)   there should be limits on dilution (not more than ten per cent in ten years) and participation (phased allocations each year based on demanding and stretching financial performance against a target group or other relevant benchmark);

(e)   the company should have the ability, in specified circumstances, to reduce all or part of an award before it has vested, or recover sums already paid; and

(f)   there should be a structure which effectively aligns the long-term interests of management and shareholders, in particular, arrangements whereby employees retain meaningful shareholdings are encouraged.

Performance conditions

3.11   The requirements on performance conditions are set out at paragraph 2.ii of the ABI Guidelines. The ABI/IMA expects performance conditions to be achieved as a basis for the vesting of awards at the end of the incentivisation period. Performance conditions should be fully explained and clearly linked to the achievement of appropriately challenging financial performance and value creation. The definition of any performance measurement should be fully disclosed to shareholders. Where comparator groups are used, vesting should also be subject to the outcome being genuinely reflective of the company's underlying financial performance.

3.12   Threshold vesting, reflecting expected performance, should not be significant by comparison with base salary. Schemes are expected to require exceptional performance for full vesting, reflecting significantly greater value creation than at threshold vesting; the greater the potential reward, the more stretching and demanding the performance conditions should be. Sliding vesting scales are required as an 'all or nothing' hurdle or 'cliff edge' vesting is seen as inappropriate (ABI Guidelines, paragraph 2.iii).

3.13   Performance periods should be linked to the implementation of strategy and are expected to run for a period of three or more years. Retesting of performance conditions is seen as unacceptable. The ABI's/IMA's hostility to retesting has almost stamped out retesting in the schemes of larger companies. Performance targets with a fixed starting point with retesting after three, four and often five years have also lost the ABI's/IMA's support as a result of the focus on annual phased grants.

3.14   Generally speaking, the ABI/IMA will not support performance conditions which apply as a condition of grant (as distinct from a condition of exercise). Any such arrangements would need to be carefully justified and disclosed, and be accompanied by 'genuinely long holding periods and significant shareholding requirements'. (ABI Guidelines, paragraph 2.xi(c))

3.15   The ABI/IMA requires performance targets to continue to apply where there is a change of control of the company and where employees leave employment early. Share incentive awards should vest on a pro-rata basis according to the amount of time which has passed (ABI Guidelines, paragraph 2.vi).

Valuation; cost to shareholders

3.16   The ABI/IMA considers that shareholders should be able to evaluate share incentive proposals upon the basis of the costs of the scheme. The costs are stated to include:

(a)   the potential value of individual awards at vesting (assessed on the basis of full vesting and expressed either by reference to the face value of the shares under the option or award at grant, or as a multiple of base salary); and

(b)   the maximum dilution which may arise through the issue of new shares (ABI Guidelines, paragraph 2.v).

Dilution limits

3.17   The ABI/IMA seeks an overall scheme limit across all schemes of ten per cent of share capital over any ten-year period. This applies not only to the issue of new shares but also to the transfer of treasury shares. Shares acquired on the market are outside the scope of the dilution limits. The full number of shares under awards should be included in the calculation, even where share-settled stock appreciation rights are granted (where only the gain over an exercise price is settled in shares) until the time that the award vests and the exact number of shares can be substituted.

3.18   The ABI/IMA does not now lay down 'flow-rate' limits relating to the issue of new shares. Previously, it required a maximum of three per cent over three years (or five per cent over five years), but now there is no prescribed limit other than a general warning to ensure the flow of allocations does not breach the overall ten per cent over ten-year limit (see **3.17** above).

3.19   The ABI/IMA does, however, state that commitments to issue shares under discretionary schemes should be limited to five per cent of share capital over any ten-year period (ABI Guidelines, paragraph 2.ix).

3.20   Although rarely followed in practice, the ABI/IMA requires that any options or awards over new shares granted at the time of a takeover as replacement (or 'rolled-over') options should also count towards these limits. The grant of such options is, however, generally seen as a cost of the transaction.

Participation

3.21 Participation in share incentive schemes should be restricted to bona fide employees and executive directors. Non-executive directors are not expected to participate as shareholders consider it inappropriate for chairmen and independent directors to receive incentive awards geared to the share price or corporate performance.

3.22 Participation in more than one share incentive scheme is not ruled out, but the appropriateness would need to be justified to shareholders.

3.23 The ABI Guidelines discourage arrangements whereby share options are granted at a discount (although this would not preclude LTIPs being granted in the form of nil-cost or nominal cost options). In matching scheme arrangements, it expects to see performance targets attached to the vesting of the shares, although the ABI/IMA is not supportive of such arrangements as potentially adding 'unnecessary complexity' to a company's remuneration arrangements (ABI Guidelines, paragraph 2.xi(a)).

Pricing of options and shares

3.24 In determining the number of shares under an option or award, the company should use a price which is not less than the mid-market price immediately preceding grant (ABI Guidelines, paragraph 2.vii). The exercise price for an executive (market value) option should be set on a similar basis.

3.25 Where grant levels are expressed as a percentage of base salary, the Remuneration Committee should consider reducing award levels in circumstances where there has been a substantial fall in share price in order to avoid windfall gains (ABI Guidelines, paragraph 2.iv).

Regrants of 'underwater' options

3.26 Underwater options are not expected to be surrendered and regranted (ABI Guidelines, paragraph 2.vii).

Timing of grants

3.27 The ABI/IMA expects schemes to restrict grants normally to a 42-day period following an announcement of results of the company (ABI Guidelines, paragraph 2.vii). In practice, most schemes also allow for exceptional grants to facilitate, for example, recruitments or to take account of Model Code restrictions on when grants may be made.

Duration of scheme

3.28   No awards should be made later than ten years after approval of the scheme, which should be by shareholders (ABI Guidelines, paragraph 2.viii).

Period for vesting

3.29   Shares and options are not expected to vest (or be exercisable) earlier than three years or later than ten years after grant (ABI Guidelines, paragraph 2. vii). On an early termination of employment, or upon a change of control, options should be exercisable for not more than one year, subject to the achievement of any performance targets and time apportionment. Where the rules of the scheme allow early exercise, performance should be pro-rated over the shorter period. The options should vest no later than the end of the initial performance period and should be finally exercisable no later than 12 months following the date of vesting (ABI Guidelines, paragraph 2.viii). The ABI/IMA also recommends that consideration is given to using additional post-vesting holding periods. Indeed, certain institutional investors are now requiring the use of such holding periods as a condition to their support for the scheme.

Subsidiary company and joint ventures

3.30   The ABI/IMA discourages the grant of share options and awards over joint venture companies and subsidiaries unless exercise is made conditional upon a flotation or sale of the subsidiary company (where a minimum return on investment is required). An exception can also be made in the case of overseas subsidiaries if 25 per cent of the share capital is listed or held outside the group.

The ABI/IMA accepts that shareholders may allow a subsidiary or joint venture scheme where the scheme is made available only to employees of that subsidiary or joint venture, the accounting treatment for the scheme and methodology for valuing shares is fully disclosed, there are appropriately challenging performance targets, dilution at subsidiary level is included in the overall dilution limits (see **3.17** above), and any entitlement to convert subsidiary shares into parent company shares is fully disclosed (ABI Guidelines, paragraph 2.x).

Employee share ownership trusts

3.31   The ABI/IMA discourages employee share ownership trusts/employee benefit trusts from holding more shares than are required to meet current liabilities. The prior approval of shareholders is required where more than five per cent of share capital is to be held (ABI Guidelines paragraph 2.xii).

Dividends

3.32   Previous ABI Guidelines made specific reference to the ABI's view that, where awards are made under a long-term incentive plan in respect of whole shares, in order to better align the interests of participants with those of shareholders, where shares vest, the participant should receive a payment equivalent in value to the dividends which would have been paid in respect of such vested shares during the performance period. The current ABI Guidelines now refer only to dividends not accruing on share options prior to exercise, although presumably this relates to market value options, rather than LTIPs structured as nil-cost or nominal cost options.

3.33   Where 'dividend equivalents' are paid, shareholders may expect the Remuneration Committee to bear this in mind when setting the size of the awards.

Chapter 4

Establishment of Schemes

INTRODUCTION

4.1   There are a number of reasons why companies establish employees' share schemes rather than enter into separate agreements with each individual employee. The first is convenience, since a scheme removes the need to set out the full rights of participants in a separate agreement on each occasion an option is granted. Second, there are considerable company law advantages. Third, certain of the tax advantages under the Income Tax (Earnings and Pensions) Act 2003 (ITEPA 2003), Pt 7 are only available in respect of 'schemes' or 'plans'. Fourth, for listed companies the use of a scheme avoids the need to obtain shareholders' specific approval of each grant of an option to a director.

COMPANIES ACT 2006

Meaning of 'employees' share scheme'

4.2   An employees' share scheme is defined by the Companies Act 2006 (CA 2006), s 1166 as follows:

'a scheme for encouraging or facilitating the holding of shares or debentures in a company by or for the benefit of –

(a)   the bona fide employees or former employees of –

(i)   the company,

(ii)   any subsidiary of the company, or

(iii) the company's holding company or any subsidiary of the company's holding company; or

(b)   the spouses, civil partners, surviving spouses, surviving civil partners, or minor children or step-children of such employees or former employees'.

4.3   There are a number of difficulties which arise in relation to the construction of this definition. First, the legislation refers to 'the ... employees ...' and 'the spouses ...' and this could mean all such persons. However, one meaning for the word 'the' when used with a noun in the plural is 'those who are' and this seems the better construction. In other words, the definition of 'employees' share schemes' sets out the categories of persons who may be included in an employees' share scheme, but it does not lay down that all persons within these categories must be included. However, it is unlikely that an arrangement intended to benefit only directors would amount to an employees' share scheme unless it is the intention that participation will be widened subsequently.

4.4   Another difficulty arises where a particular scheme allows participation by persons outside the permitted categories in CA 2006, s 1166, for instance, non-executive directors, self-employed consultants and the employees of joint venture companies or other non-subsidiaries. There is no authority on this, but the widely accepted view is that a distinction should be made between allocations to qualifying and non-qualifying persons, and the allocations to qualifying persons should be treated as made under an employees' share scheme. Allocations to non-qualifying persons should be treated as separate arrangements and, therefore, should not enjoy the company law benefits normally available in respect of allocations under employees' share schemes (see **4.5** and **4.6** below). However, the statutory tax-advantaged scheme codes now provide for employees of joint venture companies to be able to participate in one or other of the schemes of a joint owner and, to this extent, non-subsidiaries would be involved (ITEPA 2003, Sch 2, para 91; Sch 3, para 46; and Sch 4, para 34).

Directors' authority to allot shares

4.5   CA 2006, s 549 provides that directors shall not exercise any power of the company to allot shares or grant options over shares unless the company is a private company with only one class of share capital or, otherwise, they are authorised by a resolution in general meeting or under the articles of association. However, there is no prohibition on an allotment of shares in pursuance of an 'employees' share scheme' within the meaning of CA 2006, s 1166. An 'allotment' of shares includes not only the issue of new shares, but also the grant of an option over such shares (CA 2006, s 549(2)(a)).

Disapplication of pre-emption provisions

4.6   CA 2006, s 561 gives the shareholders of a company a right to be offered any proposed allotment of 'equity securities' in priority to third parties. However, by CA 2006, s 566 such pre-emption rights do not apply to an offer of equity securities under an employees' share scheme.

Prohibition of financial assistance by a public company in the purchase of own shares (CA 2006, ss 677–683)

4.7   CA 2006, s 678 provides that it is unlawful for a company to give financial assistance directly or indirectly to a person for the acquisition of its shares (where the company is a public company), or shares in any public holding company. Amongst the exceptions to this is 'the provision by a company, in good faith in the interests of the company, of financial assistance for the purposes of an employees' share scheme' (see CA 2006, s 682(2)(b)). 'Financial assistance' will be tainted if the purpose is to establish an impediment to a possible takeover (*Hogg v Cramphorn [1967] Ch 254*). 'Financial assistance' includes any loan, guarantee or other financial assistance given to 'another person', such as an Employee Benefit Trust (EBT) trustee, for the acquisition of shares. In addition, the giving of financial assistance by a public company is only allowed if the company has net assets which are not thereby reduced or, to the extent that the assets are thereby reduced, if the assistance is provided out of distributable profits. Financial assistance by private companies in the purchase of private company shares is permitted.

Memorandum and articles of association

4.8   It is common for a company's articles of association to incorporate a power enabling the company to establish employees' share schemes. A typical form of words for such a power is as follows:

'To establish, maintain, manage, support and contribute to any schemes for the acquisition of shares in the Company or its holding company by or for the benefit of any individuals who are or were at any time in the employment of, or directors or officers of:

(i)   the Company; or

(ii)   any company which is or was its holding company or is or was a subsidiary of the Company or any such holding company; or

(iii)   any other company or former company connected or associated in any way with the Company or with the whole or any part of its undertaking,

and to lend money to any such individuals or to trustees on behalf of such individuals to enable them to acquire shares in the Company or in its holding company and to establish, maintain, manage and support (financially or otherwise) any schemes for sharing profits of the Company or any other such company as aforesaid with any such individuals.'

4.9   However, the absence of any such express power will not be fatal. CA 2006, s 31 provides that where a company's articles association do not restrict the object of the company, then the objects are unrestricted, and so unless there is an express prohibition of employees' share schemes, they will be a permitted object of the company.

Directors' fiduciary duties

4.10   Under company law, there are various provisions intended to ensure that a director acts in the best interests of the company and avoids conflicts of interest. CA 2006, s 177 imposes a duty on a director to declare his interest in contracts in which he is interested. In most companies, the articles of association restrict a director voting at meetings of directors on matters in which he is personally interested (see Article 14 of the Model Articles comprised in the Companies (Model Articles) Regulations 2008). In principle, every director is potentially interested in an employees' share scheme and, therefore, voting restrictions usually need to be relaxed where an employees' share scheme is to be considered at a meeting of the directors. For this reason, the resolution to establish an employees' share scheme will often include such a relaxation. Strictly speaking, any such resolution should be passed as a special resolution if it is intended to override the provisions of the articles of association.

Prohibition of the allotment of shares at a discount to the nominal value

4.11 CA 2006, s 580 provides that no shares may be allotted at a discount. In a share option scheme, this will mean that the subscription price of new shares must be fixed at a price which is not less than the nominal value.

4.12 Whilst options may not be granted at a discount to the nominal value, many share option schemes provide for the adjustment of options in the event of certain variations of share capital such as a rights issue. This will normally involve a reduction in the price of the shares under option as well as an increase in the number of shares. The question arises whether any adjustment can be made if the adjusted option price would be less than the nominal value of a share. In order to overcome the prohibition under CA 2006, s 580, where shares are to be subscribed, the difference between the adjusted option price and the nominal value would need to be paid up out of a capitalisation of reserves. The Model Articles (Article 36) only allow for capitalisation issues in favour of 'the persons who would have been entitled 'which does not extend to optionholders and so the company's articles of association may need to be altered to allow a specific power to capitalise reserves in favour of optionholders. An appropriate power is as follows:

> 'Where, pursuant to an employees' share scheme (within the meaning of section 1166 of the Companies Act 2006) the Company has granted options to subscribe for ordinary shares on terms which provide (inter alia) for adjustments to the subscription price payable on the exercise of such options or to the number of shares to be allotted upon such exercise in the event of any increase or reduction in or other reorganisation of the Company's issued share capital and an otherwise appropriate adjustment would result in the subscription price for any share being less than its nominal value, then, subject to the provisions of the articles of association, the Directors may on the exercise of any of the options concerned and payment of the subscription price which would have applied had such adjustment been made, capitalise any profits or reserves (including share premium account and capital redemption reserve) to the extent necessary to pay up the unpaid balance of the nominal value of the

shares which fall to be allotted on the exercise of such options and to apply such amount in paying up such balance and to allot shares fully paid accordingly'.

Disclosure of directors' dealings

4.13   Under rule 3.1.2 of the Disclosure and Transparency Rules (DTRs) published by the Financial Conduct Authority (FCA), a person discharging managerial responsibility of a listed company is under an obligation to notify the company in writing of the occurrence of all transactions conducted on his own (or a connected person's) account or any financial involvements relating to those shares. Such a transaction will include the grant of an option and the receipt of an award under an LTIP. The acquisition or disposal of shares by the trustees of an EBT in which the director is a beneficiary is not a transaction by a connected person provided the EBT is an employees' share scheme within CA 2006, s 1166 and not a personal trust for the benefit of the individual concerned. As soon as possible, and no later than the end of the next business day, the company must notify an approved Regulatory Information Service ('RIS') (a list of which is maintained by the FCA) of the information disclosed pursuant to DTR, r 3.1.2.

4.14   There is no obligation under the Companies Act 2006 on a director to report share dealings to the company. However, a record will need to be maintained by listed companies to satisfy the objectives in **4.13** above.

Disclosure of notifiable interests (DTR 5.1.2)

4.15   The trustees of a SIP or other EBT holding shares in a listed company have a notifiable interest under the provisions of rule 5.1.2 of the Disclosure and Transparency Rules if their holdings of shares exceeds three per cent (or any greater percentage) of the share capital. There is no obligation of disclosure under the Companies Act 2006.

PROSPECTUS RULES

4.16   The Prospectus Rules provide that it is unlawful to offer transferable securities to the public in the UK unless an approved prospectus has been made available. Transferable securities include, for example, securities capable of being dealt in on a regulated stock exchange (even if not actually so dealt with). They will be offered to the public as a result of any communication in any form and by any means presenting sufficient information on the terms of the offer and the securities to enable an investor in any EU country to purchase or subscribe. The Prospectus Rules are derived from the EU Prospectus Directive which is based on the principle that there should be a common form of prospectus throughout the EU so that approval by the 'competent authority' in one EU country will be sufficient for an offer made in another country, subject only to registration of the document with the competent authority in the other EU country. The 'single passporting' of prospectuses throughout the EU means that companies based in non-EU countries may be faced with the preparation of a full prospectus before making an offer of shares to employees within the UK, although an extension to the employee offer exemption (see below), allows for companies not listed in the EEA to take advantage of the exemption if they are incorporated outside the EU but have securities admitted to trading on a third country market, provided that the European Commission has determined that the relevant market offers equivalent protections to those which exist in relation to EU regulated markets. Currently, the European Commission has not made any such determination, but it is anticipated that exchanges such as the New York Stock Exchange, the Tokyo Stock Exchange and the Australian Stock Exchange will qualify for equivalence.

As far as UK companies are concerned, the UKLA does not treat offers of non-transferable options as within the scope of the Prospectus Rules. In addition, as there is no consideration paid for the receipt of free shares (for example under an LTIP or SIP), these also fall outside of the Prospectus Rules. It is, therefore, probably the case that only offers of partnership shares under a SIP and share purchase offers are caught (although this may not be the case in relation to the interpretation of the Prospectus Directive in other jurisdictions). In addition, there are a number of exceptions from the prospectus requirements which can be helpful to companies wishing to make an offer of shares where the offer is made wholly or mainly to employees. In particular, these include:

(a) the employee offer exemption – securities offered to existing or former directors or employees by their employer (being with a company either having its head office or registered office in the EU, having a listing on an EU market, or otherwise where the extension referred to above applies), provided an information memorandum is made available containing:

  (i) the name of the issuer and where additional information on the issuer can be found, e.g. the website;

  (ii) the reasons for the offer, i.e. to give employees the opportunity to participate in the growth in value of the company;

  (iii) the price of the securities;

  (iv) eligibility conditions;

  (v) minimum and maximum numbers of shares offered;

  (vi) details of any scaling back provisions;

  (vii) whether shares are offered by purchase or subscription;

  (viii) the opening and closing dates of the offer;

  (ix) the method of payment; and

  (x) a summary of rights eg dividend and voting rights.

The above information will normally be included in the employee guides prepared by most companies so it will normally be fairly easy for most companies to satisfy the conditions of the employee exemption offer. Where the employee offers exemption is not available, there is the possibility for issuers without an EU listing to file a 'short-form' prospectus which excludes certain information not considered to be relevant for employee offers. This does not, however, extend to private companies.

(b)   Small offers – an offer to 150 or fewer persons is exempt and so is an offer where the total consideration payable is less than €5m.

FINANCIAL SERVICES AND MARKETS ACT 2000

4.17   The Financial Services and Markets Act 2000 (FSMA 2000) regulates investment business and includes provisions relating to employees' share schemes.

Carrying on regulated activities – exemption for employees' share schemes

4.18   A company which establishes an employees' share scheme, and any EBT to be operated in conjunction with the scheme, is likely to be carrying on a 'regulated activity' in the UK. A regulated activity is one of the activities which may be specified in secondary legislation from time to time and carried on as a business activity. By the Financial Services and Markets Act 2000 (Regulated Activities) Order 2001 (SI 2001/544), these will include:

(a)   dealing in investments (which includes dealing in shares as principal or agent);

(b)   arranging deals in investments;

(c)   managing investments;

(d)   safeguarding and administering investments; and

(e)   establishing and operating, etc a collective investment scheme.

It is an offence for a person to carry on a regulated activity in the UK, or purport to do so, unless he is either an authorised or exempt person (FSMA 2000, s 19(1)).

4.19   However, article 71 of the Order includes an exemption for group companies or relevant trustees carrying on activities by entering into, as principal, transactions for the purpose of enabling or facilitating transactions in acquiring or holding shares or debentures in connection with employees, or former employees, of that or another group company (or their spouses or dependants). This covers most activities carried on by a company in connection with issuing and allotting shares under employees' share schemes. It also covers most activities carried on by trustees, including the operation of EBTs and SIPs.

Prohibition of financial promotion: exemption for employees' share schemes

4.20 FSMA 2000, s 21 provides that a person must not, in the course of business, 'communicate an invitation or inducement to engage in investment activity' unless he is an authorised person, or the content of the communication is approved by an authorised person (FSMA 2000, s 21). However, this prohibition does not extend to any communication which is made by a person, a member of a group of companies or a relevant trustee for the purpose of an employees' share scheme and relates to shares, debentures, options or certificates in respect of securities (Financial Services and Markets Act 2000 (Financial Promotion) Order 2001 (SI 2001/1335), art 60).

LISTING RULES

4.21 The Listing Rules apply to all companies admitted to the Official List of the Financial Conduct Authority (and so does not apply to AIM companies or companies admitted to the High Growth segment of the London Stock Exchange, each of which are subject to their own rulebooks), although the provisions relating to employees' share schemes and long-term incentive schemes do not apply to overseas companies admitted to listing.

Terms used in the Listing Rules

4.22 In the Listing Rules, the terms 'deferred bonus' and 'long-term incentive scheme' have the following meanings:

(a) Deferred bonus – any arrangement pursuant to the terms of which the participant(s) may receive an award of any asset (including cash or any security) in respect of service and/or performance in a period not exceeding the length of the relevant financial year notwithstanding that any such asset may, subject only to the participant(s) remaining a director or employee of the group, be receivable by the participant(s) after the end of the period to which the award relates.

(b) Long-term incentive scheme – any arrangement (other than a retirement benefit plan, a deferred bonus or any other arrangement that is an element of an executive director's remuneration package which may involve the receipt of any asset (including cash or any security) by a director or employee of the group:

- which includes one or more conditions in respect of service and/or performance to be satisfied over more than one financial year; and

- pursuant to which the group may incur (other than in relation to the establishment and administration of the arrangement) either cost or liability, whether actual or contingent.

Requirement for shareholders' approval of an employees' share scheme and remuneration policy

4.23   Rule 9.4.1 of the Listing Rules provides that the following schemes of a listed company incorporated in the UK (and of any of its major subsidiary undertakings, even if incorporated or operating overseas) must be approved by an ordinary resolution of shareholders in general meeting prior to their adoption:

(a)   an employees' share scheme if the scheme involves, or may involve, the issue of new shares;

(b)   a long-term incentive scheme in which one or more directors of the listed company are eligible to participate with the following two exceptions:

  (i)   an arrangement under which participation is offered on similar terms to all, or substantially all, employees of the listed company or any of its subsidiary undertakings whose employees are eligible to participate in the arrangement (provided that all, or substantially all, employees are not directors of the company); and

  (ii)   an arrangement, for a single director or prospective director of the company, which is to be established specifically to facilitate, 'in unusual circumstances', the recruitment or retention of the relevant individual. However, the following information must be disclosed in the next report and accounts:

  •   all of the information prescribed in **4.24**(a)–(d) below;

  •   the name of the sole participant in the arrangement;

  •   the date on which the participant first became eligible to participate in the arrangement;

  •   an explanation of why the circumstances in which the arrangement was established were unusual;

  •   the conditions to be satisfied under the terms of the arrangement; and

  •   the maximum award(s) under the terms of the arrangement or, if there is no maximum, the basis on which awards will be determined.

  In principle, an arrangement for a single director in (ii) above will also be a 'related party' transaction requiring a shareholders' circular under Chapter 11 of the Listing Rules (see **4.40**) if it is not within the small transactions exception (see **4.42** below). However, it is understood that the UKLA will normally regard any such arrangement as outside Chapter 11, provided the information required above is disclosed in the next report and accounts. Any company proposing to enter into an arrangement should consult the UKLA in advance.

  Whether a UK-incorporated quoted company will be able to grant one-off awards on the basis of Listing Rule 9.4.2 will also depend on whether that company has reserved the right to do so within its remuneration policy which is now subject to a binding shareholder vote under CA 2006, s 439A.

Indeed, the adoption and operation of any employees' share scheme by a UK-incorporated quoted company will, in so far as directors of the company are eligible to participate, must be provided for in such an approved remuneration policy as CA 2006, s 226B provides that such a company may not make a 'remuneration payment' (which includes the receipt of any asset, including shares) to any director unless such payment is made in accordance with the terms of an approved remuneration policy. Any remuneration payment made not in accordance with such a policy could be reclaimed from the recipient (irrespective of any contractual documentation) or could be claimed from any director authorising the payment (CA 2006, s 226E).

The company's remuneration policy will include a description of each employees' share scheme, including the maximum grants, available for directors, together with details of the type of performance condition which will apply.

Contents of a circular for approval of an employees' share scheme or long-term incentive scheme

4.24 Rule 13.8.11 of the Listing Rules provides that a circular sent to shareholders in connection with the approval of an employees' share scheme, or a long-term incentive scheme, must:

(a) include either the full text of the scheme or a description of its principal terms;

(b) where directors of the company are trustees of the scheme, or have a direct or indirect interest in the trustees, include details of such trusteeship or interest;

(c) state that the provisions (if any) of the scheme relating to:

— the person to whom, or for whom, securities, cash or other benefits are provided under the scheme (the 'participants');

— limitations on the number or amount of the securities, cash or other benefits subject to the scheme;

— the maximum entitlement for any one participant;

— the basis for determining a participant's entitlement to, and the terms of, securities, cash or other benefits to be provided, and for the adjustment thereof (if any) in the event of a capitalisation issue or open offer, sub-division or consolidation of shares or reduction of capital or any other variation of capital;

cannot be altered to the advantage of participants without the prior approval of shareholders in general meeting (except for minor amendments to benefit the administration of the scheme, to take account of any change in legislation, or to obtain or maintain favourable tax, exchange control or regulatory treatment for participants in the scheme or for the company operating the scheme or for members of its group);

(d) state whether benefits under the scheme will be pensionable and, if so, the reason for this;

(e) if the scheme is not circulated to shareholders, include a statement that it will be available for inspection:

— from the date of despatch of the circular until the close of the relevant general meeting, at a place in or near the City of London or such other place as the UKLA may determine; and

— at the place of the general meeting for at least 15 minutes prior to, and during, the meeting; and

(f) comply with those requirements of Rule 13.3.1 of the Listing Rules on the contents of the circulars which are relevant to the approval of employee share schemes or long-term incentive schemes as follows:

(i) provide a clear and adequate explanation of the subject matter;

(ii) state why the shareholder is being asked to vote or, if no vote is required, why the circular is being sent;

(iii) if voting or other action is required, contain all information necessary to allow the holders of the securities to make a properly informed decision;

(iv) if voting or other action is required, contain a heading drawing attention to the importance of the document and advising holders of securities, who are in any doubt as to what action to take, to consult appropriate independent advisers;

(v) if voting or other action is required, contain a recommendation from the directors as to the voting action shareholders should take for all resolutions proposed, indicating whether or not the proposal in the circular is, in the opinion of the directors, in the best interest of the shareholders as a whole;

(vi) state that if all the shares have been sold (or transferred) by the addressee, the circular and any other relevant documents should be passed to the person through whom the sale or transfer was effected for transmission to the purchaser or transferee;

(vii) if new shares are being issued in substitution for existing shares, explain what will happen to existing documents of title;

(viii) not include any reference to a specific date on which listed shares will be marked 'ex' any benefit or entitlement which has not been agreed in advance with the recognised investment exchange on which the company's shares are or are to be traded;

(ix) if the new scheme relates to the admission of shares to listing, include a statement that application has been or will be made for the shares to be admitted and, if known, a statement of the following matters:

- when the new shares are expected to be admitted and on which dealings are expected to commence;

- how the new shares rank for dividend or interest;

- whether the new shares rank equally with any existing listed securities;

- the nature of the document of title;

- the proposed date of issue;

- the treatment of any fractions;

- whether or not the shares may be held in uncertificated form; and

- the names of the relevant investment exchange on which shares are to be traded:

(x)   if a person is named in the circular as having advised the listed company or its directors, a statement that such adviser has given and has not withdrawn its written consent to the inclusion of the reference to the advisers' name in the form and context in which it is included.

4.25   The resolution contained in the notice of meeting accompanying the circular to establish the employees' share scheme or long-term incentive scheme must refer either to:

(a)   the scheme itself (if circulated to shareholders); or

(b)   the summary of the principal terms of the scheme included in the circular.

Contents of a circular for the alteration of an employee share scheme or long-term incentive scheme

4.26   It was noted in **4.24**(c) above that a circular sent to shareholders for approval of an employees' share scheme, or long-term incentive scheme, must state that certain amendments, if to the advantage of the participants, must be first approved by shareholders. Under rule 13.8.14 of the Listing Rules, a circular sent to shareholders proposing such alterations must:

(a)   include an explanation of the effect of the proposed amendments;

(b)   include the full terms of the proposed amendments or a statement that the full text of the scheme, as amended, will be available for inspection as required in the same manner as for circulars for the approval of a new employees' share scheme (see **4.24**(e) above); and

(c)   comply with the relevant requirements on the contents of a circular (see **4.24**(f) above).

Contents of the circular for approval of discounted option arrangements

4.27   Rule 9.4.4 of the Listing Rules provides that a listed company may not, without the prior approval of shareholders, by ordinary resolution, grant to a director or employee of the company (or any subsidiary undertaking):

(a)   an option to subscribe;

(b)   a warrant to subscribe; or

(c)   other similar right to subscribe,

for shares (i.e. for new shares) in the capital of the company (or any subsidiary undertaking) at less than whichever of the following is used to calculate the exercise price:

(a)   the market value of the shares on the date when the exercise price is determined;

(b)   the market value of the shares on the business day before such date; or

(c)   the average of the market values of the shares over two or more dealing days within a period not exceeding 30 days immediately preceding such a date.

4.28   The obligation to seek shareholders' approval for discounted option arrangements does not apply to grants:

(a)   under an employees' share scheme where participation is offered on similar terms to all, or substantially all, employees of the company (and its subsidiary undertakings) eligible to participate; or

(b)   replacement options over shares in a company (or any subsidiary undertaking) following a takeover or reconstruction.

4.29   Where a shareholders' circular is required, rule 13.8.14 of the Listing Rules provides that the following information must be circulated to shareholders:

(a)   details of the persons to whom the options, warrants or rights are to be granted;

(b)   a summary of the principal terms of the options, warrants or rights; and

(c)   details complying with the relevant requirements on the contents of a circular (see **4.24**(f) above).

Authority to establish overseas schemes

4.30   A resolution approving the adoption of an employees' share scheme or long-term incentive scheme may authorise the directors to establish similar schemes, based on any scheme which has previously been approved by shareholders, but modified to take account of local tax, exchange control or securities laws in overseas territories, provided that any shares made available under such further schemes are treated as counting against any limits on individual or overall participation in the main scheme (see rule 13.8.13 of the Listing Rules).

Approval of circulars and documents by the UKLA

4.31 Circulars and documents relating to employees' share schemes do not need to be sent to the UKLA for approval in advance, unless they contain unusual features.

Lodging of documents with the UKLA

4.32 However, a listed company is required to forward to the FCA for publication through the document viewing facility two copies of any circular relating to an employees' share scheme, long-term incentive scheme or discounted option arrangement with the UKLA not later than the date of despatch.

4.33 In addition, a listed company must disclose the forwarding of relevant documents and notify where any such document is available for inspection.

MODEL CODE ON DIRECTORS' DEALINGS IN SECURITIES

4.34 The Model Code on directors' dealings in securities is set out as an Annex to Chapter 9 of the Listing Rules. It imposes wider restrictions on share dealings beyond those imposed by law with a view to ensuring directors, and other persons discharging managerial responsibilities ('restricted persons') and persons connected with them, do not abuse, and do not place themselves under suspicion of abusing, price-sensitive information that they may have (or may be thought to have), especially in periods leading up to an announcement of results.

4.35 Amongst other things, a restricted person must not deal in any securities of the listed company during a prohibited period which includes both a close period (the period of 60 days or other relevant period before an announcement of results) and at any other time when there exists inside information in relation to the company.

Clearance to deal

4.36 A director or company secretary may not deal in any securities of the listed company without first advising the chairman (or other designated director) and receiving clearance. Similar obligations are imposed on the chairman who must consult the chief executive, and/or the chief executive who must consult the chairman or the senior independent director. There are rules about when permission to deal may be given and the records which must be maintained by the company.

Seek to prohibit dealings with connected persons

4.37   Under paragraphs 20 to 22 of the Model Code, a director or other person discharging managerial responsibilities (PDMRs) must seek to prohibit any dealing by (amongst others) persons connected with him or by investment managers acting for him during a close period. Connected persons are the persons specified in CA 2006, s 96B(2). A person discharging managerial responsibilities is required to advise all connected persons and investment managers of:

(a)   the name of the listed company of which he is a PDMR;

(b)   the close periods during which they cannot deal in the company's securities; and

(c)   that they must advise the company immediately after they have dealt in any of its securities.

Meaning of 'dealing'

4.38   Under the Model Code, a 'dealing' is defined, amongst other things, as:

(a)   any sale or purchase, or agreement to sell or purchase, any securities of the company;

(b)   in relation to any option or other right or obligation, present or future, conditional or unconditional to require or dispose of securities, or any interest in securities, of the company:

•   a grant;

•   an acceptance;

•   a disposal;

•   an exercise;

•   a discharge (i.e. a surrender).

The grant of an option or award under a share scheme by the board of directors of a listed company would, therefore, also be restricted (unless an exception applies) during a prohibited period even where the grant is not to a director or PDMR.

Exceptions

4.39   There are a number of special circumstances which will not be treated as a 'dealing':

(a)   Grant of options – the grant of options by the board of directors under an employees' share scheme to individuals who are not restricted persons may be permitted during a prohibited period if such grant could not reasonably be made at another time and failure to make the grant would indicate that the company was in a prohibited period (paragraph 12 of the Model Code).

(b) Awards and grants prescribed for under an employees' share scheme – awards and grants of options to restricted persons are permitted in a prohibited period if made in accordance with terms as to timing and value set out in the employees' share scheme and failure to make the award would indicate that the company is in a prohibited period (paragraph 13 of the Model Code). However, this exception does not include discretionary awards, or awards made when a scheme is established or altered.

(c) Exercise of options – exercise may be allowed where the company has had an exceptionally long prohibited period or there have been a number of consecutive periods, and the final date for exercise falls during any prohibited period and the restricted person could not reasonably have been expected to exercise it at an earlier time when he was free to deal (paragraph 14 of the Model Code). Given that it will be very rare for a person not to have been previously free to exercise his option at some time since grant, the value of this exception is doubtful.

(d) Savings schemes, etc – a restricted person may enter into a regular commitment under which shares in the company are purchased (under a standing order, direct debit, salary deduction or dividend reinvestment instructions) if the following conditions are complied with:

- the restricted person does not enter into the arrangement during a prohibited period;

- the initial purchase of shares does not take place during a prohibited period (unless the scheme requires him to purchase at that time);

- the restricted person does not cancel or vary his participation, or carry out the sale of shares, during a prohibited period;

- a restricted person must obtain clearance to deal (see **4.36** above) before entering into, cancelling or varying the terms of his participation in the savings scheme, or carrying out the sale of shares held in the scheme.

This exception to 'dealings' will cover partnership share offers, matching share offers and dividend reinvestment arrangements under a SIP or dividend reinvestment plan. It will also cover contributions to ISAs.

(e) Approved schemes – any dealings in connection with a savings-related share option scheme or a share incentive plan (except a disposal of the shares otherwise than to a savings scheme investing only in shares of the company) is not treated as a 'dealing' for these purposes. This exception also applies to 'similar' schemes to those which satisfy the provisions of ITEPA 2003.

(f) Surrender of options – any surrender of an option under an employees' share scheme.

(g) Trading plans – provided that the restricted person enters into arrangements outside of a prohibited period, and the arrangements have been approved by the company, the restricted person may give instructions to an independent third party to deal on his or her behalf during a prohibited period. This provision in the Model Code may be useful where the restricted person needs to sell shares in order to cover a tax liability (including where there is a right for the trustee to sell shares automatically) or where the restricted person wishes to exercise options and sell shares when the share price reaches a certain level. However, if the company wishes to rely on the trading plans exemption where shares are to be sold for tax, specific clearance for the trading plan must be received at the time that awards are granted under the share scheme, as it is not possible to deem clearance to have been given by virtue of the awards having been granted, or the scheme approved, by the directors.

4.40   Chapter 11 of the Listing Rules contains certain safeguards against a 'related party' (broadly, current or recent directors, or substantial shareholders, or associates including family trustees of either) taking advantage of their position. In particular, it requires that a listed company should issue a circular to shareholders and obtain the prior approval of the company in general meeting where the listed company (or any of its subsidiaries) is proposing a transaction of a revenue nature in the ordinary course of business. The related party should not vote at a meeting of the company.

4.41   There is an exception for any transaction which involves:

(a)   the receipt of (amongst other things) shares; and

(b)   the grant of an option to acquire (amongst other things) shares,

in a group company in accordance with an employees' share scheme or long-term incentive scheme (Listing Rules, Chapter 11, Annex 1R, paragraph 3), provided that the arrangement does not have any 'unusual features'. The exception also covers the receipt of cash under long-term incentive schemes.

4.42   A transaction for the purposes of these rules would not include ordinary employee remuneration and benefits as these will be of a revenue nature in the ordinary course of business. Most incentive schemes will be within the exception in Chapter 11, Annex 1R, paragraph 3 of the Listing Rules. Most transactions with EBTs will be outside the related party transactions as an EBT is neither a related party nor an associate of the related party. Other transactions may be covered by the small transactions exception in Chapter 11, Annex 1R, paragraph 1 (transactions equal to or less than 0.25 per cent in terms of each of the accounting profits, turnover, market capitalisation or gross capital of the company).

ESTABLISHING A SCHEME OR PLAN

4.43   An appropriate form of shareholders' resolution to establish a scheme or plan is as follows:

'That the XYZ Scheme/Plan, the rules of which are summarised in the Chairman's letter dated ..., 20 ... and are now produced to the Meeting (and, for the purposes of identification, signed by the Chairman) be hereby approved and the directors be authorised to do all such acts and things necessary to adopt the Scheme/Plan and to seek approval of the Board of HM Revenue & Customs'.

It is common practice to include the phrase, 'Subject to the prior approval of the Board of HM Revenue & Customs' although this cannot be construed as giving the directors the authority to alter the scheme in order to obtain such approval. If the directors wish to reserve the power to make amendments to obtain HMRC's approval of a scheme or plan, a specific power is needed. A suitable form of wording is as follows:

'That the directors be hereby authorised to take all steps which they consider necessary or expedient to establish and carry the [scheme]/[plan] into effect, including making any changes which they consider appropriate to obtain the approval of the [scheme]/[plan] by the Board of HM Revenue & Customs under the provisions of the Income Tax (Earnings and Pensions) Act 2003'.

Any shareholders' resolution to establish a scheme may also include a relaxation of the restrictions on voting in respect of the scheme by interested directors. Unless the articles of association give the directors a power to suspend or relax restrictions on voting on matters in which they are interested, the necessary resolution will need to be approved by shareholders as a special resolution.

An appropriate form of resolution is as follows:

'That the directors be authorised to vote as directors and be counted in a quorum on any matter connected with the [scheme], notwithstanding that they may be interested in the same save that no director may vote or be counted in a quorum on any matter solely concerning his own participation in the [scheme], and any prohibition on voting by interested directors (contained in the articles of association of the Company) be hereby suspended and relaxed to that extent'.

HMRC NOTIFICATION REQUIREMENTS

Tax-advantaged schemes

4.44   Prior to 6 April 2014, other than in relation to an EMI option, tax relief was only available under ITEPA 2003 on the application to HMRC for approval of a 'scheme' or 'plan' adopted by a company. From 6 April 2014, this requirement for HMRC approval has been replaced with a self-certification regime (see **4.47** to **4.50** below). The legislation in relation to tax-advantaged schemes still requires, however, the adoption of a scheme or plan (rather than a contract between an employer and a single employee). For EMI options, whilst a scheme or plan may be adopted, each EMI option must be evidenced by a separate option agreement.

In addition to the self-certification of new schemes, all existing 'approved' schemes must also be self-certified if there are options and awards outstanding or the scheme continues to be operated. Commencing with the tax year 2014/15, all annual returns will need to be filed online, which will require the relevant scheme to have been notified (effectively, re-notified) to HMRC through the self-certification regime. The previous approved reference given to such schemes by HMRC became redundant following the submission of the annual returns for the 2013/14 tax year.

Non-tax advantaged schemes

4.45   As all annual returns, commencing with those for the tax year 2014/15, need to be filed online, this will require a similar notification of non-tax advantaged arrangements to HMRC as under the self-certification process for tax-advantaged schemes (see **4.47** to **4.50** below).

Liaising with HMRC

4.46   HMRC has established a special team which deals with employees' share schemes and, in particular, for dealing with queries on the application of the relevant legislation. Prior to 6 April 2014, this team was responsible for providing approval for the tax-advantaged share schemes and plans, but following introduction of the self-certification regime will be available only to provide assistance to companies in notifying their schemes and plans to HMRC, and to provide non-binding assistance on generic issues.

The unit's main address for correspondence is:

Employee Shares and Securities Unit
HM Revenue & Customs
1st Floor, Fitzroy House
Castle Meadow Road
Nottingham
NG2 1BD

The unit's technical team continues to be based at:

Employee Shares and Securities Unit
HM Revenue & Customs
Room G52
100 Parliament Street
London
SW1A 2BQ

Telephone enquiries: 0300 123 1079
Email: shareschemes@hmrc.gsi.gov.uk

The unit is invariably helpful in handling enquiries from companies on the tax-advantaged schemes and plans, but is also available to assist in relation to other non-tax advantaged arrangements.

Queries about Enterprise Management Incentives should go to:

Small Companies Enterprise Centre Admin Team
S0777PO Box 3900
GLASGOW
G70 6AA

Telephone enquiries: 0300 123 1079
Email: enterprise.centre@hmrc.gsi.gov.uk

Queries about share valuations should go to:

Shares and Assets Valuation
Ferrers House
PO Box 38
Castle Meadow Road
Nottingham
NG2 1BB

Tel: 0300 123 1082
Fax: 0300 056 2705

Self-certification process

4.47   From 6 April 2014, tax advantages will only be available for Share Incentive Plans (see Chapters 8–11), SAYE schemes (see Chapter 12) and Company Share Option Plans (see Chapter 5) once the company has given notice of the scheme to HMRC and has confirmed that the scheme meets the relevant legislative requirements. The scheme will qualify for tax advantages from the date of the notice to HMRC or, if the notice is given after the first share options have been granted or SIP awards made, from the date of that first grant or award.

Notice to HMRC must be given by 6 July following the end of the tax year in which the first grant or award is made under the scheme. If notice is given after this date, the scheme will only qualify for tax advantages from the tax year in which the notice is given.

The notification to HMRC must include a declaration by, or on behalf of, the company secretary confirming that the scheme meets the relevant legislative requirements at the time the notification is made.

Where notification is made after the date of the first grant or award, the declaration will be that the relevant legislative requirements were met:

(a)   at the time of the first grant or award, and

(b)   at all other times after the first grant or award whilst unexercised share options exist under the scheme or, in relation to a SIP, whilst shares were held in the plan.

As a notification to HMRC must contain a declaration relating to the scheme meeting the relevant legislative requirements at the time the notification is made, it is important that notification is made prior to any event that might cause a scheme to cease to meet the statutory requirements. For example, where options have been granted during the first year of the operation of the scheme at a time when the scheme met all of the legislative requirements, the scheme will not attract tax advantages if notification happens following an event whereby the legislative requirements would cease to be met. This could happen where options are granted prior to a takeover; if the company becomes aware that the takeover may cause its shares to cease to meet the statutory conditions (so causing the scheme to fail to meet the statutory requirements), notification of the scheme to HMRC would need to be made before the takeover became effective as this would be the only way of preserving the tax reliefs for the options already granted. After the takeover the company will be unable to make the necessary declaration as the legislative requirements will not be met after that date.

HMRC regards any scheme or plan as comprising not only the rules (and, for a SIP, the trust deed), but also:

(a) all ancillary documents to be used in operating the scheme or plan, including any application form, invitation letter, deed of grant, option or award certificate or agreement and notice of exercise;

(b) the resolution establishing the scheme or plan and any subsequent resolution to amend it;

(c) the company's articles of association;

(d) any schedule of performance conditions;

(e) any side agreement or other documents that cover arrangements made between the company and the participants; and

(f) if the scheme or plan is expressed to be a sub-scheme or plan to a wider non-ITEPA compliant scheme or plan (which is often the case where a non-UK company establishes a sub-plan to be used for its UK subsidiary's employees), the rules of the main scheme or plan.

4.48   A company operating a scheme which had been approved by HMRC before 6 April 2014 is also under an obligation to notify the scheme to HMRC and self-certify compliance with the relevant legislation. This notification must be made by 6 July 2015. SAYE options granted, and SIP shares acquired, before 6 April 2014 under such a scheme are deemed to have been granted under a scheme which satisfies the relevant legislative provisions such that the tax exemptions and other relevant legislative provisions will automatically apply to these options and shares even if the notification is not made. This will not, however, be the case for CSOP options, which will lose their tax-advantaged status effective from 6 April 2014 if the notification and self-certification is not made by the company by the strict 6 July 2015 deadline.

4.49   Notification of schemes is made through HMRC's new online service for employment related securities (ERS) which is accessed through

HMRC Online Services (a service generally accessed by companies' payroll departments, who will likely already have an organisation account). In order to make the notification, the individual accessing the online system will need a user ID and password which can be arranged by the person who first set up the account through the Government Gateway. Companies which do not have an organisation account will need to sign up to use HMRC Online Services and register for HMRC taxes. If a company wishes for share scheme information to be held within HMRC Online Services separately from other data, such as payroll data, then a new organisation account will need to be established under a different PAYE reference. Any active or live PAYE reference for any group company may be used for these purposes.

Whilst it is possible for a company to give access to the ERS service to an agent (either a third party or an individual within the company) in order to file annual returns, an agent is not able to make the initial scheme notification as this is an obligation of the company which established the scheme. In order to set up access for an agent the agent first needs to be registered for HMRC Online Services for agents. Once registered, the agent may request authorisation to access the ERS service and the company will receive a letter with an authorisation code which can be used by the agent to activate the service. An agent will be able to access details of all share schemes registered under the relevant PAYE reference, but will not have access to payroll data. Agents are therefore limited to viewing scheme details and completing and filing returns.

4.50   After logging on to HMRC Online Services, from the Main Menu the ERS service is accessed through 'Services you can use', 'PAYE for Employers', and then 'Employment Related Securities'.

Through this service companies may notify CSOP, EMI, SAYE, SIP or Other (formerly Form 42 or non-tax-advantaged arrangements). For each notification, the following process will need to be followed:

(a)   Choose the 'Scheme Type'.

(b)   On the next screen state whether the scheme was previously approved by HMRC, choose the Tax Year for the first event (grant or award) under the scheme, input a Scheme Name (each scheme must have a different name), and provide CT and CRN references.

(c)   On the next screen confirm that the information entered is correct.

(d)   The next screen is the self-certification declaration for CSOP, SAYE and SIP. A SIP, SAYE, and CSOP must meet the legislative requirements for this declaration to be made.

(e)   The next screen sets out a general declaration for all scheme types.

(f)   Finally there is a security check – the user's ID and Password must again be entered.

Once this process has been completed an acknowledgement that the scheme or arrangement has been registered will be provided.

The above process will need to be repeated for each scheme being notified, although only one notification needs to be made in respect of all non-tax advantaged arrangements which are being operated.

Each scheme being notified must be given a name that is unique. Where non-tax advantaged arrangements are being registered, HMRC has requested that the company name is included in the name given to the arrangements. Errors in naming a scheme cannot be corrected and the only way of using the correct name would be to register the scheme as a new scheme and notify HMRC that the scheme notified in error has 'ceased'.

Notice of enquiry

4.51   Whilst HMRC no longer provides approval for schemes before they are operated, the tax-advantaged status which applies once the company has notified the scheme to HMRC may be withdrawn, or HMRC may direct that amendments be made in order for a scheme to be able to continue to be operated, should HMRC so determine following an enquiry into the scheme.

Enquiry into declaration

No later than 6 July in the tax year following the tax year in which the 'initial notification deadline' falls, HMRC may send a notice of enquiry into the declaration made by the company when notifying the scheme to HMRC. The 'initial notification deadline' is 6 July in the tax year following that in which the first grant or award was made.

HMRC can enquire into whether the scheme meets the relevant legislative requirements and whether the scheme has been operated in accordance with the scheme rules.

The deadline for raising an enquiry is extended if the company has failed to notify the scheme within the requisite period, and HMRC can raise an enquiry up until 6 July in the second year following the tax year in which the notice is given.

Enquiry into continuing to meet the statutory conditions

A notice of enquiry can be issued at any time if HMRC has 'reasonable grounds' for believing that the relevant legislative requirements are not met or have not been met in relation to the scheme.

4.52   One of the main areas which will be of concern to HMRC is whether the scheme appears to contain features which are, 'neither essential nor reasonably incidental to the purpose of providing for employees and directors, benefits in the nature of shares or rights to acquire shares'. The most common problems which arise on this are as follows:

(a)   any arrangements under which cash is to be paid, either as an alternative to the making of an award, the exercise of option rights or where option rights lapse in any circumstances, will be regarded as 'not incidental to the acquisition of shares';

(b)   any arrangements under which shares may be issued and allotted (upon exercise) under a share option scheme in the name of a nominee rather than the participant will, in these circumstances, be considered by HMRC as arrangements not incidental to 'providing for employees and directors benefits in the nature of shares'; and

(c)   in the case of a SIP, the plan not being operated in a way which provides for every participant to enter into a free shares agreement in respect of free shares under ITEPA 2003, Sch 2, para 36 or a partnership share agreement in respect of partnership shares under Sch 2, para 44 and in respect of matching shares under Sch 2, para 61. Under these agreements, the participant undertakes to permit his shares to remain with the trustees during a holding period (of between three and five years) and not to assign, charge or dispose of his beneficial interest in the shares during that period.

4.53   In the case of a savings-related share option scheme or a SIP, HMRC will also require:

(a)   that there are no features in the scheme which have, or would have, the effect of discouraging any description of employees or former employees (who must normally be included in such a scheme) from actually participating in it (ITEPA 2003, Sch 2, para 7(2) (SIPs); Sch 3, para 5 (savings-related share options); and Sch 4, para 5 (approved share option schemes)); and

(b)   in the case of a group scheme, that the scheme does not have the effect of conferring benefits wholly or mainly on directors of companies in the group, or on those employees in the group who are in receipt of the higher or highest levels of remuneration (ITEPA 2003, Sch 2, para 10 (SIPs); and Sch 3, para 8 (savings-related share options)).

Closure of enquiry

4.54   An enquiry is completed when a notice is given to the company by HMRC informing the company that the enquiry has been completed and stating whether or not it has concluded that:

(a)   there has been a 'serious error', in which case the tax-advantaged status of the scheme may be withdrawn either from a date specified in the closure notice (being any date from the date the scheme failed to meet the legislative requirements) or from the date of the closure notice. A 'serious error' would include a fundamental or material error in the plan rules or in the way in which the scheme is operated and would potentially include something that could be put right by either amending or 'repairing' the plan rules. An example might be where the company's shares do not satisfy the criteria for scheme shares are not and were never eligible, or where the company was never eligible to establish and operate the scheme;

(b)   there has been a 'less serious error', in which case the company will be required to 'repair' or correct the error within 90 days of the end of the period during which an appeal can be made against the decision that the error is a 'less serious error', or the date on which any appeal against the decision is determined or withdrawn. Even if the company corrects the error within 90 days and the scheme retains its tax-advantaged status, the company may incur a penalty of up to £5,000. Should the error not be corrected, HMRC may issue a default notice in which case this will have the same effect, including on the tax-advantaged status of the scheme and penalties, as there having been a 'serious error' (see below); or

(c)   there has been no error, in which case there is no effect on the scheme or its tax-advantaged status.

The company may apply to the Tax Tribunal to direct HMRC to issue a closure notice within a specified period. The Tribunal hearing the application, which must be heard and determined in the same way as an appeal, will give a direction, unless it is satisfied that there are reasonable grounds for not giving a closure notice within a specified period.

Where the tax advantaged status of an SAYE or SIP (but not CSOP) is withdrawn, the interests of participants holding awards made, or options granted, before the date specified in the closure notice are protected in that the tax-advantaged status of their awards or options will not be removed. As well as removing the tax advantaged status for the scheme, HMRC may impose a penalty of up to twice the amount of tax and NICs relief given or due on shares awarded to, or options granted to, participants within the period prior to the date specified in the closure notice during which the scheme did not meet the relevant statutory requirements.

Costs of establishment of a scheme

4.55   The expenditure incurred by a company on the establishment of one of the statutory tax-advantaged employees' share schemes is deductible in computation of trading profits or as a management expense of certain investment companies. HMRC will usually reject claims for relief in respect of the establishment of non-tax advantaged share option schemes or EBTs. Normal expenditure on the operation and administration of the scheme will be deductible. The position is not clear as regards expenditure on the alteration of any such schemes.

SCHEME SHARES – TAX-ADVANTAGED SCHEMES UNDER ITEPA 2003

4.56   ITEPA 2003, Sch 2, paras 25–33 (SIPs); Sch 3, paras 17–22 (SAYE) and Sch 4, paras 15–20 (CSOP) set out the various requirements as to the shares to be used in the statutory tax-advantaged share schemes (for further specific detail in relation to SIPs see **8.54** to **8.65**). The self-certification declaration made by a company which operates such a scheme includes reference to the shares to be used complying with those provisions, and the continuing tax-advantaged status of the scheme is based on that declaration and the requirements continuing to be met. The various requirements are examined below.

Ordinary share capital

4.57   ITEPA 2003, Sch 2, para 26 (SIP), Sch 3, para 18 (SAYE) and Sch 4, para 16 (CSOP) provide that scheme shares must form part of the ordinary share capital of:

(a)   the company which established the scheme; or

(b)   a company which has control of the company which established the scheme; or

(c)   a company which is:

    (i)   a consortium owner of the company which established the scheme; or

    (ii)   a consortium owner of a company which controls the company which established the scheme; or

    (iii)   a company which controls any consortium owners in (i) or (ii) above.

4.58   A jointly owned company or its subsidiary can in certain circumstances use the shares of a 'joint owner'. The terms on which jointly owned companies can participate are set out in ITEPA 2003, Sch 2, para 91 (SIPs); Sch 3, para 46 (SAYE); and Sch 4, para 34 (CSOP) and are as follows:

(a)   the jointly owned company must not be controlled by any one person; and

(b)   the jointly owned company must be either:

    (i)   owned as to 50 per cent of the issued share capital by one person and 50 per cent by another; or

    (ii)   otherwise controlled by two persons taken together.

Jointly owned companies may participate in the scheme of either joint owner. However, they cannot participate in more than one of the joint owners' schemes where both joint owners have established the same type of scheme, eg a SIP.

4.59   Only the 'ordinary share capital' of any of the above companies may be used. However, 'ordinary share capital' includes any shares other than those with a right to a fixed dividend and no participation in profits; it may, therefore, include participating preference shares.

4.60   A company is a 'member of a consortium' owning another company if:

(a)   it is one of a number of companies which between them beneficially own at least 75 per cent of the other company's share capital; and

(b)   each beneficially owns at least five per cent of that share capital (ITEPA 2003, Sch 2, para 99(3), ITEPA 2003, Sch 3, para 48(2) and Sch 4, para 36(2)).

4.61   Under ITEPA 2003, Sch 2, para 27 (SIP) and Sch 3, para 19 (SAYE), scheme shares must be:

(a)   shares of a class listed on a recognised stock exchange; or

(b)   shares in a company which is not under the control of another company; or

(c)   shares in a company which is under the control of a company (other than a company which is, or would, if resident in the UK, be a close company) whose shares are listed on a recognised stock exchange.

For CSOP options (Sch 4, para 17), scheme shares may only fall within categories (a) or (b) above, but not (c) since 24 September 2010 (FA 2010, s 39(1), (2a)).

The list of 'recognised stock exchanges' is set out at Appendix 4A below. Any shares must be listed. Shares dealt in on the Alternative Investment Market (AIM), the High Growth Segment, or dealt in on a matched bargain basis, are ineligible under this criterion.

4.62   The assumption behind the conditions in **4.57** and **4.58** above is that the value of shares in subsidiary companies, particularly the subsidiaries of closely controlled companies, can be manipulated by management and, for this reason, are normally regarded as inappropriate for approved employees' share schemes.

Fully paid up and not redeemable

4.63   By virtue of ITEPA 2003, Sch 2, para 28 (SIP), Sch 3, para 20 (SAYE) and Sch 4, para 18 (CSOP), scheme shares must be:

(a)   fully paid-up; and

(b)   not redeemable (except in the case of shares in a workers' co-operative).

4.64   'Fully paid-up' means that an amount at least equivalent to the nominal value of the shares was added to the capital of the company when the shares were issued. This capital amount will normally have been paid (or provided in some other equivalent form) by the subscriber. For the purposes of SIPs only, shares will not be treated as fully paid up if there is any undertaking to pay cash at a future date to the company whose shares they are. This restriction does not apply to SAYE and CSOPs.

4.65   For options and awards made prior to 17 July 2013, shares could not be subject to any special restrictions (other than those authorised by the relevant legislation). This provision was, however, removed for options and awards made after 17 July 2013 by FA 2013, Sch 2.

4.66   Where restrictions apply to scheme shares, the company must ensure, where it is operating a SIP or SAYE, that those restrictions apply in a similar manner to all individuals eligible to participate in order that the provisions of ITEPA 2003, Sch 2, para 9 and ITEPA 2003, Sch 3, para 7 are met. Details of those restrictions must be made available to participants either by a detailed description of those restrictions or by informing participants of where those restrictions are documented and how they may obtain or access a copy of the relevant document.

4.67   HMRC does not currently consider that clawback arrangements should be able to apply to shares acquired under the all-employee tax-advantaged share schemes (SAYE and SIP), although does permit clawback to be included in the terms of a CSOP. Although restrictions on scheme shares are now permitted in relation to all of the tax-advantaged schemes, it seems that the potential discretionary nature of clawback provisions could offend the requirement for participants to receive SAYE options and SIP awards on similar terms.

Widespread ownership of shares

4.68   ITEPA 2003, Sch 3, para 22 (SAYE) and Sch 4, para 20 (CSOP) contain various rules intended to ensure that the class of ordinary share made available is owned sufficiently widely in order to reduce the risk of manipulation of its value. The rules do not apply where either there is only one class of ordinary share or, if there is more than one class, the class of shares in question are 'employee-control' shares. Shares in a company are 'employee-control shares' if the persons holding the shares are, by virtue of their holdings, together able to control the company and these persons are (or have been) employees or directors of the company (or of another company which is under the control of the company). Shares of a different class to those which are scheme shares are not taken into account.

4.69   If there is more than one class of ordinary share, then the majority of the class which are scheme shares must be 'open market shares' held by persons who acquired them otherwise than as directors and employees (or as trustees on behalf of directors and employees) of the company. An exception is made for shares acquired by a director or employee in a public offer.

4.70   The provisions set out above at **4.68** to **4.69** do not apply to SIP. ITEPA 2003, Sch 2, para 29 provides that service company shares will not be eligible to be acquired under a SIP (see **8.65**).

Material interest

4.71   ITEPA 2003, Sch 4, paras 9–14 (CSOP) excludes participation by persons who have (or have had in the previous 12 months) a 'material interest' in certain close companies. The purpose of this is to avoid giving income tax relief to persons acquiring an interest in companies in which they already hold a significant interest. For this purpose, 'participation' includes both the grant and exercise of an option. Similar provisions applied in respect of SIPs and SAYE schemes prior to 17 July 2013 but were removed by FA 2013, Sch 2).

4.72   A close company will be within the rule if:

(a)   its shares are to be used under the scheme; and

(b)   it has control of the company whose shares are to be used under the scheme; or

(c)   it is a member of a consortium which owns the company whose shares are to be used under the scheme.

4.73   A 'material interest' is more than 30 per cent of the ordinary share capital. FA 2013, Sch 2, para 44(1) substituted 30 per cent for the previous 25 per cent with effect from 17 July 2013. In determining whether a person has a 'material interest', it is necessary to aggregate all the shares of which he and any associate of his (relative, partner, certain trustees and certain co-beneficiaries – see **4.76** below) are the beneficial owners of, or able (directly or through the medium of other companies, or by any other indirect means) to control. It is also necessary to aggregate the shares in any close company in which he (or any such associate) possesses, or is entitled to acquire, such rights as would (in the event of the winding-up of that company or in any other circumstances) give an entitlement to receive more than 30 per cent of the assets which would be available for distribution amongst the participators (as defined by CTA 2010, s 454).

4.74   A 'close company' has the meaning given by CTA 2010, s 439, being a company under the control of five or fewer participants (or of participants who are directors), but excluding (amongst other things) any company not resident in the UK. In order to treat participants in schemes using the shares of UK and non-UK companies alike, the relevant legislative provisions state that a company which would be closely controlled if it were UK resident, will be so treated for the purposes of determining whether a person has a material interest under the approved share scheme legislation.

4.75   At **4.73** above, it was noted that the shares of an 'associate' are attributed to a participator in determining whether that participator has a 'material interest' in the company concerned. In particular, where the participator is a beneficiary under a trust, or is interested in part of the estate of a deceased person, the trustee or personal representatives are treated as 'associates' of the participator.

4.76   The attribution of shares held by a trustee to a participator who is a discretionary beneficiary could potentially give rise to difficulties in the case of pension trustees or the trustees of other employee benefit trusts. In order to deal with this situation, ITEPA 2003, Sch 4, para 13 provides that any shares held by the trustee of an employee benefit trust are disregarded when applying the 30 per cent test to determine whether any particular participator has a 'material interest' (see **4.73** above). For these purposes, an 'employee benefit trust' is defined by ITEPA 2003, s 550 as a trust under which all or most employees of the company are eligible to benefit; any disposals of trust property (being either shares in the company or cash paid outright) have therefore either been made in the ordinary course of trust arrangements or to benefit employees, former employees and certain spouses and dependants.

4.77   Any unappropriated shares held by the trustees of a SIP are specifically disregarded in applying the material interest test (ITEPA 2003, Sch 4, para 11(5)(a)).

4.78   The rules on employee benefit trusts and SIPs deal with the main situations in which the shares of trustees may be attributed to employee participators. However, employees may have a remote interest under a family discretionary trust on there being no surviving family members. By ITEPA 2003, Sch 4, para 14, the interest of a beneficiary under such a trust who irrevocably disclaims his interest under seal is not regarded as having an interest in the shares held under such trusts. Alternatively, the trustees may exercise any power to exclude these beneficiaries. The employee must not have received any benefit from the trust in the past 12 months.

Shares under option

4.79   In determining whether a participator has a material interest in the shares of a company it is necessary to include all unissued shares over which he and his associates hold options or are otherwise entitled to acquire. It would obviously be unfair if, in determining whether a person has a material interest, the total issued ordinary share capital (as well as the individual's percentage interest) were not diluted to reflect the number of shares that the participator (and his associates) are entitled to acquire. ITEPA 2003, Sch 4, para 11 provides for this adjustment to be made, but only in respect of unissued shares which the company is contractually bound to issue to that individual in the event of the exercise of the option. Options held by any person other than the individual concerned (or his associates) are disregarded.

4.80   Shares over which options are granted, but which will be supplied by EBT trustees on the exercise of an option, are not shares which the company is contractually bound to 'issue'. Such shares will be taken into account in determining the participator's percentage interest in the company, but not in determining the total issued ordinary share capital for these purposes. In short, the material interest rules may apply more harshly where the shares under option are held through an EBT than where they will be newly issued.

VALUATIONS OF SHARES

Market value of shares quoted on the London Stock Exchange

4.81   The market value of a share for the purposes of the statutory tax-advantaged schemes is determined in accordance with the capital gains tax rules in Part VIII of the Taxation of Chargeable Gains Act 1992. At the time of writing, a draft regulation (The Market Value of Shares, Securities and Strips Regulations 2014) has been published for consultation which would result in a simplified calculation.

Until any new regulation becomes effective, in the case of shares admitted to the Official List of the UKLA and to trading on the London Stock Exchange, market value will normally be the lesser of the 'quarter up' price and the 'mean bargain price' (if there were any recorded bargains) as quoted on the London Stock Exchange Daily Official List on the relevant date. However, these rules do not apply where, as a result of 'special circumstances', prices quoted on the London Stock Exchange are not a proper measure of market value, in which case, it is necessary to apply the normal 'open market' principles of valuing shares, or to use the prices quoted elsewhere than in the London Stock Exchange Daily Official List if those other prices reflect a more active market.

In addition, HMRC has accepted that in relation to the exercise of share options or other acquisition of shares, where the participant sells shares to fund either the exercise price and/or any PAYE/NIC liabilities at the time of exercise or vesting, then it is possible to use the actual sale value (over no more than one or two days) as the figure for the market value of the shares acquired. However, where there is no sale of shares on the open market because the participant has provided sufficient funds to cover the exercise price and/or PAYE/NICs or where the shares are not sold on the open market (for example, where the shares are purchased by a trustee or there is a private sale to a third party) the statutory market value, as described above, will continue to apply.

The draft regulation would simplify the above calculation in that, unless the proviso in relation to being a proper measure of market value applied, only the 'mean bargain price' test would be used (i.e. the lower of the two prices shown in the London Stock Exchange Daily Official List for that day as the closing price for the shares on that day plus one-half of the difference between those two figures. The draft regulation will also put on a statutory footing HMRC's accepted position in relation to same day acquisitions and sales (but only where the sale occurs on the same day as acquisition).

Market value of shares quoted on the New York Stock Exchange or American Stock Exchange

4.82   Currently, HMRC will accept that where shares are listed on the New York Stock Exchange or American Stock Exchange, market value may be derived from the published quotations in the *Wall Street Journal* without the need for any agreement with Shares and Assets Valuation. HMRC also requires that the rules provide for this price to be converted into sterling by reference to the rates of exchange for the relevant day, as shown in the London Stock Exchange Daily Official List, or to other sources acceptable to Shares and Assets Valuation such as the *Financial Times*. Shares dealt in on NASDAQ in the US are not treated as dealt in on the New York Stock Exchange and are, therefore, treated as unquoted shares (see **4.83** below).

The proposed regulation referred to in **4.80** above provides that, for shares listed on a recognised stock exchange outside the United Kingdom, market value will be the price shown in the 'foreign exchange list' for that day (or the last day on which the exchange was open) as the closing price for the shares on that day (or if more than one price is shown the lower price plus one-half of the difference between those two figures). The 'foreign exchange list' is any publication which performs a function equivalent, or broadly similar, to that performed by the London Stock Exchange Daily Official List.

A list of the overseas stock exchanges which are 'recognised' by HMRC is set out in Appendix 4A below.

Market value of shares quoted on other recognised stock exchanges

4.83   Whilst there are specific rules valuing shares quoted on the London Stock Exchange (see **4.79** above) and on the New York Stock Exchange (see **4.81** above), until the new regulation comes into effect, all shares quoted on other 'recognised stock exchanges' are treated in the same way as other unquoted shares and values must be specifically agreed with Shares and Assets Valuation on each occasion shares or options are allocated.

Market value of unquoted shares

4.84   The market value of unquoted shares for tax purposes is the 'open market' value on a sale of the shares on the assumption there is available, to any prospective purchaser, all the information which a prudent prospective purchaser might reasonably require if he were proposing to purchase it from a willing vendor. The statutory tax-advantaged schemes must provide that, for unquoted shares, the market value of those shares must be agreed with Shares and Assets Valuation in advance. As mentioned above, the same currently applies to companies whose shares are quoted on a recognised stock exchange overseas.

4.85   Although shares dealt in on the AIM, the High Growth Segment or NASDAQ are treated as unquoted shares, nevertheless, where bargains in respect of the shares have been recorded with reasonable frequency during the period prior to the proposed allocation under the scheme, HMRC will generally (in the absence of special circumstances) use the published prices in establishing the value of the shares for tax purposes. A similar approach is adopted in practice in valuing the shares of companies whose shares are dealt in under the 'over the counter' market on the London Stock Exchange, provided details of bargains are published in the London Stock Exchange Daily Official List or elsewhere.

Information required for the valuation of shares in unquoted companies

4.86   The information required by Shares and Assets Valuation to enable a value to be negotiated includes:

(a)   a copy of the company's accounts for the last three financial years not previously seen by Shares and Assets Valuation and any subsequent interim statement for the current financial year;

(b)   the relevant scheme rules;

(c)   a valuation proposal, including an explanation of how it was arrived at; and

(d)   details of any recent arm's-length transactions (including the date on which they occurred, the number of shares sold and the price paid for each share).

The address of Shares and Assets Valuation is as follows:

Shares and Assets Valuation (Share Schemes)
Ferrers House
PO Box 38
Castle Meadow Road
Nottingham
NG2 1BB

Tel: 0300 123 1082
Fax: 0300 056 2705

4.87   In the case of companies whose shares are dealt in on the AIM, the High Growth Segment or (currently) are quoted on a recognised stock exchange overseas, Shares and Assets Valuation may be prepared to allow the company to value its shares on the basis of recent bargains or the recent trading price (and, in the case of the statutory tax-advantaged schemes, for the company to notify Shares and Assets Valuation after the grant of options or award of shares as the case may be). This is regarded as satisfying the usual provision in scheme rules – that the market value must be approved by Shares and Assets Valuation.

4.88   Shares and Assets Valuation will normally deal with any valuation proposal promptly if all the necessary information is supplied.

4.89   Shares and Assets Valuation is not normally prepared to agree share values in advance in the case of non-tax advantaged schemes, although where PAYE arises on acquisition their agreement of market value should be forthcoming.

4.90   Although shares for the tax-advantaged schemes must be fully-paid, the remaining shares of the same class might be partly-paid. In such cases, HMRC will normally accept that the market value of a fully-paid share – of the class of shares which are scheme shares – might be discounted in respect of the early payment of the shares, even where this is only theoretical (as in the case of unissued shares over which options have been granted).

EMPLOYEE COMMUNICATIONS

4.91   There is no doubt that clear employee communications material will increase the take-up of any offer under a scheme, since the better an employee understands the value of the offer and how the scheme works, the more likely he is to respond to any offer. Employee communications usually comprise at least one of the following:

- a written guide;
- company newsletter or intranet articles;
- team briefings and formal presentations;
- videos;
- posters; and
- email.

Written material

4.92   Most companies appear to provide full explanatory written material about any scheme at the time it is first launched and on subsequent offers, although it is increasingly common for such material to be disseminated predominantly in electronic form. A few companies send shareholders' circulars and annual reports to employees.

4.93   Savings bodies and SIP administrators send participants annual sharesave/SIP account statements each year and will usually alert participants to the sharesave bonus date shortly before this arises.

4.94   Most savings bodies and SIP administrators are able to provide explanatory guides in a fairly standard format at a fee to cover printing costs.

Company newsletters and intranet articles

4.95   Company newsletters and intranet articles are often the most effective methods of communicating the essence of the scheme, if only because such articles tend to stick to the main points and are not cluttered by non-essential information.

Team briefings and formal presentations

4.96   The spread of team briefing procedures, relying on managers to brief their own teams, is effective in drawing the attention of employees to the existence and timing of any offers. Such informal methods always need to be supported by the provision of written material to ensure consistent and reliable information is supplied to all eligible employees. A number of companies make use of formal presentations inviting the use of specially prepared videos, slides, flip charts and scripts for speakers.

4.97   To support SAYE and SIP offers, many savings bodies and SIP administrators will provide training materials which may or may not be personalised for the particular client company. In the case of other share offers, registrars may provide a similar service, but many companies may need to prepare their own material.

Video

4.98   Video messaging can be an excellent way to ensure consistent and reliable information is supplied to employees at team briefings and formal presentations.

Posters, email and social media

4.99   Posters, email communication and postings on social media sites can be helpful in alerting employees to the timing of any offers, especially where new information needs to be quickly communicated to participants.

DURATION OF A SCHEME

Share option schemes

4.100   There are no limits, under either the tax-advantaged scheme legislation or under the Listing Rules, on the duration of any share scheme. However, a maximum duration of ten years is laid down under the ABI Guidelines.

SIPs

4.101   The ABI (now IMA) and other bodies representing institutional investors have not previously laid down any guidelines on the duration of a SIP, although the latest ABI Guidelines do not seem to make a distinction between the types of scheme to which the maximum ten year rule applies. There are no limits on the duration of a scheme in either the SIP legislation or under the Listing Rules. Under general trust law, all settlements must finally vest within certain periods. By the Perpetuities and Accumulations Act 2009, s 5, a statutory period of 125 years is now mandated.

Alterations to schemes

4.102   Most employees' share schemes contain provisions which allow for the alteration of the scheme. Alterations which are to the advantage of participants are usually subject to shareholders' approval whilst alterations which are adverse to the interests of participants are usually subject to the approval of the participants (or a specified proportion of them). Many schemes provide that any proposed alteration (which may abrogate and adversely affect participants) shall require the prior approval of the holders of options or awards when the number of shares constitute at least 75 per cent of the total number of shares under all options or awards. This broadly reflects the provisions of the Model Articles which relate to the alteration of class rights. Any amendment to a 'key feature' of one of the statutory tax-advantaged schemes must be notified to HMRC as part of the annual return process and the company must make a declaration that the amendment does not cause the scheme to fail to satisfy the relevant legislative requirements. The practice of HMRC is to regard all improvements – to the rights of exercise, improvements to the number or price of shares under option and to any acceleration or extension of the period allowed for exercise – as the creation of new rights of exercise which are unacceptable (see *IRC v Eurocopy plc [1991] STC 707* and *IRC v Reed International plc [1995] STC 889*; and see also **5.103–5.106** below).

RENEWAL OF SCHEMES

Share and share option schemes

4.103   Where the expiry date of a share scheme is reached, the company may extend the life of the scheme by altering the rules and inserting a new expiry date. Any such alteration can be made even after the expiry of the scheme. Expiry of a tax-advantaged scheme does not affect the existing participants who will be completely unaffected. Shareholders' approval may be required to renew a scheme.

SIPs

4.104   SIPs do not generally specify any final termination date although provision is made for the service of a plan termination notice.

4.105   Where the rules of a tax-advantaged scheme provide for termination of the scheme on a particular date, any awards after that date will not attract the usual tax reliefs.

Recognised Stock Exchanges

The London Stock Exchange and any stock exchange in the following countries which is a stock exchange within the meaning of the law of the particular country relating to stock exchanges (or as specified below):

- The Athens Stock Exchange;

- Austria;

- The Australian Stock Exchange (and any of its stock exchange subsidiaries);

- The Bahamas International Securities Exchange;

- Belgium;

- The Bermuda Stock Exchange (and note that the entire exchange meets the HMRC interpretation of 'listed');

- The Bond Exchange of South Africa;

- Canada (any stock exchange prescribed for the purposes of the Canadian Income Tax Act);

- The Cayman Islands Stock Exchange;

- The Colombo Stock Exchange;

- The Copenhagen Stock Exchange;

- The Cyprus Stock Exchange

- European Wholesale Securities Market

- France;

- Germany;

- Global Board of Trade;

- Guernsey;

- GXG Official List

- GXG Main Quote

- The Helsinki Stock Exchange;

- Hong Kong;

- ICAP Securities & Derivatives Exchange Ltd;

- The Iceland Stock Exchange;
- Ireland (Republic of);
- Italy;
- Japan;
- The Johannesburg Stock Exchange;
- The Korea Stock Exchange;
- The Kuala Lumpur Stock Exchange;
- LIFFE Administration and Management;
- Luxembourg;
- The Malta Stock Exchange;
- The Mexico Stock Exchange;
- The MICEX Stock Exchange
- NASDAQ OMX Tallinn
- NASDAQ OMX Vilnius
- The National Stock Exchange of Australia
- Netherlands;
- Norway;
- The New Zealand Stock Exchange;
- Portugal;
- The Rio de Janeiro Stock Exchange;
- The Sao Paulo Stock Exchange;
- The Singapore Stock Exchange;
- Spain;
- The Stockholm Stock Exchange;
- The Stock Exchange of Mauritius
- The Stock Exchange of Thailand;
- The Swiss Stock Exchange;
- The United States of America Exchanges (any exchange registered with the Securities and Exchange Commission of the United States as a national securities exchange; and the NASDAQ Stock Market as maintained through the facilities of the National Association of Securities Dealers, Inc and its subsidiaries); and
- The Warsaw Stock Exchange.

Chapter 5

Discretionary Share Option Schemes

INTRODUCTION

5.1   Discretionary share option schemes involve the grant of a right to acquire a specified number of shares at a fixed price during a specified period, although some schemes have an escalating price over time and in most schemes, particularly those of listed companies where the company is following the ABI Guidelines, the right of exercise is subject to the achievement of specified performance targets. So long as the share price rises, the optionholder will, in due course, wish to exercise the option in order to realise the gain on the shares. If the share price does not rise, then the optionholder will not exercise the option and it will eventually lapse.

PRINCIPAL DIFFERENCES BETWEEN CSOP OPTIONS AND 'UNAPPROVED' SHARE OPTIONS

5.2   Many of the discretionary share option schemes established by both public and private companies will comprise a tax-advantaged Company Share Option Scheme (CSOP), which satisfies the legislative requirements of the Income Tax (Earnings and Pensions) Act 2003 (ITEPA 2003), Sch 4, and a part which provides for the grant of non-tax advantaged (or 'unapproved') options. The key differences between CSOP and unapproved share options are as follows.

CSOP Options	*Unapproved Share Options*
Statutory limit of subsisting options over shares worth up to £30,000 at the date of grant.	No statutory limits on individual participation, although the ABI Guidelines may need to be considered.
Options should be granted at a price which is not less than the market value at the date of grant.	Options need not be granted at the market value, but the ABI Guidelines may need to be considered.
Income tax and NICs relief on the grant of an approved option (unless, in extremely limited circumstances, the option was granted at a discount).	Income tax and NICs relief on the grant of an unapproved option in all circumstances.

CSOP Options	*Unapproved Share Options*
Income tax and NICs reliefs on the exercise of share options providing they are exercised between the 3rd and 10th anniversaries of grant.	Income tax and NICs apply on exercise.
Income tax and NICs reliefs on early exercise in certain specified circumstances.	
The scheme shares must satisfy the qualifying conditions of ITEPA 2003, Sch 4, paras 15–20	
Any performance targets must be objective and satisfy HMRC requirements.	There may be more flexibility in the setting of performance targets.

In addition, EMI options are granted by many smaller, high-risk trading companies and these are dealt with in Chapter 6. A comparison between CSOP options and EMI options is set out at **6.3** below.

5.3   For most companies setting up a discretionary share option scheme, the limit on individual participation under a CSOP of subsisting options over shares with an aggregate market value at their respective dates of grant of £30,000 is insufficient to meet the requirements for executive options and it is usual to grant CSOP options up to the £30,000 limit and unapproved options over the excess. Often the scheme rules will be in two parts, a CSOP and an unapproved option part, providing for the grant of options in excess of the £30,000 limit. Specimen rules of a share option scheme, comprising a CSOP and an unapproved part, are set out in Appendix 5A below.

UNAPPROVED SHARE OPTIONS

5.4   There are three tax-related questions to be considered in relation to any event affecting unapproved share options.

- Is there an income tax liability?

- If so, is PAYE applicable?

- Finally, are National Insurance contributions (NICs) applicable?

There can be no PAYE liability, unless there is an income tax liability. NICs generally apply whenever there is a PAYE liability.

Income tax on unapproved share options

5.5   Before consideration can be given to the question of whether PAYE and NICs apply to any event involving an unapproved share option, it is first necessary to consider whether the event gives rise to an underlying income tax liability. Briefly, any income tax liability in respect of unapproved share options is as follows:

(a)   Grant of unapproved options – by virtue of ITEPA 2003, s 475(1), the grant of an unapproved option to an employee irrespective of the exercise price, is relieved from income tax in all circumstances. However, in the case of CSOP options, any discount at grant is subject to income tax in the year of grant (ITEPA 2003, s 526) (see **5.26** below);

(b)   Maturity (vesting) of unapproved options – an option matures (vests) when it first becomes exercisable. UK income tax does not apply in respect of any gains accruing when options first become exercisable (as distinct from actual exercise);

(c)   Exercise of an unapproved option – by virtue of ITEPA 2003, s 477(3) (a), gains arising to the optionholder (or any 'associated person') on the exercise of an unapproved option over shares in a company obtained by reason of a person's employment with that or any other company are chargeable to income tax under ITEPA 2003, Pt 7, Ch 5. An 'associated person' is the person exercising the option, the employee in respect of whom the option was granted or any connected person or dependant. Any gain on exercise is computed as the difference between the market value of the shares at the date of acquisition less any price payable and any deductible amounts e.g. stamp duty on a transfer of shares;

(d)   Assignment or release of options – by virtue of ITEPA 2003, s 477(3) (b), any gains arising on the assignment or release of options (whether CSOP or unapproved) obtained by an associated person in respect of shares acquired by reason of employment are chargeable to income tax (ITEPA 2003, s 477(3)). Any gains on the assignment or release of options are computed as the difference between the consideration payable for the grant of the option (if any) and the consideration payable for its assignment or release. In most cases this will merely be the cash payable for the assignment or release;

(e)   Benefits received in respect of an option – by virtue of ITEPA 2003, s 477(3)(c), any benefit in money or moneys worth received in respect of an option (whether CSOP or unapproved), including for omitting to exercise an option, is chargeable to income tax on the market value of the benefit received (ITEPA 2003, s 479(6)).

5.6   Income tax, which is payable on any of the above events, will be paid by self-assessment (unless PAYE is applicable). The circumstances where PAYE applies are explained at **5.7–5.13** below and the circumstances where NICs are payable are explained at **5.14–5.16** below.

PAYE on unapproved share options

5.7   PAYE did not apply to unapproved options granted before 27 November 1996 or approved (i.e. CSOP) options exercised without income tax relief before 9 April 2003.

5.8   PAYE applies where an income tax liability arises in respect of:

(a)   the exercise of options where the shares acquired are 'readily convertible assets' (see **5.9** below); and

(b)   in respect of the assignment or release of the option and/or the receipt of a benefit in connection with the option, as set out at **5.5** above (ITEPA 2003, s 700).

5.9   Shares in a company traded on the London or New York Stock Exchanges are 'readily convertible assets', which also includes AIM shares. By virtue of ITEPA 2003, s 702, 'readily convertible assets' also includes assets for which 'trading arrangements' are, or are likely, to come into existence under either arrangements or an understanding in existence at the time. It also includes assets consisting of debts, property subject to a warehousing regime or anything which when done by the employer may give rise to a valuable right. There is no clear guidance on when trading arrangements are 'likely to come into existence' (an imprecision which generally ensures employers bend over backwards to protect themselves by operating PAYE whenever there is any doubt or no informal agreement can be reached with the PAYE Inspector). However, it is clear that where an EBT is actively operated by a private company to provide a market in the shares, or a flotation is shortly planned (e.g. bankers are appointed), then the shares will be treated as 'readily convertible assets'. In addition, by virtue of ITEPA 2003, s 702(1)–(5), an asset which is not otherwise a readily convertible asset – in particular, shares in a private company which is a subsidiary within an unlisted group – is to be treated as a readily convertible asset if a corporation tax deduction is not available in respect of that asset under Corporation Tax Act 2009 (CTA 2009), Pt 12 (previously FA 2003, Sch 23) (Statutory Corporation Tax – see Chapter 16) upon the acquisition of the shares by employees.

5.10   By virtue of ITEPA 2003, s 696(2), the amount on which PAYE is due is based on the 'best estimate' that can reasonably be made of the income tax liability (with any necessary adjustments being made in due course by self-assessment). A provisional 'check' on the 'best estimate', without a formal valuation, can be made with Shares and Assets Valuation (PAYE Valuations) – see **4.45** above. As a result of HMRC's current guidance (which it is proposed be put on a statutory footing – see **4.81** above) in relation to market value, where shares are sold on the open market, it is possible for listed companies to match exactly the taxable amount with the PAYE which is due, by using the sale price to calculate market value (and so the gain made).

5.11   PAYE must be applied where prospective or former employees receive assessable income in the form of readily convertible assets (ITEPA 2003, ss 696 and 702(1)). An agency which engages employees to work for other businesses is responsible for operating PAYE when that individual is paid in the form of readily convertible assets (ITEPA 2003, ss 696 and 688).

5.12   PAYE should be deducted using the code number issued in respect of the employee. In respect of former employees for whom a form

P45 has been issued, PAYE is deducted under the 0T tax code (month 1, non-cumulative without tax allowances). The amount chargeable must be reported to HMRC in 'real time' (which will generally mean on or before the date on which shares are delivered) and accounted for to HMRC the Collector of Taxes within 14 days of the end of the relevant income tax month, ie by the 19th of each calendar month (or by the 22nd of the month if paying electronically in cleared funds). The amount must also be reported on forms P9D or P11D, as appropriate. Where the employer is not able to make the real time return on or before the time that shares are delivered, the information must, instead, be provided to HMRC as soon as reasonably practicable thereafter and, in any event, no later than the first to occur of (i) the time at which tax is deducted, or (ii) 14 days after the end of the tax month in which the shares are delivered.

5.13 The main problem which PAYE obligations impose on employers is obtaining repayment from the employee of the PAYE accounted for to HMRC. There is no statutory right to recover the tax from the employee, except by a deduction from pay within 90 days of the date the shares were acquired, although there is a restitutionary right. In the case of large gains, there may be insufficient income from which to make the deductions and so there will normally be some form of agreement by which the employee either reimburses the employer or agrees that the employer may arrange for a sale of sufficient shares so as to realise the amount necessary to reimburse the employer. If the employee has not reimbursed the employer within 90 days after the end of the tax year in which the chargeable event occurs, the amount which remains unrecovered by the employer is treated as additional taxable remuneration (ITEPA 2003, s 222). Prior to 6 April 2014, the period for the reimbursement was 90 days following the chargeable event. This additional tax is not discharged if the PAYE is subsequently recovered by the employer. There may be scope for a beneficial loan to be made by the company to the employee so that PAYE can be treated as recovered, and so prevent liability under ITEPA 2003, s 222. If the aggregate of any outstanding beneficial loan to an employee exceeds £10,000, then income tax under ITEPA 2003, s 175 on the benefit will arise.

National Insurance contributions on unapproved share options

5.14 No National Insurance contributions (NICs) were payable in respect of unapproved share options before 5 December 1996 (unless over the shares of a non-employing company or group). Earnings for NICs did not include 'own-company' shares and share options.

5.15 Between 6 April 1996 and 5 April 1999, NICs were only payable in limited circumstance in respect of any discount in the price at which an unapproved option was granted. In summary, therefore, whilst PAYE was due in this period on gains arising in respect of readily convertible assets on the exercise of unapproved share options, NICs were due on any discount at grant, not on gains on exercise.

5.16   Since 6 April 1999, the liability for NICs in respect of share options which are readily convertible assets has matched the PAYE liability. This means that NICs will not be payable on any discounts at grant (except in limited cases in respect of CSOP options), but will be payable in respect of gains on the exercise of options. Gains on the assignment or release of an option and/or the receipt of a benefit in connection with an option, as set out at **5.5** above, are also subject to NICs.

Passing employers' NICs onto employees

5.17   As a general rule, employers are not entitled to pass secondary NICs borne by them onto the employees concerned (Social Security Contributions and Benefits Act 1992, Sch 1, para 3A(1)). This means that they cannot make any deductions from earnings or even enter into any agreement to make deductions to recover the liability.

Agreements under paragraph 3A

5.18   However, an exception to this rule relates to share option gains arising on or after 28 July 2000 on which the employee is chargeable to income tax under ITEPA 2003, s 476 (Social Security Contributions and Benefits Act 1992, Sch 1, para 3A(2)). This could, therefore, apply both to CSOP and unapproved options, and it also extends to gains chargeable to tax under ITEPA 2003, s 426 (restricted securities) and ITEPA 2003, s 438 (convertible securities). The employer and employee may agree that the employer may recover the liability from the employee, whether by way of deduction from pay or otherwise, but no such agreement could be entered into before 19 May 2000. The format of an agreement and the manner by which the employee reimburses the employer is a matter for the parties, not HMRC.

Joint elections under paragraph 3B

5.19   As an alternative to an agreement for reimbursement of the employer's NICs by the employee (see **5.18** above), the employer and employee can enter into a joint election to transfer the employer's National Insurance liability on share option gains (Social Security Contributions and Benefits Act 1992, Sch 1, para 3B) and restricted securities and convertible securities gains. The initial reason for this alternative method of passing on the NICs liability, which was particularly designed for the UK subsidiaries of US parents, was the 'recovery' approach of US Generally Accepted Accounting Practice. Entering into an election to transfer the liability would allow for the arrangements to be structured in a way so as not to trigger a charge to the company's profit and loss, which would otherwise be required under the variable plan accounting provisions of US Generally Accepted Accounting Practice. However, there are also accounting advantages for companies reporting only in the UK under the Accounting Standards Board's UITF 25. This requires an immediate provision for NICs in respect of the option gains (although the same principle applies in respect of all share-based payments). If the share options are subject to performance tests, then the provision should be spread over the performance period (and adjusted as appropriate from year to year, depending on the likelihood of achievement of the target). This treatment would also apply in respect of all agreements under regulation 3A to recover the employers' liability. Where a joint election to transfer the employers' National Insurance liability to the employee has been entered into under regulation 3B, then no liability should appear in the accounts as the initial liability no longer rests with the employer but with the employee.

5.20   There are various conditions set out in regulation 3B, which must be satisfied for a joint election to transfer the whole, or part of, the employer's National Insurance liability:

(a)   the election must be made jointly by the secondary contributor (employer) and the employee receiving the NIC-able gains;

(b)   before the election is entered into, HMRC must have given their approval to the form of the election and the proposed arrangements for securing that the liability will be transferred – HMRC will approve a 'model' form of election, which can then be used for successive joint elections between a company and its employees (or can be used as a single 'one-off' election) but will not approve any election with includes provisions that are neither required by the legislation nor essential to implementation of the election;

(c)   the joint election must be expressed to continue in force until the earliest of the following:

(i)   it ceases to have effect in accordance with its terms;

(ii)   it is revoked jointly by both parties; or

(iii)   the company serves notice of termination.

HMRC may refuse approval of a 'model' form of election if they do not feel adequate arrangements have been made for securing the liabilities to be transferred by the proposed elections (or they do not have sufficient information to satisfy themselves). HMRC may also subsequently withdraw approval from a date specified by them in the notice of withdrawal of approval served on the company. There is a right of appeal to the Tax Tribunal against any withdrawal of approval.

5.21   The Social Security (Contributions) Regulations 2001 (SI 2001/1004), regulation 69 and Sch 5 make regulations about the content of a form of joint election under regulation 3B. The form of joint election must include:

(a)   details of the shares or options to which it relates (or of the period within which such shares will be acquired or options will be granted);

(b)   a statement that the election relates to gains on which the employee is liable to pay the employer's National Insurance contributions which have been transferred to him by the election, including a statement to that effect;

(c) the amount or proportion (as the case may be) of the employee's liability to be transferred;

(d) a statement that its purpose is to transfer the employer's liability to the employee;

(e) a statement that it does not apply to any liability arising in relation to retrospective tax legislation;

(f) a statement as to the method by which the employer will secure the liability is transferred under the election;

(g) a statement as to the circumstances in which the joint election will cease to have effect;

(h) a declaration by the employee that he agrees to be bound by the terms; and

(i) the employee's signature (or other evidence) that he agrees to be bound (which can include an electronic communication authorised by HMRC).

5.22 The election may be set out in one or more documents and must be in writing, or in such electronic form as HMRC may approve. Once the election takes effect, the company must give the employee notification that the liability has been transferred.

5.23 The following is a form of joint election under paragraph 3B of Schedule 1 to the Social Security Contributions and Benefits Act 1992:

Between: [Name] (the 'Employee') whose National Insurance number is [   ]
               [Address]

and: [   ] (the 'Secondary Contributor'), who is the employer
               [Registered Office and Registered Number]

JOINT ELECTION TO TRANSFER THE EMPLOYER'S NATIONAL INSURANCE LIABILITY TO THE EMPLOYEE

1. Purpose and scope of election

(a) This election covers

(Delete as appropriate)

   — the grant of employment related securities options

   — the award of employment related restricted securities and/ or

   — the award of employment related convertible securities

under [enter names of all Schemes/Plans/Individual awards or grants that may be used]

(Delete as appropriate)

- on [DD/MM/YYYY] or
- between [DD/MM/YYYY] and [DD/MM/YYYY] or
- on or after [DD/MM/YYYY]

(b) This joint election is made in accordance with Paragraph 3B(1) of Schedule 1 of the Social Security Contributions and Benefits Act 1992 ('SSCBA 1992').

(c) The Company requests the Employee to enter into this joint election to transfer the liability for the secondary contributor's National Insurance contributions that arise on any **relevant employment income** covered by this election from the secondary contributor to the Employee.

(d) The employer's National Insurance liability that shall transfer from the employer to the Employee under this joint election is

(Delete as appropriate)

- the whole of the secondary liability **or**
- [X %] of the secondary liability **or**
- the secondary liability on gains in excess of [£X]

Relevant employment income from securities and options specified in 2(a) on which employer's National Insurance Contributions becomes due is defined as:

(i) an amount that counts as employment income of the earner under section 426 of ITEPA 2003 (restricted securities: charge on certain post-acquisition events),

(ii) an amount that counts as employment income of the earner under section 438 of that Act (convertible securities: charge on certain post-acquisition events), or

(iii) any gain that is treated as remuneration derived from the earner's employment by virtue of section 4(4)(a) SSCBA 1992.

2. Arrangements for payment of secondary NICs

(a) In signing this joint-election the Employee authorises the Company, or other body *(if applicable)*, to recover an amount sufficient to cover the liability for the employer's National Insurance contributions transferred under this election in accordance with the arrangements summarised below[and further detailed in the attached scheme/plan/personal arrangement, *[delete where necessary]*].

- A deduction from salary or other payments due.
- The delivery in cleared funds from the Employee in sufficient time to enable the Company to make payment to H M Revenue & Customs (HMRC).
- The sale of sufficient shares acquired from the Employee's securities option following notification to the Company Secretary/Scheme Administrator *(delete as necessary or add other party if applicable)* the proceeds of which must be delivered to the Company in sufficient time for payment to be made to HMRC by the due date.
- A deduction from any cash payment, treated as Relevant Employment Income, given to the Employee.
- Where the proceeds of the gain are to be made through a third party, the Employee will authorise that party to withhold an amount from the payment or

to sell shares sufficient to cover the secondary NICs transferred. Such amount will be paid in sufficient time to enable the Company to make payment to HMRC by the due date.

(b) The Company and the Employee will ensure that payment of the liability for the secondary NICs will be made to HMRC within 14 days following the end of the Income Tax month in which the relevant employment income arises – *the due date*.

The Employee understands that in making this election he/she will be personally liable for the secondary NICs covered by this election.

3. Duration of this election

(a) This joint election shall continue in force from the time it is made until whichever of the following first takes place subject to (c) below.

• The Company gives notice to the Employee terminating the joint election, **or**

• it is cancelled jointly by the Company and the Employee, **or**

• it ceases to have effect in accordance with the terms of the joint election, **or**

• HMRC serves notice on the Company that the approval of the joint election has been withdrawn.

(b) The terms of this joint-election will continue in full force regardless of whether the Employee ceases to be an employee of the Company.

(c) This joint election will not apply to the extent that it relates to relevant employment income which is employment income of the earner by virtue of Chapter 3A of Part 7 of ITEPA 2003 (employment income: securities with artificially depressed market value).

(d) This election does not apply in relation to any liability, or any part of any liability, arising as a result of regulations being given retrospective effect by virtue of section 4B(2) of either the Social Security Contributions and Benefits Act 1992 or the Social Security Contributions and Benefits (Northern Ireland) Act 1992.

HMRC HAS APPROVED THE FORM OF THIS ELECTION (REFERENCE:).

4. Declaration

In signing this joint election both the Company and the Employee agree to be bound by its terms as stated above.

Signature of Employee: ....

Date: ....

....

Signature for the Company....................................

Position in company: ....

Date: ....

Hedging NICs liability

5.24   Some companies, instead of passing on the employer's NICs liability to employees, have preferred to set up hedging arrangements to provide for the amount of NICs liability payable by the employer. This is normally achieved by funding an EBT to acquire additional shares, any increase in the value of which can be used by the trustee to make interest payments on loans provided by the company which can then be used to cover the employers' National Insurance contributions liability. Care needs to be taken to ensure that in structuring the arrangements, the prohibition on financial assistance for the purchase of shares under CA 2006, s 678 is not breached inadvertently (see **4.7** above).

CSOP OPTIONS

5.25   ITEPA 2003, s 475 provides that CSOP options will not be chargeable to income tax on grant unless the option is granted at a discount (ITEPA 2003, s 526). Given that CSOP options cannot be granted at 'manifestly' less than market value, and this is an extremely limited provision, it is unlikely that in practice tax will ever arise on the grant of a CSOP option. A CSOP option will also not be chargeable to income tax on exercise except where the option is exercised before three years (other than an exercise within six months of leaving in certain specified circumstances – see **5.93–5.96** below), or more than ten years after grant (ITEPA 2003, s 524), in which case the gains will be taxed in the same way as for an unapproved option (see **5.5** above).

5.26   Where income tax is chargeable on any gains at exercise, or on the assignment or release of the option and/or the receipt of a benefit in connection with the option, the tax is collected through PAYE (although, in relation to exercise, only if the shares are 'readily convertible assets'). The company is responsible for returning, on an annual basis, the details of any gains, whether chargeable to income tax or not, via HMRC's online service (see **18.20** below).

5.27   NICs are payable in respect of CSOP options in all circumstances PAYE is payable, in particular, exercises of options within three years of grant other than exercises in certain specified circumstances – see **5.93–5.96** below. Where NIC arises, it is possible for the employer to pass employer NICs on to the employee (see **5.17** above).

ELIGIBILITY CRITERIA IN SHARE OPTION SCHEMES

Eligibility in CSOPs

5.28   Under ITEPA 2003, Sch 4, para 8, a person is only eligible to obtain rights under a CSOP if he is a 'full-time director' or a 'qualifying employee'. A person is treated as a 'full-time director' if he normally works a minimum number of hours each week for the company, regardless of whether he works under a service contract specifying at least such number of hours – the minimum number is 25 hours if meal breaks are excluded or 30 hours if they are included. A non-executive director who normally works the required number of hours for the relevant company or companies will, therefore, be treated as eligible. However, most schemes are specifically drafted so that the test must be applied by reference to the number of contractual hours.

5.29   Under ITEPA 2003, Sch 4, para 8, a 'qualifying employee' includes all full-time and part-time employees, which would include executive directors irrespective of hours worked.

5.30   Where the scheme does not extend to other participating companies, the directorship or employment must be with the company which established the scheme. Where the scheme is extended to other participating companies, hours worked for different participating companies (but not associated companies) may be aggregated in calculating the number of hours.

5.31   It does not matter if a person, who is either a full-time director or qualifying employee at the time of grant, ceases to satisfy these conditions following the grant of the option. A CSOP may allow the exercise of options by a person who has ceased employment or, indeed, the personal representatives of an optionholder who has died.

5.32   There are restrictions in CSOPs on the eligibility and right to exercise options by persons with a 'material interest' (see **4.71–4.80** above).

Institutional investors

5.33   The ABI Guidelines provide that participation in share incentive schemes should be restricted to bona fide employees and executive directors. This is intended to prevent directors who work for two or more groups of companies obtaining share options from each group of companies. Non-executive directors are expressly discouraged from participating in any form of share incentive scheme or share option scheme in order to avoid compromising their independent status (UK Corporate Governance Code, paragraph D.1.3), although a number of public companies now encourage non-executive directors to acquire shares in the company with some or all of the fees payable for their services.

Selection of optionholders

5.34   Discretionary share option schemes involve the participation of selected eligible employees in the scheme. Normally, prospective optionholders are selected at the absolute discretion of the directors without the need to obtain the prior approval of shareholders or any other person. In the case of listed companies, the selection is usually approved by a Remuneration Committee comprising the chairman and non-executive directors to which board powers are delegated. Under the UK Corporate Governance Code, all listed companies are expected to establish Remuneration Committees consisting exclusively of non-executive directors with no personal financial interest other than as shareholders and which, through the chairman, should report to shareholders on questions relating to directors' remuneration. Under ABI Guidelines, the Remuneration Committee should be responsible for the operation of any share incentive scheme for directors and senior executives.

Practical pointers – who gets options?

5.35   Each company will identify the persons who will be selected for the grant of options according to the company's own remuneration policies and its own culture. Consequently, there is an enormous variety in the extent to which options are offered to less senior employees. However, there are a number of practical considerations which always need to be taken into account as follows:

(a)   the amount of share capital available for the grant of options may be limited (although this may be overcome by the use of equity-settled stock appreciation rights whereby the gains on the exercise of unapproved options, but not CSOP options, are converted into a number of shares with the same market value, thus reducing the number of shares required to satisfy the option and alleviating the participant from having to fund the exercise price);

(b)   where a company has a savings-related share option scheme, it may be appropriate to grant discretionary share options only to a limited number of senior executives;

(c)   if the optionholder may need to raise significant amounts of finance in order to be able to exercise an option, it is generally considered that such schemes are best targeted at a limited group of senior executives (although, for companies with tradable shares, a 'cashless' exercise facility (see **2.8** above) may be made available to enable participants to fund the exercise price from a sale of the shares to be acquired);

(d)   it may be considered inappropriate to grant options to middle management and below where exercise is subject to the satisfaction of prescribed performance targets which are designed to be appropriate for senior executives (for instance, performance criteria based on total shareholder return or share price improvement, or earnings per share); and

(e)   UK listed companies will be bound by the terms of their shareholder-approved remuneration policy which will set out the maximum grant levels for directors and will likely include provisions relating to the performance conditions which may be set (see **4.23** above).

GRANT OF OPTIONS

Time of grant

5.36   There is nothing in the CSOP legislation which limits the grant of options at any time. In order to benefit from tax advantaged status, the CSOP must be notified to HMRC by 6 July in the tax year following that in which the first CSOP options are granted. Most schemes of listed companies will also provide that options are granted only within the 42-day period following the announcement of results, and not later than the 10th anniversary of the approval of the scheme, although these provisions reflect the ABI Guidelines, rather than the CSOP legislation (see ABI Guidelines, paragraphs 2.vii and2. viii respectively). Setting such a grant period may also be useful for unlisted companies which may have to agree a valuation of their shares with Shares and Assets Valuation at HMRC.

ABI Guidelines

5.37   ABI Guidelines provide that options must be granted within a period of 42 days following the date of publication of results of the company. The reason for this is to ensure that optionholders are granted options at a time when the maximum possible financial information about the company is in the public domain. At one time, the ABI even suggested that invitations of applications for the grant of options should be issued to optionholders during the period of 14 days following an announcement of results by the company, but as most companies now grant options under deed this practice is now largely academic. Although not reflected in the Guidelines, the ABI/IMA accepts that the initial grant of options may be made during the period of 42 days following either the listing of the company's shares or the approval of the scheme by the shareholders, provided the initial grant does not coincide with a close period preceding the announcement of results.

5.38   In addition, the ABI/IMA accepts in practice (although increasingly reluctantly) the grant of options at any time the directors consider there are exceptional circumstances which justify the grant of options. This provision, which was originally allowed to cover circumstances such as the grant of options to a newly appointed senior executive, can be used by directors in a variety of circumstances, provided they are satisfied that the circumstances in fact justify a grant of options at that time.

Model Code

5.39   The Model Code set out in the Listing Rules (Annex 1 to LR 9) restricts dealings by PDMRs (persons discharging managerial responsibility) of listed companies. Amongst other things, it restricts the grant of discretionary share options to, and their subsequent exercise by, PDMRs during:

(a)   the period of 60 days immediately preceding the preliminary announcement of the company's annual results or, if shorter, the period from the relevant financial year end up to, and including, the time of the announcement;

(b)   the period of 60 days immediately preceding the publication of the company's annual financial report or, if shorter, the period from the relevant financial year end up to, and including, the time of such publication; and

(c)   either:

    (i)   where the company reports half-yearly, the period from the end of the financial period up to, and including, the announcement; or

    (ii)   where the company reports quarterly, the period of 30 days immediately preceding a quarterly announcement (or from the end of the period to the announcement, if shorter), except in the case of the announcement of annual results.

These restrictions apply to listed companies, regardless of anything to the contrary contained in the scheme, and apply not only to the grant and exercise of options, but also to the surrender of options (as well as other sales and acquisitions of shares).

PROCEDURE

Offer and acceptance/grants under deed

5.40   As for any other legal contract, an option will only be enforceable if consideration is given for its grant or the option is executed as a deed.

5.41   Options may be granted by the company sending out invitations to eligible employees and requiring consideration to be paid for the option grant. Generally speaking, the alternative procedure of granting an option under deed is much simpler. The grant of options under deed saves time and effort since it is not necessary to wait for the optionholder to respond to the invitation by applying for the option, or even requiring him to pay the consideration (which is often a nominal amount of, say, £1). In particular, it does not matter if the proposed optionholder is absent on business or holiday. For these reasons, most companies now grant options under deed involving a pre-printed certificate, countersigned by a director and secretary as may be required by the company's articles of association, although normally the signatures will be pre-printed as well. Options may, alternatively, be granted under a single (global) deed of grant which sets out a list of the options being granted in a schedule. In this case, optionholders need only receive a certificate which does not need to be executed.

5.42   Any payment for the grant of an option will be deducted in calculating any gain for income tax purposes accruing on the exercise of an unapproved option or approved option exercised within three years (ITEPA 2003, s 478).

PRICE

CSOP options

5.43   ITEPA 2003, Sch 4, para 22 provides that the price at which shares may be acquired on the exercise of an approved option must be stated at the time of grant. The exercise price may be stated in a currency other than sterling and may be expressed as 'X or such higher market value as is agreed with Shares and Assets Valuation at HMRC', which allows options to be granted over unlisted shares without waiting for Shares and Assets Valuation to agree the market value of the shares. The acquisition price of the shares is so fundamental to a legally binding contract that it is difficult to envisage any grant of an option without stating the exercise price.

5.44   Although unusual, a CSOP can be drafted to allow for a variable exercise price during the life of the option. For instance, the exercise price may be increased on each anniversary of the date of grant by an amount representing the increase in the retail prices index over the previous year, or the price may increase from time-to-time to reflect the carrying costs of the option shares during the option period (ie interest costs on a notional loan to purchase the shares less the amount of dividends payable on that number of shares). So long as the exercise price of a CSOP option is determinable at any time, the requirement for the exercise price to be stated at the time of grant would be satisfied.

5.45   CSOP options must be granted at a price which is not manifestly less than the market value of shares of the same class at the time of grant. Options may be granted at a higher price than the market value. CSOP options granted at a discount are subject to income tax (ITEPA 2003, s 526).

5.46   The value of shares which are included in the London Stock Exchange Daily Official List (but not AIM shares) will normally be derived from the quoted prices for the relevant day (or an average over the relevant days). The market value is taken from TCGA 1992, s 272, which currently provides for the lower of:

(a)   the quarter-up price (the lower of the two prices shown for the relevant day plus 25 per cent of the difference); or

(b)   the mean bargain price (halfway between the highest and lowest prices) recorded on the relevant day (unless there have been any special circumstances).

At the time of writing, a draft regulation (The Market Value of Shares, Securities and Strips Regulations 2014) has been published for consultation which would result in a simplified calculation – see **4.81** above.

5.47   Non-quoted shares are valued at the price which such shares might reasonably be expected to fetch on a sale in the open market (ITEPA 2003, Sch 4, para 36(1) and TCGA 1992, s 272(1)). Although the market value of shares quoted on overseas stock exchanges currently needs to be agreed with Shares and Assets Valuation, the prices on the New York Stock Exchange or the American Stock Exchange (but not NASDAQ) as derived from the Wall Street Journal will normally be accepted as market value. This requirement will likely change as a result of the proposed regulation referred to at **4.82** and **4.83** above.

5.48   Problems often arise in valuing shares for the purposes of the statutory tax advantaged schemes where the company proposes to float. Any grant of a CSOP option taking effect on or after the date on which shares are floated should be based on market prices derived from the Daily Official List (see **5.47** above), which will not necessarily be the flotation price. Where options are granted on the day of flotation the issue arises in that there will be no readily available market value determined by this methodology. Where options are granted not later than the day of any offer for sale, then Shares and Assets Valuation may be prepared to treat the offer for sale price as the market value, provided there is a fixed price and the grant takes effect unconditionally no later than the day of the flotation. If HMRC are consulted in advance and will not accept the offer for sale price as market value on the day of flotation, for example because of significant 'grey market' trading, then the grant of options may need to occur in advance of flotation. It is often the case that the shareholders of a company proposing a flotation do not wish to see unconditional grants of options prior to flotation and, in such cases, the scheme rules may provide for the lapse of options if the proposed flotation does not take place within a specified number of days after grant.

5.49   Where the scheme provides for an invitation of applications, HMRC will normally not permit the exercise price to be ascertained by reference to the market value of the shares on a day earlier than 30 days prior to the date of grant. Where options are granted under deed, unilaterally, by the company, HMRC will not normally agree to value the shares by reference to the market value over more than five dealing days prior to the grant. Similarly, where applications for the grant of options are invited, HMRC will not normally agree to value the shares by reference to the average market value over more than five dealing days before the date of invitation. Any such five-day period must, in any event, fall within the 30-day period.

5.50   CSOP options must be granted at a price which is not 'manifestly' less than the market value of the shares at the material time. 'Manifestly' is strictly interpreted by HMRC and so, where fractions of a share are involved, the fractional amount should be rounded up. HMRC emphasise that if an exercise price is not determined exactly in accordance with the rules of the approved scheme, the option will not qualify for income tax relief. HMRC specifically seeks information, through the annual return, of the basis on which the market value of the shares was determined, including, in the case of unquoted shares and, currently, shares quoted on any overseas recognised stock exchange, the date Shares and Assets Valuation agreed to the market value.

5.51   By virtue of ITEPA 2003, s 526, any undervalue on the grant of approved options is taxable as income of the tax year in which the option is granted. Any amount charged to income tax under ITEPA 2003, s 526 is deducted in calculating the income tax charge which may arise on the exercise of the option and is taken into account for capital gains tax purposes in determining the cost of the shares on any subsequent disposal. It appears that if a CSOP option is granted at less than the market value of the shares, then the option will inevitably have been granted otherwise than in accordance with the CSOP legislative requirements (and any gains on exercise will, therefore, be subject to income tax).

Unapproved options

5.52   In unapproved share option schemes, the grant of an option at less than the market value will not be chargeable to income tax (ITEPA 2003, s 475(1)).

5.53   Prior to 15 April 2003, an unapproved option was only relieved from income tax in respect of gains arising on grant if it was capable of exercise for no more than ten years from grant. Most schemes continue to limit the lifespan of an option to ten years as a result of ABI Guidelines (ABI Guidelines, paragraph 2.viii).

Board resolution to grant options

5.54   Under most schemes, the authority to grant options is given to the board of directors or, more specifically in listed companies, the Remuneration Committee. An appropriate form of board resolution for the grant of share options is as follows:

'Directors' resolution

IT WAS RESOLVED THAT [CSOP]/[Part B (unapproved)] options be hereby granted under the [   ] Share Option Scheme to the following employees:

Name and address of optionholders	Number of shares	Exercise price	Terms or performance targets
[Details]	[Details]	[Details]	[Details]

The Secretary be hereby instructed to prepare and issue the option certificates and to make all necessary regulatory notifications accordingly.'

5.55   Boards of directors and Remuneration Committees often agree the options to be granted in advance of the actual date of grant. In such cases, the exercise price cannot be ascertained at the time the directors, or the Remuneration Committee, meets, but there is no reason why options cannot be determined in advance based on an aggregate acquisition price. An appropriate form of board resolution is as follows:

'Directors' resolution

IT WAS RESOLVED THAT with effect from [date], [CSOP]/[Part B (unapproved)] options be hereby granted at a price equal to the [market value]/[mid-market closing price] on [specified date of grant] under the [   ] Share Option Scheme to the following employees:

Name and address of optionholders	Number of shares	Exercise price	Terms or performance targets
[Details]	[Details]	[Details]	[Details]

PROVIDED THAT the number of shares above shall be limited, where appropriate, to such lesser number of shares as shall not exceed any limit on the number of shares available to that individual under the Scheme rules.'

Option certificate

5.56 ITEPA 2003, Sch 4, para 21A requires optionholders to receive certain specified information on grant (as denoted by * in **5.57** below), which will usually form part of an option certificate or statement to be given to optionholders.

5.57 Any form of option certificate should contain the following:

- the identity of the optionholder;

- the name of the company;

- the name of the scheme;

- the maximum number of shares under option*;

- the exercise price (per share)*;

- a description of the shares which may be acquired*;

- details of any restrictions which apply to the shares to be acquired*;

- the period during which the option may be exercised*;

- the circumstances in which the option may lapse*;

- a statement that the option is not transferable, and that the option rights will lapse upon the occasion of any assignment, charge, disposal or other dealing with the rights conveyed by it or in any other circumstances; and

- any performance targets or special conditions of exercise (if these were not included in any invitation)*.

HMRC accepts that the option certificate need not set out in detail all of the above information but may cross-refer to the provisions of the scheme rules.

5.58 HMRC's Model Scheme, which is included on the HMRC website, includes provisions for options to be granted under deed or as a result of an invitation of applications and payment of nominal consideration for the grant of the option. Most schemes now provide for the grant of options solely under deed.

5.59 The manner in which a company may execute a document must be ascertained from the articles of association.

5.60   A recommended form of option certificate for options granted under seal is as follows.

'SHARE OPTION CERTIFICATE

[   ] plc/Limited

SHARE OPTION SCHEME

Date of grant	Normal first exercise date	Exercise price per share	Number of shares
[Details]	[Details]	[Details]	[Details]

This is to certify that: .... of ....has been granted an Option to acquire the number of ordinary shares of [ ]p each fully paid in the Company at the exercise price shown above under the Rules of the [..................................] Share Option Scheme.

The option may not be exercised later than the tenth anniversary of the date of grant.

Executed as a deed)

by [a person] on behalf)

of [a company])

in the presence of:)

[Director]

[Secretary]

NOTES:

(1)   The Option is not transferable, and will lapse upon any assignment, charge, disposal or other dealing.

(2)   The option may be exercised and may lapse in other circumstances as set out in the scheme rules.

(3)   A copy of the Scheme rules is available for inspection upon request to [   ].

THIS CERTIFICATE IS IMPORTANT AND SHOULD BE KEPT IN A SAFE PLACE'

5.61   Many schemes allow the company to issue a balance certificate where an option is exercised in part; the option certificate may be called in for endorsement or cancellation and replacement in appropriate circumstances, for example, where the number and price of option shares has been adjusted following any variation of share capital (see Chapter 14).

Disclaimer of options

5.62   Many public company schemes provide for an optionholder, who so wishes, to disclaim an option granted to him within a specified period following the date of grant. In principle, this is unnecessary since an optionholder always has the right to unilaterally surrender his option under seal at any time.

5.63   However, express provisions in the scheme rules allowing the disclaimer of options to be made under hand, has the advantage that this will avoid the need for a disclaimer to be made under seal. A written disclaimer under the provisions of the scheme is not liable to stamp duty.

NON-TRANSFERABILITY OF AN OPTION

5.64   Normally, scheme rules will provide that an option will not be capable of transfer, assignment or charge. Previously, ABI Guidelines specifically excluded any right of transfer, but the current Guidelines contain no such prohibition. The non-transferability of options does, however, assist with such options not being subject to the prospectus rules (see **4.16** above).

CSOP options

5.65   ITEPA 2003, Sch 4, para 23 specifically excludes any transfer of option rights under a CSOP. The only exception to this is the transmission of shares to the personal representatives of a deceased participant.

Tax on transfers of option rights

5.66   Where a gain is realised upon the transfer of an option, income tax is chargeable on the amount of the gain under the provisions of ITEPA 2003, ss 471–484. For this purpose, the gain will be the difference between any price paid for the transfer and any sum paid for the grant of the option (ITEPA 2003, s 478) (see **5.5** above).

5.67   PAYE has been liable on any such gains since 6 April 1998 (ITEPA 2003, s 700(3)). NICs are payable on any gains arising from the assignment of any options granted since 6 April 1999.

5.68   An option is a chargeable asset for capital gains tax purposes. Any gain arising on the transfer of an option may be chargeable to capital gains tax. However, as the consideration chargeable to income tax under ITEPA 2003, ss 471–484 will be deductible for the purposes of computing any chargeable gains, it is unlikely any capital gains tax will be payable (TCGA 1992, s 38).

INDIVIDUAL PARTICIPATION LIMIT

Introduction

5.69   Most share option schemes set out limits on individual participation. These will normally include one or more of the following:

(a)   the CSOP limit of £30,000 (under ITEPA 2003, Sch 4, para 6); and

(b)   an annual multiple of salary each year, which is the limit preferred by the ABI/IMA (see **5.76** below).

5.70   In general, the schemes of listed companies will be in two parts: CSOP and unapproved parts. The individual limit will apply across both parts. CSOP options will be granted within the £30,000 limit.

Limits under 'discretionary' CSOPs

5.71   CSOPs must provide that no person shall obtain rights under it which (at the time they are obtained) would cause the aggregate market value of the shares comprised in subsisting options under that, or any other CSOP, established by that company, or by any associated company, to exceed (or further exceed) £30,000 (ITEPA 2003, Sch 4, para 6).

5.72   The market value of subsisting options over shares under other CSOPs established by the company (or by any associated company) which established the scheme, must be taken into account in applying the £30,000 limit. An 'associated company' is defined by ITEPA 2003, Sch 4, para 35(1). Broadly speaking, it includes any company which at the relevant time (or at any time in the previous 12 months) is, or has been, the controlling company of the company which established the scheme (or any subsidiary of that company), where control is defined in CTA 2010, s 450. However, the market value of shares allocated under any savings-related share option scheme are not taken into account.

ABI Guidelines

5.73   The ABI Guidelines do not lay down detailed rules on the size of individual participation. Rather, at paragraph 2.i, the ABI Guidelines simply provide that 'scheme and individual participation limits must be fully disclosed' and, at paragraph 2.iv, that where grant are expressed as a percentage of salary, potential windfalls, where there has been a drop in share price, should be avoided.

5.74   Paragraph 3.1 of the previous ABI Guidelines stated that:

'The regular phasing of share incentive awards and option grants, generally on an annual basis, is strongly encouraged because:

- it reduces the risk of unanticipated outcomes that arise out of share price volatility and cyclical factors;

- it eliminates the perceived problem that a limit on subsisting options encourages early exercise;

- it allows the adoption of a single performance measurement period; and

- it lessens the possible incidence of "underwater" options, where the share price falls below the exercise price'.

Parallel options

5.75 A parallel option is an option granted over shares on alternative terms as to exercise. In particular, the alternative terms may relate to the price, the period during which the option is exercisable and any performance targets to be satisfied as a condition of exercise. Two separate options may be granted over the same shares under separate schemes. Alternatively, the two options may be granted 'in parallel' under the same scheme if the scheme so provides, including an approved share option scheme. To the extent an option is exercised upon one set of terms, it may not be exercised on the alternative set of terms and vice versa. Such arrangements are unusual but can be useful where an original grant of options was made on terms which leave gaps in the rights of exercise and it is proposed that parallel options are granted conferring rights in these circumstances.

Excess options

5.76 Options may, in error, be granted to a person in excess of either the £30,000 limit or any limit on the number of shares available under the scheme. Any such excess option cannot be granted 'in accordance with the provisions of a Schedule 4 CSOP' (ITEPA 2003, s 522). An excess option may not, therefore, enjoy the tax reliefs available to CSOP options, even if it appears to be granted under a CSOP.

5.77 Where a CSOP option is granted in excess of either the £30,000 limit, or any scheme limit, it would appear that, absent any specific provisions in the scheme rules to deal with the issue, the position is as follows:

(a) no tax reliefs will be available under ITEPA 2003, Sch 4 in respect of that option;

(b) the option is enforceable at the instance of the optionholder on the terms of the scheme, provided the option was granted under deed or for some consideration; and

(c) the grant of an option would seem to be made under an employees' share scheme and, therefore, no breach of CA 2006, s 549 applies (and there is no need for any disapplication of the pre-emption provisions under CA 2006, s 570).

The company will need to report the grant of the option as an unapproved share option or, if it has previously reported it as a CSOP option, it will also need to contact HMRC, explaining the position, so that an appropriate adjustment to the tax liability of the optionholder can be made.

5.78 A company which has both a CSOP and an unapproved option scheme can grant options expressed to be made, so far as possible, under the CSOP, with any excess being granted under the unapproved scheme.

5.79   One way of avoiding the risk of granting options in excess of the £30,000 limit, or for that matter any scheme limit, is for the scheme to provide for any grant of options to take effect within any relevant limit. HMRC has confirmed that it would be acceptable for the scheme rules to include a provision which states that, 'Any Option … shall be limited to take effect so that it does not exceed [the prescribed limit]'.

SCHEME LIMITS

Listing Rules

5.80   The Listing Rules contain no limits on the number of shares which may be made available.

ABI Guidelines

5.81   The ABI Guidelines, paragraph 2.ix, limits discretionary share options to five per cent of the ordinary share capital over any ten-year period unless vesting is dependent on achieving 'significantly more stretching performance criteria'.

5.82   Under ABI Guidelines, listed companies are also required to adhere to an overall limit of ten per cent in ten years for all schemes, but there are no longer any prescriptive flow rate limits of three per cent in three years or five per cent in five years.

EXERCISE OF OPTIONS

ABI Guidelines

5.83   ABI Guidelines have substantially shaped the rights of exercise in discretionary share option schemes established by listed companies. It has long been a fundamental principle of the ABI Guidelines that options should not normally be exercised by an employee before the third anniversary of grant. However, an exception is made in the case of employees who die or if there is a takeover. In the case of employees who leave employment early for 'good leaver' reasons, the ABI Guidelines provide that performance should be measured over the original performance period, with vesting thereafter, unless the Remuneration Committee considers this not to be appropriate, in which case early vesting may be permitted (ABI Guidelines, paragraph 2.viii).

CSOP options

5.84   ITEPA 2003, Sch does not contain any rules relating to the time or manner in which approved options must be exercised, except that where a CSOP provides for a right of exercise following an optionholder's death, option must be capable for exercise for, but no longer than the end of, a period of one year after the date of the optionholder's death (ITEPA 2003, Sch 4, para 25, as amended from 6 April 2014 by FA 2014). Such exercise period will take precedence over any lapse date provided for in the rules other than where there has been a winding up of the company as, in this situation, there would be no possibility of acquiring shares.

Income tax applies on the exercise of an option within three years of the date of grant other than in certain specified circumstances (see **5.93–5.96** below). In addition, there is no income tax relief on the exercise of an option after the 10th anniversary of grant (ITEPA 2003, s 524). It should be noted that whilst the income tax relief normally applies from the third anniversary of grant, there is in fact no prohibition on the exercise of approved options before the third anniversary of grant.

EXERCISE BY EMPLOYEES

CSOP options

5.85   The Model Scheme (see Appendix 5A) provides for CSOP options to be exercisable from the third anniversary of the date of grant. This simply reflects the tax rules which provide for any gains on the exercise of a CSOP option prior to the third anniversary of grant to be chargeable to income tax. The Model Scheme provides that a CSOP option will lapse on the tenth anniversary of grant in order to mirror the tax relief provisions under ITEPA 2003, s 524.

Unapproved schemes

5.86   Until FA 2003, unapproved share option schemes were usually drafted so that options lapsed on the 10th anniversary at the latest. This was to ensure that there was no risk of any charge to income tax at the date of grant, as the legislation previously provided that no charge to income tax would arise on the grant of an unapproved option where the option was not capable of being exercised more than ten years after the date of grant. However, since 1 September 2003, ITEPA 2003, s 475 provides that there will be no liability to income tax on the grant of unapproved options. Consequently, there are no tax constraints on the duration of an unapproved option.

EXERCISE BY FORMER EMPLOYEES

ABI Guidelines

5.87   Under ABI Guidelines, options may be exercised after a director or employee leaves employment, although it should generally be the case that options held by employees who resign or are dismissed for cause should lapse. Where options are exercisable, ABI Guidelines recommend that only a portion of the options will vest, to the extent of the service period that has been completed but subject to the achievement of relevant performance criteria. In general, the originally stipulated performance measurement period should continue to apply, but with an ability for the Remuneration Committee to vest options early where appropriate, or otherwise necessary (for example on death), in which case options should vest by reference to performance criteria achieved over the period to date.

5.88 Following ABI Guidelines, most listed companies will only allow exercise in the following involuntary circumstances:

(a)   injury;

(b)   disability;

(c)   redundancy;

(d)   retirement; or

(e)   the employment ceasing to be with a participating company as a result of the sale or transfer of the subsidiary or business in which the optionholder works to a person who is not a participating company.

Most schemes also usually provide for a right of exercise by persons who leave for any other reason in the absolute discretion of the directors or the Remuneration Committee, a provision which provides a useful flexibility in dealing with unexpected cessations of employment.

5.89 Exercise may be allowed where an employee retires, although care should be taken to avoid discrimination on the grounds of age which may be caught by the provisions of the Employment Equality (Age) Regulations 2006 (SI 2006/1031). Provided that the company applies a definition of 'retirement' which complies with the legislation (i.e. is not directly or indirectly age-related), it is likely that a right of exercise would not be seen as discriminatory, particularly where the rules allow for exercise in the circumstances of other 'non-fault' terminations and where the ability to exercise is restricted based on the length of time that the option has been held.

In order for CSOP options to retain their tax relief where the option is exercised due to retirement within three years of grant it must be exercise not more than six months after leaving employment. The previous requirement for the scheme rules to provide for a 'specified age' (ie an age not less than 55 and the same for both men and women) was removed from 17 July 2013 by FA 2013, Sch 2.

5.90 A number of schemes allow optionholders who are transferred to a foreign jurisdiction in which the exercise of the option may not be practicable or tax efficient to exercise early at the discretion of the directors. Although this is not specifically included in the ABI Guidelines, it is understood that such a provision is acceptable to the ABI/IMA. Tax reliefs for CSOP options are not available in these circumstances.

CSOP options

5.91   There are no restrictions under ITEPA 2003, Sch 4 on the rights of exercise which may be granted under a CSOP in respect of former employees.

5.92   HMRC does not consider that a scheme which provides no absolute rights of exercise, but allows the directors a discretion to permit exercise in any circumstances they deem fit, to satisfy the requirements for there to have been the grant of an 'option', being a legally enforceable right to acquire shares. However, HMRC does accept that a CSOP may contain such a discretion, provided there is an absolute right of exercise whether upon reaching a specified date and/or upon achieving performance conditions, or upon leaving employment in certain 'core circumstances', such as injury, disability or redundancy.

5.93   Where a CSOP option is exercised by a former employee within three years from the date of grant, tax reliefs will only be available where the option is exercised within six months from the date of leaving and provided that the reason for leaving is injury, disability, redundancy, retirement, a TUPE transfer or the optionholder's employer ceases to be controlled by the company which established the scheme. Where tax advantages are not available, the CSOP option is taxed in the same way as an unapproved option.

Exercise by personal representatives

5.94   The personal representatives of a deceased optionholder will normally be allowed to exercise an option during the period following the death of the deceased. For CSOP options, if such a right of exercise is included, a period of one year for exercise must be specified (which will take precedence over any other lapse provisions other than following a winding up). Normally, an option held at the date of death will form part of the estate of the deceased for inheritance tax purposes and, in valuing any option, any restrictions on transfer are disregarded (Inheritance Tax Act 1984, s 163(1)). There are no income tax or NIC charges in relation to options exercised following death (ITEPA 2003, s 477(2)).

Takeover, etc

5.95   Most schemes provide for a right of exercise in the event of a takeover, a scheme of arrangement under CA 2006, s 899 or a voluntary winding-up, which affects the scheme shares (see Chapter 13). Many CSOPs also have a provision for optionholders with the agreement of any acquiring company to rollover their options (see **13.15–13.21** below).

Where a CSOP option is exercised within three years from the date of grant, tax reliefs will only be available where the option is exercised in connection with the takeover, scheme of arrangement or, for non-UK companies, a 'non-UK company reorganisation arrangement' in circumstances where the optionholder receives cash consideration (and no other assets) for the shares acquired on the exercise of the CSOP option. The tax advantages are, however, lost if it would have been possible for the optionholder to rollover his options rather than exercising. Where tax advantages are not available, the CSOP option is taxed in the same way as an unapproved option.

5.96 Where, following a takeover (or similar event) the shares which are to be acquired on the exercise of an option would cease to satisfy the relevant legislative requirements, exercise will only be permitted during a period of 20 days following the takeover if the rules provide that, during such period, the legislative provisions relating to scheme shares need not apply. Such a provision may be added to scheme rules at any time, and would then apply both to subsisting and new options.

CSOP rules may also include a provision which allows for the options to be exercised conditionally during a period of 20 days prior to a takeover (or similar event), with the exercise deemed to be ineffective if the takeover does not occur within the relevant period.

PERFORMANCE TARGETS

5.97 A scheme may provide that options will only be exercisable if specified conditions of exercise are satisfied. These may include the achievement of a specified performance target.

Institutional investor guidelines

5.98 Almost all listed companies now incorporate performance targets in option grants. Schedule A to the UK Corporate Governance Code provides that payouts or grants under all incentive schemes, including new grants under existing share option schemes, should be subject to 'challenging performance criteria reflecting the company's objectives, including non-financial metrics where appropriate.'

5.99 Whilst responsibility is now placed squarely on the Remuneration Committees of listed companies to formulate appropriate performance targets and justify them to its shareholders, there is no doubt that different institutional investors have preferences for particular performance measures. The ABI/IMA has periodically reviewed various absolute and comparative performance targets which they indicate may be acceptable to institutional investors. It has generally been the case that, for share options, an absolute measure, based on the achievement of a percentage increase in earnings per share over the rate of increase in the retail prices index, has been adopted. Initially, options were subject to 'cliff vesting' (ie a single hurdle after which the option would have become exercisable in full), but it is now the case that vesting schedules will include 'target' and 'stretch' vesting hurdles. As far as comparative measures are concerned, the following may be acceptable:

(a)   Earnings per share – out-performance against a peer group;

(b)   Net asset value per share – achieved against a pre-defined peer group or index; net asset value would usually be appropriate for the property or mining sectors;

(c)   Total shareholder return – out-performance against a benchmark within a pre-defined peer group. The ABI's/IMA's view is that this performance target depends substantially on an improvement in share price and the selection of the peer group is important. It also considers that there should be a secondary criterion 'validating a sustained and significant improvement, in the underlying financial performance'. This is generally interpreted as an additional performance target based on the achievement of an absolute measure based on earnings per share increasing at a rate in excess of the rate of increase in the retail prices index;

(d)   Comparative share price – achievement against a pre-defined peer group with a secondary performance target as for total shareholder return because of the reliance on improvement in the share price.

CSOP options

5.100   HMRC's view is that additional conditions of exercise may be included in CSOPs provided that they are either clearly specified in the scheme, or the rules of the scheme must contain clear 'objective guidelines' by which those additional conditions will be determined. HMRC consider that the scheme rules may provide for conditions to be set based on the attainment of targets by the optionholder which might reasonably be considered to be a fair measure of the performance of the optionholder's job, and to be attainable. Performance targets may, therefore, be individually set (although it would be normal for any performance target to apply to a group of participants).

5.101   Many listed companies do not wish to incorporate the precise terms of any performance target in the scheme rules, particularly if any changes in future years will require shareholders' prior approval. It is generally accepted, however, that changes to performance targets are a matter for the Remuneration Committee, rather than shareholders.

5.102   Scheme rules will, therefore, usually authorise the directors to set objective exercise conditions, with the flexibility to change the performance targets in later years without resorting to shareholders on each occasion. The detailed performance targets will be set out in the documents issued to optionholders at the time of grant.

Variations of performance targets

5.103   One of the areas of greatest difficulty, in respect of CSOP options, has been the question of altering subsisting option rights and, in particular, performance targets under subsisting options. HMRC's approach to option rights is that once set they cannot be varied except in accordance with their original terms.

5.104   In *IRC v Burton Group plc [1990] STC 242*, Burton Group plc had established a share option scheme and proposed to amend it so that performance conditions could be set or varied after the date on which an option had been granted under the scheme. The court held that the scheme could be altered to allow performance targets to be varied in certain circumstances. In particular, the mechanism for altering the performance targets needs to be set out in the scheme rules and a variation must be made in a way which is intended to represent a fairer measure of performance. In *IRC v Eurocopy plc [1991] STC 707*, the court endorsed HMRC's usual approach to the variation of option rights. The case involved a proposed alteration to a scheme to reduce the earliest date of exercise of options from nine to six years. HMRC argued that such an alteration was so fundamental to the original option that it amounted to the grant of a new right to acquire shares. The *Burton* and *Eurocopy* cases are obviously, to some extent, in conflict. HMRC generally construes the *Burton* case in the narrowest possible way.

5.105   HMRC's guidance on its website reflects the decision in the *Eurocopy* case (see **5.104** above) and provides that conditions or targets may only be varied or waived after they have been set if it is clearly specified in the scheme (and therefore in the terms of the option itself) when and to what extent they may be varied. The guidance states that normally the extent of any variation should be an adjustment which the directors reasonably consider would be neither more nor less difficult to satisfy than were the original conditions when first set. This requirement that any variation should be neither more nor less difficult is an attempt to reconcile the *Eurocopy* and *Burton* cases. The *Eurocopy* case makes it clear that an alteration of a significant term of an option is the grant of a new right; the *Burton* case suggests that there are circumstances in which performance targets can be varied after the grant of the option. However, HMRC's view that varied rights should be no less onerous is difficult to apply in practice. In most cases, the only reason why a company may wish to vary or waive a performance target is because a change in market conditions has made the satisfaction of the performance target significantly less capable of achievement.

5.106   HMRC's guidance states that any variation should take the form of an adjustment which the directors reasonably consider will be no more onerous. It is not clear whether HMRC will normally be prepared to accept the variation envisaged by the directors or will apply its own judgment in respect of any application to vary performance targets.

AMENDMENTS TO CSOPS

5.107   In addition to the requirements to seek shareholder approval for certain amendments to share schemes which have already received shareholder approval (Listing Rules, rule 13.8.11), ITEPA 2003, Sch 4, para 28B(6) provides that any amendment to a 'key feature' of a CSOP must be notified to HMRC via the online annual return process. A 'key feature' is defined as any provision which is necessary in order to meet the legislative requirements relating to CSOPs.

Discretionary Share Option Scheme Rules

Set out below is a precedent for a discretionary share option scheme appropriate to a listed company. It is split into two parts: Parts A and B. Part A is intended to comply with the requirements of ITEPA 2003, Sch 4 and, therefore, provides for the grant of tax-advantaged options within the £30,000 limit under ITEPA 2003, Sch 4, para 6. Part B provides for the grant of non tax-advantaged share options and, therefore, the £30,000 limit does not apply. Both Part A and Part B are subject to an annual phased grant limit. Certain provisions in the precedent (eg references to the London Stock Exchange, grant periods, the scheme limits, the alteration provisions and the performance target) would not normally be included in the scheme of a private company.

Rules of the [   ] Share Option Scheme

PART A: SCHEDULE 4 CSOP

1   DEFINITIONS

1.1   In this Scheme, the following words and expressions shall bear, unless the context otherwise requires, the meanings set forth below:

'Appropriate Limit' means the limit set out in Paragraph 6 of Schedule 4 to ITEPA;

'Appropriate Period' means the relevant period of time as set out in Paragraph 26(3) of Schedule 4 to ITEPA;

'Associated Company' means an associated company of the Company within the meaning that the expression bears in Paragraph 35 of Schedule 4 of ITEPA;

'Basic Salary' means, in relation to an Eligible Employee an amount equal to his basic annual rate of earnings from time to time from his employing company excluding any bonuses and pension contributions;

'Board' means the board of directors of the Company, or a duly authorised committee thereof or, following an event specified in Rule 5, shall be the board of directors or duly authorised committee as constituted immediately prior to such event;

'Close Company' means a close company as defined in Paragraph 37 of Schedule 4 to ITEPA;

'Company' means [COMPANY] [Limited/plc] (registered in England and Wales under No [NUMBER]);

'**Control**' has the meaning given by Section 995 of the Income Tax Act 2007;

'**Date of Grant**' means the date on which the Board grants an Option;

'**Dealing Day**' means any day on which the London Stock Exchange is open for the transaction of business;

'**Eligible Employee**' means any individual who:

(A)   is a director (who is required to work at least 25 hours per week exclusive of meal breaks) or any employee (other than one who is also a director) of a Participating Company; and

(B)   has not at the Date of Grant, and has not had within the preceding 12 months, a Material Interest in a Close Company which is:

    (i)   the Company; or

    (ii)   a company which has Control of the Company or is a Member of a Consortium which owns the Company;

'**Employees' Share Scheme**' has the meaning given by Section 1166 of the Companies Act 2006;

'**Exercise Price**' means the total amount payable in relation to the exercise of an Option, whether in whole or in part, being an amount equal to the relevant Option Price multiplied by the number of Shares in respect of which the Option is exercised;

'**Grant Period**' means the period of 42 days commencing on any of the following:

(A)   the Dealing Day immediately following the day on which the Company makes an announcement of its results for the last preceding financial year, half-year or other period; and

(B)   any day on which the Board resolves that exceptional circumstances exist which justify the grant of Options;

'**Key Feature**' has the meaning given by Paragraph 28B(8) of Schedule 4 to ITEPA;

'**ITEPA**' means the Income Tax (Earnings and Pensions) Act 2003;

'**London Stock Exchange**' means London Stock Exchange plc;

'**Market Value**' means, in relation to a Share on any day:

(A)   if and so long as the Shares are admitted to listing by the UK Listing Authority and traded on the London Stock Exchange, its middle market quotation (as derived from the Daily Official List of the London Stock Exchange); or

(B)   subject to (A) above, its market value, determined in accordance with Part VIII of the Taxation of Chargeable Gains Act 1992 (but where any Shares are subject to a Restriction, determined as if there was no such Restriction) and agreed in advance with Shares and Assets Valuation at HM Revenue and Customs;

'**Material Interest**' has the meaning given by Paragraph 10 of Schedule 4 to ITEPA;

'**Member of a Consortium**' has the meaning given by Paragraph 36(2) of Schedule 4 to ITEPA;

['Non-UK Company Reorganisation' has the meaning given by Paragraph 35ZA of Schedule 4 to ITEPA;]

'Option' means a right to acquire Shares under the Scheme which is either subsisting or (where the context so admits or requires) is proposed to be granted;

'Option Price' means the price per Share, as determined by the Board, at which an Eligible Employee may acquire Shares upon the exercise of an Option being not less than:

(A)   the Market Value of a Share:

    (i)   on the Date of Grant; or

    (ii)   if the Board so determines, either on the Dealing Day (being a Dealing Day within the Grant Period) or averaged over the three Dealing Days (all being Dealing Days within the Grant Period) immediately preceding the Date of Grant; and

(B)   if the Shares are to be subscribed, their nominal value,

but subject to any adjustment pursuant to Rule 9;

'Original Market Value' means, in relation to any Share to be taken into account for the purposes of the limits in Rule 2.5 and 2.6, its Market Value as determined for the purposes of the grant of the relevant Option;

'Part A' means Part A of the Scheme;

'Part B' means Part B of the Scheme;

'Participant' means a director or employee, or former director or employee, to whom an Option has been granted or (where the context so admits or requires) the personal representatives of any such person;

'Participating Company' means:

(A)   the Company; and

(B)   any other company which is under the Control of the Company and is for the time being designated by the Board as a Participating Company;

'Restriction' has the meaning given by Paragraph 36(3) of Schedule 4 to ITEPA;

'Schedule 4 CSOP' has the meaning given by Paragraph 1 of Schedule 4 to ITEPA;

'Scheme' means the [COMPANY] Share Option Scheme in its present form comprising Part A and Part B or as from time to time amended in accordance with the provisions hereof;

'Share' means:

(A)   for the purposes of Part A:

    (i)   an ordinary share in the capital of the Company which satisfies the conditions specified in Paragraphs 16 to 18 and 20 of Schedule 4 to ITEPA (provided that such conditions need not be satisfied at the date of exercise of the Option where such Option is exercised within 20 days after the date on which Options become exercisable pursuant to Rule 5); and

    (ii)   for the purposes of the limit set out in Rule 2.5, an ordinary share in the capital of any Associated Company over which the Participant has been granted an option under another Schedule 4 CSOP; and

(B) for the purposes of Part B, an ordinary share in the capital of the Company;

'**Subsidiary**' has the meaning given by Section 1159 and Schedule 6 of the Companies Act 2006;

'**Treasury Shares**' means Shares to which Sections 724 to 732 of the Companies Act 2006 apply; and

'**UK Listing Authority**' means the Financial Services Authority as the competent authority for listing in the United Kingdom under Part VI of the Financial Services and Markets Act 2000.

1.2 In the Scheme, unless the context requires otherwise:

1.2.1 the headings are inserted for convenience only and do not affect the interpretation of any Rule;

1.2.2 a reference to a Rule is a reference to a Rule of this Scheme;

1.2.3 a reference to a statute or statutory provision includes a reference:

(A) to that statute or statutory provision as from time to time consolidated, modified, re-enacted or replaced by any statute or statutory provision;

(B) to any repealed statute or statutory provision which it re-enacts (with or without modification); and

(C) to any subordinate legislation made under it;

1.2.4 words in the singular include the plural, and vice versa;

1.2.5 a reference to the masculine shall be treated as a reference to the feminine, and vice versa;

1.2.6 a reference to a person shall include a reference to a body corporate; and

1.2.7 any reference to writing or written form shall include any legible format capable of being reproduced on paper, irrespective of the medium used.

2. GRANT OF OPTIONS

2.1 An Option may be granted by the Board only to an Eligible Employee.

2.2 Options may be granted only during a Grant Period

2.3 All Options shall be granted subject to objective performance targets or such other objective conditions of exercise as the Board may determine from time to time.

2.4 Any performance target or condition in respect of an Option granted under Part A may only be altered if events happen which mean that the Board considers that the original target or condition is no longer appropriate and that an altered target or condition reflects a fairer measure of the performance required. Such an alteration may only be effected to the extent that the Board reasonably considers that it will subsequently be no more difficult for a Participant to satisfy the target or condition as so altered than it was for him to achieve the target or condition in its original form at the Date of Grant.

2.5   Any Option granted to an Eligible Employee shall be limited to take effect so that, immediately following such grant, the aggregate of the Original Market Value of all Shares over which he has been granted option rights which are subsisting under:

2.5.1 Part A; and

2.5.2 any other Schedule 4 CSOP which has been adopted by the Company or an Associated Company,

shall not exceed or further exceed the Appropriate Limit.

2.6   Any Option granted to an Eligible Employee shall be limited to take effect so that, immediately following such grant, the aggregate of the Original Market Value of all the Shares over which he has been granted option rights in any year under the Scheme shall not exceed an amount equal to [two times] the Base Salary of that Eligible Employee at that time.

2.7   In determining the limits in Rule 2.6, no account shall be taken of any Shares where the Option was released without being exercised within 30 days of its grant.

2.8   The Company shall issue to each Participant an option certificate or statement in such form (not inconsistent with the provisions of the Scheme) as the Board may from time to time prescribe. Each such certificate or statement shall specify:

2.8.1 the Date of Grant of the Option;

2.8.2 the number and class of Shares over which the Option is granted;

2.8.3 whether the Option has been granted under Part A or Part B;

2.8.4 the Option Price;

2.8.5 details of the times at which the Option may be exercised, or information as to where such details are available in a clear and accessible manner;

2.8.6 the full terms of the applicable objective performance target and any other conditions of exercise which the Board has determined shall apply to the Option (including details of the terms of Rule 2.4 and of any other term pursuant to which the performance target or condition may be varied) or information as to where such details are available in a clear and accessible manner;

2.8.7 whether the Shares over which the Option is granted are subject to any Restriction and, if so, the details of that Restriction (including details of any terms pursuant to which such Restriction may be varied) or information as to where such details are available in a clear and accessible manner;

2.8.8 any further information required to be so included by Schedule 4 to ITEPA, or information as to where such details are available in a clear and accessible manner.

2.8.9 details of the terms of Rule 8; and

2.9   The grant of an Option shall be made under seal or in such other manner as to take effect in law as a deed.

2.10   Except as provided in the Scheme, every Option shall be personal to the Participant to whom it is granted and shall not be transferable.

2.11   No amount shall be paid in respect of the grant of an Option.

2.12 The Participant may release an Option without it being exercised within 30 days of its grant. Where the Participant does not release the Option within this period the Participant shall be deemed to have accepted the Option on the terms set out in the Rules.

3 SCHEME ALLOCATION LIMITS

3.1 The maximum number of Shares which may be allocated under the Scheme on any day shall not, when added to the aggregate of the number of Shares which have been allocated in the previous 10 years under the Scheme and under any other discretionary Employees' Share Scheme adopted by the Company, exceed such number as represents five per cent of the ordinary share capital of the Company in issue immediately prior to that day.

3.2 The maximum number of Shares which may be allocated under the Scheme on any day shall not, when added to the aggregate of the number of Shares which have been allocated in the previous 10 years under the Scheme and under any other Employees' Share Scheme adopted by the Company, exceed such number as represents 10 per cent of the ordinary share capital of the Company in issue immediately prior to that day.

3.3 References in this Rule 3 to the 'allocation' of Shares shall mean:

3.3.1 in the case of any option, conditional share award or other similar award pursuant to which Shares may be acquired:

(A) the grant of the option, conditional share award or other similar award to acquire Shares, pursuant to which Shares may be issued; and

(B) in so far as not previously taken into account under (A) above from the date of grant, any subscription for Shares which are issued for the purpose of satisfying any option, conditional share award or other similar award to acquire Shares; and

3.3.2 in relation to other types of Employees' Share Scheme, the issue and allotment of Shares,

and references to 'allocated', in this Rule 3, shall be construed accordingly.

3.4 In determining the above limits no account shall be taken of:

3.4.1 any allocation (or part thereof) where the option, conditional share award or other similar award to acquire Shares was released, lapsed or otherwise became incapable of vesting;

3.4.2 any allocation (or part thereof) in respect of which the Board has determined shall be satisfied otherwise than by the issue of Shares; and

3.4.3 such number of additional Shares as would otherwise have been issued on the exercise of an option for monetary consideration (*the exercise price*) but in respect of which the exercise price is not paid, in substitution for the issue of such lesser number of shares as have a market value equal only to the gain which the optionholder would have made on exercise (*equity-settled SAR alternative*).

3.5 References to the issue and allotment of Shares shall include the transfer of Treasury Shares, but only until such time as the guidelines issued by institutional investor bodies cease to provide that they need to be included.

4. RIGHTS OF EXERCISE AND LAPSE OF OPTIONS

4.1 Save as provided in Rules 4.5, 4.6, 4.8 and Rule 5, an Option shall not be exercised earlier than the third anniversary of the Date of Grant.

4.2 Save as provided in Rules 4.5, 4.6 and Rule 5, an Option may only be exercised by a Participant whilst he is a director or employee of a Participating Company.

4.3 An Option may not be exercised by a Participant if he has, or has had at any time within the 12-month period preceding the date of exercise, a Material Interest in the issued ordinary share capital of a Close Company which is the Company or a company which has Control of the Company or is a Member of a Consortium which owns the Company.

4.4. An Option may only be exercised if and to the extent that the conditions of exercise pursuant to Rules 2.3 and 2.4 have previously been fulfilled.

4.5 An Option may be exercised by the personal representatives of a deceased Participant within one year following the date of his death.

4.6 An Option may be exercised within six months following the date on which the Participant ceases to hold an office or employment with a Participating Company if such cessation is as a result of:

4.6.1 injury or disability;

4.6.2 redundancy within the meaning of the Employment Rights Act 1996 or the Employment Rights (Northern Ireland) Order 1996;

4.6.3 retirement;

4.6.4 a relevant transfer within the meaning of the Transfer of Undertakings (Protection of Employment) Regulations 2006;

4.6.5 the company which employs him ceasing to be under the Control of the Company; or

4.6.6 any other reason, at the discretion of the Board or Committee acting fairly and reasonably,

PROVIDED THAT if the Participant ceases to hold the said office or employment as a result of any of the reasons specified in 4.6.1 to 4.6.6 above, the Board may, in addition to the period of exercise specified above, allow exercise of the Option during such period or periods as the Board shall determine acting fairly and reasonably, ending not later than the date which is six months after the third anniversary of the Date of Grant.

4.7 [Where the Participant exercises an Option pursuant to Rule 4.6, the number of Shares in respect of which that Option would otherwise have been exercisable shall be limited to a pro rata number on the basis of the number of whole months which have elapsed from the Date of Grant to the date the Participant ceased to hold an office or employment with a Participating Company, as compared to 36 months. Any remainder of the Option shall lapse.]

4.8 If it is proposed that a Participant, whilst continuing to hold an office or employment with a Participating Company, is to be transferred to work in another country and as a result of that transfer the Participant will either:

4.8.1 become subject to income tax on his remuneration in the country to which he is transferred and the Board is satisfied that as a result he will suffer a tax disadvantage upon exercising an Option; or

    4.8.2 become subject to restrictions on his ability to exercise an Option or to deal in the Shares issuable upon the exercise of that Option by reason of, or in consequence of, the securities laws or exchange control laws of the country to which he is transferred,

the Participant may exercise the Option in the period commencing three months before the proposed date of his transfer and ending three months after the date of his actual transfer.

4.9   Options shall lapse upon the occurrence of the earliest of the following events:

    4.9.1 the conclusion of the day on the 10th anniversary of the Date of Grant, or such earlier date as shall be determined by the Board prior to the grant of such Options;

    4.9.2 the expiry of any of the periods specified in Rules 4.5 and 4.6 (save that if at the time any of the periods specified in Rule 4.6 expire, time is running under the period specified in Rule 4.5, the Option shall not lapse by reason of this Rule 4.9.2 until the expiry of the period specified in Rule 4.5);

    4.9.3 the expiry of any of the periods specified in Rules 5.4, 5.5, 5.6 or 5.7 save where an Option is released in consideration of the grant of a New Option over New Shares in the Acquiring Company (during one of the periods specified in Rules 5.4, 5.5 or 5.6) pursuant to Rules 5.9 (and further save that if at the time any of the periods specified in Rules 5.4,5.5, 5.6 or 5.7 expire, time is running under the period in Rule 4.5, the Option shall not lapse by reason of this Rule 4.9.3 until the expiry of the period under Rule 4.5);

    4.9.4 the Participant ceasing to hold an office or employment with a Participating Company in any circumstances other than:

        (A)   where the cessation of office or employment arises on any of the grounds specified in Rules 4.5 and 4.6; or

        (B)   where the cessation of office or employment arises on any ground whatsoever during any of the periods specified in Rule 5;

    4.9.5 subject to Rule 5.7, the passing of an effective resolution, or the making of an order by the Court, for the winding-up of the Company; and

    4.9.6 the Participant being deprived (otherwise than on death) of the legal or beneficial ownership of the Option by operation of law, or doing or omitting to do anything which causes him to be so deprived or becomes bankrupt.

4.10 A Participant shall not be treated as ceasing to hold an office or employment with a Participating Company until he no longer holds any office or employment with any Participating Company.

5.   **TAKEOVER, COMPROMISE OR ARRANGEMENT, AND LIQUIDATION**

5.1   If any person obtains Control of the Company as a result of making a general offer to acquire all of the Shares (other than Shares held by the person making the offer or by any person connected to that person) which is either unconditional or is made on a condition such that if it is satisfied the person making the offer will have Control of the Company, an Option may be exercised within six months of the time when the person making the offer has obtained Control of the Company and any condition subject to which the offer is made has been satisfied or waived.

5.2   If, having or having obtained Control of the Company, a person makes a general offer to acquire all of the Shares (other than Shares held by the person making the offer or by any person connected to that person), an Option may be exercised within six months of the time when the offer becomes unconditional in all respects (or, if made on an unconditional basis, from the time the offer is made).

5.3   For the purposes of Rules 5.1 and 5.2 a person shall be deemed to have Control, or have obtained Control, of the Company if he and others acting in concert with him together have Control of it or have obtained Control of it.

5.4   If any person becomes bound or entitled to acquire Shares under Sections 979 to 982 or 983 to 985 of the Companies Act 2006, an Option may be exercised within one month of the date on which that person first became so bound or entitled.

5.5   If, under Section 899 of the Companies Act 2006, the Court sanctions a compromise or arrangement applicable to or affecting:

5.5.1   all of the Shares; or

5.5.2   all of the Shares which are held by a class of shareholders identified otherwise than by reference to their employment or directorships or their participation in the Scheme or any Schedule 4 CSOP,

an Option may be exercised within six months of the Court sanctioning the compromise or arrangement PROVIDED THAT an Option may not be exercised pursuant to this Rule 5.5 where the purpose and effect of the compromise or arrangement is that the Company becomes a Subsidiary of another company, such other company having substantially the same shareholders and approximate shareholdings as those of the Company immediately prior to the compromise or arrangement taking effect and an offer of a New Option is made pursuant to Rules 5.9 and5.10.

5.6   [If a Non-UK Company Reorganisation applicable to or affecting:

5.6.1   all of the Shares; or

5.6.2   all of the Shares which are held by a class of shareholders identified otherwise than by reference to their employment or directorships or their participation in the Scheme or any Schedule 4 CSOP,

becomes binding on the shareholders covered by it, an Option may be exercised within six months of such date PROVIDED THAT an Option may not be exercised pursuant to this Rule 5.6 where the purpose and effect of the Non-UK Company Reorganisation is that the Company becomes a Subsidiary of another company, such other company having substantially the same shareholders and approximate shareholdings as those of the Company immediately prior to the Non-UK Company Reorganisation becoming binding and an offer of a New Option is made pursuant to Rules 5.9 and 5.10.]

5.7   If notice is duly given of a resolution for the voluntary winding-up of the Company, an Option may be exercised within two months from the date of the resolution.

5.8   [Where the Participant exercises an Option pursuant to any of Rules 5.1 to5.7, the number of Shares in respect of which that Option would otherwise have been exercisable shall be limited to a pro rata number on the basis of the number of whole months which have elapsed from the Date of Grant to the date of the event which gives rise to the right of exercise, as compared to 36 months. Any remainder of the Option shall lapse.]

5.9 If any company (the 'Acquiring Company'):

5.9.1 obtains Control of the Company as a result of making a general offer to acquire all of the Shares (other than Shares held by the person making the offer or by any person connected to that person) which is either unconditional or made on a condition such that if it is satisfied the Acquiring Company will have Control of the Company;

5.9.2 obtains Control of the Company as a result of a compromise or arrangement sanctioned by the Court under Section 899 of the Companies Act 2006;

5.9.3 [obtains control of the Company as a result of a Non-UK Company Reorganisation which became binding on the shareholders covered by it;] or

5.9.4 becomes bound or entitled to acquire Shares under Sections 979 to 982 or 983 to 985 of the Companies Act 2006,

any Participant may at any time within the Appropriate Period, by agreement with the Acquiring Company, release any Option which has not lapsed (the 'Old Option') in consideration of the grant to him of an option (the 'New Option') which (for the purposes of Paragraph 27 of Schedule 4 to ITEPA) is equivalent to the Old Option but relates to shares in a different company (whether the Acquiring Company itself or some other company falling within Paragraph 16(b) or (c) of Schedule 4 to ITEPA).

5.10 The New Option shall not be regarded for the purposes of Rule 5.9 as equivalent to the Old Option unless the conditions set out in Paragraph 27(4) of Schedule 4 to ITEPA are satisfied, but so that the provisions of the Scheme shall for this purpose be construed is if:

5.10.1 the New Option were an option granted under the Scheme at the same time as the Old Option;

5.10.2 except for the purposes of the definition of 'Participating Company' in Rule 1, the reference to '[COMPANY] [Limited/plc]' in the definition of 'Company' in Rule 1 were a reference to the different company mentioned in Rule5.9 (provided that the Scheme Organiser (as defined in Schedule 4 to ITEPA) shall continue to be the Company); and

5.10.3 Rule 11.2 was omitted.

6. MANNER OF EXERCISE

6.1 An Option may be exercised, in whole or in part, by the delivery to the Secretary of the Company, or its duly appointed agent, of a notice of exercise in such form as the Board may prescribe, duly completed and signed by the Participant (or by his duly authorised agent) together with either:

6.1.1 a remittance for the Exercise Price payable;

6.1.2 an assurance, in such form as the Board may accept, that the Exercise Price will be remitted to the Company as soon as reasonably practicable (including a remittance to be made out of the proceeds of sale of at least some of the Shares to be acquired on exercise) payable in respect of the Shares over which the Option is to be exercised; or

6.1.3   an application for bridging finance to exercise the Option duly completed and signed, in such form as the Board may prescribe, in respect of the Shares over which the Option is to be exercised.

6.2   Delivery of the notice of exercise shall not be treated as effecting the exercise of an Option unless and until any conditions to which exercise of the Option is subject have been fulfilled.

6.3   All such Shares shall be allotted or transferred (as the case may be) into the name of the Participant, or as he may direct pursuant to any finance arrangement provided that beneficial ownership of the Shares remains with the Participant until any sale of the Shares takes effect.

6.4   As a condition of exercise, the Board may require the Participant to enter into an election to which paragraph 3B of Schedule 1 to the Social Security Contributions and Benefits Act 1992 applies.

7.   ISSUE OR TRANSFER OF SHARES

7.1   Shares to be issued pursuant to the exercise of an Option shall be allotted within 30 days following the effective date of exercise of the Option.

7.2   The Board shall procure the transfer of any Shares (including any Treasury Shares) to be transferred pursuant to the exercise of an Option within 30 days following the effective date of exercise of the Option.

7.3   Shares issued and allotted pursuant to the Scheme will rank pari passu in all respects with the Shares then in issue at the date of such allotment, except that they will not rank for any rights attaching to Shares by reference to a record date preceding the date of allotment.

7.4   Shares to be transferred pursuant to the Scheme (including any Treasury Shares) will be transferred free of all liens, charges and encumbrances and together with all rights attaching thereto, except they will not rank for any rights attaching to Shares by reference to a record date preceding the date of transfer.

7.5   If and so long as the Shares are admitted to listing by the UK Listing Authority and traded on the London Stock Exchange or are admitted to trading on any stock exchange, stock market or other recognised exchange (the 'Relevant Exchange'), the Company shall apply for any Shares issued and allotted pursuant to the Scheme to be admitted to listing by the UK Listing Authority, or to be listed or traded on the Relevant Exchange, as soon as practicable after the allotment thereof.

7.6   Shares acquired pursuant to the exercise of an Option shall be subject to the Company's Articles of Association as amended from time to time.

8.   TAX LIABILITY

8.1   If, on the exercise of an Option (whether in whole or in part), a Tax Liability arises, then unless:

8.1.1   the Participant has agreed that he will make a payment to the Company or his employer or former employer of an amount equal to the Tax Liability; and

     8.1.2 the Participant makes such payment within 7 days of being notified by the Company of the amount of the Tax Liability,

the Company shall only be obliged to deliver (or procure the delivery of) legal title to such proportion of the Shares in respect of which that Option is exercised as shall be determined as follows (notwithstanding that beneficial title shall otherwise pass):

$$\frac{A - B}{A}$$

Where:

A   is the aggregate Relevant Value of the Shares in respect of which that Option is exercised; and

B   is the amount of the Tax Liability arising as a result of the exercise.

8.2   The Participant authorises the Company to arrange for a trustee or nominee on behalf of the Participant to sell the proportion of the Shares which the Company is not obliged to deliver, under Rule 8.1, to the Participant (the 'Retained Shares') on the date on which those Shares would otherwise be delivered to the Participant and for that trustee or nominee to remit the proceeds of the sale of the Retained Shares to the Company or the Participant's employer or former employer in order to reimburse it for the Tax Liability arising as a result of the exercise of the Option.

8.3   To the extent that the full amount of the Tax Liability is not reimbursed to the Company or the Participant's employer or former employer, or the Participant has agreed with the Company that Rules 8.1 and 8.2 shall not apply, the Participant authorises the Company to make such adjustments through payroll as are necessary to ensure that the correct amount is reimbursed to the Company or the Participant's employer or former employer in respect of the Tax Liability arising as a result of the exercise of the Option.

8.4   In this Rule 8, 'Relevant Value' shall mean 'the market value of a Share determined in accordance with Part VIII of the Taxation of Chargeable Gains Act 1992' and all fractions of a Share shall be ignored.

8.5   In this Rule 8, 'Tax Liability' shall include any amount of tax and/or social security (or similar) contributions which the Company or the Participant's employer becomes liable on behalf of the Participant to pay to the appropriate authorities, together with all or such proportion (if any) of employer's social security contributions which would otherwise be payable by the Company or the Participant's employer as is determined to be recoverable from the Participant (to the extent permitted by law) by the Board at the Date of Exercise, save to the extent that such employer's social security contributions are subject to recovery pursuant to an election to which paragraph 3B of Schedule 1 to the Social Security Contributions and Benefits Act 1992 applies.

9.   ADJUSTMENTS

9.1   The number of Shares over which an Option has been granted and the Option Price thereof shall be adjusted in such manner as the Board shall determine following any capitalisation issue (other than a scrip dividend), rights issue, subdivision, consolidation, reduction of share capital or any other variation of share capital of the Company to take account of such event, provided that such adjustment must secure that:

9.1.1 each of (i) the total Market Value of the Shares which may be acquired by the exercise of the Option; and (ii) the total Exercise price of the Option, is immediately after the adjustment substantially the same as it was immediately before the adjustment; and

9.1.2 following such adjustment the requirements of Schedule 4 to ITEPA continue to be met,

and any adjustment pursuant to this Rule 9.1 shall be notified to HM Revenue & Customs in accordance with Paragraph 28B(6) of Schedule 4 to ITEPA.

9.2 Subject to Rule 9.3, an adjustment may be made under Rule 9.1 which would have the effect of reducing the Option Price of unissued shares to less than the nominal value of a Share but only if and to the extent that the Board shall be authorised to capitalise from the reserves of the Company a sum equal to the amount by which the nominal value of the Shares in respect of which the Option is exercisable exceeds the adjusted Exercise Price, and so that on the exercise of any Option in respect of which the Option Price has been so reduced, the Board shall capitalise and apply such sum (if any) as is necessary to pay up the amount by which the aggregate nominal value of the Shares in respect of which the Option is exercised exceeds the Exercise Price for such Shares.

9.3 Where an Option subsists over both issued and unissued Shares, an adjustment permitted by Rule 9.2 may only be made if the reduction of the Option Price of both issued and unissued Shares can be made to the same extent.

9.4 The Board may take such steps as it may consider necessary to notify Participants of any adjustment made under this Rule 9 and to call in, cancel, endorse, issue or reissue any option certificate consequent upon such adjustment.

10. ADMINISTRATION

10.1 Any discretion of the Board (including pursuant to which any amendment may be made to any term of the Option) must be exercised on a fair and reasonable basis.

10.2 Any notice or other communication made under, or in connection with, the Scheme may be given by personal delivery or by sending the same by post or such other suitable mode of communication deemed appropriate in the circumstances by the Board, in the case of a company to its registered office and in the case of an individual to his last known address, or, where he is a director or employee of the Company or an Associated Company, either to his last known address or to the address of the place of business at which he performs the whole or substantially the whole of the duties of his office or employment. Where a notice or other communication is given by first-class post, it shall be deemed to have been received 48 hours after it was put into the post properly addressed and stamped.

10.3 The Company may distribute to Participants copies of any notice or document normally sent by the Company to the holders of Shares.

10.4 If any option certificate shall be worn out, defaced or lost, it may be replaced on such evidence being provided as the Board may require.

10.5 The Company shall at all times keep available for allotment unissued Shares at least sufficient to satisfy all Options under which Shares may be subscribed, or procure that sufficient Shares (which may include Treasury Shares) are available for transfer to satisfy all Options under which Shares may be acquired.

10.6 The decision of the Board in any dispute relating to an Option or the due exercise thereof or any other matter in respect of the Scheme shall be final and conclusive.

10.7 The costs of introducing and administering the Scheme shall be borne by the Company.

11. ALTERATIONS

11.1 Subject to Rule 11.2, the Board may at any time alter or add to all or any of the provisions of the Scheme in any respect, provided that an alteration or addition to a Key Feature of Part A shall be notified to HM Revenue & Customs in accordance with Paragraph 28B(6) of Schedule 4 to ITEPA.

11.2 Subject to Rule 11.3, no alteration or addition to the advantage of present or future Participants or employees relating to eligibility, scheme limits, the Option Price, the basis of individual entitlement or to the provisions for the adjustment of Options on a variation of share capital under Rule 9 shall be made without prior approval by ordinary resolution of the members of the Company in general meeting.

11.3 Rule 11.2 shall not apply to any alteration or addition which is necessary or desirable in order to ensure that Part A complies or continues to comply with the requirements of Schedule 4 to ITEPA or any other enactment, or to comply with or take account of the provisions of any proposed or existing legislation, law or other regulatory requirements or to take advantage of any changes in legislation, law or other regulatory requirements, or to obtain or maintain favourable taxation, exchange control or regulatory treatment of the Company, any Subsidiary or any Participant or to make minor amendments to benefit the administration of the Scheme.

11.4 No alteration or addition shall be made under Rule 11.1 which would abrogate or adversely affect the subsisting rights of a Participant unless it is made:

11.4.1 with the consent in writing of such number of Participants as hold Options under the Scheme to acquire not less than 75 per cent. of the Shares which would be issued or transferred if all Options granted and subsisting were exercised in respect of the maximum number of Shares the subject thereof;

11.4.2 by a resolution at a meeting of Participants passed by not less than 75 per cent. of the Participants who attend and vote either in person or by proxy; or

11.4.3 in the case of an Option granted under Part A, pursuant to a decision of HM Revenue & Customs under paragraph 28I of Schedule 4 to ITEPA (such that it is required to ensure that the Scheme complies or continues to comply with the requirements of Schedule 4 to ITEPA)

and for the purpose of Rule 11.4.1 and 11.4.2 the Participants shall be treated as the holders of a separate class of share capital and the provisions of the Articles of Association of the Company relating to class meetings shall apply mutatis mutandis.

11.5 The Board may, in respect of Eligible Employees who are or who may become subject to taxation outside the UK on their remuneration, establish such schemes or sub-schemes (which may not qualify as Schedule 4 CSOPs) based on the Scheme but subject to such modifications as the Board considers necessary or desirable to take account of or to mitigate or to comply with relevant overseas taxation, securities or exchange control laws, provided that the terms of options granted under such schemes or sub-schemes are not overall more favourable than the terms of Options granted under the Scheme and provided that options granted, and shares issued, pursuant to such schemes or sub-schemes shall count towards the limits in Rule 3.

11.6 As soon as reasonably practicable after making any alteration or addition under Rule 11.1, the Board shall give written notice thereof to any Participant affected thereby.

12   GENERAL

12.1 The Scheme shall terminate on the 10th anniversary of its adoption or at any earlier time by the passing of a resolution by the Board or an ordinary resolution of the Company in general meeting. Termination of the Scheme shall be without prejudice to the subsisting rights of Participants.

12.2 The Company and any Subsidiary of the Company may provide money to the trustees of any trust or any other person to enable them or him to acquire Shares to be held for the purposes of the Scheme, or enter into any guarantee or indemnity for these purposes, to the extent that such is not prohibited by Chapter 2 of Part 2 of the Companies Act 2006.

12.3 The rights and obligations of any individual under the terms of his office or employment with the Company, any past or present Participating Company, Subsidiary, or Associated Company shall not be affected by his participation in the Scheme and the Scheme shall not form part of any contract of employment between the individual and any such company.

12.4 An Eligible Employee shall have no right to be granted an Option under the Scheme.

12.5 By participating in the Scheme, the Participant waives all and any rights to compensation or damages in consequence of the termination of his office or employment with any such company mentioned in Rule 12.3 for any reason whatsoever, whether lawfully or otherwise, insofar as those rights arise or may arise from his ceasing to have rights under or being entitled to exercise any Option under the Scheme as a result of such termination, or from the loss or diminution in value of such rights or entitlements, including by reason of the operation of the terms of the Scheme, any determination by the Board pursuant to a discretion contained in the Scheme or the provisions of any statute or law relating to taxation.

12.6 Benefits under the Scheme shall not form part of a Participant's remuneration for any purpose and shall not be pensionable.

12.7 By participating in the Scheme, the Participant consents to the collection, processing, transmission and storage by the Company, in any form whatsoever, of any data of a professional or personal nature which is necessary for the purposes of introducing and administering the Scheme. The Company may share such information with any Participating Company or Associated Company, its registrars, brokers, other third party administrator or any person who obtains Control of the Company or acquires the company, undertaking or part-undertaking which employs the Participant, whether within or outside of the European Economic Area.

12.8   The invalidity or non-enforceability of any provision or Rule of the Scheme shall not affect the validity or enforceability of the remaining provisions and Rules of the Scheme which shall continue in full force and effect.

12.9   These Rules shall be governed by and construed in accordance with English Law.

12.10 The English courts shall have exclusive jurisdiction to determine any dispute which may arise out of, or in connection with, the Scheme.

PART B: UNAPPROVED PART

1.   DEFINITIONS

In this Part B, the words and expressions used in Part A shall bear, unless the context otherwise requires, the same meaning herein save to the extent these Rules shall provide to the contrary.

2.   APPLICATION OF THE SCHEME

Save as modified by the Rules below, all the provisions in the Rules of Part A (including any Appendices thereto) shall be incorporated into this Part B as if fully set out herein and so as to be part of Part B and (for avoidance of doubt) Shares allocated under this Part B shall be taken into account for the purposes of Rule 3 of Part A.

3.   REVENUE NOTIFICATION

Any requirement in Part A to make any notification to HM Revenue and Customs shall not apply in this Part B.

4.   INDIVIDUAL LIMIT

Rule 2.5 of Part A shall not apply in this Part B.

5.   MATERIAL INTEREST

Section (B) of the definition of 'Eligible Employee' in Rule 1.1 and Rule 4.3 shall not apply in this Part B.

Chapter 6

Enterprise Management Incentives

INTRODUCTION

6.1   Enterprise Management Incentives (EMIs) under Income Tax (Earnings and Pensions) Act 2003 (ITEPA 2003), ss 527–541 and Sch 5 are another type of discretionary share option. An EMI provides particularly attractive reliefs from income tax and National Insurance contributions. On the other hand, the qualifying conditions, particularly those relating to eligible companies, mean that far fewer companies are able to take advantage of the reliefs available. EMIs were introduced to provide incentives to enterprising key managers to work in small high-risk companies.

6.2   The qualifying conditions for EMI option tax reliefs are set out in ITEPA 2003, Sch 5. The main conditions are as follows:

(a)   EMI options may be held by full-time employees of the relevant company or its subsidiaries (essentially employees who work 25 hours per week or who devote 75% of their working time to the relevant employment) over shares worth £250,000 (£120,000 prior to 16 June 2012) at the market value per person at the date of grant;

(b)   EMI options must be granted to individuals by reason of their employment for commercial reasons to recruit and retain employees (and not as part of a tax avoidance scheme);

(c)   EMI options must be granted over shares in a qualifying company; this means the company must satisfy tests relating to independence, its gross assets (which must be no more than £30m) and its trading activities, and all its subsidiaries must be qualifying subsidiaries; and

(d)   EMI options may be held over £3m worth of shares in total in the company.

COMPARISON WITH CSOP OPTIONS

6.3   Companies wishing to introduce a discretionary share option scheme should consider each of EMIs, CSOP options and unapproved share options in that order in view of their descending tax favourability. The key differences between EMIs and CSOP options are as follows:

103

EMIs	*CSOP Options*
Limit of shares worth up to £250,000	Limit of shares worth up to £30,000
NICs relief	NICs relief
Options may be granted at a discount – tax on the discount element is deferred until exercise	Options must be granted at market value at date of grant
Qualifying company conditions relating to trading activities carried on and gross assets of company	
EMIs may be granted by agreement which is notified to HMRC within 92 days after grant	Approved options granted under scheme rules which must be notified to HMRC by 6 July in the following tax year
Accrued tax relief generally not affected by any disqualifying events	Tax reliefs lost on a disqualifying event

QUALIFYING OPTIONS

6.4   The favourable tax position is available for 'qualifying options'. These are options which are granted by reason of the individual's employment with the relevant company (or group) and:

(a)   satisfy the requirements of ITEPA 2003, Sch 5, as at the date of grant; and

(b)   have been notified to HMRC within 92 days of grant (including a declaration that the qualifying conditions are satisfied) (ITEPA 2003, Sch 5, Pt 7).

The onus is therefore on the company not only to grant options in accordance with the qualifying conditions but also to then notify HMRC within a strict timeframe.

Companies are under an obligation to make the notification to HMRC through HMRC's online system (ITEPA 2003, Sch 5, para 44(8)) unless the company considers that it is unable to file online in which case it should provide full details of why this is the case to the Employee Shares and Securities Team at Room G47, 100 Parliament Street, London, SW1A 2BQ (E-mail: shareschemes@hmrc.gsi.gov.uk).

In order to make the online declaration that all of the qualifying conditions are satisfied, companies are required to seek a declaration from the optionholder that he or she satisfies the working time commitment (see **6.22** below). This declaration may be in written or electronic form and must be provided to the optionholder within seven days of it being signed, and must be retained by the company for inspection by HMRC. It is acceptable for the employee's working time declaration to be contained within the option agreement itself, provided that the option agreement is signed by the employee and the employee receives a copy of the option agreement within seven days of such signature.

A failure to make a notification to HMRC of the grant of the option within 92 days will mean that the option does not meet the legislative conditions for being an EMI option. If the company believes that it has a reasonable excuse for a delayed notification, the company should provide details to HMRC as to why the delay as taken place and, provided that HMRC accept the company's explanation, will provide the company with a reasonable excuse unique reference number which will need to be used by the Company in submitting the declaration via the online system.

If the option is granted by a third party, for example the trustee of an employee benefit trust or another shareholder, the employer remains bound by the requirement to notify the grant of the option and will need to obtain the relevant information from the third party in order to comply with the notification requirements.

REQUIREMENTS TO BE SATISFIED

General requirements

Purpose of the grant

6.5   ITEPA 2003, Sch 5, para 4 provides that an EMI option must be granted for commercial reasons in order to recruit or retain employees in a company (it is no longer necessary that the employees are 'key' employees) and not for the purposes of a tax avoidance scheme. Such a 'purpose test' is unsatisfactory in that for most companies the true purpose will be to incentivise existing executives rather than specifically to recruit or retain, but probably in practice this test presents little problem except in any case which HMRC (justifiably or not) regards as a flagrant tax avoidance device.

£250,000 individual entitlement

6.6   The limit on individual entitlement is £250,000 worth of shares (valued at the market value at the date of grant) (ITEPA 2003, Sch 5, para 5). EMI options granted by different members of the group are aggregated. If an option will, in part, exceed the £250,000 limit, it is not a qualifying option in respect of the excess. No qualifying option can be granted if the limit has already been exceeded.

6.7   In principle, a new EMI option can be granted up to the £250,000 limit once a previous EMI option has been exercised. Where EMI options over shares worth a total value of £250,000 have been granted, however, no new grant may be made within three years of the date of the last grant as a qualifying option (ITEPA 2003, Sch 5, para 6). It is possible, however, for a new EMI grant to be made within three years of the last EMI grant, provided that the previous grants were over shares with a value of £249,999 or less. EMI options, therefore qualify for relief if, at the time of grant, there has been no previous qualifying option granted in excess of the £250,000 limit in the previous three years.

6.8   In determining the £250,000 limit, unexercised CSOP options are treated as unexercised EMI options. This means that if the maximum £30,000 CSOP options are subsisting, only up to £220,000 worth of EMI options may be granted.

No limits on the number of participants

6.9   There is no limit on the number of employees who may hold qualifying options in respect of shares in the relevant company but there is an overall limit of £3m worth of subsisting EMI options (ITEPA 2003, Sch 5, para 7).

Qualifying companies

6.10   Part 3 of ITEPA 2003, Sch 5 lays down restrictions on the types of company which may grant EMI options and these restrictions mark out EMI options relief as more 'targeted' than CSOP options.

Independence test

6.11   ITEPA 2003, Sch 5, para 9 provides that companies must not be:

(a)   a 51 per cent subsidiary of another company (ie a company in which another holds 51 per cent of the shares);

(b)   under the control (within ITA 2007, s 995) of another company; or

(c)   under the control of another company and any other person connected with it (without being a 51 per cent subsidiary).

There must also be no arrangements in existence by virtue of which the company could become a 51 per cent subsidiary or come under the control of another company (other than as a result of a 'qualifying exchange of shares' within ITEPA 2003, Sch 5 – see **6.46** below). Where an investment has been made by one or more venture capital investors and others then a shareholder agreement will usually be entered into in order to lay down how the business will be run. Technically, any such agreement might amount to the company being under the control of another company and any connected persons. It is understood that HMRC do not intend to apply this test aggressively, but care will always need to be taken when there is any form of shareholders' agreement in existence.

Qualifying subsidiaries test

6.12   Where a company ('the parent') has subsidiaries, all those subsidiaries must be 'qualifying subsidiaries': ITEPA 2003, Sch 5, para 10. A subsidiary is a company which is under the control within the meaning of CTA 2010, ss 450 and 451 of another company (and any connected persons).

6.13   A company is a 'qualifying subsidiary' of another company ('the parent') if all the following conditions are met:

(a)   that the subsidiary is a 51 per cent subsidiary of its holding company;

(b)   no person (other than the parent or its subsidiaries) has control of the company; and

(c)   there are no arrangements in existence as a result of which any of the above conditions would cease.

There are provisions which make it clear that the above conditions will not be treated as having ceased to apply where either a winding up or disposal of a subsidiary (whereby it will cease to be a qualifying subsidiary) is carried out for bona fide commercial reasons, ie not for the purposes of tax avoidance (ITEPA 2003, Sch 5, para 11(4)–(7)), or where anything is done as a consequence of the company being in administration or receivership (ITEPA 2003, Sch 5, para 11(8)–(10)).

A subsidiary which is a property managing subsidiary, ie one whose business consists wholly or mainly in the holding of managing of land, buildings or interest in land, will not, however, be a qualifying subsidiary if the parent does not satisfy various 90 per cent tests – it must hold at least 90 per cent of the issued share capital, 90 per cent of the votes, 90 per cent of the assets available for distribution on a winding up and 90 per cent of the profits available for distribution (ITEPA 2003, Sch 5, para 11A(1)).

Gross assets and employees tests

6.14   ITEPA 2003, Sch 5, para 12 provides for a gross assets test in respect of the company (or group of companies) granting EMI options. The limit is gross assets of £30m. Where there is more than one member of the group of companies, the £30m test applies to the consolidated value of the group, disregarding any interests in other group companies. ITEPA 2003, Sch 5, para 12A was introduced in 2008 to limit the availability of EMI options to companies and groups with less than 250 full-time equivalent employees: in calculating the number of full-time equivalent employees, part-time employees are counted on a pro rated basis, but employees on maternity/paternity leave and students on vocational training are excluded. HMRC regard a full-time employee as someone whose standard working week (excluding lunch breaks and overtime) is at least 35 hours, although any employee who works in excess of 35 hours would still only count as one full-time employee. The purpose of these two tests is to limit EMI options to small companies.

UK permanent establishment and trading activities tests

6.15   ITEPA 2003, Sch 5, para 14A provides that, in relation to a single company, that in order to be able to grant EMI options the company must have a permanent establishment in the UK. For a group, this requirement is met is any other member of the group has a permanent establishment in the UK. In either case, the trading activities test must be met by the company with the permanent establishment in the UK.

ITEPA 2003, Sch 5, paras 13 and 14 set out alternative tests on trading activities depending on whether a single company or a parent company of a group is involved.

6.16   In the case of a single company, the company must exist wholly for the purpose of carrying on one or more qualifying trades (see **6.18** below) and is so carrying on such a trade, or preparing to do so, ignoring any incidental activities (e.g. holding property for one or more qualifying trades carried on by it).

6.17   In the case of a group of companies, at least one group member must satisfy the tests in **6.16** above. In addition, disregarding any incidental activities, the business of the group taken as a whole must not consist wholly, or as to a substantial part, in the carrying on of non-qualifying activities, other than incidental activities, e.g. the holding of shares in a subsidiary, making loans to another group company, or holding property used in qualifying trades carried on by a group company (see **6.19** below). Non-qualifying activities means all excluded activities or activities carried on otherwise than in the course of a trade. HMRC generally consider that activities amounting to more than 20 per cent of the trade form a substantial part of the whole.

6.18   By virtue of ITEPA 2003, Sch 5, para 15(1), a trade is a qualifying trade if it:

(a)   is conducted on a commercial basis with a view to the realisation of profits; and

(b)   does not consist wholly or mainly (or as to a substantial part) in the carrying on of excluded activities (see **6.19** below).

Research and development by the company (or a company in the group) prior to commencement of a qualifying trade, which it is intended to carry on, is treated as carrying on the qualifying trade. However, preparation for carrying on such research and development is not the carrying on of a qualifying trade.

6.19   A number of activities are treated as excluded activities so that companies carrying them out cannot grant qualifying options. These activities are:

(a)   Dealing in land, in commodities and futures or in shares, securities or other financial instruments.

(b)   Dealing in goods otherwise than in the course of an ordinary trade of wholesale or retail distribution.

'Wholesale distribution' means a trade where goods are offered for sale or for resale (or processing and resale) to members of the public for their use and consumption. 'Retail distribution' means a trade where goods are offered for sale to members of the general public for their use and consumption (ITEPA 2003, Sch 5, para 17).

A trade is not 'an ordinary trade of wholesale or retail distribution' if it consists, to a substantial extent, in dealing in goods of a kind which are collected or held as an investment (or a mix of that and some other excluded activity), or if goods are held for a significantly longer period than would reasonably be expected.

It is an indication of the carrying on of 'an ordinary trade of wholesale or retail distribution' if the goods are bought in quantities larger than they are sold, or if the goods are bought and sold by the dealer in different markets, or if the person employs staff and incurs expenses in the trade in addition to the cost of the goods and (in the case of a trade carried on by a company) any remuneration paid to any person connected with it. It is an indication that the activities are not 'an ordinary trade of wholesale or retail distribution' if there are purchases of sales from and to a person who are connected with the trader, or if the purchases are matched with forward sales or vice versa, or if the goods are held by that person for longer than is normal for goods of the kind in question, or if the trade is carried on otherwise than at a place or places commonly used for wholesale or retail trade, or if the person does not take physical possession of the goods.

(c)   Banking, insurance, moneylending, debt-factoring, hire purchase financing or other financial activities.

(d)   Leasing (including letting ships on charter or other assets on hire).

Letting of ships – ITEPA 2003, Sch 5, para 18 provides supplementary information on the letting of ships (but does not apply to offshore installations or pleasure craft). A trade shall not be excluded from being a qualifying trade by reason only of its consisting in letting ships on charter if the following requirements are met:

–   every ship let on charter is beneficially owned by the company;

–   every ship beneficially owned by the company is registered in the UK;

–   the company is solely responsible for arranging the marketing of the services of its ships; and

–   the following conditions are satisfied:

   •   the letting is for a period not exceeding 12 months and there is no provision for extending it (other than at the option of the charterer);

- during the letting there is no provision for a new letting (other than at the option of the charterer) which will end more than 12 months after the provision is made;

- the letting is by way of a bargain made at arm's length between the company and a person who is not connected with it;

- under the charter, the company is responsible as principal for managing the ship and defraying expenses in connection with the ship (other than those of a particular voyage); and

- no arrangements exist for someone to be appointed as manager of the ship.

(e) Receiving royalties or licence fees.

Receipt of royalties and licence fees – ITEPA 2003, Sch 5, para 19 provides supplementary information on royalties and licence fees. A trade shall not be excluded from being a qualifying trade by reason only that it consists to a substantial extent in the receiving of royalties or licence fees if the royalties and licence fees (or substantially all) are attributable to the exploitation of intangible assets (in accordance with normal accountancy practice), the whole or greater part of the value of which has been created by the company or a qualifying subsidiary, including most forms of intellectual property which have been created by the company (alone or with others).

(f) Providing legal or accountancy services.

(g) Property development.

ITEPA 2003, Sch 5, para 20 provides supplementary information in relation to property development which is defined as the development of land by a company which has (or at any time has had) an interest in land, with the sole or main object of realising a gain from the disposal of an interest in the land when it is developed. Interests in land include any estate, interest or right including options over such estate, interest or right but do not include the interests of creditors or mortgages.

(h) Farming or market gardening.

(i) Holding, managing or occupying woodlands, any other forestry activities or timber production.

(j) Operating or managing hotels or comparable establishments, or managing property used as a hotel or comparable establishment.

ITEPA 2003, Sch 5, para 21 provides supplementary information on hotels and comparable establishments which is defined as a guest house, hostel or other establishment the main purpose of maintaining which is the provision of facilities for overnight accommodation (with or without catering services). The activities will only be excluded if the person has an estate or interest, or is in occupation of, the hotel or comparable establishment in question.

(k)   Operating or managing nursing homes or residential care homes, or managing property used as a nursing home or residential care home.

ITEPA 2003, Sch 5, para 22 provides supplementary information on nursing homes and residential care homes. Nursing homes are defined as establishments which exist wholly or mainly for the provision of nursing care for persons suffering from sickness, injury or infirmity or for women in maternity wards. Residential care homes are defined as establishments that exist wholly or mainly for the provision of residential accommodation (with board and personal care) for persons in need of personal care by reason of old age, mental or physical disability, alcoholic or drug dependence, any past illness, past or present mental disorder. Any such activities are excluded activities if the company has an estate or interest in, or is in occupation of, the nursing home or residential care home in question.

(l)   Providing services or facilities for another person carrying on an excluded activity.

ITEPA 2003, Sch 5, para 23 provides that the provision of services or facilities for a business carried on by another person is excluded if it consists, to a substantial extent, of excluded activities and a controlling interest in the business is held by a person who also has a controlling interest in the business carried on by the company providing the services or facilities. Control of the business is extended in the case of a close company to cases where the person and his associates (being a director of the company) beneficially own 30 per cent of the ordinary share capital or are able directly or indirectly to control more than 30 per cent of that share capital or not less than one half of the business could, for the purposes of CTA 2010, s 942, be regarded as belonging to them for the purposes of CTA 2010, s 941 (company reconstructions without a change of control).

(m)   Shipbuilding (for options granted from 21 July 2008).

The definition of shipbuilding is set out in ITEPA 2003, Sch 5, para 20A by reference to European legislation on state aid.

(n)   Producing coal (for options granted from 21 July 2008).

ITEPA 2003, Sch 5, para 20B provides that coal is defined in accordance with European legislation on state aid, and includes the extraction of coal.

(o)   Producing steel (for options granted from 21 July 2008).

ITEPA 2003, Sch 5, para 20C provides that the definition of steel includes any of the steel products listed in Annex 1 to the European guidelines on national regional aid (OJ [2006] C54/08) published in the Official Journal on 4 March 2006.

It is possible to seek comfort from HMRC before options are granted as to whether it considers that a company will qualify for the grant of EMI options by writing to the Small Company Enterprise Centre (SCEC) at:

Local Compliance
Small Company Enterprise Centre Admin Team
S0777
PO Box 3900
Glasgow
G70 6AA

The SCEC will only give its view on the qualifying requirements, and not in relation to other aspects of an EMI option, such as whether an individual is an eligible employee.

Eligible employees

6.20   Part 4 of ITEPA 2003, Sch 5 lays down three eligibility tests relating to individuals which must be satisfied. These three eligibility tests are a requirement that the individual is employed with the relevant company, a requirement in relation to his commitment of working time and a requirement that he has no material interest.

The requirement of employment with the relevant company

6.21   ITEPA 2003, Sch 5, para 25 provides that an individual will only be eligible if he is an employee of the company whose shares are the subject of the option or of a qualifying subsidiary (see **6.13** above) of that company.

Commitment of working time test

6.22   ITEPA 2003, Sch 5, para 26 provides that an employee will only be eligible if they satisfy one of the two tests in respect of the time they are required to spend on their duties ('committed time'). These alternative tests are that their committed time amounts to:

(a)   at least 25 hours a week; or

(b)   if less, 75 per cent of their working time (all gainful work including self-employment).

Committed or working time includes any time which the employee would have been required to spend on their duties in relevant employment (ITEPA 2003, Sch 5, para 26(2)–(4)) but for injury, disability, pregnancy, childbirth, maternity or paternity leave or parental leave, reasonable holiday entitlement or any garden leave. Relevant employment means employment with the relevant company or (if the relevant company is a parent company) employment with any group company.

The 'no material interest' requirement

6.23   ITEPA 2003, Sch 5, para 28 excludes participation by individuals who have a material interest (see **6.24** below) in the company (or any 51 per cent subsidiary). An individual has a material interest if they (with or without their associates) or any associate (with or without their associates) has a material interest. An associate means, in relation to an individual, their relatives (lineal predecessors or descendants) or partner, trustees of any settlement set up by them (or any relative of theirs) and the trustees of any settlement (except certain employee benefit trusts) under which they are excluded as a beneficiary or the personal representatives of any estate (in either case, where the individual is a beneficiary) which is interested in shares of the company (ITEPA 2003, Sch 5, paras 31–33).

6.24   By virtue of ITEPA 2003, Sch 5, para 29, a material interest in a company means:

(a)   beneficial ownership of (or the ability to control) directly or indirectly, more than 30 per cent of the ordinary share capital;

(b)   (where the company is a close company) the possession of, or entitlement to acquire such rights as would, upon the winding up of the company or in other circumstances, give a right to 30 per cent of the assets available for distribution. A close company includes a company that would be a close company, but for its non-UK residence under CTA 2010, s 442(a) or its exclusion under CTA 2010, ss 446 and 447 (exclusion of certain quoted companies). For these purposes, a person has the ability to control shares if he has a right to subscribe for them (ie the shares are unissued).

6.25   In determining whether any person has a material interest, shares under EMI options and unappropriated shares held under a SIP are disregarded. Thus the 30 per cent test will be applied to a smaller number of shares.

Terms of options

6.26   Part 5 of ITEPA 2003, Sch 5 lays down requirements as to the terms of the options which must be satisfied. These terms relate to the types of shares that may be acquired when the option is capable of being exercised, the terms to be agreed in writing and the non-assignability of the option.

Type of shares that may be acquired

6.27   By virtue of ITEPA 2003, Sch 5, para 35 options must be over shares which:

(a)   form part of the ordinary share capital of the relevant company (see **6.21** above);

(b)   are fully paid up; and

(c)   are not redeemable.

Option capable of exercise within ten years

6.28   An option must be capable of being exercised within 10 years of the date of grant (ITEPA 2003, Sch 5, para 36). This does not mean that an EMI option is not capable of exercise after ten years, only that it must be capable of being exercised before ten years; there is nothing to prevent EMI options remaining exercisable for some years after the 10th anniversary of grant although if they are exercised after ten years, then there will be no income tax relief and the whole of any gain will be subject to income tax under ITEPA 2003, s 476 and, if readily convertible assets, PAYE and NICs (in the same way as for any unapproved share option).

6.29   If exercise is dependent on the satisfaction of conditions, whether the condition will be satisfied (or not) must be able to be determined within ten years (ITEPA 2003, Sch 5, para 36(2)). If the condition cannot be satisfied within ten years, then the option cannot be a qualifying option.

Option terms to be agreed in writing

6.30   ITEPA 2003, Sch 5, para 37 states that an EMI option must take the form of a written agreement between the grantor and the employee which meets certain requirements set out below. Although the majority of EMI options are granted under separate agreements, there is nothing to prevent the grant of options under the terms of plan rules, which are incorporated into a written agreement or certificate. However, in order to constitute an 'agreement' it will be necessary for both parties to either give consideration or for the agreement to be executed as a deed. It is doubtful that the promise to perform the terms of an existing employment contract constitutes consideration from the employee and so, unless executed as a deed, a payment of a nominal amount, say £1, would seem to be necessary. It is more usual, however, for the agreement to be executed both by the grantor and employee as a deed.

6.31   As far as the content of any written agreement is concerned: ITEPA 2003, Sch 5, para 37(2) states that the following must be included:

(a)   the date on which the option is granted, ie the date on which the agreement is concluded (not the date of any director's resolution approving the grant of options);

(b)   a statement that the option is granted under the provisions of ITEPA 2003, Sch 5;

(c)   the number (or maximum number) of shares that may be acquired;

(d)   the exercise price (if any) or the method by which the exercise price is to be determined; and

(e)   when and how the option may be exercised.

In addition, the written agreement must also set out (in so far as applicable):

(a)   any performance conditions affecting the term or extent of the employee's entitlement; and

(b)   details of any restrictions applying to 'restricted shares' within the meaning of ITEPA 2003, s 423.

Non-assignability of rights

6.32   ITEPA 2003, 5 Sch 5, para 38 provides that a qualifying option must:

(a)   prohibit the transfer of any rights to another person; and

(b)   prohibit exercise more than 12 months after the optionholder's death (assuming the agreement even provides for exercise by the personal representatives after the optionholder's death).

INCOME TAX

6.33   ITEPA 2003, Pt 7, Ch 9 gives income tax relief in respect of the grant and exercise of a qualifying option (including a replacement qualifying option) within ten years of the date of grant. However, there is no relief for an EMI option in respect of the following income tax charges:

(a)   on any gain arising on the surrender of a qualifying option under ITEPA 2003, s 477;

(b)   on the removal of restrictions, etc, or on special benefits (attaching to shares acquired pursuant to the exercise of qualifying options) under ITEPA 2003, ss 427 and 477; and

(c)   on shares acquired pursuant to a qualifying option ceasing to be restricted shares under ITEPA 2003, s 427, or upon the conversion of shares under ITEPA 2003, s 439.

No income tax on grant

6.34   ITEPA 2003, s 528 provides that income tax is not chargeable in respect of gains accruing on the grant of an option.

6.35   Unlike SAYE and CSOP options under ITEPA 2003, Schs 3 and 4 respectively, there is no lower limit on the exercise price which must be paid on the exercise of an EMI option. EMI options may, therefore, be granted at an exercise price which is less than the market value of the shares at the date of grant or even as a nil-cost option. In such cases, the amount of the undervalue at the date of grant (or the gain at exercise, if less) will be liable to income tax at the time of the exercise of the option.

Income tax reliefs on exercise

Options to acquire shares at market value

6.36   ITEPA 2003, s 530 provides that income tax is not chargeable in respect of any gains accruing on the exercise of a qualifying option (or a replacement qualifying option) where the original option was granted at a price which was not less than the market value of the shares at the date of grant.

6.37   However, income tax may be chargeable on all or part of the gain if the exercise takes place later than the period allowed after a disqualifying event (see **6.41** below).

Options to acquire shares at less than market value (as at the date of grant) or for nil consideration

6.38   ITEPA 2003, s 531 applies where options are granted at a price which is less than the market value of the shares at the date of grant (ie at a discount), including the gain which is chargeable to income tax under ITEPA 2003, s 476. It is taken to be:

(a)   the amount of the discount (at grant); or

(b)   (if less) the amount of the gain which accrues on exercise (and if there is no gain, then no income tax is chargeable).

Broadly speaking, therefore, no part of the increase in the market value of the shares following the date of grant is subject to income tax. It is only the discount at grant which is taxed and even this is limited to the amount of any gains – and if there are no gains since grant, there will be no tax.

6.39   ITEPA 2003, s 531 also applies where the option (or the original option if it has been replaced) was granted for nil consideration. In these circumstances, the income tax charge under ITEPA 2003, s 476 is simply on the market value at the date of the grant (or, the market value at the date of exercise, if less).

Disqualifying events

6.40   ITEPA 2003, ss 534–536 set out nine disqualifying events (see **6.41** below). If any of these disqualifying events occur before the exercise of the EMI option, then the gains on exercise will only be relieved from income tax if the option is exercised within 90 days of the disqualifying event. If it is exercised more than 90 days after the disqualifying option, then (in effect) the gain in the period down to immediately before the disqualifying event retains its tax relief but the gain in the period from the disqualifying event is subject to income tax under ITEPA 2003, s 477 (and, if the shares are readily convertible assets (see **5.9** above), National Insurance contributions as well). Such apportionment of the gains may mean that even though the optionholder exercises the option after the 90-day period, substantially all the gains may still qualify for income tax relief.

6.41   The following are 'disqualifying events' in relation to a qualifying option:

(a)   The relevant company's loss of independence.

ITEPA 2003, s 534(1) provides that a disqualifying event will occur if the relevant company either becomes a 51 per cent subsidiary (see **6.11** above) of another company or it comes under the control of another company or it comes under the control of another company (together with any connected persons) without being a 51 per cent subsidiary. However, there will be no disqualifying event where by agreement upon a company reorganisation (see **6.46** below) a new qualifying option (over the shares of a company in the acquiring group) is granted to replace the option over the original company.

(b) The relevant company ceasing to meet the trading activities requirement.

(c) The employee:

  • ceasing employment with the relevant company (see **6.21** above); or

  • ceasing to meet the commitment of working time (see **6.22** above); this relates to the number of hours they are required to work (however, a disqualifying event also occurs if the actual number of hours worked falls below 25 hours a week or, if less, 75 per cent of their working time (see also (i) below)).

(d) Any change to the terms of the option which:

  • increases the market value of the shares under the option;

  • is contrary to the requirement of ITEPA 2003, Sch 5.

(e) Any alteration of share capital which:

  • affects the value of the shares (or would do so if the alteration were taken alone);

  • consists of or includes the creation, variation or removal of a right or arrangements relating to the shares in the relevant company (or the imposition, variation or removal of restrictions on such shares),

in circumstances in which it appears that the effect of the alteration is to increase share values other than for commercial reasons or which result in the option ceasing to comply with the requirements for qualifying options.

(f) Conversions of the shares subject to the option.

ITEPA 2003, s 538 excludes conversions which apply to all shares in the company (or all the shares of one class of shares in the company) and the majority of the shares are either held by non-employees, or the company is an employee-controlled company. HMRC has also accepted that a conversion of shares contemplated by the company's articles of association at the time of grant would also not result in a disqualifying event occurring.

(g) The grant to the employee of a CSOP option if immediately after it is granted, the employee holds unexercised approved and qualifying options in respect of shares with a total market value (ie at grant) of more than £250,000.

(h)　The relevant company was only a qualifying company by reason of preparations by it, or a group company, to carry on a qualifying trade, but preparations have either ceased or two years have passed since the date of grant, without any commencement of the trade.

(i)　If the employee's relevant working time in the current tax year amounts to less than 25 hours a week or, if less, 75 per cent of their working time.

ITEPA 2003, s 535 provides that an employee's actual relevant working time is the time they in fact spend as an employee in relevant employment on the business of the relevant company (or, if the relevant company is a parent company, on the business of the group). The time at which the disqualifying event occurs is determined by, first, calculating whether over the tax year to date (ie starting 6 April) the employee's relevant working time amounts to less than 25 hours a week or, if less, 75 per cent of their working time and, if it does, taking the disqualifying event to have occurred at the end of the previous calendar month in that tax year (or in March at the end of the previous tax year) where the calculation is done in April at the start of the tax year). If the actual relevant working time in the tax year falls before the grant of the option then the option is treated as if it had never been granted.

Effect of a disqualifying event

6.42　Where a qualifying option is exercised within 90 days of a disqualifying event, then the full income tax relief on exercise remains available.

6.43　If, on the date of exercise, more than 90 days have passed since the disqualifying event, income tax may be payable under ITEPA 2003, s 532. Where the qualifying option had been granted with an exercise price equal to the market value of the shares at the date of grant, income tax is payable on any gain accruing in the period from immediately before the disqualifying event to the date of exercise. Where the qualifying option had been granted with an exercise price of less than market value (or at nil cost), then the amount of the gain arising under ITEPA 2003, s 476 on the undervalue at grant (by virtue of ITEPA 2003, s 531) will be increased by any gain accruing in the period from immediately before the disqualifying event to the date of exercise which is brought in to charge to income tax. However, the amount chargeable under ITEPA 2003, s 476, where the options were granted at less than market value (or nil cost), can never exceed the amount which would be chargeable based on the increase in value of the shares since the date of grant (ITEPA 2003, s 532(6)).

CAPITAL GAINS TAX

6.44　Shares acquired on the exercise of a qualifying option (including any replacement qualifying options) are assets for capital gains tax purposes and any gains arising on their disposal may be chargeable to capital gains tax. The acquisition cost of the shares will include any amount on which income tax was payable under ITEPA 2003, s 476.

Capital gains tax is payable at 18 per cent for lower rate tax payers or 28 per cent for higher and additional rate tax payers. However, the sale of shares acquired pursuant to the exercise of an EMI option may qualify the optionholder to take advantage of entrepreneurs' relief, which results in the effective rate of capital gains tax reducing to 10 per cent.

Entrepreneurs relief on the sale of EMI shares will be available if the EMI option was granted at least 12 months prior to the date of the sale of shares and that, during that period of 12 months to the date of sale, the individual has been an office or employee of the of the company or one or more members of the group, and the company has been a trading company or holding company of a trading group (TCGA 1992, s169I(7A)).

Where the company ceases to meet the trading company requirements, then provided that the shares were acquired before, and are sold within three years of, such date (the 'cessation date'), the option had been granted at least 12 months prior to the cessation date and the above employment and trading company provisions were met during that 12-month period up to the cessation date, entrepreneurs' relief will continue to be available (TCGA 1992, s169I(7B)).

Where a disqualifying event has occurred in relation to the EMI option, entrepreneurs' relief will only be available where the option was exercised within 90 days of the disqualifying event (TCGA 1992, s169I(7E)).

Special rules apply where the option which is exercised was acquired in connection with a qualifying exchange of shares pursuant to ITEPA 2003, Sch 5, para 40.

REPLACEMENT OPTIONS ON A CHANGE OF CONTROL

6.45   As mentioned at **6.41**(a) above, the loss of independence of a company will be a disqualifying event (see **6.41** above) for both income tax and capital gains tax purposes in relation to any qualifying options. The only exception to this is where replacement options relating to shares in the acquiring company (or group) are granted to the optionholder by agreement on a company reorganisation (see **6.46** below).

6.46   The types of company reorganisation where replacement options may be granted are where the acquiring company:

(a)   obtains control of the company whose shares are subject to qualifying options as a result of a general offer to acquire all of the shares in the company or shares of the same class as the shares over which the option is granted;

(b)   obtains control in pursuance of a court-approved scheme of arrangement under Companies Act 2006 (CA 2006), s 899;

(c)   becomes bound or entitled under CA 2006, ss 979–982 to acquire shares of the same class as the shares comprised in the qualifying option;

(d)   obtains all the shares of a company whose shares are subject to such a qualifying option as a result of a qualifying exchange of shares. A qualifying exchange of shares has the meaning given in ITEPA 2003, Sch 5, para 40 and is basically limited to a group reorganisation where a 'mirror image' new holding company is imposed on a group of companies.

6.47   ITEPA 2003, Sch 5, para 42 lays down the time limits for the grant of replacement options. This will be six months from the date control is obtained (or any period during which the acquiring company remains bound or entitled under CA 2006, 979–982).

6.48   ITEPA 2003, Sch 5, para 43 provides that an option will only qualify as a replacement option if the following additional conditions are satisfied:

(a)   the new option is granted by reason of the optionholder's employment with the acquiring company or member of the group, e.g. the acquired company;

(b)   at the time of the grant of the replacement option, the requirements as to the purpose of the option (see **6.5** above) and the maximum value of options (ie the £3m limit, but as it applied at the date of grant of the original options) will be satisfied;

(c)   at that time the independence requirement and the trading activities requirement are satisfied in relation to the acquiring company;

(d)   at that time the optionholder is an eligible employee in relation to the acquiring company;

(e)   at that time the requirements as to the terms of the option are satisfied;

(f)   the new and old options have equal market value at the time of the replacement; and

(g)   the total amount payable for the new and old options is unchanged.

ANNUAL RETURNS

6.49   As mentioned at **6.4** above, grants of EMI options must be notified to HMRC within 92 days of the date of grant. In addition, ITEPA 2003, Sch 5, para 52 requires a company whose shares are the subject of a qualifying option at any time during a tax year to make a return to HMRC (using HMRC's online system) within three months of the end of the tax year. The return must be made whether or not any options have been granted or exercised during the tax year.

HMRC POWER TO REQUIRE INFORMATION

6.50   HMRC may give a notice of enquiry into an option. Such notice must be given within 12 months of the end of the 92-day period after grant (see **6.4**(b) above) or longer if misleading information has been given (ITEPA 2003, Sch 5, para 46). In addition, HMRC has wide powers to require any person to furnish them within not less than three months with information which they consider necessary for the performance of their functions (ITEPA 2003, Sch 5, para 51).

SHARE VALUATIONS

6.51   The market value of an option must be determined at the time an option is granted, upon a disqualifying event, at exercise (if income tax is payable) and upon certain exchanges of options.

6.52   Market value has the same meaning as for capital gains tax purposes (ITEPA 2003, Sch 5, para 55). Where EMI options are granted over shares which are subject to restrictions, the shares will have both an actual and unrestricted market value. Provided that the price to acquire the shares under option is equal to or in excess of the actual market value (the capital gains tax value) at the date of grant, the options are not regarded as being granted at a discount and so can be exercised without incurring a charge to tax. The unrestricted market value at the date of grant is only used for the purpose of the individual and company limits.

6.53   HMRC and the employer company may agree the market value based on such date or dates, or an average of the values on a number of dates.

6.54   Shares and Assets Valuation at HMRC has issued a form of application (Form VAL 231) for valuation which may be used by the employer company.

Enterprise Management Incentive Agreement

Set out below is a precedent for an enterprise management incentive agreement.

Enterprise Management Incentive share option agreement pursuant to Schedule 5 to Income Tax (Earnings and Pensions) Act 2003

This Agreement is entered into on [   ] 20

Between:

(1)   [   ] (registered number [   ]) with registered office at [   ] (the 'Company'); and

(2)   [   ] of [   ] (the 'Employee').

Recitals

(A)   The Employee is an employee of [the Company/a Qualifying Subsidiary of the Company] and is obliged to spend, on the business of the [group/relevant company], at least 25 hours per week or, if less, 75% of the Employee's Working Time.

(B)   The Company is desirous of retaining the employment services of the Employee.

(C)   The Employee does not hold, directly or indirectly, a Material Interest in any member of the Group.

(D)   The gross assets of the Group do not exceed £30,000,000.

(E)   The number of Full-Time Equivalent Employees of the Group does not exceed 250.

(F)   Details of all restrictions attaching to the shares comprised in the option are set out in the Schedule to this Agreement.

(G)   The Company has decided, for commercial reasons, to grant to the Employee an option to acquire part of the Company's ordinary share capital pursuant to the provisions of Schedule 5 to ITEPA 2003.

(H)   The Employee's employing company shall notify the grant of the option to HMRC within 92 days of the date of this Agreement as required by Paragraph 44 of the Schedule.

(I)   The Company shall provide a copy of this Agreement to the Employee within 7 days of the date of this Agreement.

1.   DEFINITIONS

1.1   In this Agreement, the following words and expressions shall bear, unless the context otherwise requires, the meanings set forth below:

'Appropriate Limit' means the limit set out in Paragraph 5(1)(1) of the Schedule;

'Appropriate Period' means the relevant period of time as set out in Paragraph 42 of the Schedule;

'Board' means the board of directors of the Company, or a duly authorised committee thereof or, following an event specified in Clause 4, shall be the board of directors or duly authorised committee as constituted immediately prior to such event;

'Control' has the meaning given by Section 995 of the Income Tax Act 2007;

'Date of Grant' means the date on which this Agreement is executed;

'Disqualifying Event' has the meaning given by Section 533 of ITEPA;

'Exercise Price' means the total amount payable in relation to the exercise of the Option, whether in whole or in part, being an amount equal to the Option Price multiplied by the number of Shares in respect of which the Option is exercised;

'Full-Time Equivalent Employees' has the meaning given by Paragraph 12A of the Schedule;

'Group' has the meaning given by Paragraph 58 of the Schedule;

'Initial Market Value' means, in relation to any Share to be taken into account for the purposes of the limits paragraph 6 of the Schedule, its Market Value as determined for the purposes of the grant of the Option;

'ITEPA' means the Income Tax (Earnings and Pensions) Act 2003;

'Market Value' has the meaning given by Paragraphs 55 and 56 of the Schedule, save that in respect of the determination of Initial Market Value, the provisions of Paragraph 5(7) of the Schedule shall also apply;

'Material Interest' has the meaning given by Paragraph 29 of the Schedule;

'Option' means the right to acquire [*number*] Shares under this Agreement;

'Option Price' means [£] per Share, but subject to any adjustment pursuant to Clause 8, being the price at which the Employee may acquire Shares upon the exercise of the Option;

'Qualifying Company' has the meaning given by Paragraph 8 of the Schedule;

'Qualifying Exchange of Shares' means an event falling within paragraph 40 of the Schedule;

'Qualifying Option' means an option to which the provisions of the Schedule apply, being an 'Enterprise Management Incentive' (**'EMI'**);

'Schedule' means Schedule 5 to ITEPA;

'Share' means an ordinary share in the capital of the Company which satisfies the conditions specified in Paragraph 35 of the Schedule; and

'**Working Time**' has the meaning given in Paragraph 27 of the Schedule.

1.2   In this Agreement, unless the context requires otherwise:

    1.2.1   the headings are inserted for convenience only and do not affect the interpretation of any Clause;

    1.2.2   a reference to a Clause is a reference to a Clause of this Agreement;

    1.2.3   a reference to a statute or statutory provision includes a reference:

        (A)   to that statute or statutory provision as from time to time consolidated, modified, re-enacted or replaced by any statute or statutory provision;

        (B)   to any repealed statute or statutory provision which it re-enacts (with or without modification); and

        (C)   to any subordinate legislation made under it;

    1.2.4   words in the singular include the plural, and vice versa;

    1.2.5   a reference to the masculine shall be treated as a reference to the feminine, and vice versa;

    1.2.6   a reference to a person shall include a reference to a body corporate; and

    1.2.7   any reference to writing or written form shall include any legible format capable of being reproduced on paper, irrespective of the medium used.

2.   GRANT OF OPTIONS

2.1   The Option is hereby granted subject to the terms herein and the performance target attached as Appendix A (the '**Performance Target**').

2.2   The Performance Target may be altered if events happen which mean that the Board considers that the original target is no longer appropriate and that an altered target reflects a fairer measure of the performance required. Such an alteration may only be effected to the extent that the Board reasonably considers that it will subsequently be no more difficult for the Employee to satisfy the target as so altered than it was for him to achieve the target in its original form.

2.3   The Option is intended to be a Qualifying Option to the extent that, immediately following such grant, the aggregate of the Initial Market Value of all Shares over which the Employee has been granted option rights in connection with his employment with the Group and which are subsisting under:

    2.3.1   any Qualifying Option; and

    2.3.2   any other share option scheme approved under Schedule 4 to ITEPA,

does not exceed or further exceed the Appropriate Limit.

2.4   The Option shall only be a Qualifying Option if, within three years prior to the Date of Grant, the Employee has not been granted a Qualifying Option resulting in the Employee holding subsisting Qualifying Options over Shares with an aggregate Initial Market Value equal to the Appropriate Limit.

2.5   The Option is intended to be a Qualifying Option to the extent that, immediately following such grant, the aggregate of the Initial Market Value of all Shares over which the Company has granted Qualifying Options which are subsisting does not exceed £3,000,000.

2.6   The Option shall be personal to the Employee and shall not be transferable.

2.7   No amount shall be payable in respect of the grant of the Option.

3.   RIGHTS OF EXERCISE AND LAPSE OF OPTIONS

3.1   Save as provided in Clauses 3.4, 3.5, 3.7 and Clause 4, the Option shall not be exercised earlier than [the third anniversary of the Date of Grant].

3.2   Save as provided in Clauses 3.4, 3.5, 3.7 and Clause 4, the Option may only be exercised by the Employee whilst he is a director or employee of a company within the Group.

3.3   The Option may only be exercised if and to the extent that the conditions of exercise pursuant to Clauses 2.1 and 2.2 have previously been fulfilled.

3.4   The Option may be exercised, subject to sub-clause 3.8.2 below, by the personal representatives of the Employee within 1 year following the date of his death.

3.5   The Option may be exercised, subject to sub-clause 3.8.2 below, within six months following the date on which the Employee ceases to hold an office or employment with a company within the Group if such cessation is as a result of:

   3.5.1   injury or disability;

   3.5.2   redundancy within the meaning of the Employment Rights Act 1996 or the Employment Rights (Northern Ireland) Order 1996;

   3.5.3   retirement;

   3.5.4   the company which employs him ceasing to be under the Control of the Company;

   3.5.5   the transfer or sale of the undertaking or part-undertaking in which he is employed to a person who is neither under the Control of the Company; or

   3.5.6   any other reason, at the discretion of the Board.

3.6   [Where the Employee exercises the Option pursuant to Clause 3.5, the number of Shares in respect of which that Option would otherwise have been exercisable shall be limited to a pro rata number on the basis of the number of whole months which have elapsed from the Date of Grant to the date the Employee ceased to hold an office or employment with a company within the Group, as compared to 36 months. Any remainder of the Option shall lapse.]

3.7   The Board may, at its discretion, allow exercise of the Option within the period of 90 days following the occurrence of a Disqualifying Event.

3.8   Options shall lapse upon the occurrence of the earliest of the following events:

   3.8.1   the conclusion of the day on the 10th anniversary of the Date of Grant;

   3.8.2   if the Board in its absolute discretion determines, the conclusion of the day on the ninetieth day following a Disqualifying Event;

   3.8.3   the expiry of any of the periods specified in Clauses 3.4 and 3.5 (save that if at the time any of the applicable periods under Clause 3.5 expire, time is running under the period in Clause 3.4, the Option shall not lapse by reason of this sub-clause 3.8.3) until the expiry of the period under Clause 3.4);

3.8.4 the expiry of any of the periods specified in Clauses 4.4, 4.5 and 4.6, save where the Option is released in consideration of the grant of a New Option pursuant to Clause 4.8;

3.8.5 the Employee ceasing to hold an office or employment with a company within the Group in any circumstances other than:

    (A) where the cessation of office or employment arises on any of the grounds specified in Clauses 3.4 and 3.5; or

    (B) where the cessation of office or employment arises on any ground whatsoever during any of the periods specified in Clause 4;

3.8.6 subject to Clause 4.6, the passing of an effective resolution, or the making of an order by the Court, for the winding-up of the Company; and

3.8.7 the Employee being deprived (otherwise than on death) of the legal or beneficial ownership of the Option by operation of law, or doing or omitting to do anything which causes him to be so deprived or becomes bankrupt;

3.9 The Employee shall not be treated as ceasing to hold an office or employment with a company within the Group until he no longer holds any office or employment with any company within the Group.

4.   TAKEOVER, COMPROMISE OR ARRANGEMENT, AND LIQUIDATION

4.1 If any person obtains Control of the Company as a result of making a general offer to acquire Shares which is either unconditional or is made on a condition such that if it is satisfied the person making the offer will have Control of the Company, the Option may be exercised, subject to sub-clause 3.8.2 above, within six months of the time when the person making the offer has obtained Control of the Company and any condition subject to which the offer is made has been satisfied or waived.

4.2 If, having or having obtained Control of the Company, a person makes a general offer to acquire Shares, the Option may be exercised, subject to sub-clause 3.8.2 above, within six months of the time when the offer becomes unconditional in all respects (or, if made on an unconditional basis, from the time the offer is made).

4.3 For the purposes of Clauses 4.1 and 4.2 a person shall be deemed to have Control, or have obtained Control, of the Company if he and others acting in concert with him together have Control of it or have obtained Control of it.

4.4 If any person becomes bound or entitled to acquire Shares under Sections 979 to 982 of the Companies Act 2006, the Option may, subject to sub-clause 3.8.2 above, be exercised within one month of the date on which that person first became so bound or entitled.

4.5 If, under Section 899 of the Companies Act 2006, the Court sanctions a compromise or arrangement, the Option may be exercised, subject to sub-clause 3.8.2 above, within six months of the Court sanctioning the compromise or arrangement PROVIDED THAT the Option may not be exercised pursuant to this Clause 4.5 where the purpose and effect of the compromise or arrangement is that the Company becomes a Subsidiary of another company, such other company having substantially the same shareholders and approximate shareholdings as those of the Company immediately prior to the compromise or arrangement taking effect and an offer of a New Option is made pursuant to Clauses 4.8 and 4.9.

4.6   If notice is duly given of a resolution for the voluntary winding-up of the Company, the Option may be exercised, subject to sub-clause 3.8.2 above, within two months from the date of the resolution.

4.7   [Where the Employee exercises the Option pursuant to any of Clauses 4.1 to 4.6, the number of Shares in respect of which that Option would otherwise have been exercisable shall be limited to a pro rata number on the basis of the number of whole months which have elapsed from the Date of Grant to the date of the event which gives rise to the right of exercise, as compared to 36 months. Any remainder of the Option shall lapse.]

4.8   If any company (the 'Acquiring Company'):

4.8.1 obtains Control of the Company as a result of making:

(A)   a general offer to acquire the whole of the issued ordinary share capital of the Company which is made on a condition such that if it is satisfied the Acquiring Company will have Control of the Company; or

(B)   a general offer to acquire all the shares in the Company which are of the same class as the Shares which may be acquired by the exercise of Options,

in either case ignoring any Shares which are already owned by it or a member of the same group of companies;

4.8.2 obtains Control of the Company in pursuance of a compromise or arrangement sanctioned by the Court under Section 899 of the Companies Act 2006;

4.8.3 becomes bound or entitled to acquire Shares under Sections 979 to 982 of the Companies Act 2006; or

4.8.4 obtains all the shares of the Company as a result of a Qualifying Exchange of Shares,

the Employee may at any time within the Appropriate Period, by agreement with the Acquiring Company, release the Option, to the extent that it has not lapsed (the 'Old Option') in consideration of the grant to him of an option (the 'New Option') which is equivalent to the Old Option but relates to shares in the Acquiring Company.

4.9   The New Option shall not be regarded for the purposes of Clause 4.8 as equivalent to the Old Option unless all of the conditions set out in Paragraph 43 are satisfied, but so that the provisions of this Agreement shall for this purpose be construed as if:

4.9.1 the New Option were an option granted under this Agreement at the same time as the Old Option; and

4.9.2 the reference to '[COMPANY] [Limited/plc]' in the definition of 'Company' were a reference to Acquiring Company.

5.   MANNER OF EXERCISE

5.1   The Option may be exercised, in whole or in part, by the delivery to the Secretary of the Company, or its duly appointed agent, of a notice of exercise in such form as the Board may prescribe, duly completed and signed by the Employee (or by his duly authorised agent) together with a remittance for the Exercise Price payable.

5.2   Delivery of the notice of exercise shall not be treated as effecting the exercise of the Option unless and until any conditions to which exercise of the Option is subject have been fulfilled.

5.3   As a condition of exercise, the Board may require the Employee to enter into an election to which paragraph 3B of Schedule 1 to the Social Security Contributions and Benefits Act 1992 applies.

6.   ISSUE OR TRANSFER OF SHARES

6.1   Shares to be issued pursuant to the exercise of the Option shall be allotted within 30 days following the effective date of exercise of the Option.

6.2   The Board shall procure the transfer of any Shares (including any Treasury Shares) to be transferred pursuant to the exercise of the Option within 30 days following the effective date of exercise of the Option.

6.3   Shares issued and allotted pursuant to the exercise of the Option will rank pari passu in all respects with the Shares then in issue at the date of such allotment, except that they will not rank for any rights attaching to Shares by reference to a record date preceding the date of allotment.

6.4   Shares to be transferred pursuant to the exercise of the Option (including any Treasury Shares) will be transferred free of all liens, charges and encumbrances and together with all rights attaching thereto, except they will not rank for any rights attaching to Shares by reference to a record date preceding the date of transfer.

6.5   If and so long as the Shares are admitted to listing and/or trading on any stock exchange, stock market or other recognised exchange (the 'Relevant Exchange'), the Company shall apply for any Shares issued and allotted pursuant to the Option to be admitted to be listed or traded on the Relevant Exchange, as soon as practicable after the allotment thereof.

6.6   Shares acquired pursuant to the exercise of the Option shall be subject to the Company's Articles of Association as amended from time to time.

7.   TAX LIABILITY

7.1   If, on the exercise of the Option (whether in whole or in part), a Tax Liability arises, then unless:

7.1.1   the Employee has agreed that he will make a payment to the Company or his employer or former employer of an amount equal to the Tax Liability; and

7.1.2   the Employee makes such payment within 7 days of being notified by the Company of the amount of the Tax Liability,

the Company shall only be obliged to deliver (or procure the delivery of) legal title to such proportion of the Shares in respect of which that Option is exercised as shall be determined as follows (notwithstanding that beneficial title shall otherwise pass):

$$\frac{A - B}{A}$$

Where:

A   is the aggregate Relevant Value of the Shares in respect of which that Option is exercised; and

B   is the amount of the Tax Liability arising as a result of the exercise.

7.2   The Employee authorises the Company to arrange for a trustee or nominee on behalf of the Employee to sell the proportion of the Shares which the Company is not obliged to deliver, under Clause 7.1, to the Employee (the 'Retained Shares') on the date on which those Shares would otherwise be delivered to the Employee and for that trustee or nominee to remit the proceeds of the sale of the Retained Shares to the Company or the Employee's employer or former employer in order to reimburse it for the Tax Liability arising as a result of the exercise of the Option.

7.3   To the extent that the full amount of the Tax Liability is not reimbursed to the Company or the Employee's employer or former employer, or the Employee has agreed with the Company that Clauses 7.1 and 7.2 shall not apply, the Employee authorises the Company to make such adjustments through payroll as are necessary to ensure that the correct amount is reimbursed to the Company or the Employee's employer or former employer in respect of the Tax Liability arising as a result of the exercise of the Option.

7.4   In this Clause 7, 'Relevant Value' shall mean 'the market value of a Share determined in accordance with Part VIII of the Taxation of Chargeable Gains Act 1992' and all fractions of a Share shall be ignored.

7.5   In this Clause 7, 'Tax Liability' shall include any amount of tax and/or social security (or similar) contributions which the Company or the Employee's employer becomes liable on behalf of the Employee to pay to the appropriate authorities, together with all or such proportion (if any) of employer's social security contributions which would otherwise be payable by the Company or the Employee's employer as is determined to be recoverable from the Employee (to the extent permitted by law) by the Board at the Date of Exercise, save to the extent that such employer's social security contributions are subject to recovery pursuant to an election to which paragraph 3B of Schedule 1 to the Social Security Contributions and Benefits Act 1992 applies.

8.   ADJUSTMENTS

8.1   The number of Shares over which the Option has been granted and the Option Price shall be adjusted in such manner as the Board shall determine following any capitalisation issue (other than a scrip dividend), rights issue, subdivision, consolidation, reduction of share capital or any other variation of share capital of the Company to the intent that (as nearly as may be without involving fractions of a Share or an Option Price calculated to more than two decimal places) the Exercise Price payable in respect of the Option shall remain unchanged.

8.2   The Board shall notify the Employee of any adjustment made under this Clause 8 and shall endorse this Agreement consequent upon such adjustment.

9. AMENDMENT

9.1 The Company and the Employee may at any time, and by the execution of a deed, alter or add to any of the provisions of this Agreement in any respect.

10. ADMINISTRATION

10.1 Any notice or other communication made under, or in connection with, this Agreement may be given by personal delivery or by sending the same by post or such other suitable mode of communication deemed appropriate in the circumstances by the Board, in the case of the Company to its registered office and in the case of the Employee to his last known address, or, where remains a director or employee of the Company or any member of the Group, either to his last known address or to the address of the place of business at which he performs the whole or substantially the whole of the duties of his office or employment. Where a notice or other communication is given by first-class post, it shall be deemed to have been received 48 hours after it was put into the post properly addressed and stamped.

10.2 The Company may distribute to the Employee copies of any notice or document normally sent by the Company to the holders of Shares.

10.3 This Agreement, if worn out, defaced or lost, may be replaced on such evidence being provided as the Board may require.

10.4 The Company shall at all times keep available for allotment unissued Shares at least sufficient to satisfy the Option, where Shares are to be subscribed, or procure that sufficient Shares (which may include Treasury Shares) are available for transfer to satisfy the Option where Shares are to be acquired.

10.5 The decision of the Board in any dispute relating to the Option or the due exercise thereof or any other matter in respect of this Agreement shall be final and conclusive.

11. GENERAL

11.1 The rights and obligations of the Employee under the terms of his office or employment with the Company or any past or present member of the Group shall not be affected by his entering into this Agreement and this Agreement shall not form part of any contract of employment between the Employee and any such company.

11.2 The Employee shall have no right to be granted further options by the Company.

11.3 The Employee hereby waives all and any rights to compensation or damages in consequence of the termination of his office or employment with any such company mentioned in Clause 11.1 for any reason whatsoever, whether lawfully or otherwise, insofar as those rights arise or may arise from his ceasing to have rights under or being entitled to exercise the Option as a result of such termination, or from the loss or diminution in value of such rights or entitlements, including by reason of the operation of the provisions of this Agreement, any determination by the Board pursuant to a discretion contained in this Agreement or the provisions of any statute or law relating to taxation.

11.4 The Employee hereby waives all and any rights to compensation or damages in respect of the Option losing its tax-favoured status by reason of the requirements of the Schedule not being met, the occurrence of a Disqualifying Event, or otherwise.

11.5   The Option and any benefits thereunder shall not form part of the Employee's remuneration for any purpose and shall not be pensionable.

11.6   The Employee hereby consents to the collection, processing, transmission and storage by the Company, in any form whatsoever, of any data of a professional or personal nature which is necessary for the purposes of administering the terms of this Agreement. The Company may share such information with any company within the Group, the trustee of any employee benefit trust, its registrars, brokers, other third party administrator or any person who obtains Control of the Company or acquires the company, undertaking or part-undertaking which employs the Employee, whether within or outside of the European Economic Area.

11.7   The invalidity or non-enforceability of any provision or Clause of this Agreement shall not affect the validity or enforceability of the remaining provisions and Clauses of this Agreement which shall continue in full force and effect.

11.8   This Agreement shall be governed by and construed in accordance with English Law and the English courts shall have exclusive jurisdiction to determine any dispute which may arise out of, or in connection with, this Agreement.

12.   WORKING TIME DECLARATION

12.1   The Employee hereby declares that, as at the date of this Agreement, the Employee works for the Company or for another member of the Company's Group for at least (i) 25 hours per week; or (ii) 75% of the Employee's Working Time.

Schedule

[Attach the Company's Articles of Association and details of any other restrictions that will apply to option shares, eg investors' agreements. These must form part of the EMI option agreement.]

As witness this Agreement has been duly executed as a Deed by each of the parties on the day and year first above written.

Chapter 7

LTIPs: Performance, Deferred, Matching, Restricted and Convertible Shares

INTRODUCTION

7.1   The term 'Long Term Incentive Plan' (or 'LTIP') is usually understood as referring to a discretionary incentive plan which has the following characteristics:

(a)   it is usually intended for directors and senior executives, particularly of listed companies;

(b)   the incentive is usually based on a three- (sometimes four- and/or five-) year period;

(c)   it usually involves 'own company' shares rather than cash;

(d)   shares are often delivered through an EBT as, unlike share options, the shares are usually acquired for no payment;

(e)   the value of the reward received by the participant is invariably linked to the performance of the company, particularly the company's comparative performance in relation to other companies in the same sector.

7.2   LTIPs normally take one of the following forms:

(a)   Performance Share Awards – awards of free shares which vest to the extent set performance targets are achieved after three (or more) years;

(b)   Restricted Shares – shares in which the employee acquires a beneficial interest (subject to a risk of forfeiture or some other factor which reduces their initial market value); or

(c)   Convertible Shares – shares in which the employee acquires a beneficial interest and which are convertible into other (usually more valuable) shares.

Similar to LTIPs are deferred share awards which take the form either of an award of shares (structured in the same way as an LTIP) in lieu of a portion of the participant's annual bonus, or of an acquisition of shares with a portion of the participant's annual bonus, which are released after a specified period into the name of the participant, provided he has not left employment. Some deferred share schemes also provide for matching share awards – an award of additional free shares often made if deferred shares are held for a specified period and further performance conditions have been met.

Listed companies which establish LTIPs usually prefer awards of performance, deferred and matching shares. Restricted shares and convertible shares in which the employee acquires the beneficial interest in the shares are less common.

7.3   LTIPs can be categorised under the following tax regimes.

(a)   *'Unsecured promises' of shares* – the benefit of free shares which are delivered on vesting under an LTIP are treated as 'general earnings' under the Income Tax (Earnings and Pensions) Act 2003 (ITEPA 2003), s 62.

(b)   *'Securities options'* which confer a 'right' to acquire shares pursuant to a share option or otherwise fall under ITEPA 2003, Pt 7, Ch 5 – this provides income tax relief on the acquisition (ie grant) of any securities option but imposes income tax on any subsequent 'chargeable event' (acquisition of securities, assignment or receipt of any benefit in money or money's worth) under ITEPA 2003, s 477. This tax treatment applies either where the individual has a right only to receive shares at a particular time, or if the individual has the right to exercise an option to acquire shares over the course of a specified exercise period. See also **7.79** below where the company has the right to substitute a cash payment for shares.

(c)   *'Restricted securities'* under ITEPA 2003, Pt 7, Ch 2 – restricted securities involve the acquisition of the beneficial interest in the securities subject to restrictions which reduce their market value, for instance, a risk of forfeiture if performance targets are not satisfied, or restrictions on disposal of the securities but without any risk of forfeiture. Where the beneficial interest is acquired, the employee will be entitled to dividends, voting rights and other shareholder rights. There are no taxing provisions under Ch 2 at the time of acquisition, rather Ch 2 acts to delay an income tax charge from the time of acquisition (either in whole or in part). Any income tax arising on acquisition will be under the general charging provisions of ITEPA 2003, s 62 or ITEPA 2003, Pt 7, Ch 5 (if pursuant to a securities option). Few of the LTIPs established by listed companies involve restricted securities.

(d)   *'Convertible securities'* under ITEPA 2003, Pt 7, Ch 3 – convertible securities contain a right to convert (or provide for a conversion) into securities of a different (and usually more valuable) security. As with restricted shares, where the beneficial interest is acquired the employee will be entitled to dividends, voting rights and other shareholder rights (if any). As with restricted securities, there are no taxing provisions under Ch 3 at the time of acquisition, rather any income tax arising on acquisition will be under the general charging provisions of ITEPA

2003, s 62 or ITEPA 2003, Pt 7, Ch 5 (if pursuant to a securities option). Only upon the occurrence of a chargeable event (conversion, disposal, surrender or receipt of a benefit) do the provisions of ITEPA 2003, Pt 7, Ch 3 impose income tax charges. Few listed companies have established schemes involving convertible securities.

7.4   ITEPA 2003, Pt 7 also includes various anti-avoidance provisions relating to employee share acquisitions:

(a)   securities with an artificially depressed market value (ITEPA 2003, Pt 7, Ch 3A) – where the value of shares have been reduced in value by at least 10 per cent as a result of a depreciatory non-commercial transaction in the seven years before acquisition, income tax on acquisition will be charged as if the depreciatory transaction were disregarded;

(b)   securities with an artificially enhanced market value (ITEPA 2003, Pt 7, Ch 3B) – where the value of shares have been increased in value by at least 10 per cent as a result of a non-commercial transaction in the seven years after acquisition, tax is charged on the basis of yearly valuations during the seven-year period after acquisition on the incremental excess over market value as a result of the transaction;

(c)   securities acquired for less than market value (ITEPA 2003, Pt 7, Ch 3C) – where shares are acquired for a deferred or discounted payment, the employee acquiring the shares will be treated as receiving the benefit of a notional loan equal to the whole amount of the undervalue and income tax will be applied each year until the undervalue is paid. This charge to income tax does not apply where income tax on the benefit applies under ITEPA 2003, s 62, or as a taxable benefit, or upon the acquisition by conversion of securities, or acquisition pursuant to a securities option;

(d)   securities disposed of for more than market value (ITEPA 2003, Pt 7, Ch 3D) – where shares are acquired for more than their market value, the excess is chargeable to income tax as earnings.

7.5   Listed companies are required under the Listing Rules to seek shareholders' approval for all long-term incentive schemes which, broadly speaking, covers all incentive schemes other than deferred bonuses, in which directors participate, with performance periods, or periods of service, of more than one year. There is no need to obtain shareholders' approval for annual cash bonus schemes or deferred bonus schemes. A deferred bonus scheme involves a bonus which is crystallised in respect of one financial year but will not be paid for several years and may be lost altogether if the participant leaves employment during the retention period. Whilst schemes involving performance and matching shares will usually require shareholders approval because of the presence of performance targets over a period of more than one year, deferred shares should not require such approval. Irrespective of Listing Rule requirements, any of these arrangements to be adopted by a UK quoted company would need to be in line with the company's approved remuneration policy if directors are to participate, otherwise specific shareholder approval would be required.

PERFORMANCE SHARES

Development of performance share schemes

7.6   Until the 1990s, most UK companies relied upon share option schemes for providing executive share incentives. The concept of performance shares grew in popularity for a number of reasons:

(a)   the reduction in the top rate of income tax to 40 per cent in FA 1986 meant that it was more practicable to consider arrangements outside the approved share option scheme legislation (which in any event was severely reduced in value with the introduction of the £30,000 limit from 17 July 1995);

(b)   the volatility of option gains became more evident with the increasing share price volatility of the period 1987 to 1992;

(c)   Remuneration Committees, which become widely established in listed companies following the recommendations of the Cadbury Committee (1992), took an increasingly active part in the design and operation of executive share incentive schemes;

(d)   there was growing consensus, particularly after the publication of the Greenbury Report (1995), that the benefits derived from executive share incentive schemes must be more proportionate to the company's achievement of its objectives; and

(e)   the increasing availability of comparative financial performance data made the adoption of performance targets, such as total shareholder return, based on comparative rather than absolute performance measures, both more economic and more practical.

7.7   By the end of the 1990s, performance share schemes had become as popular as conventional share options amongst the larger as well as some of the smaller public companies. However, smaller public companies and private companies generally retained share options. Some companies which had adopted performance share schemes for directors have resumed the use of share options instead of LTIPs for levels of management below that of director and senior executive. There is also a substantial proportion, about 50 per cent, of the FTSE 250 companies, which used both LTIPs and share options at director and senior executive level despite the recommendation of the Greenbury Report that only one scheme should be used.

7.8   Many of the early performance share schemes were established using only existing shares. Prior to changes made to the Listing Rules in 1996, there was no obligation on a listed company to obtain shareholders' approval for any employees' share scheme which was restricted to existing shares and was not designed solely to benefit directors.

7.9   Until 1996, therefore, proposals to establish new performance share schemes were rarely put before shareholders and a variety of different designs for performance share schemes developed, particularly as the ABI/IMA steadfastly refused to lay down formal guidelines on the new types of scheme which were emerging. This, however, has changed in the last few years, with the ABI Guidelines now reflecting share incentives as well as options.

7.10   Since late 1996, as a result of changes in the Listing Rules, all performance share schemes in which directors may participate have been subject to shareholder approval and this has meant greater uniformity in the design and size of allocations under different schemes.

Design of performance share schemes

7.11   Performance share schemes are the most common type of LTIP in public companies and typically involve:

(a)   annual or phased awards of performance shares often worth 100 per cent or more of base salary;

(b)   a fixed performance period of three or possibly four years;

(c)   the company's performance will usually be measured against a specified comparator group in terms of total shareholder return, earnings per share or share price improvement;

(d)   although the shares may be released early in specified 'good leaver' circumstances or in the event of a takeover or reconstruction, this will usually only be to the extent the company's performance is in line with the performance target and, in conformity with ABI Guidelines, on a time-apportioned basis unless the Remuneration Committee considers that it is appropriate for this not to be the case;

(e)   upon vesting, the shares will be transferred for no (or only nominal) consideration into the name of the participants by the EBT trustees subject to any PAYE and NICs obligations;

(f)   often the participant will receive a cash payment, or additional shares of equivalent value, representing the dividends which would have been paid on the vested shares over the performance period; and

(g)   in some cases, there may be an additional one or two-year period when the shares continue to be held by trustees on behalf of the participant (or, alternatively, the award may vest with shares delivered over the three to five-year period, but with performance having been measured over the original three-year period), which is becoming increasingly popular with institutional investors.

7.12   Performance shares may be made available in any of the following ways:

(a)   an 'unsecured promise' of free shares if certain conditions are satisfied to be delivered through an EBT which is taxable under general principles of employment income on release of the shares (under ITEPA 2003, s 62);

(b)   a 'right' to acquire the shares for no (or only nominal) consideration if certain conditions are satisfied (e.g. 'a nil price option' which is taxable on acquisition of the shares under ITEPA 2003, Pt 7, Ch 5); or

(c)   'restricted securities' which pass the beneficial interest in those shares to the participant subject to forfeiture if certain conditions are not satisfied and which is taxable under ITEPA 2003, Pt 7, Ch 2.

7.13   It makes little or no difference to the participant whether an allocation is made in either of the ways set out in **7.12**(a) or (b) above. Income Tax (PAYE and National Insurance contributions (NICs) where the shares are 'readily convertible assets') will not be payable on 'allocation' but on 'vesting'. The same will normally apply to the acquisition of restricted securities (referred to in **7.12**(c) above) provided that the restrictions will cease to apply within five years, as income tax will be payable not on acquisition but on a subsequent chargeable event (cessation or variation of restrictions, or disposal of the securities). However, where the shares are subject to risk of forfeiture, the employee may jointly elect with the employer (within 14 days of acquisition) in a form approved by HMRC for the shares to be taxed on acquisition as if the shares were not subject to any restrictions (ITEPA 2003, s 425(3)) instead of at the time of any subsequent chargeable event. Where an election is made, the taxable amount (basically the untaxed proportion of the original value of the shares) is taxed as if the outstanding restrictions did not apply. In the case of securities subject to a risk of forfeiture (other than where an election to tax upfront is entered into) it will be possible for the employer to pass on the employer's Class I NICs under the Social Security Contributions and Benefits Act 1992, Sch 1, paras 3A and 3B in the same way as for rights/options (see **5.17** to **5.22** above).

7.14   The shares which are transferred to participants on 'vesting' may either be existing shares purchased on the market, newly subscribed shares or shares held in treasury. Other than where shares are transferred by the company from treasury (which may be for nil consideration), the shares will normally be acquired by EBT trustees, with financial assistance provided by the company, and then transferred to the participants at the appropriate time. The use of an EBT is necessary where shares are to be newly issued, as shares may only be issued, as a matter of UK companies law, at nominal (or 'par') value and not for nil cost – the EBT will therefore be funded to subscribe for shares at not less than this amount. Following the introduction of the 'disguised remuneration' legislation (see (see **16.71–16.74** below), it has become increasingly important to ensure that LTIPs and the use of EBTs are structured so as not to result in an upfront income tax charge on the participant at any time during which the trustee holds shares in connection with LTIP awards.

7.15   An EBT is usually established offshore, often in the Channel Islands or the Isle of Man, but UK resident trusts are not necessarily at any disadvantage if all the participants are resident in the UK.

Performance targets

7.16   In accordance with ABI Guidelines and the UK Corporate Governance Code published by the Financial Reporting Council, Remuneration Committees are responsible for determining appropriate long-term incentive schemes for directors with challenging performance targets. Details must then be reported to shareholders in the Remuneration Report in the annual report and accounts (in accordance with the amended Large and Medium-sized Companies and Groups (Accounts and Reports) Regulations 2008 (SI 2008/410)). Institutional investors approach the subject of performance share plans by deciding whether the potential rewards under any scheme are proportionate to the company's level of performance, particularly against the background of its business forecasts and objectives. There are no longer any prescribed performance tests although different institutional investors do express preferences for particular performance measures. It follows, therefore, that what might be acceptable for one company may not be acceptable to another. The Remuneration Committee must make a judgement about the proposed performance targets and will then usually visit its key institutional investors to check whether it is likely to obtain an appropriate level of support for any new scheme. A scheme is only likely to receive support if it contains performance targets which are both 'challenging and stretching'. In support of institutional investors, a number of representative bodies such as the ABI (now the IMA), ISS and PIRC regularly monitor all proposals for new schemes and regularly report to their subscribers on the content of those schemes.

Performance measures

7.17   The appropriate choice of performance measure is now central to the design of any performance share plan. Most institutional investors wish to see performance measures which align the participants' interests with those of the shareholders, and in particular wish to see measures based on the company's comparative performance against its peer group or some benchmark. The choice of performance measure is now usually made from the following:

(a)   Total shareholder return – total shareholder return is based on both share price improvement and dividends and is therefore regarded as a more balanced measure of performance than share price improvement on its own. Indices of the total shareholder return of all listed companies and sectors are now available on a daily basis for the purposes of comparison. Institutional investors expect a comparison to be made with the relevant sector or peer group of companies. However, the ABI/IMA has doubts about whether a total shareholder return measure on its own is evidence of 'sustained and significant underlying financial performance' and therefore has traditionally encouraged a secondary target based on earnings per share growth. However, it is content for companies to rely on total shareholder return measures if it is tested against the performance of a comparator group.

(b)   Earnings per share – earnings per share is the performance measure which traditionally has been encouraged by the ABI/IMA. In share options, an absolute test based on a rate of increase in excess of inflation has been recommended for many years. In the context of LTIPs, the ABI/IMA has advocated a performance target based on the company's comparative earnings per share against a specified peer group of companies. The problem with earnings per share tests is obtaining consistency, particularly in relation to the treatment of exceptional items. The ABI/IMA has therefore recommended that 'normalised' earnings per share figures should be used. UK companies are required to report earnings per share in accordance with Accounting Standard FRS 22 which implements in the UK the international standard IAS 33.

(c)   Share price improvement – the ABI/IMA has indicated that share price improvement relative to a peer group is an acceptable alternative to total shareholder return provided there is a secondary performance criterion 'validating sustained and significant improvement in underlying financial performance over the same period'. This is usually understood to mean an earnings per share test.

(d)   Net assets per share – the ABI/IMA has said that net assets per share is an acceptable performance measure against a specified peer group or an appropriate index. This is the measure which is perhaps most appropriate in the property sector.

The ABI Guidelines do not prescribe any particular performance target but place responsibility on the Remuneration Committee to formulate appropriate measures based on the forecast performance of the company.

Performance period

7.18   Institutional investors expect a fixed performance period of at least three years. Most performance-related allocations are made for this period. Historically, a number of schemes provided for a rolling three-year performance period with annual retests or for a three-year period starting from a fixed base point and retesting of the performance target on a proportionate basis after four years – and even in some schemes – five years. A scheme which provides for retesting of performance conditions would unlikely now receive shareholder approval as a result of institutional investor requirements on scheme design.

Individual allocations

7.19   The ABI/IMA recommends that allocations should be phased. Most performance share schemes are operated annually. Allocations for directors are generally about 100 per cent of base pay, but the recent trend has been for this to be increased to 200 per cent or more in larger public companies, particularly where the Remuneration Committee considers there have been exceptional circumstances. In practice, a smaller proportion of base pay will be made available each year to lower levels of management.

Vesting schedules

7.20   As the objective is to provide challenging and stretching performance targets, taking into account the company's level of achievement against its business objectives, it is not surprising that the vesting schedules in performance share schemes are more sophisticated than the absolute performance targets usually found in share options. Institutional investors expect performance targets to involve a payout for better than median performance and a maximum release of shares if the performance ranks in the upper quartile or decile when compared to the comparator group. Between the median and the upper quartile (or decile), shares may normally be released on a straightline growth basis.

Income tax and NICs

7.21   The income tax treatment of the different types of performance share schemes are set out in **7.12** above. PAYE will be deductible if the shares are 'readily convertible assets' (ITEPA 2003, s 702). In relation to the processes involved in the operation of PAYE, see **5.10–5.13** above.

7.22   Where PAYE is deductible on any gains from share acquisitions, NICs will also be payable.

Precedent

7.23   A precedent for a performance share scheme involving a right to receive free shares is set out at Appendix 7A below.

DEFERRED SHARES

7.24   The term 'deferred shares' refers to a variety of arrangements intended to retain the services of the employee. The number of shares will not vary or depend on the company's performance – only continued employment.

7.25   Deferred shares may be delivered in one of a number of different forms:

(a)   bonus shares which are beneficially owned by the employee but lodged with trustees – usually these have been acquired by the investment of the employee's annual bonus and can be withdrawn at any time but with the result that the employee will lose some other benefit, e.g. an award of matching shares which would have been made if he left the shares with the trustee for a minimum period (see matching shares at **7.30–7.35** below);

(b)   restricted securities which are awarded subject to forfeiture if the employee leaves employment (see restricted shares at **7.36–7.45** below);

(c)   a conditional award which constitutes either a 'right' to acquire shares without payment provided the employee remains in employment for a minimum period or an unsecured promise to the shares provided that these conditions are met; and

(d)   a nil-cost option exercisable for a specified period provided that the employee has remained in employment for a minimum period.

Bonus shares

7.26   A number of listed companies have looked for ways to make directors and senior executives keep part of their annual bonuses in the form of shares in the company. This is usually with a view to exposing directors and senior executives to the same investment risks as shareholders generally. Typically, this involves:

(a)   participants having the opportunity to invest part of their post-tax annual bonus in the form of shares – usually no more than 50 per cent of the gross bonus;

(b)   as a term of the arrangement, the participant will leave the shares with EBT trustees for a number of years (usually three years) so as to qualify for some benefit, usually Matching Shares (see **7.30–7.35**). Alternatively, the benefit could be delivered upfront in the form of an increased bonus amount provided that the increase is deferred under these arrangements;

(c)   the participant will be beneficially entitled to receive dividends on the shares and may, other than in the increased bonus situation referred to in (b) above, withdraw the shares at any time (although any Matching Shares would be lost in such circumstances).

Most bonus share schemes provide for the annual bonuses of the participants to be applied in the purchase of shares in the company through the stock exchange. PAYE income tax and NICs are borne on the annual bonus before any investment in shares. The shares will, therefore, be acquired at market value and there will, in most cases, be no question of any further charge to income tax on the acquisition of the shares. On a disposal, any increase in value will be subject solely to capital gains tax.

Restricted shares

7.27   Deferred share schemes which involve the acquisition of shares in which the employee acquires the beneficial interest and which are subject to forfeiture if the employee ceases employment within a specified period are 'restricted securities' and are taxed under the restricted securities regime (see **7.36–7.45** below). In such case, the arrangements may be structured such that the employee's pre-tax bonus is used to acquire shares, which would then be taxable at the end of the forfeiture period under ITEPA 2003, Pt 7, Ch 2 (restricted securities). As the shares will normally have been acquired at the open market value on the Stock Exchange, if acquired with post-tax bonuses there should be no discount to the open market value which would be the subject of a post-acquisition tax liability under ITEPA 2003, Pt 7, Ch 2.

Deferred shares awards and options

7.28 Deferred shares awards involve the employee receiving either a 'right' to acquire the shares provided they remain in employment and so will fall within the 'securities option' tax regime in ITEPA 2003, Pt 7, Ch 5 (see **7.3**(b) above) or an unsecured promise to the shares in such circumstances, in which case the acquisition of the shares would be chargeable to income tax under ITEPA 2003, s 62. Where the employee receives a 'right', it is not necessary for the scheme to require any right of exercise – an automatic transfer of shares on vesting will be sufficient. However, some schemes provide for a nil price option to be granted in place of the award of deferred shares. This enables the participants to exercise the option at a time of his choice. If the option is granted automatically over existing shares under the terms of the annual bonus scheme, then the participant may only be liable to income tax and any NICs when he exercises the option, assuming he was not at any time entitled to the annual cash bonus. In principle, an option over shares equal in value to the amount of an annual cash bonus would seem to satisfy the requirements for a 'deferred bonus' for the purposes of the UKLA Listing Rules. The acquisition of a nil price share option will mean that the grant and exercise will be within the securities option regime in ITEPA 2003, Pt 7, Ch 5. A precedent for a deferred shares award which allows for the release of shares provided the participant remains in employment for three years is set out at Appendix 7B below.

UKLA and shareholder approval

7.29 Deferred share schemes have been established by a number of large companies in recent years. The scheme will normally satisfy the conditions for a 'deferred bonus' for the purposes of the UKLA Listing Rules and will not, therefore, require shareholders' approval (as a long-term incentive) provided that only market-purchased shares may be used. The fundamental principle of the 'deferred bonus' exception under the Listing Rules is that there must be no fluctuation in the number of shares which may be released as a result of performance after the date of the award. However, the shares can be forfeited (in whole or in part) if the employee leaves employment. A deferred share scheme will not, however, be able to be established by a UK quoted company if directors are to participate unless the adoption of such arrangement is in line with the company's approved remuneration policy, or specific shareholder approval is sought.

MATCHING SHARES

7.30 Matching shares are additional free shares which are awarded by the company or an EBT if qualifying shares are retained for a specified period, usually three years or more. A matching award is often also subject to a performance target in accordance with institutional investor guidelines.

7.31   The views of institutional investors about matching awards can be generally summarised as follows:

(a)   the basis of matching should be no more generous than one additional free share for every two bonus (or qualifying) shares unless there are very challenging performance targets;

(b)   there should in any event be appropriate performance targets as a condition of vesting;

(c)   the additional matching shares should not normally be released before the expiry of three years.

However, institutional investors wish to assess in each case whether the vesting of the additional free shares is proportionate to the company's level of achievement against its objectives.

7.32   Where matching shares are awarded in conjunction with a deferred share scheme as an incentive to participants in a deferred share scheme to retain their shares, it would be usual for those additional matching shares to be forfeited if the employee sells or otherwise disposes of the deferred shares to which those matching shares relate.

7.33   Matching share awards will generally only vest if performance targets are satisfied. In the vast majority of cases, the performance target will be based on similar targets to those employed in performance share schemes over a period of three years.

7.34   As matching shares do not involve the acquisition of any beneficial interest in the shares until the shares vest, income tax will not be chargeable until the award vests. Income tax will be chargeable at vesting on the market value of the shares either under the general principles of earned income (ITEPA 2003, s 62), as a securities option (ITEPA 2003, Pt 7, Ch 5) or, in a limited number of schemes, restricted securities (ITEPA 2003, Pt 7, Ch 2). PAYE and NICs will be payable if the shares are 'readily convertible assets'.

7.35   A precedent for a deferred/matching shares scheme is set out at Appendix 7C below.

RESTRICTED SHARES

7.36   Listed companies generally prefer schemes where the incidence of income tax on gains arises when the employee can realise his shares and so fund the tax payable. 'Unsecured promises' of shares which are taxed as general earnings on receipt under ITEPA 2003, s 62, and 'securities options' which involve a 'right to acquire shares' which are taxed on acquisition of the shares under ITEPA 2003, Pt 7, Ch 5, do not involve the employee acquiring the beneficial interest in the shares until 'vesting' or 'exercise' and so will be the normal structure adopted for most share schemes. On the other hand, 'restricted shares' involve the employee acquiring the beneficial interest in the shares 'up front'. Most companies are wary about using 'restricted shares' because any tax paid up front cannot be reclaimed from HMRC if subsequently the shares reduce in value, are forfeited or otherwise fall foul of the restrictions imposed on them. 'Restricted shares' have, therefore, always been a relatively specialised type of scheme involving relatively sophisticated employee participants. Prior to 2003, one reason for employees taking the risks involved in 'restricted shares' was the possibility of acquiring the shares at a discount on account of the restrictions, whilst also benefiting from capital gains tax business assets taper relief running from the acquisition of the shares rather than the end of the restricted period. However, following a major overhaul of the taxation of restricted securities (now ITEPA 2003, Pt 7, Ch 2) and the abolition of CGT taper relief in FA 2008, these tax benefits have been withdrawn. Broadly speaking, the position now is that if the shares are subject to a risk of forfeiture for a period of up to five years, income tax will be charged not on acquisition but on any post-acquisition chargeable events (although the employee and the employer can elect at the time of acquisition for tax to be charged early which may have advantages for the employee in a rapidly rising market). In all other cases (ie where the risk of forfeiture may run for five years or more, or there are 'non-forfeitable' restrictions, then there is the potential for income tax to arise both on the acquisition of the shares and upon any subsequent chargeable events (which will include the shares ceasing to be subject to the relevant restrictions).

7.37 By virtue of ITEPA 2003, s 423, restricted securities are securities which are acquired by reason of a person's employment which:

(a) are subject to any agreement, arrangement or condition which imposes restrictions on the securities; and

(b) as a result, are lower in value at the time of acquisition than if the restrictions did not apply. As an example, Shares and Assets Valuation would generally agree that shares which cannot be transferred for five years would be reduced in value by about 25 per cent.

The restrictions may take the form of:

(a) a risk of forfeiture of the securities if the employee ceases employment, or a performance or other condition is not achieved;

(b) a restriction on the rights of the employee to dispose of the shares or exercise rights conferred by the shares;

(c) a restriction on the right to receive dividends or vote the shares; or

(d) provisions which impose some disadvantage on the employee if he seeks to dispose or exercise the rights conferred by the shares. However, shares which are subject to liens for unpaid calls on shares and employee pre-emption rights are not restricted securities. Also, a requirement to sell or transfer the securities (whether or not in the articles of association) in the event of 'misconduct' would not be a 'restriction' for these purposes.

Acquisition of restricted securities

7.38   There is no income tax liability in respect of the acquisition of restricted shares if they are subject to a risk of forfeiture for a period of less than five years. On the other hand, the acquisition of shares which are subject to a risk of forfeiture for five years or more, or are subject to restrictions not involving any forfeiture, are chargeable to income tax on acquisition under general principles (ITEPA 2003, s 62) and will also be chargeable on any post-acquisition 'chargeable event' (ITEPA 2003, s 426).

7.39   However, there will be income tax on the acquisition of restricted securities (even in circumstances where the shares are subject to a forfeiture provision lasting less than five years) in the following circumstances:

(a)   the acquisition arises by reason of a conversion within ITEPA 2003, Pt 7, Ch 3 (see **7.46** below);

(b)   the acquisition is chargeable to tax in respect of the undervalue by reason of ITEPA 2003, Pt 7, Ch 3C (see **7.4**(c) above);

(c)   the acquisition arises by reason of the exercise of a share option under ITEPA 2003, Pt 7, Ch 5 (see Chapter 5); and

(d)   the employer and employee irrevocably elect that any restricted securities which are subject to risk of forfeiture are to be subject to income tax on acquisition – any such election must be made in a form approved by HMRC within 14 days of the date of acquisition: ITEPA 2003, s 425(5). The effect of any election is that income tax will apply on acquisition under the general principle of earned income as if the restrictions did not apply (ITEPA 2003, s 62).

There are a number of different types of election which may be entered into between the employer and the employee. These include:

(a)   an election entered into on the acquisition of forfeitable securities to ignore the forfeiture provision for tax purposes (a 's 425 election');

(b)   an election entered into on the acquisition of non-forfeitable securities, but which are restricted in some other manner, to ignore all (a 's 431(1) election') or some (a 's 431(2) election') of the restrictions for tax purposes; and

(c)   an election entered into at the time of a chargeable event where there continue to be other applicable restrictions (a 's 430 election'), to ignore the remaining restrictions tax purposes.

In each case the election may be entered into as a one-part election between the employer and a single employee or as a two-part election where each employee completes Part A of an election and the employer completes a single Part B to the election.

Any election made at the time of the acquisition of the restricted securities must be made within 14 days of the acquisition, and income tax will then be applied at acquisition taking account of the election.

Examples of the above elections can be found on the HMRC website at www.hmrc.gov.uk/manuals/ersmmanual/ERSM30450.htm.

Post-acquisition chargeable events

7.40   By virtue of ITEPA 2003, s 427, the following are post-acquisition chargeable events:

(a)   restricted securities ceasing to be subject to restrictions;

(b)   any variation of the restrictions; and

(c)   any disposal of the restricted securities.

7.41   ITEPA 2003, Pt 7, Ch 2 contains a complicated formula which imposes tax on the untaxed proportion of the value of the shares on a post-acquisition chargeable event. For example, if a share which would be worth £1 without any restrictions has a restricted market value of 75p then the tax liability would be as follows:

on acquisition:

– unrestricted value	£1
– restricted security worth	75p (untaxed proportion 25%)

on lifting of all restrictions:

– market value at the time of lifting of all restrictions	£5
– charge is £5 × 25%	£1.25

If there are successive chargeable events (e.g. lifting of restrictions) then the untaxed proportion of the value of the shares will be subject to successive tax charges until all the untaxed proportion has been taxed.

7.42   If the shares increase in value rapidly, then the amount of income tax payable on any post-acquisition chargeable event may be significantly greater than if the untaxed proportion had been taxed on acquisition. The employer and employee may, therefore, make an irrevocable election within 14 days of acquisition in order that income tax may be correctly applied at acquisition.

7.43   The new restricted securities regime affects the acquisition of shares on earn-outs, MBOs and many private equity arrangements. Shares in listed companies are normally acquired by employees under awards which do not confer the beneficial interest in shares until vesting (LTIPs) or exercise (options). Shares acquired under share option schemes within ITEPA 2003, Pt 7, Ch 5 (securities options) are also outside the regime.

7.44   A joint election can also be made by the employer and employees so that on any chargeable event, the existence of any outstanding restrictions can be ignored and income tax charged on the balance of the untaxed proportion as if the restrictions did not apply.

7.45 The operation of the income tax charges on chargeable events can be illustrated by the following three examples.

Example 1

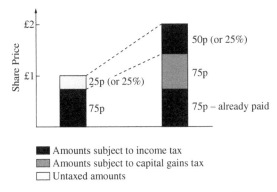

■ Amounts subject to income tax
▦ Amounts subject to capital gains tax
☐ Untaxed amounts

- Employee gifted shares subject to five-year sale restriction (no forfeiture).

- Restriction reduces market value by 25 per cent.

- Income tax paid on 75 per cent of value (25 per cent remains untaxed).

- After five years restriction falls away and 25 per cent of value then charged to income tax (50p).

- If shares immediately sold, remaining gain of 75p subject to capital gains tax.

Example 2

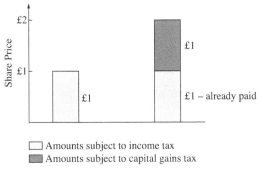

☐ Amounts subject to income tax
▦ Amounts subject to capital gains tax

- Employee gifted shares subject to five-year sale restriction (no forfeiture).

- Employee elects with employer to disregard restrictions.

- Income tax paid on full unrestricted market value.

- On lifting of restrictions after five years no further change to income tax.

- On sale any gain since acquisition charged to capital gains tax only.

Example 3

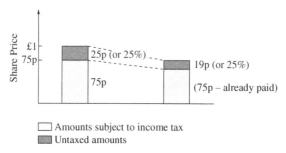

Amounts subject to income tax
Untaxed amounts

• Employee gifted shares subject to five-year sale restriction (no forfeiture).

• Restriction reduces market value by 25 per cent.

• Income tax paid on 75 per cent of value (25 per cent remains untaxed).

• After five years restriction falls away and 25 per cent of value then charged to income tax (19p).

• If shares immediately sold, capital loss of 19p.

CONVERTIBLE SECURITIES

7.46   ITEPA 2003, Pt 7, Ch 3 sets out the regime for the taxation of 'convertible securities'. These are securities in which the employee obtains the beneficial interest from the outset and which:

(a)   confer on the holder an immediate or conditional right to convert them into securities of a different description; or

(b)   contain an agreement which either authorises or requires the grant of such a right if circumstances arise or do not arise; or

(c)   contain an agreement which makes provision for the conversion of the securities (otherwise than by the holder) into different securities.

Income tax adjustment on acquisition

7.47   On acquisition, convertible securities are treated as if no rights on conversion exist and income tax on general earnings under ITEPA 2003, s 62, or pursuant to a securities option under ITEPA 2003, Pt 7, Ch 5, is adjusted accordingly (ITEPA 2003, s 437).

Income tax on post-acquisition chargeable events

7.48   Convertible securities are charged to income tax on the gain arising upon any post-acquisition chargeable event. These include:

(a)   the conversion of the securities into securities of a different description;

(b)   the disposal of the securities for a consideration;

(c)   the release of the securities for a consideration;

(d)   the receipt by an associated person of a benefit in money or moneys worth in connection with the entitlement to convert.

7.49   The amount of the gain on which income tax is chargeable is the amount of the gain on the occurrence of the chargeable event (ie the value of the new securities at the time of the conversion, less the value of the old securities which are converted) less any consideration given for the right to convert. ITEPA 2003, s 441 explains how the amount of gain released on the occurrence of different chargeable events is calculated and ITEPA 2003, s 442 explains how the amount of consideration for the entitlement to convert is calculated.

7.50   The convertible securities income tax charge on chargeable events does not apply if either the company is employee controlled or the majority of the share capital is held by non-employees and, in either case, all the shares are convertible (ITEPA 2003, s 443).

ACCOUNTING FOR LTIPs

7.51   A discussion of accounting issues is to be found in Chapter 15. In calculating the 'fair value' of LTIP awards, as there is generally no exercise price to pay to acquire shares, the initial value of the awards (before taking into account the potential for vesting and, to the extent possible, performance conditions) will be the full market value of the underlying shares.

THE COMPANY'S TAX POSITION

Introduction

7.52   The EBT trustees who will make, or satisfy, LTIP awards (whether performance shares or matching shares) will sooner or later need to be financed either by outright contributions or by loans which may not be repaid and would therefore need to be written off. The reason for this is that there is no reimbursement of the acquisition costs of the shares upon the exercise of any options as there is in the case of an EBT linked to a discretionary share option scheme.

7.53   The question which arises, therefore, in establishing any LTIP providing performance shares is whether the company's contributions to the EBT trustees will be paid:

(a)   at the time of allocation;

(b)   at the time of vesting; or

(c)   from time to time, possibly matching the timing of the profit and loss charges for accounting purposes.

Obviously, where the EBT trustees wish to hedge the cost of acquiring the shares in the market, it will be necessary to borrow the acquisition costs of the shares. It is likely that the only source of borrowed funds for this purpose will be the company. If so, then the EBT trustees will need to apply any future receipts in repayment of loans made by the company.

Deductibility of contributions for tax purposes

7.54   Any contribution made by the company to the trustees of an EBT for providing shares is likely not to be deductible in computing trading profits as a result of Corporation Tax Act 2009 ('CT A 2009'), s 1038 (previously FA 2003, Sch 23, para 25) as the value of the shares on acquisition by employees will be deductible for corporation tax purposes under CTA 2009, Pt 12 (previously FA 2003, Sch 23) (see Chapter 15).

TRUSTEES' TAX POSITION

Capital gains tax

7.55   At vesting, the participant becomes absolutely entitled to the shares as against the trustee. Consequently, the trustee (if UK resident) is treated as making a disposal of the shares for capital gains tax purposes under TCGA 1992, s 71. A disposal is treated as made for a consideration equal to the market value of the shares since the disposal is made in connection with the participant's employment (see TCGA 1992, s 17).

7.56   Under TCGA 1992, s 239ZA (previously Extra-Statutory Concession D35), relief from capital gains tax is available on certain disposals by EBT trustees where:

(a)   the EBT transfers the chargeable asset for no consideration (a transfer pursuant to the exercise of a share option would therefore be ineligible);

(b)   the employee to whom the asset is transferred is chargeable to income tax on the value received;

(c)   the EBT must be an employee trust within the meaning of IHTA 1984, s 86, subject to two modifications. First, the restriction in IHTA 1984, s 86(3) does not need to be satisfied; in other words, it is not necessary that the trust property is held for 'all or most' of the employees of the company concerned. Secondly, the employee receiving the transfer of the asset must not be to a person of the kind described in IHTA, s 28(4) and not excluded by subsection (5), that is to say, he must not, broadly speaking, hold, together with his associates, 5 per cent or more of the equity of the company.

Inheritance tax

7.57   An EBT trustee will normally hold trust property on discretionary trusts. As for any EBT, the inheritance tax treatment will depend upon whether it falls within IHTA 1984, s 86, that is to say, a trust for the benefit of all or most of the company's employees.

Section 86 trust

7.58   An EBT which qualifies as a section 86 trust normally enjoys full relief from any inheritance tax charge where any distribution is made to a qualifying beneficiary and in respect of the ten-year tax charge. However, property comprised in a 'qualifying interest in possession' will not be treated as held on exempt section 86 trusts. An interest in five per cent or more of the whole of the trust will be treated as such a qualifying interest in possession (IHTA 1984, ss 72(1) and 86(4)(b)).

7.59   Where any allocation of shares under an LTIP within section 86 involves five per cent or more of the whole of the trust this will be treated as the creation of an interest in possession trust and will give rise to a charge to inheritance tax under IHTA 1984, s 72(2)(a). This tax charge will only be relieved to the extent income tax is paid by the employee on the allocation (IHTA 1984, ss 70(3) and 72(5)). However, as there is normally no income tax charge at allocation, inheritance tax will normally apply, assuming the employee has an interest in possession in more than five per cent of the whole of the employee trust as a result of the allocation.

7.60   Furthermore, on termination of the five per cent interest in possession (on forfeiture or on sale of the shares for cash) the employee will be treated as making a lifetime transfer of value (IHTA 1984, s 52). On vesting, there will be no charge to tax since the employee is treated as beneficially entitled to the property (IHTA 1984, s 49).

7.61   Consequently, allocations of shares under an LTIP where the property is held on trusts within IHTA 1984, s 86 should be limited to no more than five per cent of the whole of the property so that such interest is not treated as the creation of a 'qualifying interest in possession' with the result that inheritance tax applies at that time.

Non-section 86 trusts

7.62   A non-section 86 trust is subject to inheritance tax in the normal way for discretionary trusts as follows:

(a)   where a distribution is made out of the trust (IHTA 1984, s 65(1)(a));

(b)   where value is transferred out of the trust without a distribution (IHTA 1984, s 65(1)(b));

(c)   every 10th anniversary of the trust.

However, there is relief from inheritance tax on any distribution which is subject to income tax in the hands of the recipient (an employee, former employee or relative of an employee). This will cover the vast majority of distributions at the time of vesting, but it will not apply to the original allocation of shares to the extent that this is a distribution for inheritance tax purposes. It is advisable, therefore, to ensure that allocations are made within 90 days of the establishment of the EBT since no inheritance tax charge will arise under the relief in IHTA 1984, s 65(4). In any event, any charge to inheritance tax on a distribution during the first ten years should be minimal, particularly if the trustee's acquisition of shares is funded by loan and in any event the 10-year charge can be avoided by distributing the trust assets shortly beforehand.

OTHER STRUCTURING ISSUES

UK resident or offshore trust

7.63   At **7.56** above it was noted that under TCGA 1992, s 239ZA, EBT trustees may be relieved from capital gains tax in respect of the transfer of shares to employees who pay UK income tax on the value received.

7.64   However, TCGA 1992, s 239ZA does not apply if any consideration (even £1) is payable for the transfer of the shares or in respect of a transfer of shares to an employee who is outside the scope of UK income tax. There is also no relief from capital gains tax where the trustee sells shares which are not required to satisfy LTIP awards (for example where an award has lapsed) in circumstances where a gain is realised.

7.65   In order to remove the EBT from the scope of UK capital gains tax, an EBT operating in connection with an LTIP will normally be set up offshore.

Disguised remuneration

7.66   The legislation, titled 'Employment income provided through third parties', but more commonly referred to as the 'disguised remuneration' legislation, was introduced by the Finance Act 2011 with effect from 6 April 2011 (see ITEPA 2003, Part 7A) which was designed to counter tax avoidance arising from the use of trusts which provided employees with benefits in a way that defers, or even avoids completely, a liability to tax. However, the legislation was very broadly drafted, and can therefore potentially apply to employee benefit trusts used to deliver shares under LTIPs.

7.67   The legislation, amongst other things, creates a tax charge where a third party, most commonly a trustee, 'earmarks' an amount or any asset (for example, shares) in favour of a beneficiary. The concept of "earmarking" is very broad, and any action by an EBT trustee to allocate (however informally) shares in favour of specified beneficiaries will be caught. The tax charge will arise at the time of the earmarking, notwithstanding that the beneficiary has no interest in the shares at that time.

7.68   In the context of an LTIP, were the trustees to be deemed to have earmarked shares in respect of awards made to specific participants, those participants would suffer an income tax charge at the time of the earmarking, notwithstanding that the participants' awards may not have vested, or may never in fact vest.

7.69   The legislation includes exemptions from the tax charge for certain acts in connection with employee share schemes (see **16.72** below). However, relying solely on an exemption to avoid the application of the new legislation creates a risk of a tax charge arising if any one of the conditions of the exemption is breached, even if such breach occurs unintentionally. Further, the exemptions are complex, and the application of the legislation, and HMRC's interpretation and guidance, have not yet been tested in practice.

7.70   The more prudent course of action would be to ensure that no 'earmarking' of shares occurs, such that the tax charge will not arise in the first place and so that there will be no need to rely on the exemptions is respect of future grants and awards. HMRC's published guidance states that, in general, there will be no earmarking where:

(a)   there is a pool of shares (held by the trust) and a pool of employees;

(b)   the trustee has not made the awards to the employees; and

(c)   the trustee does not know the number of shares to be awarded to any particular employee.

The guidance goes on to state that, for example, no earmarking will have occurred if the trustee only knows that 'x' shares have been granted to 'y' employees of a particular company, or only knows that 'x' shares in total have been granted to a group of named employees but does not know how many of those shares have been awarded to particular individuals.

7.71   As a result of the above HMRC guidance, companies will generally enter into a share supply agreement with their EBT trustee, under which the trustee agrees to satisfy LTIP awards, but in respect of which the trustee will not receive details of the beneficiaries, or the number of shares to be transferred to any specific beneficiary, until such time as the LTIP awards vest.

Clawback

7.72   Over the last few years, clawback provisions have become a much more common feature in share schemes, and in LTIPs in particular. A clawback will generally operate to reduce unvested awards, or awards which have vested but in respect of which shares have not yet been issued or transferred (often referred to as 'soft clawback' or 'malus') or will require a participant to transfer shares back to the company, or make a payment of an equivalent amount (often referred to as 'hard clawback' or, simply, 'clawback').

7.73 Section D of the September 2014 reissue of the UK Corporate Governance Code deals with the design of performance-related remuneration for executive directors, and provides (at para D.1.1) that schemes should include provisions that would enable the company to recover sums paid or withhold the payment of any sum, and specify the circumstances in which it would be appropriate to do so (the previous version of the UK Corporate Governance Code provided only that consideration should be given to the use of provisions that permit the company to reclaim variable components in exceptional circumstances of misstatement or misconduct).

7.74 Clawback is also referred to in the ABI Guidelines, which provide that companies should include in their incentive arrangements provisions that allow the company, in specified circumstances, to forfeit all or part of a bonus or long-term incentive award before it has vested and been paid and/or recover sums already paid.

7.75 The most common circumstances in which clawback will therefore apply include where:

(a) the financial accounts of the company used to determine the outcome of performance conditions are restated; or

(b) the participant's conduct prior to vesting would, if it had been known at the relevant time, have resulted in his or her dismissal, with a consequent lapse of the share awards which vested.

7.76 Clawback provisions which do not impose a penalty on the participant, and which do not interfere with the individual's ability to move to another job, should be enforceable under English law. Care needs to be taken, however, if clawback may apply post-termination that it is not used either as a penalty or a restraint of trade. Consideration also needs to be given to the length of time following vesting that clawback will apply, and whether the full amount will need to be returned to the company, or whether clawback will be limited to a net of tax amount.

7.77 HMRC does not currently consider that clawback provisions being operated result in the employee being able to make a claim for tax paid on the amounts clawed back. In relation to cash bonuses, there is currently an outstanding dispute as to whether amounts clawed back should constitute 'negative earnings' leading to the ability to off-set against other income, and potentially reclaim tax already paid. Even if the taxpayer is ultimately successful in this claim, the legislation relating to share-based payments is drafted differently, and it would be unlikely that, without legislative changes, HMRC would be willing to permit income tax reclaims.

7.78 In relation to tax-advantaged schemes, see **4.44** above.

Cash alternatives

7.79   Where an LTIP provides a right for the company to substitute a
cash payment in place of a transfer of shares to the participant, there has
been debate as to whether this will result in the participant no longer having
a 'right' to acquire shares (where the LTIP was intended to be structured as
a securities option under ITEPA 2003, Pt 7, Ch 5). HMRC has confirmed
that, where the ability to receive a cash payment in lieu of shares is a choice
for the participant, this will not affect the tax treatment of the participant's
award. Where the company has the ability to unilaterally substitute a cash
payment, HMRC accept that, provided that the award has been accounted
for as an option, then until the company exercises its right to substitute cash,
the award will continue to be subject to securities option tax treatment. If
the company habitually relies on this right of substitution in relation to UK
resident employees, then the award will not be treated as a securities option,
and instead will be taxable as general earnings under ITEPA 2003, s 62.

Performance Share Awards

Set out below is a precedent for the rules of an LTIP providing for performance share awards which are taxed as a right to receive shares under ITEPA 2003, Pt 7, Ch 5.

Performance share awards

1. **INTERPRETATION AND CONSTRUCTION**

1.1   For the purposes of the Plan, the following terms shall have the meaning indicated below unless the context clearly indicates otherwise:

'**Award**' means a conditional right to receive Shares under the Plan which may be transferred into the name of the Participant following the Vesting Date in accordance with Rule 6.2;

'**Award Certificate**' means a certificate in such form as the Board shall determine (which may include electronic form), but containing the information specified in Rule 3.6;

'**Award Date**' means the date on which an Award is granted;

'**Award Period**' means the period of 42 days commencing on any of the following:

(A)   the Dealing Day following the day on which the Company makes an announcement of its results for the last preceding financial year, half-year or other period; and

(B)   any day on which the Board resolves that exceptional circumstances exist which justify the making of an Award;

'**Board**' means the board of directors of the Company or committee duly authorised by the board of directors or, following any Corporate Action, the Board or duly authorised committee as constituted immediately prior to the Corporate Action;

'**Company**' means [COMPANY] [Limited/plc] (registered in England and Wales under No [NUMBER]);

'**Control**' has the meaning given by Section 995 of the Income Tax Act 2007;

'**Corporate Action**' means any of the following:

(A)   a person obtaining Control of the Company as a result of making a general offer to acquire Shares;

(B)   a person, having obtained Control of the Company, making a general offer to acquire Shares;

(C)   the Court sanctioning a compromise or arrangement under Section 899 of the Companies Act 2006 SAVE where the purpose and effect of the compromise or arrangement is a reconstruction whereby the Company becomes a subsidiary of another company, such other company having substantially the same shareholders and approximate shareholdings as those of the Company immediately prior to the compromise or arrangement taking effect;

(D)   the passing of a resolution for the voluntary winding up of the Company; or

(E)   if the Board so determines, the announcement of the terms of a demerger of a substantial part of the Group's business, special dividend or similar event affecting the value of Shares subject to Awards;

'Dealing Day' means any day on which the London Stock Exchange is open for the transaction of business;

'Eligible Employee' means an employee (including an executive director) of the Company or of any Subsidiary;

'Employees' Share Scheme' has the meaning given by Section 1166 of the Companies Act 2006;

'Employing Company' means the Member of the Group which employs the Participant;

'Group' means the Company and its Subsidiaries from time to time, and the expression **'Member of the Group'** shall be construed accordingly;

'London Stock Exchange' means London Stock Exchange plc;

'Market Value' means, in relation to a Share on any day:

(A)   if and so long as the Shares are admitted to listing by the UK Listing Authority and traded on the London Stock Exchange, its closing mid-market quotation on that day; or

(B)   subject to (A) above, its market value, determined in accordance with Part VIII of the Taxation of Chargeable Gains Act 1992;

'Participant' means an Eligible Employee who has received an Award to the extent it has not been renounced or forfeited;

'Performance Target' means the performance target determined by the Board from time to time;

'Plan' means this [Company] Long Term Incentive Plan, as amended from time to time;

'Rule' means a rule of this Plan;

'Salary' means, in relation to an Eligible Employee, his annual rate of basic salary excluding any bonuses or pension contributions;

'Share' means a fully paid ordinary share in the capital of the Company or any share representing the same after any takeover or reconstruction or any variation of the share capital of the Company;

'**Subsidiary**' means a company which is a subsidiary of the Company within the meaning of Section1159 and Schedule 6 of the Companies Act 2006;

'**Treasury Shares**' means Shares to which Sections 724 to 732 of the Companies Act 2006 apply;

'**UK Listing Authority**' means the Financial Services Authority as the competent authority for listing in the United Kingdom under Part VI of the Financial Services and Markets Act 2000; and

'**Vesting Date**' means the earlier of:

(A)   the third anniversary of the Award Date (or, if not a Dealing Day, then the next Dealing Day);

(B)   save where Rule 9 applies, the date of a Corporate Action; and

(C)   such date as may be determined by the Board under Rule 6.5.

1.2   In this Plan unless the context requires otherwise:

1.2.1   the headings are inserted for convenience only and do not affect the interpretation of any Rule;

1.2.2   a reference to a statute or statutory provision includes a reference:

(A)   to that statute or provision as from time to time consolidated, modified, re-enacted or replaced by any statute or statutory provision;

(B)   to any repealed statute or statutory provision which it re-enacts (with or without modification); and

(C)   to any subordinate legislation made under it;

1.2.3   words in the singular include the plural, and vice versa;

1.2.4   a reference to the masculine shall be treated as a reference to the feminine and vice versa;

1.2.5   a reference to a person shall include a reference to a body corporate; and

1.2.6   a reference to writing or written form shall include any legible format capable of being reproduced on paper, irrespective of the medium used.

2.   PLAN ALLOCATION LIMITS

2.1   The maximum number of Shares which may be allocated under the Plan on any day shall not, when added to the aggregate of the number of Shares which have been allocated in the previous 10 years under the Plan and under any other discretionary Employees' Share Scheme adopted by the Company, exceed such number as represents 5 per cent of the ordinary share capital of the Company in issue immediately prior to that day.

2.2   The maximum number of Shares which may be allocated under the Plan on any day shall not, when added to the aggregate of the number of Shares which have been allocated in the previous 10 years under the Plan and under any other Employees' Share Scheme adopted by the Company, exceed such number as represents 10 per cent of the ordinary share capital of the Company in issue immediately prior to that day.

2.3 References in this Rule 2 to the 'allocation' of Shares shall mean:

    2.3.1 in the case of any option, conditional share award or other similar award pursuant to which Shares may be acquired:

        (A) the grant of the option, conditional share award or other similar award to acquire Shares, pursuant to which Shares may be issued; and

        (B) in so far as not previously taken into account under (A) above from the date of grant, any subscription for Shares which are issued for the purpose of satisfying any option, conditional share award or other similar award to acquire Shares; and

    2.3.2 in relation to other types of Employees' Share Scheme, the issue and allotment of Shares,

and references to 'allocated' in this Rule 2 shall be construed accordingly.

2.4 In determining the above limits no account shall be taken of:

    2.4.1 any allocation (or part thereof) where the option, conditional share award or other similar award to acquire Shares was released, lapsed or otherwise became incapable of vesting;

    2.4.2 any allocation (or part thereof) in respect of which the Board has determined shall be satisfied otherwise than by the issue of Shares; and

    2.4.3 such number of additional Shares as would otherwise have been issued on the exercise of an option for monetary consideration (*the exercise price*) but in respect of which the exercise price is not paid, in substitution for the issue of such lesser number of shares as have a market value equal only to the gain which the optionholder would have made on exercise (*equity-settled SAR alternative*).

2.5 References to the issue and allotment of Shares shall include the transfer of Treasury Shares, but only until such time as the guidelines issued by institutional investor bodies cease to provide that they need to be so included.

3. AWARDS

3.1 The Board may resolve at any time during an Award Period in its absolute discretion to grant Awards to such Eligible Employees as it may determine.

3.2 The maximum number of Shares which may be subject to an Award to an Eligible Employee in any year shall be the number resulting from the following formula:

$$\frac{V}{ASP}$$

Where:

    V is an amount equal to such percentage, not exceeding [200] per cent, of the Eligible Employee's Salary (expressed in pounds sterling, where applicable converted at such rate as the Board may determine) as may be determined by the Board; and

    ASP is the middle market quotation for a Share on the Dealing Day (or averaged over up to five Dealing Days, all being days within the Award Period, if the Board so determines) immediately preceding the Award Date.

3.3   The grant of an Award shall be made under seal or in such other manner as to take effect in law as a deed.

3.4   An Award shall be evidenced by an Award Certificate which shall be issued to the Participant within 30 days of the Award Date.

3.5   No payment for an Award shall be made by the Participant.

3.6   The Award Certificate shall specify:

3.6.1   the Award Date;

3.6.2   the number and class of Shares which are subject to the Award;

3.6.3   the Vesting Date; and

3.6.4   the full terms of the Performance Target, together with a statement that the transfer of Shares comprised in an Award is subject to the achievement of such Performance Target.

3.7   The interest of a Participant in an Award may not be transferred, assigned, pledged, charged or otherwise disposed of by a Participant.

3.8   A Participant may renounce an Award (in whole but not in part) by written notice to the Company to take effect from the date of receipt of such notice by the Company.

4.   PERFORMANCE TARGET

4.1   Whether and, if so, the extent to which the number of Shares subject to an Award may be transferred to the Participant, or to his personal representative(s), under the Plan shall be determined by reference to the Performance Target.

4.2   If events happen which cause the Board to consider that the Performance Target is no longer a fair measure of the Company's performance, the Board may alter the terms of the Performance Target as it considers appropriate but not so that the revised target is materially less challenging than the target as originally set.

5.   FORFEITURE

5.1   An Award shall be forfeit:

5.1.1   to the extent that, at the expiry of such period over which performance is measured, the Performance Target has not been satisfied;

5.1.2   immediately upon the Participant ceasing to be an employee of any Member of the Group by reason of dismissal for misconduct;

5.1.3   should the Participant purport to assign, pledge, charge or otherwise dispose of his interest in an Award contrary to Rule 3.7; and

5.1.4   should the Participant become bankrupt, unless or to the extent otherwise determined by the Board.

5.2   At any time prior to the Vesting Date, an Award shall be forfeit immediately upon the Participant ceasing to be an employee of any Member of the Group for any reason other than those specified in Rule 5.3.

5.3 A Participant's Award shall not be forfeit pursuant to Rule 5.2 if he has ceased to be an employee of any Member of the Group as a result of:

5.3.1 death;

5.3.2 injury, disability or ill-health;

5.3.3 redundancy (within the meaning of the Employment Rights Act 1996);

5.3.4 retirement;

5.3.5 the sale of the Subsidiary which is the Participant's Employing Company, or the sale of the business for which he works, outside of the Group; or

5.3.6 any reason, other than those specified in sub-rules 5.3.1 to 5.3.5, as determined by the Board.

6. **TRANSFER**

6.1 Subject to the forfeiture of the whole or any part of an Award under Rule 5.1, 6.3 or 6.4, an Award shall not be forfeit at any time on or after the Vesting Date.

6.2 The Company shall procure that, if and to the extent that the Performance Target has been met, the number of Shares subject to an Award shall be transferred to the Participant, or to his personal representatives, on or as soon as practicable following the Vesting Date.

6.3 [Where the Participant has ceased to be an employee of any Member of the Group for a reason specified in Rule 5.3, the number of Shares which would be transferred pursuant to Rule 6.2 shall be limited to a pro rata number on the basis of the number of whole months which have elapsed from the Award Date to the date the Participant ceased to be an employee of any Member of the Group as compared to 36 months. Any remainder of the Award shall be forfeit.]

6.4 [In the event of a Corporate Action (save where Rule 9 applies), the number of Shares which would be transferred pursuant to Rule 6.2 shall be limited to a pro rata number on the basis of the number of whole months which have elapsed from the Award Date to the date of the Corporate Action as compared to 36 months. Any remainder of the Award shall be forfeit.]

6.5 Where a Participant ceases to be an employee of any Member of the Group for a reason specified in Rule 5.3, the Board may determine that the Vesting Date in relation to an Award made to that Participant shall be the date of cessation of employment or any date thereafter.

6.6 No Shares shall be transferred to Participants (or to any personal representative) at any time during which the Company is in a prohibited period under the Model Code published by the UK Listing Authority.

7. **PAYE DEDUCTION**

7.1 The Company shall be obliged at the time of any transfer of Shares to a Participant to transfer (or procure the transfer of) legal title to only such proportion of the Shares as shall be determined as follows:

$$\frac{A - B}{A}$$

Where:

A   is the aggregate Relevant Value of the Shares which Shares are to be transferred pursuant to Rule 6; and

B   is the aggregate amount of the Tax Liability which arises as a result of the delivery of such Shares to the Participant.

7.2   The Participant authorises the Company to sell, or procure the sale of, such proportion of the Shares, legal title to which it is not obliged to deliver to the Participant (the **'Retained Shares'**), on the date on which those Shares would otherwise be delivered to the Participant and to remit the proceeds of sale of the Retained Shares either to the appropriate authorities of the jurisdiction in which the Participant is subject to tax or to the Employing Company in order to reimburse it for any Tax Liability arising upon the delivery of the Shares to the Participant.

7.3   The Participant authorises the Employing Company to make any further adjustments through payroll to ensure that the correct amount is remitted to the appropriate authorities of the jurisdiction to which the Participant is subject to tax in respect of the Tax Liability arising upon the delivery of the Shares to the Participant.

7.4   For the purposes of this Rule 7:

7.4.1   all fractions of a Share shall be ignored;

7.4.2   **'Relevant Value'** shall mean the market value of a Share determined in accordance with Part VIII of the Taxation of Chargeable Gains Act 1992; and

7.4.3   references to **'Tax Liability'** shall include any amount of tax and/or social security (or similar) contributions which the Company or the Employing Company becomes liable on behalf of the Participant to pay to the appropriate authorities in any jurisdiction.

8.   VARIATION OF CAPITAL

8.1   In the event of a variation of the share capital of the Company by way of a capitalisation, rights issue, consolidation, sub-division, split, reclassification or reduction of Shares or other reorganisation of the share capital of the Company, the Board may make such adjustments to Awards as it may determine to be appropriate.

8.2   In the event of the demerger of a substantial part of the Group's business, a special dividend or similar event affecting the value of Shares subject to Awards to a material extent, where the Board does not determine that such event shall be a Corporate Action, the Board may make such adjustments to Awards as it may determine to be appropriate.

8.3   The Board may take such steps as it may consider necessary to notify Participants of any adjustment made under this Rule 8 and to call in, cancel, endorse, issue or reissue any Award Certificate subsequent upon such adjustment.

9.   TAKOVER OR REORGANISATION

9.1   If, as a result of any Corporate Action, a company (the "Acquiring Company") will obtain Control of the Company the Board may, with the agreement of the Acquiring Company, determine that this Rule 9 shall apply.

9.2   Where this Rule 9 applies, the Award shall not vest as a result of the Corporate Action (and for the avoidance of doubt the date of the Corporate Action shall not be a "Vesting Date"), and instead the Award (the "Old Award") shall lapse on the occurrence of the Corporate Action, and the New Parent Company shall grant a replacement right to receive shares (the "New Award") over such number of shares in the New Parent Company which are of equivalent value to the number of Shares in respect of which the Old Award was outstanding. The New Award shall be granted on the terms of the Plan, but as if the New Award had been granted at the same time as the Old Award and shall continue to be subject to the Performance Target.

9.3   For the purposes of this Rule 9:

9.3.1   the "New Parent Company" shall be the Acquiring Company, or, if different the company that is the ultimate parent company of the Acquiring Company within the meaning of section 1159 of the Companies Act 2006; and

9.3.2   the terms of the Plan shall following the date of the relevant Corporate Action shall be construed as if:

(A)   the reference to "[COMPANY] [Limited/PLC]" in the definition of "Company" in Rule 1 were a reference to the company which is the New Parent Company, and

(B)   save where the New Parent Company is listed, Rule 12.3 were omitted.

10.   CLAWBACK

10.1   The Board may determine that a claw-back shall apply where:

10.1.1   within [3] years of the Vesting Date of an Award the Board determines that the Award vested in respect of a larger number of Shares that it would otherwise have done as a result of the financial accounts of the Company on the basis of which the Performance Target was assessed having been misstated; or

10.1.2   it is discovered that the Participant committed an act or omission at any time prior to the Vesting Date that would have constituted grounds for summary termination.

10.2   Where the Board determines that a claw-back shall apply, the Board may:

10.2.1   require the Participant to transfer to the Company a number of Shares up to the excess number of Shares in respect of which the Award vested (as determined by the Board); or

10.2.2   require the Participant to make a cash payment to the Company of up to an amount calculated as the number of excess Shares referred in Rule 10.2.1 multiplied by the Market Value of a Share on the Vesting Date.

10.3   The Participant irrevocably acknowledges that where he is required to transfer Shares or pay a cash sum pursuant to Rule 10.2, the Board may:

10.3.1   reduce, by up to the number of excess Shares referred to in Rule 10.2.1, the number of Shares which are otherwise due to be transferred to the Participant pursuant to any other Award or an award under any other Employees' Share Scheme operated by the Company (other than an

Employees' Share Scheme which satisfies the requirements of any of Schedules 2 to 4 of the Income Tax (Earnings and Pensions) Act 2003); and/or

10.3.2 deduct up to the amount referred to in Rule 10.2.2 from any payment otherwise due to the Participant from any Member of the Group.

10.4 The number of Shares that would otherwise be due to be transferred to the Participant pursuant to the vesting of an Award granted under this Plan may be reduced by such number as may be determined by the Board to effect a claw-back pursuant to the terms of any other Award and/or other Employees' Share Scheme operated by the Company.

11. REGULATORY MATTERS

11.1 Any transfer of Shares to the Participant, or to his personal representative(s), under the Plan shall be subject to such consent, if any, of any authorities wherever situate, as may from time to time be required and the Participant, or his personal representative(s), shall be responsible for complying with the requirements of or to obtain or obviate the necessity for such consents.

11.2 Where the transfer of Shares is prohibited pursuant to Rule 11.1, or where Rule 6.6 applies, such transfer of Shares shall be delayed until the transfer is no longer prohibited.

12. ADMINISTRATION AND AMENDMENT

12.1 The Plan shall in all respects be administered by the Board, which may make such rules not being inconsistent with the terms and conditions hereof for the conduct of the Plan as it thinks fit provided that such rules do not prejudice any existing rights of Participants.

12.2 Subject to Rule 12.5, the Board may at any time by resolution add to or alter the Plan, or any Award made thereunder, in any respect.

12.3 Subject to Rule 12.4, no addition or alteration to the advantage of present or future Participants relating to eligibility, the limits on participation, the overall limits on the issue of shares or the transfer of Treasury Shares, the basis for determining a Participant's entitlement to, or the terms of, Shares provided pursuant to the Plan and the provisions for adjustments on a variation of share capital shall be made without the prior approval by ordinary resolution of the shareholders of the Company in general meeting.

12.4 Rule 12.3 shall not apply to any alteration or addition which is necessary or desirable in order to comply with or take account of the provisions of any proposed or existing legislation, law or other regulatory requirements or to take advantage of any changes to the legislation, law or other regulatory requirements, or to obtain or maintain favourable taxation, exchange control or regulatory treatment of the Company, any Subsidiary or any Participant or to make minor amendments to benefit the administration of the Plan.

12.5 No alteration or addition shall be made under Rule 12.2 which would abrogate or adversely affect the subsisting rights of a Participant unless it is made:

12.5.1 with the consent in writing of such number of Participants as hold Awards under the Plan to acquire 75 per cent of the Shares which would be issued or transferred if all Shares comprised in all Awards were transferred; or

12.5.2 by a resolution at a meeting of Participants passed by not less that 75 per cent of the Participants who attend and vote either in person or by proxy,

and for the purpose of this Rule 12.5 the Participants shall be treated as the holders of a separate class of share capital and the provisions of the Articles of Association of the Company relating to class meetings shall apply *mutatis mutandis*.

12.6 The Board may take such steps as it may consider necessary to notify Participants of any alteration or addition made under this Rule 12 and to call in, cancel, endorse, issue or reissue any Award Certificate subsequent upon such alteration or addition.

12.7 The Board may, in respect of Eligible Employees who are or who may become subject to taxation outside the United Kingdom on their remuneration, establish such plans or sub-plans based on the Plan but subject to such modifications as the Board considers necessary or desirable to take account of or to mitigate or to comply with relevant overseas taxation, securities or exchange control laws, provided that the terms of Awards made under such plans or sub-plans are not overall more favourable than the terms of Awards made under the Plan and that Awards made, and shares issued, pursuant to such plans or sub-plans shall count towards the limits set out in Rules 2 and 3.

13. GENERAL

13.1 The Plan shall terminate on the 10th anniversary of its adoption or at any earlier time by the passing of a resolution by the Board or an ordinary resolution of the shareholders in general meeting. Following such termination no further Awards shall be made, but such termination shall be without prejudice to the subsisting rights of Participants.

13.2 The Company and any Subsidiary of the Company may provide money to the trustees of any trust or any other person to enable them or him to acquire Shares to be held for the purposes of the Plan, or enter into any guarantee or indemnity for these purposes, to the extent that such is not prohibited by Chapter 2 of Part 2 of the Companies Act 2006.

13.3 Any disputes regarding the interpretation of the Rules or the terms of any Award shall be determined by the Board (upon such advice as it shall consider necessary) and any decision in relation thereto shall be final and binding.

13.4 Participants shall not be entitled to:

13.4.1 receive copies of accounts or notices sent to holders of Shares;

13.4.2 exercise voting rights; or

13.4.3 receive dividends,

in respect of Shares which have not been transferred to such Participants pursuant to the Plan.

13.5 If any Award Certificate shall be worn out, defaced or lost, it may be replaced on such evidence being provided as the Board may require.

13.6 Any notice or other communication under or in connection with this Plan may be given by the Company to Participants personally, by email or by post, and to the Company or any Member of the Group either personally or by post to the Secretary of the Company. Items sent by post shall be pre-paid and shall be deemed to have been received 48 hours after posting. Items sent by email shall be deemed to have been received immediately.

13.7 Nothing in the Plan shall in any way be construed as imposing upon any Member of the Group a contractual obligation as between the Member of the Group and an employee to contribute or to continue to contribute to the Plan.

13.8 The rights and obligations of any individual under the terms of his office or employment with the Company or any past or present Subsidiary shall not be affected by his participation in the Plan and the Plan shall not form part of any contract of employment between the individual and any such company.

13.9 An Eligible Employee shall have no right to receive an Award under the Plan.

13.10 By participating in the Plan, the Participant waives all and any rights to compensation or damages in consequence of the termination of his office or employment with the Company or any past or present Subsidiary for any reason whatsoever, whether lawfully or otherwise, insofar as those rights arise or may arise from his ceasing to have rights under the Plan as a result of such termination, or from the loss or diminution in value of such rights or entitlements, including by reason of the operation of the terms of the Plan, any determination by the Board pursuant to a discretion contained in the Plan or the provisions of any statute or law relating to taxation.

13.11 Benefits under the Plan shall not form part of a Participant's remuneration for any purpose and shall not be pensionable.

13.12 By participating in the Plan, the Participant consents to the collection, processing, transmission and storage by the Company, in any form whatsoever, of any data of a professional or personal nature which is necessary for the purposes of introducing and administering the Plan. The Company may share such information with any Member of the Group, its registrars, brokers, other third party administrator or any person who obtains Control of the Company or acquires the company, undertaking or part-undertaking which employs the Participant, whether within or outside of the European Economic Area.

13.13 The invalidity or non-enforceability of any provision or Rule of the Plan shall not affect the validity or enforceability of the remaining provisions and Rules of the Plan which shall continue in full force and effect.

13.14 These Rules shall be governed by and construed in accordance with English Law.

13.15 The English courts shall have exclusive jurisdiction to determine any dispute which may arise out of, or in connection with, the Plan.

Appendix 7B

Deferred Share Awards

Set out below is a precedent for the rules of an LTIP providing for the grant deferred share awards to be made in connection with annual bonuses, and which are taxed as forfeitable shares under ITEPA 2005, Pt 7, Ch 2.

Deferred Share Awards

1. INTERPRETATION AND CONSTRUCTION

1.1   For the purposes of the Scheme, the following terms shall have the meaning indicated below unless the context clearly indicates otherwise:

'Acquisition Date' means the date on which Deferred Shares are acquired on behalf of a Participant;

'Annual Bonus' means, in relation to an Eligible Employee, his bonus for any period not exceeding one financial year;

'Board' means the board of directors of the Company or committee duly authorised by the board of directors or, following any Corporate Action, the Board or duly authorised committee as constituted immediately prior to the Corporate Action;

'Company' means [COMPANY] registered in England and Wales under Number [NUMBER];

'Control' has the meaning given by Section 995 of the Income Tax Act 2007;

'Corporate Action' means any of the following:

(A)   a person obtaining Control of the Company as a result of making a general offer to acquire Shares;

(B)   a person, having obtained Control of the Company, making a general offer to acquire Shares;

(C)   the Court sanctioning a compromise or arrangement under Section 899 of the Companies Act 2006 SAVE where the purpose and effect of the compromise or arrangement is a reconstruction whereby the Company becomes a subsidiary of another company, such other company having substantially the same shareholders and approximate shareholdings as those of the Company immediately prior to the compromise or arrangement taking effect;

(D)   the passing of a resolution for the voluntary winding up of the Company; or

(E)   if the Board so determines, the announcement of the terms of a demerger of a substantial part of the Group's business, special dividend or similar event affecting the value of Shares;

'Dealing Day' means any day on which the London Stock Exchange is open for the transaction of business;

'Deferred Shares' means Shares acquired by a Nominee on behalf of an Eligible Employee, 'on a compulsory basis pursuant to Rule 3.2, with a portion of that Eligible Employee's Annual Bonus;

'Eligible Employee' means an employee (including an executive director) of the Company or of any Subsidiary;

'Employees' Share Scheme' has the meaning given by Section 1166 of the Companies Act 2006;

'Employing Company' means the Member of the Group which employs the Participant;

'Group' means the Company and its Subsidiaries from time to time, and the expression **'Member of the Group'** shall be construed accordingly;

'London Stock Exchange' means London Stock Exchange plc;

'Market Value' means, in relation to a Share on any day:

(A)   if and so long as the Shares are admitted to listing by the UK Listing Authority and traded on the London Stock Exchange, its closing mid-market quotation on that day; or

(B)   subject to (A) above, its market value, determined in accordance with Part VIII of the Taxation of Chargeable Gains Act 1992;

'Nominee' means any person appointed by the Company from time to time to hold legal title to the Deferred Shares on behalf of the Participant in accordance with these Rules;

'Participant' means an Eligible Employee in respect of whom a Nominee holds Deferred Shares;

'Rule' means a rule of this Scheme;

'Scheme' means this [COMPANY] Deferred Share Scheme, as amended from time to time;

'Share' means a fully paid ordinary share in the capital of the Company or any share representing the same after any takeover or reconstruction or any variation of the share capital of the Company;

'Subsidiary' means a company which is a subsidiary of the Company within the meaning of Section 1159 and Schedule 6 of the Companies Act 2006;

'Treasury Shares' means Shares to which Sections 724 to 732 of the Companies Act 2006 apply;

'UK Listing Authority' means the Financial Services Authority as the competent authority for listing in the United Kingdom under Part VI of the Financial Services and Markets Act 2000; and

'**Vesting Date**' means the earlier of:

(A)   the third anniversary of the Acquisition Date (or, if not a Dealing Day, then the next Dealing Day); and

(B)   save where Rule 8 applies, the date of a Corporate Action.

1.2   In this Scheme unless the context requires otherwise:

1.2.1   the headings are inserted for convenience only and do not affect the interpretation of any Rule;

1.2.2   a reference to a statute or statutory provision includes a reference:

(A)   to that statute or provision as from time to time consolidated, modified, re-enacted or replaced by any statute or statutory provision;

(B)   to any repealed statute or statutory provision which it re-enacts (with or without modification); and

(C)   to any subordinate legislation made under it;

1.2.3   words in the singular include the plural, and vice versa;

1.2.4   a reference to the masculine shall be treated as a reference to the feminine and vice versa;

1.2.5   a reference to a person shall include a reference to a body corporate; and

1.2.6   a reference to writing or written form shall include any legible format capable of being reproduced on paper, irrespective of the medium used.

2.   SCHEME ALLOCATION LIMITS

2.1   The maximum number of Shares which may be allocated under the Scheme on any day shall not, when added to the aggregate of the number of Shares which have been allocated in the previous 10 years under the Scheme and under any other discretionary Employees' Share Scheme adopted by the Company, exceed such number as represents 5 per cent of the ordinary share capital of the Company in issue immediately prior to that day.

2.2   The maximum number of Shares which may be allocated under the Scheme on any day shall not, when added to the aggregate of the number of Shares which have been allocated in the previous 10 years under the Scheme and under any other Employees' Share Scheme adopted by the Company, exceed such number as represents 10 per cent of the ordinary share capital of the Company in issue immediately prior to that day.

2.3   References in this Rule 2 to the 'allocation' of Shares shall mean:

2.3.1   in the case of any option, conditional share award or other similar award pursuant to which Shares may be acquired:

(A)   the grant of the option, conditional share award or other similar award to acquire Shares, pursuant to which Shares may be issued; and

(B)   in so far as not previously taken into account under (A) above from the date of grant, any subscription for Shares which are issued for the purpose of satisfying any option, conditional share award or other similar award to acquire Shares; and

2.3.2 in relation to other types of Employees' Share Scheme, the issue and allotment of Shares,

and references to 'allocated', in this Rule 2, shall be construed accordingly.

2.4 In determining the above limits no account shall be taken of:

2.4.1 any allocation (or part thereof) where the option, conditional share award or other similar award to acquire Shares was released, lapsed or otherwise became incapable of vesting;

2.4.2 any allocation (or part thereof) in respect of which the Board has determined shall be satisfied otherwise than by the issue of Shares; and

2.4.3 such number of additional Shares as would otherwise have been issued on the exercise of an option for monetary consideration (*the exercise price*) but in respect of which the exercise price is not paid, in substitution for the issue of such lesser number of shares as have a market value equal only to the gain which the optionholder would have made on exercise (*equity-settled SAR alternative*).

2.5 References to the issue and allotment of Shares shall include the transfer of Treasury Shares, but only until such time as the guidelines issued by institutional investor bodies cease to provide that they need to be so included.

3. OPERATION OF THE SCHEME

3.1 The Board may determine that the Scheme shall be operated in connection with the annual bonus arrangements in respect of such Eligible Employees as it may, in its absolute discretion, determine.

3.2 Where the Board determines that the Scheme is to be operated, the Board shall specify a proportion of the Annual Bonus which would otherwise be received by an Eligible Employee, not being less than [ ] per cent of such Annual Bonus, which shall be deferred .

3.3 The Board shall procure that the Nominee shall receive and shall hold on behalf of the Participant as Deferred Shares such number of Shares as:

3.3.1 in aggregate have a Market Value (to the nearest whole Share) equal to the amount which is deferred under Rule 3.2; or

3.3.2 may be acquired by purchase on the London Stock Exchange with an amount equal to that which is deferred under Rule 3.2.

3.4 The Eligible Employee shall have no entitlement to receive the proportion of his Annual Bonus which is deferred under Rule 3.2, otherwise than in accordance with this Scheme.

3.5 Deferred Shares shall be held by the Nominee until transfer pursuant to Rule 5.2.

4. FORFEITURE OF DEFERRED SHARES

4.1 A Participant's Deferred Shares shall be forfeit:

4.1.1 immediately upon the Participant ceasing to be an employee of any Member of the Group by reason of dismissal for misconduct;

4.1.2 should the Participant purport to assign, pledge, charge or otherwise dispose of his interest in Deferred Shares;

4.1.3 should the Participant become bankrupt, unless or to the extent otherwise determined by the Board;

4.1.4 to the extent that the Board determines that the number of Deferred Shares is greater than it would otherwise have been as a result of the amount of the Participant's Annual Bonus, a proportion of which was deferred pursuant to Rule 3.2, being greater than it would otherwise have been as a result of the financial accounts of the Company on the basis of which the amount of such Annual Bonus was determined having been misstated; and

4.1.5 to the extent (including in full) as may be determined by the Board to be necessary to effect a claw-back pursuant to the terms of any other Employees' Share Scheme operated by the Company.

4.2 At any time prior to the Vesting Date, Deferred Shares shall be forfeit immediately upon the Participant ceasing to be an employee of any Member of the Group for any reason other than those specified in Rule 4.3.

4.3 A Participant's Deferred Shares shall not be forfeit pursuant to Rule 4.2 if he has ceased to be an employee of any Member of the Group as a result of:

4.3.1 death;

4.3.2 injury, disability or ill-health;

4.3.3 redundancy (within the meaning of the Employment Rights Act 1996);

4.3.4 retirement;

4.3.5 the sale of the Subsidiary which is the Participant's Employing Company, or the sale of the business for which he works, outside of the Group; or

4.3.6 any reason, other than those specified in sub-rules 4.3.1 to 4.3.5, as determined by the Board.

5. TRANSFER AND RELEASE

5.1 Subject to the forfeiture of Deferred Shares under Rule 4.1, Deferred Shares shall not be forfeit at any time on or after the Vesting Date.

5.2 The Nominee shall transfer to the Participant, or to his personal representatives, legal title to the Deferred Shares held on behalf of the Participant on or as soon as practicable following the Vesting Date.

5.3 No Shares shall be transferred to Participants (or to any personal representative) at any time during which the Company is in a prohibited period under the Model Code published by the UK Listing Authority.

6. PAYE DEDUCTION

6.1 The Nominee shall be obliged at the time of any transfer of Shares to a Participant to transfer legal title to only such proportion of the Shares as shall be determined as follows:

$$\frac{A - B}{A}$$

Where:

A   is the aggregate Relevant Value of the Shares which are to be transferred pursuant to Rule 5; and

B   is the aggregate amount of the Tax Liability which arises as a result of the delivery of such Shares to the Participant.

6.2   The Participant authorises the Nominee to sell, or procure the sale of, such proportion of the Shares, legal title to which it is not obliged to deliver to the Participant (the **'Retained Shares'**), on the date on which those Shares would otherwise be delivered to the Participant and to remit the proceeds of sale of the Retained Shares either to the appropriate authorities of the jurisdiction in which the Participant is subject to tax or to the Employing Company in order to reimburse it for any Tax Liability arising upon the delivery of the Shares to the Participant.

6.3   The Participant authorises the Employing Company to make any further adjustments through payroll to ensure that the correct amount is remitted to the appropriate authorities of the jurisdiction to which the Participant is subject to tax in respect of the Tax Liability arising upon the delivery of the Shares to the Participant.

6.4   For the purposes of this Rule 6:

6.4.1   all fractions of a Share shall be ignored;

6.4.2   **'Relevant Value'** shall mean the market value of a Share determined in accordance with Part VIII of the Taxation of Chargeable Gains Act 1992; and

6.4.3   references to **'Tax Liability'** shall include any amount of tax and/or social security (or similar) contributions which the Company or the Employing Company becomes liable on behalf of the Participant to pay to the appropriate authorities in any jurisdiction.

7.   VARIATION OF CAPITAL

7.1   In the event of the receipt, by holders of Shares, of any rights to acquire shares, securities or rights of any description, the Nominee shall, on behalf of the Participant, in respect of the Participant's Deferred Shares, sell such rights nil paid to the extent necessary to enable to Nominee to take up the balance of such unsold rights (and the Trustee shall not otherwise take up such rights); and

7.2   Where the Nominee receives, on behalf of the Participant, proceeds in relation to the Participant's Deferred Shares following the occurrence of any variation of the share capital of the Company, a demerger involving the Company, the payment of a capital distribution or special dividend, or any other circumstances similarly affecting Shares (including where the Nominee takes up rights pursuant to Rule 7.1), any such proceeds shall be subject to the terms of the Scheme which shall continue to apply mutatis mutandis as they do to the Participant's Deferred Shares in respect of which the proceeds were received.

8. TAKEOVER OR REORGANISATION

8.1 If, as a result of any Corporate Action, a company (the "Acquiring Company") will obtain Control of the Company the Board may, with the agreement of the Acquiring Company, determine that this Rule 8 shall apply.

8.2 Where this Rule 8 applies Deferred Shares shall not vest as a result of the Corporate Action (and for the avoidance of doubt the date of the Corporate Action shall not be a "Vesting Date"), and instead the proceeds from the relevant Corporate Action received by the Nominee in respect of the Deferred Shares on behalf of the Participant, whether in cash or securities (and the Nominee shall accept any offer of securities in preference to the receipt of cash), shall continue to be held on behalf of the Participant subject to the terms of the Scheme which (subject to Rule 8.3) shall continue to apply mutatis mutandis as they do to the Participant's Deferred Shares in respect of which the proceeds were received, provided that a proportion of such proceeds as is of equal value to the amount of any Tax Liability arising in respect of the Award at such time shall vest and shall be dealt with in accordance with Rule 6.

8.3 For the purposes of this Rule 8 the terms of the Scheme shall following the date of the relevant Corporate Action shall be construed as if:

8.3.1 the reference to "[COMPANY] [Limited/PLC]" in the definition of "Company" in Rule 1 were a reference to the company which is the New Parent Company, and

8.3.2 save where the New Parent Company is listed, Rule 11.3 were omitted.

9. REGULATORY MATTERS

9.1 Any transfer of Shares to the Participant, or to his personal representative(s), under the Scheme shall be subject to such consent, if any, of any authorities wherever situate, as may from time to time be required and the Participant, or his personal representative(s), shall be responsible for complying with the requirements of or to obtain or obviate the necessity for such consents.

9.2 Where the transfer of Shares is prohibited pursuant to Rule 10.1, or where Rule 5.3 applies, such transfer of Shares shall be delayed until the transfer is no longer prohibited.

10. ADMINISTRATION AND AMENDMENT

10.1 The Scheme shall in all respects be administered by the Board which may make such rules not being inconsistent with the terms and conditions hereof for the conduct of the Scheme as it thinks fit, provided that such rules do not prejudice any existing rights of Participants.

10.2 Subject to Rule 10.5, the Board may at any time by resolution add to or alter the Scheme in any respect.

10.3 Subject to Rule 10.4, no addition or alteration to the advantage of present or future Participants relating to eligibility, the limits on participation, the overall limits on the issue of shares or the transfer of Treasury Shares, the basis for determining a Participant's entitlement to, or the terms of, Shares provided pursuant to the Scheme and the provisions for adjustments on a variation of share capital shall be made without the prior approval by ordinary resolution of the shareholders of the Company in general meeting.

10.4 Rule 10.3 shall not apply to any alteration or addition which is necessary or desirable in order to comply with or take account of the provisions of any proposed or existing legislation, law or other regulatory requirements or to take advantage of any changes to the legislation, law or other regulatory requirements or to obtain or maintain favourable taxation, exchange control or regulatory treatment of the Company, any Subsidiary or any Participant or to make minor amendments to benefit the administration of the Scheme.

10.5 No alteration or addition shall be made under Rule 10.2 which would abrogate or adversely affect the subsisting rights of a Participant unless it is made:

10.5.1 with the consent in writing of such number of Participants on behalf of whom the Nominee holds at least 75 per cent. of the Deferred Shares held by the Nominee; or

10.5.2 by a resolution at a meeting of Participants passed by not less that 75 per cent of the Participants who attend and vote either in person or by proxy,

and for the purpose of this Rule 10.5 the Participants shall be treated as the holders of a separate class of share capital and the provisions of the Articles of Association of the Company relating to class meetings shall apply mutatis mutandis.

10.6 The Board may take such steps as it may consider necessary to notify Participants of any alteration or addition made under this Rule 10.

10.7 The Board may, in respect of Eligible Employees who are or who may become subject to taxation outside the United Kingdom on their remuneration, establish such schemes or sub-schemes based on the Scheme but subject to such modifications as the Board considers necessary or desirable to take account of or to mitigate or to comply with relevant overseas taxation, securities or exchange control laws, provided that the terms of deferred shares acquired pursuant to such schemes or sub-schemes are not overall more favourable than the terms of Deferred Shares under the Scheme and that deferred shares issued, pursuant to such schemes or sub-schemes shall count towards the limits set out in Rule 2.

11. GENERAL

11.1 The Scheme shall terminate on the 10th anniversary of its adoption or at any earlier time by the passing of a resolution by the Board or an ordinary resolution of the shareholders in general meeting. Following such termination no further Deferred Shares shall be acquired, but such termination shall be without prejudice to the subsisting rights of Participants.

11.2 The Company and any Subsidiary of the Company may provide money to the trustees of any trust or any other person to enable them or him to acquire Shares to be held for the purposes of the Scheme, or enter into any guarantee or indemnity for these purposes, to the extent that such is not prohibited by Chapter 2 of Part 2 of the Companies Act 2006.

11.3 Any disputes regarding the interpretation of the Rules or the terms on which Deferred Shares are held shall be determined by the Board (upon such advice as it shall consider necessary) and any decision in relation thereto shall be final and binding.

11.4 The Participant shall be entitled to direct the Nominee to vote any Deferred Shares. The Nominee shall not be obliged to seek directions from the Participant to vote any Deferred Shares and, in the absence of such directions, shall take no action.

11.5 The Participant shall be entitled to receive any dividends paid on Deferred Shares, and the Nominee shall remit to the Participant any dividends received as soon as is reasonably practicable following receipt.

11.6 Any notice or other communication under or in connection with this Scheme may be given by the Company or Nominee to Participants personally, by email or by post, and to the Nominee, Company or any Member of the Group either personally or by post to the Secretary of the Company. Items sent by post shall be pre-paid and shall be deemed to have been received 48 hours after posting. Items sent by email shall be deemed to have been received immediately.

11.7 Nothing in the Scheme shall in any way be construed as imposing upon any Member of the Group a contractual obligation as between the Member of the Group and an employee to contribute or to continue to contribute to the Scheme.

11.8 The rights and obligations of any individual under the terms of his office or employment with the Company or any past or present Subsidiary shall not be affected by his participation in the Scheme and the Scheme shall not form part of any contract of employment between the individual and any such company.

11.9 An Eligible Employee shall have no right to participate in the Scheme.

11.10 By participating in the Scheme, the Participant waives all and any rights to compensation or damages in consequence of the termination of his office or employment with the Company or any past or present Subsidiary for any reason whatsoever, whether lawfully or otherwise, insofar as those rights arise or may arise from his ceasing to have rights under the Scheme as a result of such termination, or from the loss or diminution in value of such rights or entitlements, including by reason of the operation of the terms of the Scheme, any determination by the Board pursuant to a discretion contained in the Scheme or the provisions of any statute or law relating to taxation.

11.11 Benefits under the Scheme shall not form part of a Participant's remuneration for any purpose and shall not be pensionable.

11.12 By participating in the Scheme, the Participant consents to the collection, processing, transmission and storage by the Company, in any form whatsoever, of any data of a professional or personal nature which is necessary for the purposes of introducing and administering the Scheme. The Company may share such information with any Member of the Group, the Nominee, its registrars, brokers, other third party administrator or any person who obtains Control of the Company or acquires the company, undertaking or part-undertaking which employs the Participant, whether within or outside of the European Economic Area.

11.13 The invalidity or non-enforceability of any provision or Rule of the Scheme shall not affect the validity or enforceability of the remaining provisions and Rules of the Scheme which shall continue in full force and effect.

11.14 These Rules shall be governed by and construed in accordance with English Law.

11.15 The English courts shall have exclusive jurisdiction to determine any dispute which may arise out of, or in connection with, the Scheme.

Matching Shares Awards

Set out below is a precedent for the rules of an LTIP providing for the acquisition of shares by the participant out of post-tax bonus, which can be matched by the grant of a 'matching award', with the matching award constituting a right to receive shares taxed under ITEPA 2003, Pt 7, Ch. 5.

Deferred and Matching Share Awards

1. **INTERPRETATION AND CONSTRUCTION**

1.1 For the purposes of the Scheme, the following terms shall have the meaning indicated below unless the context clearly indicates otherwise:

   'Annual Bonus' means, in relation to an Eligible Employee, his bonus for any period not exceeding one financial year;

   'Award Certificate' means a certificate in such form as the Board shall determine (which may include electronic form), but containing the information specified in Rule 4.5;

   'Award Date' means the date on which an Award is granted;

   'Award Period' means the period of 42 days commencing on any of the following:

   (A)   the Dealing Day following the day on which the Company makes an announcement of its results for the last preceding financial year, half-year or other period; and

   (B)   any day on which the Board resolves that exceptional circumstances exist which justify the making of an Award;

   'Board' means the board of directors of the Company or committee duly authorised by the board of directors or, following any Corporate Action, the Board or duly authorised committee as constituted immediately prior to the Corporate Action;

   'Company' means [COMPANY] registered in England and Wales under Number [NUMBER];

   'Control' has the meaning given by Section 995 of the Income Tax Act 2007;

   'Corporate Action' means any of the following:

   (A)   a person obtaining Control of the Company as a result of making a general offer to acquire Shares;

   (B)   a person, having obtained Control of the Company, making a general offer to acquire Shares;

(C)   the Court sanctioning a compromise or arrangement under Section 899 of the Companies Act 2006 SAVE where the purpose and effect of the compromise or arrangement is a reconstruction whereby the Company becomes a subsidiary of another company, such other company having substantially the same shareholders and approximate shareholdings as those of the Company immediately prior to the compromise or arrangement taking effect;

(D)   the passing of a resolution for the voluntary winding up of the Company; or

(E)   if the Board so determines, the announcement of the terms of a demerger of a substantial part of the Group's business, special dividend or similar event affecting the value of Shares subject to Awards;

'Dealing Day' means any day on which the London Stock Exchange is open for the transaction of business;

'Deferred Shares' means Shares acquired by the Nominee on behalf of an Eligible Employee, on a voluntary basis pursuant to Rule 3.2, with a portion of that Eligible Employee's Annual Bonus;

'Eligible Employee' means an employee (including an executive director) of the Company or of any Subsidiary;

'Employees' Share Scheme' has the meaning given by Section 1166 of the Companies Act 2006;

'Employing Company' means the Member of the Group which employs the Participant;

'Group' means the Company and its Subsidiaries from time to time, and the expression **'Member of the Group'** shall be construed accordingly;

'ITEPA' means the Income Tax (Earnings and Pensions) Act 2003;

'London Stock Exchange' means London Stock Exchange plc;

'Market Value' means, in relation to a Share on any day:

(A)   if and so long as the Shares are admitted to listing by the UK Listing Authority and traded on the London Stock Exchange, its closing mid-market quotation on that day; or

(B)   subject to (A) above, its market value, determined in accordance with Part VIII of the Taxation of Chargeable Gains Act 1992;

'Matching Award' means a conditional right to receive Shares under the Scheme which may be transferred into the name of the Participant following the Vesting Date in accordance with Rule 8.2;

'Nominee' means any person appointed by the Company from time to time to hold legal title to the Deferred Shares on behalf of the Participant in accordance with these Rules;

'Participant' means an Eligible Employee who has received a Matching Award to the extent it has not been renounced or forfeited;

'Performance Target' means the performance target determined by the Board from time to time;

'Rule' means a rule of this Scheme;

'**Scheme**' means this [COMPANY] Deferred and Matching Share Scheme, as amended from time to time;

'**Share**' means a fully paid ordinary share in the capital of the Company or any share representing the same after any takeover or reconstruction or any variation of the share capital of the Company;

'**Subsidiary**' means a company which is a subsidiary of the Company within the meaning of Section 1159 and Schedule 6 of the Companies Act 2006;

'**Treasury Shares**' means Shares to which Sections 724 to 732 of the Companies Act 2006 apply;

'**UK Listing Authority**' means the Financial Services Authority as the competent authority for listing in the United Kingdom under Part VI of the Financial Services and Markets Act 2000; and

'**Vesting Date**' means the earlier of:

(A)   the third anniversary of the Award Date (or, if not a Dealing Day, then the next Dealing Day);

(B)   save where Rule 11 applies, the date of a Corporate Action; and

(C)   any earlier date determined by the Board under Rule 8.6.

1.2   In this Scheme unless the context requires otherwise:

1.2.1   the headings are inserted for convenience only and do not affect the interpretation of any Rule;

1.2.2   a reference to a statute or statutory provision includes a reference:

(A)   to that statute or provision as from time to time consolidated, modified, re-enacted or replaced by any statute or statutory provision;

(B)   to any repealed statute or statutory provision which it re-enacts (with or without modification); and

(C)   to any subordinate legislation made under it;

1.2.3   words in the singular include the plural, and vice versa;

1.2.4   a reference to the masculine shall be treated as a reference to the feminine and vice versa;

1.2.5   a reference to a person shall include a reference to a body corporate; and

1.2.6   a reference to writing or written form shall include any legible format capable of being reproduced on paper, irrespective of the medium used.

2.   SCHEME ALLOCATION LIMITS

2.1   The maximum number of Shares which may be allocated under the Scheme on any day shall not, when added to the aggregate of the number of Shares which have been allocated in the previous 10 years under the Scheme and under any other discretionary Employees' Share Scheme adopted by the Company, exceed such number as represents 5 per cent of the ordinary share capital of the Company in issue immediately prior to that day.

2.2   The maximum number of Shares which may be allocated under the Scheme on any day shall not, when added to the aggregate of the number of Shares which have been allocated in the previous 10 years under the Scheme and under any other Employees' Share Scheme adopted by the Company, exceed such number as represents 10 per cent of the ordinary share capital of the Company in issue immediately prior to that day.

2.3   References in this Rule 2 to the 'allocation' of Shares shall mean:

    2.3.1   in the case of any option, conditional share award or other similar award pursuant to which Shares may be acquired:

       (A)   the grant of the option, conditional share award or other similar award to acquire Shares, pursuant to which Shares may be issued; and

       (B)   in so far as not previously taken into account under (A) above from the date of grant, any subscription for Shares which are issued for the purpose of satisfying any option, conditional share award or other similar award to acquire Shares; and

    2.3.2   in relation to other types of Employees' Share Scheme, the issue and allotment of Shares,

and references to 'allocated', in this Rule 2, shall be construed accordingly.

2.4   In determining the above limits no account shall be taken of:

    2.4.1   any allocation (or part thereof) where the option, conditional share award or other similar award to acquire Shares was released, lapsed or otherwise became incapable of vesting;

    2.4.2   any allocation (or part thereof) in respect of which the Board has determined shall be satisfied otherwise than by the issue of Shares; and

    2.4.3   such number of additional Shares as would otherwise have been issued on the exercise of an option for monetary consideration (*the exercise price*) but in respect of which the exercise price is not paid, in substitution for the issue of such lesser number of shares as have a market value equal only to the gain which the optionholder would have made on exercise (*equity-settled SAR alternative*).

2.5   References to the issue and allotment of Shares shall include the transfer of Treasury Shares, but only until such time as the guidelines issued by institutional investor bodies cease to provide that they need to be so included.

3.   OPERATION OF THE SCHEME

3.1   The Board may determine that the Scheme shall be operated in connection with the annual bonus arrangements in respect of such Eligible Employees as it may, in its absolute discretion, determine.

3.2   Where the Board determines that the Scheme is to be operated, the Board shall invite the Eligible Employee to specify a proportion of the post-tax Annual Bonus which would otherwise be paid to the Eligible Employee as shall be deferred and used by the Nominee in the acquisition of Deferred Shares.

3.3   The proportion of the Eligible Employee's post-tax Annual Bonus deferred pursuant to Rule 3.2 shall not be paid to the Eligible Employee, and shall instead be paid to the Nominee on behalf of the Eligible Employee.

3.4   The Board shall procure that, as soon as practicable following receipt of the monies representing the portion of the Eligible Employee's post-tax Annual Bonus deferred pursuant to Rule 3.2, the Nominee shall use such monies in the acquisition of Shares by:

3.4.1 purchase on the London Stock Exchange; or

3.4.2 by subscription or transfer from treasury at Market Value on such date.

3.5 Deferred Shares shall be held by the Nominee until transfer pursuant to Rule 8.3.

4. MATCHING AWARDS

4.1 The Board may resolve at any time during an Award Period in its absolute discretion to make Matching Awards to such Eligible Employees as it may determine.

4.2 The maximum number of Shares which may be subject to a Matching Award to an Eligible Employee shall be determined as a multiple, not exceeding [two], of the number of Deferred Shares acquired by the Nominee on behalf of the Participant.

4.3 The grant of a Matching Award shall be made under seal or in such other manner as to take effect in law as a deed.

4.4 A Matching Award shall be evidenced by an Award Certificate which shall be issued to the Participant by the Nominee within 30 days of the Award Date.

4.5 No payment for a Matching Award shall be made by the Participant.

4.6 The Award Certificate shall specify:

4.6.1 the Award Date;

4.6.2 the number and class of Shares which are subject to the Matching Award;

4.6.3 the number of Deferred Shares to which the Matching Award relates;

4.6.4 the Vesting Date; and

4.6.5 the full terms of the Performance Target, together with a statement that the transfer of Shares comprised in a Matching Award is subject to the achievement of such Performance Target.

4.7 The interest of a Participant in a Matching Award may not be transferred, assigned, pledged, charged or otherwise disposed of by a Participant.

4.8 A Participant may renounce a Matching Award (in whole but not in part) by written notice to the Company to take effect from the date of receipt of such notice by the Company.

5. PERFORMANCE TARGET

5.1 Whether and, if so, the extent to which the number of Shares subject to a Matching Award may be transferred to the Participant, or to his personal representative(s), under the Scheme shall be determined by reference to the Performance Target.

5.2 If events happen which cause the Board to consider that the Performance Target is no longer a fair measure of the Company's performance, the Board alter the terms of the Performance Target as it considers appropriate but not so that the revised target is materially less challenging than the target as originally set.

6.   FORFEITURE OF MATCHING AWARD

6.1   A Matching Award shall be forfeit:

6.1.1   to the extent that, at the expiry of such period over which performance is measured, the Performance Target has not been satisfied;

6.1.2   immediately upon the Participant ceasing to be an employee of any Member of the Group by reason of dismissal for misconduct;

6.1.3   should the Participant purport to assign, pledge, charge or otherwise dispose of his interest in a Matching Award contrary to Rule 4.7;

6.1.4   should the Participant assign, pledge, charge or otherwise dispose of his interest in Deferred Shares or request a transfer of Deferred Shares from the Nominee, but only in respect of the Matching Award (or proportion thereof) which relates to such Deferred Shares; or

6.1.5   should the Participant become bankrupt, unless or to the extent otherwise determined by the Board.

6.2   At any time prior to the Vesting Date, a Matching Award shall be forfeit immediately upon the Participant ceasing to be an employee of any Member of the Group for any reason other than those specified in Rule 6.3.

6.3   A Participant's Matching Award shall not be forfeit pursuant to Rule 6.2 if he has ceased to be an employee of any Member of the Group as a result of:

6.3.1   death;

6.3.2   injury, disability or ill-health;

6.3.3   redundancy (within the meaning of the Employment Rights Act 1996);

6.3.4   retirement;

6.3.5   the sale of the Subsidiary which is the Participant's Employing Company, or the sale of the business for which he works, outside of the Group; or

6.3.6   any reason, other than those specified in sub-rules 6.3.1 to 6.3.5, as determined by the Board.

7.   FORFEITURE OF DEFERRED SHARES

7.1   A Participant's Deferred Shares shall be forfeit:

7.1.1   immediately upon the Participant ceasing to be an employee of any Member of the Group by reason of dismissal for misconduct;

7.1.2   should the Participant become bankrupt, unless or to the extent otherwise determined by the Board;

7.1.3   to the extent that the Board determines that the number of Deferred Shares is greater than it would otherwise have been as a result of the amount of the Participant's Annual Bonus, a proportion of which was deferred pursuant to Rule 3.2, being greater than it would otherwise have been as a result of the financial accounts of the Company on the basis of which the amount of such Annual Bonus was determined having been misstated; or

7.1.4   to the extent (including in full) as may be determined by the Board to be necessary to effect a claw-back pursuant to the terms of any other Employees' Share Scheme operated by the Company.

8.   **TRANSFER AND RELEASE**

8.1   Subject to the forfeiture of the whole or any part of a Matching Award under Rules 6.1, 8.4 and 8.5, a Matching Award shall not be forfeit at any time on or after the Vesting Date.

8.2   The Company shall procure that, if and to the extent that the Performance Target has been met, the number Shares subject to a Matching Award shall be transferred to the Participant, or to his personal representatives, on or as soon as reasonably practicable following the Vesting Date.

8.3   The Nominee shall transfer to the Participant, or to his personal representatives, legal title to the Deferred Shares held on behalf of the Participant on or as soon as reasonably practicable following the Vesting Date.

8.4   [Where the Participant has ceased to be an employee of any Member of the Group for a reason specified in Rule 6.3, the number of Shares which would be transferred pursuant to Rule 8.2 shall be limited to a pro rata number on the basis of the number of whole months which have elapsed from the Award Date to the date the Participant ceased to be an employee of any Member of the Group as compared to 36 months. Any remainder of the Matching Award shall be forfeit.]

8.5   [In the event of a Corporate Action (save where Rule 11 applies), the number of Shares which would be transferred pursuant to Rule 8.2 shall be limited to a pro rata number on the basis of the number of whole months which have elapsed from the Award Date to the date of the Corporate Action as compared to 36 months. Any remainder of the Award shall be forfeit.]

8.6   Where a Participant ceases to be an employee of any Member of the Group for a reason specified in sub-rule 6.3, the Board may determine that the Vesting Date in relation to a Matching Award made to that Participant shall be the date of cessation of employment or any date thereafter.

8.7   No Shares shall be transferred to Participants (or to any personal representative) at any time during which the Company is in a prohibited period under the Model Code published by the UK Listing Authority.

9.   **PAYE DEDUCTION**

9.1   The Company shall be obliged at the time of any transfer of Shares to a Participant pursuant to a Matching Award to transfer (or procure the transfer of) legal title to only such proportion of the Shares as shall be determined as follows:

$$\frac{A - B}{A}$$

Where:

A   is the aggregate Relevant Value of the Shares which are to be transferred pursuant to Rule 8; and

B   is the aggregate amount of the Tax Liability which arises as a result of the delivery of such Shares to the Participant.

9.2   The Participant authorises the Company to sell, or procure the sale of, such proportion of the Shares, legal title to which it is not obliged to deliver to the Participant (the **'Retained Shares'**), on the date on which those Shares would otherwise be delivered to the Participant and to remit the proceeds of sale of the Retained Shares either to the appropriate authorities of the jurisdiction in which the

Participant is subject to tax or to the Employing Company in order to reimburse it for any Tax Liability arising upon the delivery of the Shares to the Participant.

9.3 The Participant authorises the Employing Company to make any further adjustments through payroll to ensure that the correct amount is remitted to the appropriate authorities of the jurisdiction to which the Participant is subject to tax in respect of the Tax Liability arising upon the delivery of the Shares to the Participant.

9.4 For the purposes of this Rule 9:

9.4.1 all fractions of a Share shall be ignored;

9.4.2 **'Relevant Value'** shall mean the market value of a Share determined in accordance with Part VIII of the Taxation of Chargeable Gains Act 1992; and

9.4.3 references to **'Tax Liability'** shall include any amount of tax and/or social security (or similar) contributions which the Company or the Employing Company becomes liable on behalf of the Participant to pay to the appropriate authorities in any jurisdiction.

10. VARIATION OF CAPITAL

10.1 In the event of a variation of the share capital of the Company by way of a capitalisation, rights issue, consolidation, sub-division, split, reclassification or reduction of Shares or other reorganisation of the share capital of the Company, the Board may make such adjustments to Matching Awards as it may determine to be appropriate.

10.2 In the event of the demerger of a substantial part of the Group's business, a special dividend or similar event affecting the value of Shares subject to Awards to a material extent, where the Board does not determine that such event shall be a Corporate Action, the Board may make such adjustments to Matching Awards as it may determine to be appropriate.

10.3 The Board may take such steps as it may consider necessary to notify Participants of any adjustment made under this Rule 10 and to call in, cancel, endorse, issue or reissue any Award Certificate subsequent upon such adjustment.

10.4 In the event of the receipt, by holders of Shares, of any rights to acquire shares, securities or rights of any description, the Nominee shall, on behalf of the Participant, in respect of the Participant's Deferred Shares, sell such rights nil paid to the extent necessary to enable the Nominee to take up the balance of such unsold rights (and the Nominee shall not otherwise take up such rights); and

10.5 Where the Nominee receives, on behalf of the Participant, proceeds in relation to the Participant's Deferred Shares following the occurrence of any variation of the share capital of the Company, a demerger involving the Company, the payment of a capital distribution or special dividend, or any other circumstances similarly affecting Shares (including where the Nominee takes up rights pursuant to Rule 10.4), any such proceeds shall be subject to the terms of the Scheme which shall continue to apply mutatis mutandis as they do to the Participant's Deferred Shares in respect of which the proceeds were received.

11. TAKEOVER OR RECONSTRUCTION

11.1 If, as a result of any Corporate Action, a company (the "Acquiring Company") will obtain Control of the Company the Board may, with the agreement of the Acquiring Company, determine that this Rule 11 shall apply.

11.2 Where this Rule 11 applies, Deferred Shares and the related Matching Award shall not vest as a result of the Corporate Action (and for the avoidance of doubt the date of the Corporate Action shall not be a "Vesting Date"), and instead:

11.2.1 the proceeds from the relevant Corporate Action received by the Nominee in respect of the Deferred Shares on behalf of the Participant, whether in cash or securities (and the Nominee shall accept any offer of securities in preference to the receipt of cash), shall continue to be held on behalf of the Participant subject to the terms of the Scheme; and

11.2.2 the Matching Award (the "**Old Matching Award**") shall lapse on the occurrence of the Corporate Action, and the New Parent Company shall grant a replacement right to receive shares (the "**New Matching Award**") over such number of shares in the New Parent Company which are of equivalent value to the number of Shares in respect of which the Old Matching Award was outstanding. The New Matching Award shall be granted on the terms of the Scheme, but as if the New Award had been granted at the same time as the Old Matching Award and shall continue to be subject to the Performance Target.

For this purpose the Rules of the Scheme shall (subject to Rule 11.3) continue to apply in respect of the proceeds referred to in Rule 11.2.1 and the New Matching Award mutatis mutandis as they do to the Participant's Deferred Shares and the Old Matching Award.

11.3 For the purposes of this Rule 11:

11.3.1 the "New Parent Company" shall be the Acquiring Company, or, if different the company that is the ultimate parent company of the Acquiring Company within the meaning of section 1159 of the Companies Act 2006; and

11.3.2 the terms of the Scheme shall following the date of the relevant Corporate Action shall be construed as if:

(A) the reference to "[COMPANY] [Limited/PLC]" in the definition of "Company" in Rule 1 were a reference to the company which is the New Parent Company, and

(B) save where the New Parent Company is listed, Rule 15.3 were omitted.

12.   CLAWBACK

12.1 The Board may determine that a claw-back shall apply where:

12.1.1 within [3] years of the Vesting Date of a Matching Award the Board determines that the Matching Award vested in respect of a larger number of Shares that it would otherwise have done as a result of the financial accounts of the Company on the basis of which the Performance Target was assessed having been misstated; and/or

12.1.2 it is discovered that the Participant committed an act or omission at any time prior to the Vesting Date that would have constituted grounds for summary termination.

12.2 Where the Board determines that a claw-back shall apply, the Board may:

12.2.1 require the Participant to transfer to the Company a number of Shares up to the excess number of Shares in respect of which the Matching Award vested (as determined by the Board); or

12.2.2 require the Participant to make a cash payment to the Company of up to an amount calculated as the number of excess Shares referred in Rule 12.2.1 multiplied by the Market Value of a Share on the Vesting Date.

12.3 The Participant irrevocably acknowledges that where he is required to transfer Shares or pay a cash sum pursuant to Rule 12.2, the Board may:

12.3.1 reduce, by up to the number of excess Shares referred to in Rule 12.2.1, the number of Shares which are otherwise due to be transferred to the Participant pursuant to any other Award or any award under any other Employees' Share Scheme operated by the Company (other than an Employees' Share Scheme which satisfies the requirements of any of Schedules 2 to 4 of ITEPA); and/or

12.3.2 deduct up to the amount referred to in Rule 12.2.2 from any payment otherwise due to the Participant from any Member of the Group.

12.4 The number of Shares that would otherwise be due to be transferred to the Participant pursuant to the vesting of a Matching Award granted under this Scheme may be reduced by such number as may be determined by the Board to be necessary to effect a claw-back pursuant to the terms of any other Matching Award and/or other Employees' Share Scheme operated by the Company.

13.   REGULATORY MATTERS

13.1 Any transfer of Shares to the Participant, or to his personal representative(s), under the Scheme shall be subject to such consent, if any, of any authorities wherever situate, as may from time to time be required and the Participant, or his personal representative(s), shall be responsible for complying with the requirements of or to obtain or obviate the necessity for such consents.

13.2 Where the transfer of Shares is prohibited pursuant to Rule 13.1, or where Rule 8.7 applies, such transfer of Shares shall be delayed until the transfer is no longer prohibited.

14.   RESTRICTED SECURITIES ELECTION

14.1 The Participant shall, if requested to do so by the Company or the Nominee, enter into an election (in such form as the Board shall determine) with the Participant's Employing Company pursuant to Section 431(1) or Section 431(2) of ITEPA in relation to the Deferred Shares purchased to be purchased by the Nominee on behalf of such Participant (and the purchase of Deferred Shares by the Nominee on behalf of the Participant and/or the grant to the Participant of a Matching Award may be determined to be conditional on the Participant entering into such election within such period specified by the Board).

15.   ADMINISTRATION AND AMENDMENT

15.1 The Scheme shall in all respects be administered by the Board which may make such rules not being inconsistent with the terms and conditions hereof for the conduct of the Scheme as it thinks fit, provided that such rules do not prejudice any existing rights of Participants.

15.2 Subject to Rule 15.5, the Board may at any time by resolution add to or alter the Scheme, or any Matching Award made thereunder, in any respect.

15.3 Subject to Rule 15.4, no addition or alteration to the advantage of present or future Participants relating to eligibility, the limits on participation, the overall limits on the issue of shares or the transfer of Treasury Shares, the basis for determining a Participant's entitlement to, or the terms of, Shares provided pursuant to the Scheme and the provisions for adjustments on a variation of share capital shall be made without the prior approval by ordinary resolution of the shareholders of the Company in general meeting.

15.4 Rule 15.3 shall not apply to any alteration or addition which is necessary or desirable in order to comply with or take account of the provisions of any proposed or existing legislation, law or other regulatory requirements or to take advantage of any changes to the legislation, law or other regulatory requirements or to obtain or maintain favourable taxation, exchange control or regulatory treatment of the Company, any Subsidiary or any Participant or to make minor amendments to benefit the administration of the Scheme.

15.5 No alteration or addition shall be made under Rule 15.2 which would abrogate or adversely affect the subsisting rights of a Participant unless it is made:

    15.5.1 with the consent in writing of such number of Participants as hold Deferred Shares and Matching Awards under the Scheme which represent 75 per cent of the Shares which would be issued or transferred if Deferred Shares were released and all Shares comprised in all Matching Awards were transferred; or

    15.5.2 by a resolution at a meeting of Participants passed by not less that 75 per cent of the Participants who attend and vote either in person or by proxy,

and for the purpose of this Rule 15.5 the Participants shall be treated as the holders of a separate class of share capital and the provisions of the Articles of Association of the Company relating to class meetings shall apply mutatis mutandis.

15.6 The Board may take such steps as it may consider necessary to notify Participants of any alteration or addition made under this Rule 15 and to call in, cancel, endorse, issue or reissue any Award Certificate subsequent to such alteration or addition.

15.7 The Board may, in respect of Eligible Employees who are or who may become subject to taxation outside the United Kingdom on their remuneration, establish such schemes or sub-schemes based on the Scheme but subject to such modifications as the Board considers necessary or desirable to take account of or to mitigate or to comply with relevant overseas taxation, securities or exchange control laws, provided that the terms of matching awards made under such schemes or sub-schemes are not overall more favourable than the terms of Matching Awards made under the Scheme and that matching awards made, and shares issued, pursuant to such schemes or sub-schemes shall count towards the limits set out in Rules 2 and 4.2.

16. GENERAL

16.1 The Scheme shall terminate on the 10th anniversary of its adoption or at any earlier time by the passing of a resolution by the Board or an ordinary resolution of the shareholders in general meeting. Following such termination no further Matching Awards shall be made, but such termination shall be without prejudice to the subsisting rights of Participants.

16.2 The Company and any Subsidiary of the Company may provide money to the trustees of any trust or any other person to enable them or him to acquire Shares to be held for the purposes of the Scheme, or enter into any guarantee or indemnity for these purposes, to the extent that such is not prohibited by Chapter 2 of Part 2 of the Companies Act 2006.

16.3 Any disputes regarding the interpretation of the Rules, the terms of any Matching Award or the terms on which Deferred Shares are held shall be determined by the Board (upon such advice as it shall consider necessary) and any decision in relation thereto shall be final and binding.

16.4 Participants shall not be entitled to:

16.4.1 receive copies of accounts or notices sent to holders of Shares;

16.4.2 exercise voting rights; or

16.4.3 receive dividends,

in respect of Shares comprised in a Matching Award which have not been transferred to such Participants pursuant to the Scheme.

16.5 The Participant shall be entitled to direct the Nominee to vote any Deferred Shares. The Nominee shall not be obliged to seek directions from the Participant to vote any Deferred Shares and, in the absence of such directions, shall take no action.

16.6 The Participant shall be entitled to receive any dividends paid on Deferred Shares, and the Nominee shall remit to the Participant any dividends received as soon as is reasonably practicable following receipt.

16.7 If any Award Certificate shall be worn out, defaced or lost, it may be replaced on such evidence being provided as the Board may require.

16.8 Any notice or other communication under or in connection with this Scheme may be given by the Company to Participants personally, by email or by post, and to the Nominee, Company or any Member of the Group either personally or by post to the Secretary of the Company. Items sent by post shall be pre-paid and shall be deemed to have been received 48 hours after posting. Items sent by email shall be deemed to have been received immediately.

16.9 Nothing in the Scheme shall in any way be construed as imposing upon any Member of the Group a contractual obligation as between the Member of the Group and an employee to contribute or to continue to contribute to the Scheme.

16.10 The rights and obligations of any individual under the terms of his office or employment with the Company or any past or present Subsidiary shall not be affected by his participation in the Scheme and the Scheme shall not form part of any contract of employment between the individual and any such company.

16.11 An Eligible Employee shall have no right to acquire Deferred Shares, nor to receive a Matching Award under the Scheme.

16.12 By participating in the Scheme, the Participant waives all and any rights to compensation or damages in consequence of the termination of his office or employment with the Company or any past or present Subsidiary for any reason whatsoever, whether lawfully or otherwise, insofar as those rights arise or may arise from his ceasing to have rights under the Scheme as a result of such termination, or from the loss or diminution in value of such rights or entitlements, including by reason of the operation of the terms of the Scheme, any determination by the Board pursuant to a discretion contained in the Scheme or the provisions of any statute or law relating to taxation.

16.13 Benefits under the Scheme shall not form part of a Participant's remuneration for any purpose and shall not be pensionable.

16.14 By participating in the Scheme, the Participant consents to the collection, processing, transmission and storage by the Company, in any form whatsoever, of any data of a professional or personal nature which is necessary for the purposes of introducing and administering the Scheme. The Company may share such information with any Member of the Group, the Nominee, its registrars, brokers, other third party administrator or any person who obtains Control of the Company or acquires the company, undertaking or part-undertaking which employs the Participant, whether within or outside of the European Economic Area.

16.15 The invalidity or non-enforceability of any provision or Rule of the Scheme shall not affect the validity or enforceability of the remaining provisions and Rules of the Scheme which shall continue in full force and effect.

16.16 These Rules shall be governed by and construed in accordance with English Law.

16.17 The English courts shall have exclusive jurisdiction to determine any dispute which may arise out of, or in connection with, the Scheme.

Chapter 8

Share Incentive Plans or SIPs – General

INTRODUCTION

8.1   This tax-advantaged share plan was introduced in the Finance Act 2000 to provide tax relief for the acquisition of free shares (see Chapter 9), partnership shares (see Chapter 10), matching shares (see Chapter 11) and dividend shares (see **8.68–8.76**), with effect from 28 July 2000. Previously known as the 'All-Employee Share Ownership Plan' (or AESOP), it was renamed the SIP on 29 October 2001. Following the introduction of the Income Tax (Earnings and Pensions) Act 2003 (ITEPA 2003), the Share Incentive Plan (SIP) provisions, referred to collectively as the 'SIP Code', are now found at ITEPA 2003, ss 488–515 and Sch 2; FA 2001, s 95; TCGA 1992, Sch 7D, paras 1–8; ITTOIA 2005, ss 392–395, 405–408 and 770; ITA 2007, ss 488–490; and CTA 2009, ss 983–998 (previously ICTA 1988, Sch 4AA).

8.2   Full tax relief is available where the shares are held under the plan (ie by the trustees) for five years. It is a condition of participation that the employee agrees that any free or matching shares will be held under the plan for at least three years. There are special provisions which apply where the participant withdraws shares from the plan before the end of five years including where they cease to be in relevant employment (see **8.48–8.50**).

TYPES OF PLAN

8.3   A SIP is a plan established under a qualifying UK resident trust by a company providing for:

(a)   free shares to be appropriated without payment; or

(b)   partnership shares to be acquired at the cost of employees out of sums deducted from their salary (in addition, the plan may also provide for matching shares to be appropriated without payment pro rata to the number of partnership shares acquired by the employee).

8.4   The plan rules may provide for any of the following:

(a)   free shares;

(b)   partnership shares (with or without matching shares);

189

(c)   free and partnership shares (with or without matching shares); or

(d)   any of the above combinations (with or without dividend shares).

In practice, plans are drafted providing maximum flexibility by allowing the company to offer any of the different types of shares at different times.

Group plans

8.5   A SIP may be established by a single company for its own employees. Alternatively, a SIP may be established by a parent company of a group of companies to cover some or all of the companies which it controls (see **8.28** below).

APPOINTMENT, RETIREMENT AND REMOVAL OF TRUSTEES

Establishment under trust

8.6   The plan must provide for the establishment of trustees who are required:

(a)   in the case of free or matching shares, to acquire shares and appropriate them in accordance with the plan;

(b)   in the case of partnership shares, to apply monies deducted from pay in acquiring shares on behalf of employees in accordance with the plan; and

(c)   in the case of dividend shares, to apply cash dividends in acquiring shares on behalf of participants in accordance with the plan.

Nature of appointment

8.7   The powers and duties of the trustees must be set out in a trust instrument which is constituted under the law of a part of the UK. ITEPA 2003, Sch 2, paras 70–80 sets out specific statutory duties which must be incorporated in any trust instrument as a condition of the SIP meeting the requirements of ITEPA 2003, Sch 2 (see **8.21–8.27**). Following the stamp duty changes in FA 2008, once executed, the trust deed no longer requires stamping with the previous £5 duty.

8.8   As far as trusts expressed to be made under English law are concerned, the Trustee Act 2000 sets out a number of general powers held by trustees including several which would normally apply to the trustees of a SIP, for instance, the power to deposit documents for safe custody (Trustee Act 2000, s 17) and the power to employ agents (Trustee Act 2000, s 11) including scheme administrators. In addition, trustees will normally be entitled to the benefit of the implied indemnity of trustees under the Trustee Act 2000, s 23.

Persons who can be appointed trustees

8.9   ITEPA 2003, Sch 2, para 71(1) refers to a 'body of persons' who may be appointed trustees. This would seem to imply that at least two or more persons must be appointed to act but, in practice, it will be acceptable for a single company to act as trustee, but not a sole individual. However, any trustee must be resident in the UK and, where there is more than one trustee, HMRC will insist upon at least one of them being resident in the UK.

8.10   If a participant may be appointed trustee, the trust deed should provide that any such trustee will not be liable to account to other participants for any benefits derived from participation in the scheme.

8.11   In the case of listed companies, ABI Guidelines do not make any specific recommendations about the persons who may be appointed trustee. However, the ABI has previously taken the view that where directors and employees are appointed trustee, at least one of the trustees should be a non-executive director or a person independent of the company. Given the restrictions on the powers of the trustees under most SIPs, the identity of the trustees is less important than under other trusts.

8.12   ITEPA 2003, Sch 2, para 71 sets out a framework to enable companies to involve their employees more closely in the operation of the SIP by setting up a board of trustees for the Plan which may include employee representatives. This is not, however, obligatory.

8.13   It is generally considered more appropriate for the company establishing the SIP to appoint either a professional trustee which will also act as administrator of the plan, or a subsidiary to act as trustee of a SIP. The main advantage of appointing a corporate trustee is continuity as deeds of appointment will be unnecessary upon successive changes of administrator.

8.14   In practice, most companies establishing a SIP have appointed the scheme administrator to also act as trustee. Most administrators will take on the trusteeship and indeed a number of specialist SIP administrators have emerged to fulfil this role.

Protection of trustees

8.15   Although the trustees of a SIP are entitled to the benefit of the statutory indemnity under the Trustee Act 2000, s 23, many trust deeds nevertheless contain an express indemnity of the trustees including exoneration of any liability on the part of the trustees for the negligence or fraud of any agent unless the trustee was at fault in appointing the particular agent in the first place. The Model Trust Deed at Appendix 11A below contains an express power to this effect.

8.16   Trustees have a general duty to invest trust monies even where such funds are to be held short term. In order to obviate the need for the trustees to

invest monies short term a trust deed should specifically authorise the trustees
to hold uninvested trust monies.

Retirement and removal

8.17   A SIP trust instrument should make provision for the retirement
and removal of any trustee. The Model Trust Deed (Appendix 11A below)
provides for existing trustees to retire by giving three months' written notice
served upon the trustee, provided there are at least two trustees remaining or a
corporate trustee immediately after the retirement.

POWERS AND DUTIES OF TRUSTEES

Specific statutory powers of trustees

Power of trustees to borrow

8.18   ITEPA 2003, Sch 2, para 76 provides that the trustees may have the
power to borrow:

(a)   to acquire shares for the purposes of the plan; and

(b)   for such other purposes as may be specified in the trust instrument,
e.g. trust expenses.

This means that SIP trustees can acquire shares in advance of appropriation
(as free or matching shares) or allocation (as partnership shares). However,
the Taxation of Chargeable Gains Act 1992 (TCGA 1992), Sch 7D, para 2
restricts the availability of capital gains tax relief for SIP trustees in respect
of gains arising on the appropriation or acquisition of shares where the shares
have been held by the trustees for more than two years (five years if the
shares are not readily convertible assets) since acquisition (see **8.86** below).
In practice, the trustees are likely to borrow any monies from the company
and often this will be on interest-free terms but, provided the trust deed makes
specific provision, there is no reason why the trustees cannot pay a market rate
of interest even though ITEPA 2003, Sch 2 is silent on the point.

Tail-swallowing on a rights issue

8.19   ITEPA 2003, Sch 2, para 72(1) provides that SIP trustees must only
deal with a participant's rights on a rights issue in accordance with directions
of the participant but otherwise must not deal with his rights. ITEPA 2003,
Sch 2, para 77 provides the trustees with the power, on a rights issue, to sell
sufficient rights in order to raise money to subscribe for the remainder of the
rights shares; a practice commonly known as 'tail-swallowing'. However, this
is subject to any direction given by the participant.

Accounting for PAYE

8.20   A plan must provide for the trustees to sell plan shares (if the participants do not reimburse the trustees directly) so that the trustee can meet any PAYE obligations arising in respect of plan shares (ITEPA 2003, Sch 2, para 79(1)). A PAYE obligation on the trustee may arise where any plan shares cease to be subject to the plan because the participant ceases relevant employment or directs the trustee to sell shares (ITEPA 2003, ss 510–512). Shares are deemed to be disposed of where the beneficial interest in the shares is disposed of other than as a result of personal insolvency (TCGA 1992, Sch 7D, para 6). If the transaction is not at arm's length then the disposal of the beneficial interest is deemed to be at market value.

Specific statutory duties of trustees

Notification of awards

8.21   ITEPA 2003, Sch 2, para 75 provides that the trust instrument must require the trustee as soon as practicable to notify the details (number and description) of awards of free and matching shares and notices of allocations of partnership and dividend shares. In practice, HMRC will accept that this duty is fulfilled where annual award/allocation statements are issued. In addition, notices must include the following details in respect of:

(a)   free and matching shares – their market value on the date of award and the duration of the holding period (see **9.11–9.13** below);

(b)   partnership shares – the amount of monies deducted from earnings applied by the trustee in acquiring the shares on behalf of the participant and the market value of the shares on the acquisition date (being, if there is no accumulation period (see **10.12** below), a date fixed by the trustee not more than 30 days after the date on which acquisition monies were deducted from salary or, if there is an accumulation period, a date fixed by the trustee not more than 30 days after the end of the accumulation period);

(c)   dividend shares – their market value on the acquisition date (being a date fixed by the trustee not more than 30 days after the dividend is received by them), that the shares will be subject to a holding period of three years (ITEPA 2003, Sch 2, para 67), and information on any balance of dividends received which have not been reinvested and will be carried forward to be added to the next reinvestment (ITEPA 2003, Sch 2, para 68). Where overseas dividends are received in respect of plan shares, the trustee must give the participant notice of the amount of overseas tax deducted prior to payment.

Plan shares held by the trustees

8.22   ITEPA 2003, Sch 2, para 72(1) provides that the trust instrument must require the trustees only to dispose of a participant's shares (including dealing with any rights issue in respect of those shares) upon a direction given by or on behalf of the participant concerned. Directions need not necessarily be in writing and can be given in such general or specific terms as may be provided for in the plan (ITEPA 2003, Sch 2, para 72(3)).

8.23 However, any plan must prevent the participant giving the trustee directions to dispose of any free, matching or dividend shares (partnership shares can be disposed of at any time) during any applicable holding period (see **9.11–9.13** below) unless:

(a) the direction is to accept a general offer (ITEPA 2003, Sch 2, para 37);

(b) the direction is to tail-swallow on a rights issue of plan shares (ITEPA 2003, Sch 2, para 77): see **8.19**;

(c) the trustees sell plan shares to meet any PAYE liability falling on the trustee (assuming the participant will not be reimbursing the trustee) as a result of any shares ceasing to be subject to the plan or a sale of plan shares at the direction of the participant (ITEPA 2003, Sch 2, para 79);

(d) where the company has terminated a plan under ITEPA 2003, Sch 2, para 89 and the employee consents to withdrawal of his shares from the plan at a time when PAYE still applies on those shares (ITEPA 2003, Sch 2, para 90(5)).

Accounting to the participant for any dividends or benefits on plan shares

8.24 ITEPA 2003, Sch 2, para 74 provides that the trust instrument must require the trustee to account to the participant as soon as practicable for any dividend or non-cash benefits (e.g. securities) received in respect of plan shares.

8.25 However, there are exceptions to this obligation to account to participants for dividends or non-cash benefits:

(a) cash dividends which are to be reinvested under the plan as dividend shares;

(b) new shares issued upon a takeover or reconstruction which qualifies as an exchange of shares for capital gains tax purposes under ITEPA 2003, Sch 2, para 87;

(c) where shares (which are readily convertible assets) cease to be held subject to the scheme (including where the participant leaves employment) and, because there is no employing company or HMRC so direct, the trustee is obliged by HMRC to account for PAYE (as if the trustee were the employer) on the shares leaving the plan (ITEPA 2003, ss 510 and 511);

(d) where the trustee receives a capital receipt (see **8.77** below) in respect of plan shares (which are readily convertible assets) which is chargeable to

PAYE, then the trustee shall deduct the PAYE out of the capital receipt (ITEPA 2003, ss 513 and 514).

Duty to maintain tax records

8.26   ITEPA 2003, Sch 2, para 80 provides that the trust instrument must require the trustee to maintain such PAYE records as may be necessary to satisfy the trustee and the employee's PAYE obligations. In addition, the trustee must maintain records to be able to inform participants of any tax liabilities arising under ITEPA 2003 or ITTOIA 2005 Pt 4, Ch 3 or Ch 4 in relation to the SIP.

Duty to monitor participants in connected plans

8.27   The trustees are under a duty to maintain records of participants who have participated in one or more approved plans established by the company or a connected company (see **8.52–8.53**).

GROUP PLANS

8.28   ITEPA 2003, Sch 2, para 4 provides that where a company which has established a scheme has control of another company or companies, the scheme may be expressed to extend to all or any of these companies and is known as 'a group plan'. A company which establishes a plan cannot extend the plan to holding companies, although the shares of a holding company may be used under the plan. Strictly speaking, only companies under the 'control' (within the meaning of ITA 2007, s 995) of the company which established the plan may participate in it. However, jointly-owned companies may participate in a plan established by one of the joint owners but not in the plans of both joint owners (ITEPA 2003, Sch 2, para 91). A jointly-owned company may also set up a plan using the shares of one of the joint owners (but not both).

Anti-abuse

8.29   ITEPA 2003, Sch 2, para 10(3) provides that if the company which establishes the plan is a member of a group of companies, the plan must not have the effect of conferring benefits wholly or mainly on directors or on higher-paid employees in group companies. Apart from this provision, which is intended to avoid abuse, a company which establishes a plan has a discretion as to the companies under its control which may be admitted as participating companies.

Admission of other participating companies

8.30   The Model Trust Deed (at Appendix 11A below) provides for other participating companies to be admitted to the plan by execution of a deed of adherence by which it agrees to be bound in all respects by the trust deed and rules of the plan for so long as it remains under the control of the company which established the plan. In practice, HMRC does not require formal deeds of adherence by participating companies and plans may provide for the adherence of subsidiaries by board resolution. As with the main trust deed, any deed of adherence which is executed is not liable to stamp duty.

8.31   Where a new participating company is admitted to the plan, the company which established the plan should advise details of the new participating company (name, registered office and number and tax district) to HMRC as part of the annual return process.

Cessation of participation

8.32   The Model Trust Deed (see Appendix 11A below) provides that any company which ceases to be under the control of the company which established the plan shall cease to be a participating company. The Model Trust Deed also provides that the directors may resolve that a company, even if it remains under the control of the company which established the plan, shall cease to be a participating company. HMRC will be concerned to ensure that where the directors remove any company from the plan that this will not leave only higher-paid employees in the plan contrary to ITEPA 2003, Sch 2, para 10(3). As in the case of the admission of a new participating company, HMRC should be notified of any cessation of participation as part of the annual return process.

TAX-ADVANTAGED STATUS OF A PLAN

8.33   The tax reliefs for a SIP are only available if the requirements of ITEPA 2003, Sch 2 are satisfied. Following its establishment, whether by the company or duly authorised directors, the SIP must be notified to HMRC via the online service by 6 July in the tax year following the tax year in which the first SIP awards are made (ITEPA 2003, Sch 2, paras 81A and 81D(1)).

8.34   HMRC has the right to open an enquiry into any SIP notified via the online service to ensure compliance with the legislative requirements. Any such enquiry must be opened by 6 July in the tax year following the tax year in which the notification deadline falls (ITEPA 2003, Sch 2, para 81F). General requirements of a plan

Purpose of the plan

8.35   ITEPA 2003, Sch 2, para 7(1) provides that the purpose of a plan must be to provide share benefits to employees which give them a continuing stake in the company. This statement of principle seems self-evident and indeed unnecessary given the detailed requirements of Schedule 2 which have this effect anyhow.

8.36 ITEPA 2003, Sch 2, paras 7(1A) and (1B) state that the SIP must not provide benefits otherwise than in accordance with Schedule 2, and in particular should not provide cash as an alternative to shares. This requirement replaces, from 6 April 2014, the requirement that the SIP must not contain (and its operation must not involve) features which are neither essential nor reasonably incidental to its purpose of providing share benefits. HMRC had generally applied this requirement so as to prevent ancillary arrangements which entitled participants to elect for a cash alternative to free or matching shares, unless such arrangements were completely discretionary, and this has now been put on a statutory footing.

All-employee nature of the plan

8.37 SIPs are intended to provide share benefits to all (or substantially all) employees (ITEPA 2003, Sch 2, para 8). The eligibility criteria are set out in ITEPA 2003, Sch 2, paras 13–24 (or Part 3): see **8.46–8.55**.

8.38 A plan must provide that every eligible employee under the plan who is chargeable to income tax under ITEPA 2003, s 15 (UK resident employees) in respect of his employment in that tax year must be invited to participate in an award. The plan must not contain any feature which has, or would have, the effect of discouraging any eligible employees from participating (ITEPA 2003, Sch 2, para 8(3)). Examples of such discouraging features include invitation periods of less than 14 days (as such a period may be too short for employees on annual leave or absent due to sickness), invitations by poster which may not be seen by employees who regularly work away from the company's premises and invitations aimed at specific groups of employee.

8.39 Employees who meet the eligibility requirements but who are not chargeable to tax under ITEPA 2003, s 15 may be allowed to participate under the plan (ITEPA 2003, Sch 2, para 8(5)). A decision can be made about the participation of such employees on each occasion an award is made.

Participation on same terms

8.40 ITEPA 2003, Sch 2, para 9 provides that every employee who is invited to participate in an award must be invited to do so (and those who do participate must actually do so) on the same terms.

8.41 However, an award made by reference to:

(a)   remuneration;

(b)   length of service; or

(c)   the number of hours worked,

can be treated as made on the 'same' terms. For instance, participants may be allocated three shares for each year of service and five shares for each £1,000 of pay. The 'same' terms test will be applied separately to both elements, without regard to whether the total entitlement satisfied any same terms test. In applying these elements, however, the company operating the SIP must be mindful of the provisions of the Employment Equality (Age) Regulations 2006 (SI 2006/1031), one of the results of which is that benefits provided which relate to length of service must be objectively justified unless the period relates to only the first five years of service.

8.42   Free shares may be awarded on the basis of performance allowances (ie targets) which determine the extent to which shares are awarded (see **9.3–9.10** below). Since such allowances may result in the participants of some business units receiving a greater or lesser number of shares than their colleagues in other business units covered by the plan, ITEPA 2003, Sch 2, para 9(5) makes it clear that the same terms test can be satisfied notwithstanding the effect of performance allowances.

No preferential treatment for directors

8.43   ITEPA 2003, Sch 2, para 10(1) provides that no feature of the plan must have or be likely to have the effect of conferring benefits wholly or mainly on directors or employees receiving higher levels of remuneration. As far as group schemes are concerned, ITEPA 2003, Sch 2, para 10(3) prevents this result being obtained by employing, on the one hand, directors and the higher paid in one company and, on the other hand, the lower paid in another company.

No special conditions

8.44   ITEPA 2003, Sch 2, para 11 provides that no conditions of participation may be imposed under the plan other than those imposed or allowed by ITEPA 2003, Sch 2.

No loan arrangements

8.45   ITEPA 2003, Sch 2, para 12 prevents arrangements (whether legally enforceable or not) which involve loans being associated with participation in the plan. This is intended to expressly exclude arrangements whereby participants are advanced a sum of money which is repayable in some way or another when the award of shares is released in due course. Such arrangements are in any event not reasonably incidental to the purpose of providing share benefits and so would seem to be prevented by ITEPA 2003, Sch 2, para 7(2) anyhow. This provision is therefore in the nature of 'belt and braces'.

ELIGIBILITY

Timing of eligibility

8.46   The time at which eligibility to participate in a plan is determined in accordance with ITEPA 2003, Sch 2, para 14 and depends on the type of plan.

Eligibility for free shares is determined at the time the award is made. In the case of partnership shares, the timing of eligibility depends on whether there is an accumulation period. Where there is an accumulation period then eligibility is determined when the first deduction of partnership share money is made. Where there is no accumulation period then eligibility is determined at the date on which the partnership share money is deducted. For matching shares, eligibility is on the same date as for the partnership shares to which they relate.

The eligibility requirements

8.47   There are three requirements which must be satisfied if a UK resident employee is to be eligible to participate in an award:

(a)   the employment requirement (ITEPA 2003, Sch 2, para 15);

(b)   the non-simultaneous participation in connected plans requirement (ITEPA 2003, Sch 2, para 18); and

(c)   the requirement in relation to successive participation in connected plans (ITEPA 2003, Sch 2, para 18A).

Plans may impose further eligibility requirements in the case of employees who are non-UK resident. For instance, a non-UK resident employee might need to earn in excess of a specified amount. Any such further eligibility requirements will need to be set out in the plan.

The employment requirement

8.48   Where there is no qualifying period (see **8.51** below) in the plan, an individual must be an employee of the company (or a participating company in the case of a group plan) when the award is made.

8.49   If the plan sets out a qualifying period, then an individual must have been an employee of a qualifying company at all times during the qualifying period and must be an employee of the company or a participating company at the date of the award. Whether a company is a participating company is tested at the end of the qualifying period so that an employee of a newly acquired company in a group may be eligible provided he has been an employee of that company throughout the qualifying period.

8.50   The definition of qualifying company is set out in ITEPA 2003, Sch 2, para 17 and means:

(a)   except in the case of a group plan, the company or a company that when the individual was employed by it was an associated company of the company or of another qualifying company; and

(b)   where the plan is a group plan, a company that is a participating company at the end of the qualifying period or a company that when the individual was employed by it was a participating company, or a company that when the individual was employed by it was an associated company of a company qualifying as set out above, or another company being a qualifying company.

8.51   There is a maximum period which may be fixed as the qualifying period for each type of award (ITEPA 2003, Sch 2, para 16):

(a)   in the case of free shares, up to 18 months ending on the date of the award;

(b)   in the case of partnership or matching shares, the length of period depends on whether there is an accumulation period. If there is no accumulation period then the period is up to 18 months ending with the deduction of partnership share money relating to the award. If there is an accumulation period, the period is up to six months ending with the start of the accumulation period.

Any qualifying period must apply to all the participants in an award. However, the plan may authorise the company to specify different qualifying periods in respect of different awards of shares.

Non-simultaneous participation in connected plans

8.52   ITEPA 2003, Sch 2, para 18 prevents participation in a free, matching or partnership shares award under a plan by an individual who would, at the same time, participate in another SIP established by the company or a connected company, which includes all group companies plus consortium members owning the company and companies owned partly by the company as a consortium member.

Successive participation in connected plans

8.53   Where, in the same tax year, a participant is eligible to participate in more than one connected plan, ITEPA 2003, Sch 2, para 18A provides that the limits in relation to:

(a)   the maximum award of free shares (ITEPA 2003, Sch 2, para 35); and

(b)   the maximum amount of partnership share money deductions (ITEPA 2003, Sch 2, para 46),

should apply to the plans together as if they were a single plan, rather than applying to each plan separately.

TYPES OF SHARE THAT MAY BE USED

8.54   ITEPA 2003, Sch 2, para 25 summarises the requirements which must be satisfied in respect of plan shares (which may include fractions of shares, under ITEPA 2003, Sch 2, para 99(2), which form part of the share capital of a non-UK company, where such fractions are recognised in the company's country of registration). The requirements for eligible shares are as follows:

(a)   must be ordinary share capital (ITEPA 2003, Sch 2, para 26);

(b)   requirements as to listing, etc (ITEPA 2003, Sch 2, para 27);

(c)   must be fully paid up and not redeemable (ITEPA 2003, Sch 2, para 28);

(d)   must not be shares in a service company (ITEPA 2003, Sch 2, para 29).

In order to benefit from a tax-advantaged status, HMRC requires a declaration to be made that these requirements are satisfied. The requirements are similar to those applying to approved schemes under ITEPA 2003, Schs 3 and 4.

Ordinary share capital

8.55   Eligible shares must be part of the ordinary share capital (as defined by ICTA 1988, s 832) of:

(a)   the company; or

(b)   a company which has control of the company; or

(c)   a company which either is (or has control of) a member of a consortium which owns the company (or a company having control of such consortium member).

Requirements as to listing, etc

8.56   Eligible shares must be:

(a)   shares of a class listed on a recognised stock exchange (see Appendix 4A above);

(b)   shares in a company which is not under the control of another company; or

(c)   although the shares are in a company which is under the control of another company, the shares in the parent company are listed on a recognised stock exchange (provided the company is not, or could not be if UK resident, a close company).

In short, therefore, shares in a subsidiary of an unquoted group cannot be eligible shares. Only the shares in the parent company of an unquoted group can be used. The position is different in the case of a listed group – the shares of a subsidiary as well as the parent company can be eligible shares provided the company is not closely controlled.

Fully paid up and not redeemable

8.57   Eligible shares must be:

(a)   fully paid up; and

(b)   not redeemable – unless they are shares in a co-operative society.

To be fully paid up, there must be no undertaking to pay up the shares at a future date. Redeemable shares include shares which may become redeemable at a later date.

Service companies

8.58   Eligible shares must not be shares in a service company, or an intermediate holding company of a service company. Service companies are companies which substantially carry on the business of providing the services of persons employed by it to a person (or partners) who have control of the company (or its associate company). The purpose of this restriction is to ensure the common form of service company previously established in conjunction with registered profit-related pay schemes operated by many professional partnerships cannot be used to provide SIP plan benefits.

Restrictions

8.59   Prior to 6 April 2013, eligible shares could not be subject any restrictions other than:

(a)   the holding period restrictions (see **9.11–9.13**);

(b)   restrictions affecting all ordinary shares in the company;

(c)   those permitted by ITEPA 2003, Sch 2, in respect of shares without voting rights, forfeiture provisions and pre-emption conditions (see **8.64**).

8.60   The requirements set out in **8.59** above were removed by FA 2013, Sch 2, resulting in the potential to operate SIPs in a much more flexible manner.

8.61   Whilst it had always been possible to impose forfeiture conditions on free and matching shares, the ability to do so was limited to a period of three years following the award. Shares could also not be subject to forfeiture in the specified 'good leaver' circumstances (for example, death, injury, disability, retirement, redundancy, or leaving the group due to TUPE transfer or sale of the employing subsidiary). These limitations on forfeiture have now been removed, leaving the company to determine, if at all, when and how forfeiture restrictions may apply. Where shares are subject to any restrictions, the trustee is under an obligation to provide details of those restrictions to the participant (ITEPA 2003, Sch 2, paras 75(2)(aa) and 75(3)(aa). In practice, restrictions on shares will generally be incorporated into the free or partnership share agreement.

8.62   It remains the case that forfeiture of partnership and dividend shares is prohibited. FA 2014 has, however, introduced the ability to impose compulsory sale provisions on partnership and dividend shares provided that the shares are required to be offered for sale at a price no less than the amount of partnership share money (or dividend) used in the acquisition of the shares, or, if lower, their market value at the time that the shares are subject to the offer for sale (ITEPA 2003, Sch 2, para 43(2B) and (2C) and para 65(2) and (3)). These new provisions are wider than the previously permitted pre-emption rights on leaving employment as the compulsory sale provisions may also apply to continuing employees whilst their shares remain in the SIP (for example, pursuant to drag-along rights in the company's articles).

8.63   It is likely to remain the case that the most common forfeiture provisions attaching to free and matching (shares will be in circumstances where:

(a)   the participant ceases to be in relevant employment;

(b)   the participant attempts to withdraw the shares from the plan; and

(c)   in the case of matching share awards, the participant withdraws the partnership shares in respect of which the matching shares were awarded.

8.64   As there is now no limitation on the length of the forfeiture period, such forfeiture conditions may continue to apply to the shares throughout the relevant holding period which, under the SIP, may not extend past five years after the date of the award.

8.65   It would now be possible to supplement any holding period with a further 'no sale' restriction once the shares have ceased to be subject ot the SIP. This would act in a similar manner to an extended holding period but the shares would no longer benefit from the tax shelter of being held within the SIP trust. Shares could continue to be held by the same trustee as operates the SIP trust, but this would be in the form of a nominee arrangement (or 'bare trust') and would need to be separately agreed with the trustee. Reinvestment of cash dividends.

8.66   ITEPA 2003, Sch 2, paras 62–69 (or Part 8) provides for the reinvestment of cash dividends in respect of plan shares. The shares so acquired are known as 'dividend' shares and must be of the same class and have identical rights to those on which they are paid and must not be subject to forfeiture in any circumstances (ITEPA 2003, Sch 2, para 65). Dividend shares may, since 6 April 2014, be subject to compulsory sale provisions (see **8.63** above).

8.67   A plan may provide for the company to direct that:

(a)   all or a proportion of the cash dividends paid on plan shares must be reinvested; or

(b)   participants may elect to reinvest their cash dividends.

A direction can be revoked by the company. Dividends not reinvested must be accounted for to the participants as soon as practicable.

Reinvestment limit

8.68   The previous reinvestment limit of £1,500 in any tax year was removed by FA 2013. Instead, where the company is to impose dividend reinvestment, the company must specify either the amount of the dividend that is to be reinvested, or how that amount is to be determined.

Acquisition of dividend shares

8.69   ITEPA 2003, Sch 2, para 66 provides that the plan must as a general principle treat participants fairly and equally when exercising its power to acquire dividend shares. Dividend shares must be acquired by the trustees by a date set by them within 30 days after the date of receipt of the dividend. The date set by the trustees is known as 'the acquisition date'. The number of dividend shares allocated to each participant will be determined by reference to the market value of the shares on that date.

Holding period for dividend shares

8.70   The plan must include a holding period for dividend shares of three years from the date of the award (ITEPA 2003, Sch 2, para 67). The holding period for dividend shares, therefore, differs to free and matching shares in that there is no flexibility to set the duration of the holding period. However, as in the case of the holding period for free and matching shares, the obligation of the participant to leave his shares with the trustees ends if he ceases to be in relevant employment. The trustees may accept instructions to accept takeover offers or deal with the shares on a reconstruction, and can dispose of the shares to meet any PAYE obligations on them under the plan or to remove shares from the plan on an early termination of the plan.

Carry forward of amounts not reinvested

8.71   ITEPA 2003, Sch 2, para 68 provides that any amount that is not reinvested (because there is insufficient money to buy a whole number of shares) may be retained by the trustees and carried forward to be added to the amount of the next cash dividend. However, any dividends held by the trustees must be accounted for to the participant as soon as possible if:

(a)   the participant ceases to be in relevant employment; or

(b)   a plan termination notice is issued in respect of the plan.

The previous requirement that dividends must be reinvested with in three years of payment no longer applies.

No income tax on reinvestment of cash dividends

8.72   ITTOIA 2005, s 770 provides that the amount applied by the trustees in acquiring dividend shares is exempt from income tax (and, not surprisingly, there are no tax credits attaching to them). However, dividend shares withdrawn from the plan within the three-year period after receipt of the dividend are subject to tax (see **8.74** below). The obligation on a nominee under ICTA 1988, s 234A(4) to give information about distributions to a beneficial owner is lifted for dividends reinvested in dividend shares (but still applies in the case of dividends not reinvested into shares and where the dividend shares cease to be subject to the plan within three years).

HMRC has given guidance in relation to companies which have converted into Real Estate Investment Trusts. Dividends from these companies, which are referred to as Property Income Dividends (or PIDs), are subject to a withholding tax at basic rate which results in the SIP trustee only having the remainder to reinvest in dividend shares. The exemption from income tax in ITTOIA 2005, s 770 applies only to the reinvested amount, with the result that income tax is due in respect of the amount withheld, and only the net PID is available to be used under the SIP.

8.73   The exemption from income tax also extends to the small unallocated amounts carried forward for future reinvestment and there is, therefore, no tax credit in respect of such amount (under ITEPA 2003, s 496). However, if the carried forward dividend is later paid out then the participant becomes chargeable to tax under ITTOIA 2005, ss 393 or 406 on these amounts not reinvested. Tax will apply under ITTOIA 2005, Pt 4, Ch 3 (ITTOIA 2005, Pt 4, Ch 4 if an overseas cash dividend) for the year in which the dividend is paid over. The tax credit then attaching to the dividend is at the rate in force on the date on which the cash dividend was originally received by the trustee.

Income tax on dividend shares ceasing to be subject to the plan

8.74   ITTOIA 2005, ss 394 and 407 provide that where dividend shares cease to be subject to the plan within three years after acquisition (ie during the period any holding period would apply) then the participant is chargeable to income tax under ITTOIA 2005, Pt 4, Ch 3 (ITTOIA 2005, Pt 4, Ch 4 in respect of an overseas cash dividend) on the amount of the original cash dividend used to buy the shares for the tax year in which the shares cease to be subject to the plan. Any tax credit is given at the rate in force when the shares cease to be subject to the plan (ITTOIA 2005, ss 394(5) and 407(4A)). There is no charge to tax, however, where the dividend shares cease to be subject to the plan on account of the participant ceasing to be in relevant employment as a result of injury or disability, dismissal by reason of redundancy, a TUPE transfer, a change of control, retirement or on his death.

INCOME TAX ON A SIP – GENERAL PRINCIPLES

8.75   ITEPA 2003, s 490 provides that:

(a)   the award of free, matching or partnership shares; and

(b)   the acquisition of dividend shares,

does not give rise to a taxable amount. In addition, under ITEPA 2003, s 499, any incidental expenditure of the trustees, the company or the employer (if different) is not treated as a benefit of employees giving rise to a charge to income tax.

8.76 Although the blanket exemption of ITEPA 2003, s 421G, in relation to the operation of ITEPA 2003, Pt 7, Chs 2–4 in respect of SIP shares, has been removed, such provisions will only apply to the extent that HMRC considers that there are measures in place which are designed to avoid tax or National Insurance (other than as provided for by the SIP Code).

Capital receipts in respect of participants' shares

8.77 ITEPA 2003, s 501 provides that capital receipts received by a participant in respect of any plan shares are charged to income tax as employment income if they are received within five years of acquisition (three years in the case of dividend shares). All money or money's worth is a capital receipt unless (or to the extent that) it is (or would be apart from ITEPA 2003, ss 489–498) income of the participant for income tax purposes, or it consists of the disposal proceeds of shares, or it consists of shares which consist of a new holding for capital gains tax purposes on a company reconstruction, or it is the proceeds of a disposal under a tail-swallowing on a rights issue of shares (see **8.19** above). Capital receipts received by personal representatives after a participant has died are not taxed as capital receipts by virtue of ITEPA 2003, s 501(6).

8.78 The plan may provide that capital receipts of less than £3 may be retained by the trustee. There will be no charge to income tax where capital receipts of less than £3 are retained.

8.79 Income tax is chargeable upon the occurrence of a number of specified events affecting plan shares, for instance, when shares cease to be subject to the plan. Details of these tax charges on free, matching and partnership shares are set out in ITEPA 2003, ss 503–508 (see **9.14–9.20** and **10.30–10.32** below).

PAYE AND NICs

Readily convertible assets

8.80 Where income tax (other than in respect of dividends and dividend shares) is payable in respect of plan shares (on shares ceasing to be subject to the plan; on capital receipts; on the disposal of the beneficial interest in shares during the holding period and on partnership share money paid over to the employee) and the plan shares are 'readily convertible assets', then the tax will be collected through PAYE. A 'readily convertible asset' has the same meaning (basically, a tradeable asset) as in ITEPA 2003, ss 701 and 702 (excluding ITEPA 2003, s 702 (5A)–(5D)) except that, for SIP purposes, the readiness of the trustees in acquiring shares solely for the purposes of the plan is disregarded (ITEPA 2003, s 509(5)). If the readiness of the SIP to acquire shares were not disregarded then all shares made available to employees through SIPs would be treated as readily convertible assets. This would be counter to the Government's wish to encourage many small private companies to establish SIPs.

8.81   Similarly, National Insurance contributions will be payable in the same circumstances.

PAYE on shares ceasing to be subject to the plan and on a disposal of the beneficial interest in shares

8.82   PAYE is the obligation of the employing company. ITEPA 2003, s 510 provides, therefore, that where PAYE applies on shares ceasing to be subject to the plan the trustees must, if the participant is not so obliged by the plan, pay to the employer company a sum which is sufficient to enable it to account for the PAYE to HMRC. ITEPA 2003, s 509(3) makes it clear that the employer is only liable to account for his best estimate of the amount of income tax due. PAYE does not have to be operated on the exact amount which will eventually be chargeable as employment income. In most cases, where the shares are listed or dealt with on a recognised stock exchange, there should be no problem for the employer to value the shares; however, in the case of unlisted shares which are readily convertible assets, any agreement on valuation is unlikely to be concluded with Shares and Assets Valuation at HMRC within the time available for operating PAYE and National Insurance contributions.

8.83   After accounting for the PAYE to HMRC, any remaining amount is paid to the participant.

8.84   If, when a participant is chargeable to income tax upon shares ceasing to be subject to the plan, there is either no employer company which can deduct the PAYE, or HMRC rule that it is 'impracticable' for it to do so, then the trustees are under a secondary liability to deduct the PAYE under ITEPA 2003, s 511. Any such payment will be made under the 0T tax code which applies to former employees (non-cumulative, month one rates without any allowances.)

8.85   Similar procedures apply where the participant disposes of his beneficial interest in plan shares. TCGA 1992, Sch 7D, para 6 provides that any disposal by the participant of his beneficial interest in plan shares (except on an insolvency) shall be treated as a deemed disposal by the trustees for the same price as was obtained by the participant for his beneficial interest (or at market value if the disposal was not at arm's length). Accordingly, ITEPA 2003, s 512 provides that the trustees must pay a sufficient sum to the employer company to enable it to operate PAYE on the deemed disposal proceeds in the same way as if an actual disposal of the plan shares had taken place. National insurance contributions will also apply in these circumstances.

CAPITAL GAINS TAX

Awards of plan shares

8.86   The award by the trustees of free, matching and partnership shares (or the acquisition of dividend shares) is a disposal for capital gains tax purposes on which the gain, in principle, would be based on the market value where the shares have been awarded for less than the full market value. However, TCGA 1992, Sch 7D, para 2 relieves the trustees from any capital gains tax where the shares are awarded, or acquired as dividend shares, within a certain period of time since acquisition by the trustees. This period of time is:

(a)   where any shares in the company are readily convertible assets at the time shares are acquired by the trustees – two years;

(b)   where any shares in the company become readily convertible assets after the acquisition of shares by the trustees – two years from the date they became readily convertible assets;

(c)   where none of the shares in the company were readily convertible assets when shares were acquired by the trustees – five years.

If, however, the shares were acquired by the trustees using monies in respect of which a deduction has been allowed under CTA 2009, s 989 (previously ICTA 1988, Sch 4AA, para 9), the above periods are extended to ten years.

Shares are identified for this purpose on a first-in, first-out basis.

Deduction for contributions to plan trust

8.87   In addition to the corporation tax deductions allowed in respect of the award of shares (see **9.21–9.23** and **10.19** below) and the costs of setting up and running the plan (see **8.102** below), ESSA 2002 introduced provisions (now contained in CTA 2009, s 989 (previously ICTA 1988, Sch 4AA, para 9) which provide for corporation tax relief for block purchases of shares.
Where a payment is made by a company to the SIP trustees which is then used to acquire shares in that company or a company which controls it, and the shares are acquired from persons other than a company, then an up-front corporation tax deduction will be available in relation to the payment. This will only be the case provided that at the end of the period of 12 months beginning with the date of the acquisition, the trustees hold shares to be used in the plan trust that:

(a)   constitute at least ten per cent of the ordinary shares in the company; and

(b)   carry rights to at least ten per cent of any distributable profits and any assets of the company that would be available for distribution to shareholders on a winding-up.

Shares that have been awarded under the plan continue to be counted towards the 10 per cent limit until such time as they cease to be subject to the plan.

Withdrawal of deduction for contribution to plan trust

8.88 Under CTA 2009, s 990 (previously ICTA 1988, Sch 4AA, para 10), HMRC may, however, direct that the corporation tax deduction received under CTA 2009, s 989 (previously ICTA 1988, Sch 4AA, para 9) is withdrawn where:

(a) less than 30 per cent of the shares acquired with the payment have been awarded within five years of the date of acquisition; or

(b) not all the shares acquired with the payment have been so awarded within ten years of that date.

Plan shares

8.89 The participant is treated as being absolutely entitled against the trustees in respect of plan shares for capital gains tax purposes (TCGA 1992, Sch 7D, para 3).

Shares ceasing to be subject to the plan

8.90 The circumstances when shares cease to be subject to a plan are set out in ITEPA 2003, Sch 2, para 97 and include the withdrawal of shares by the participant or his personal representatives, the cessation of relevant employment or a disposal by the trustees to meet PAYE obligations under ITEPA 2003, Sch 2, para 79. TCGA 1992, Sch 7D, para 5 provides that where shares cease to be subject to the plan, the shares will be released for capital gains tax purposes at market value. In this way, there is no chargeable gain on an event where income tax normally applies or where there is relief from income tax or where the shares are simply released from the plan at the expiry of the five-year period (three years in the case of dividend shares).

Forfeiture of shares

8.91 TCGA 1992, Sch 7D, para 7 provides that if any of the participant's plan shares are forfeited to the trustee, they are treated as disposed of (and acquired by the trustees) at market value at the date of forfeiture and any chargeable gain arising is relieved from tax.

Tail-swallowing of rights shares

8.92 TCGA 1992, Sch 7D, para 8 provides that no capital gains tax will be chargeable on the trustees where rights attaching to plan shares are tail-swallowed (see **8.19** above) provided all shareholders have similar rights.

MISCELLANEOUS

Company reconstructions and rights issues

8.93   ITEPA 2003, Sch 2, paras 87 and 88 contain provisions which allow a new holding of shares received on a company reconstruction (e.g. a share exchange on a takeover, or upon a scheme of arrangement, or a bonus or rights issue) to be treated as if it were the original holding and therefore provides relief from income tax and capital gains tax on any gains arising on the disposal of the original holding involved in the transaction. The relief is available where the new holding is equated with the original holding for capital gains tax purposes, including a transaction where the new holding consists of, or includes, a qualifying corporate bond (within the meaning given by TCGA 1992, s 117). However, the relief is not available where the new holding consists of redeemable shares, a bonus issue which follows an earlier repayment of share capital, or a stock dividend taxable as income under ICTA 1988, s 249.

8.94   Where in respect of plan shares the trustees subscribe for new shares on the same terms as all other shareholders under a rights issue then the rights shares taken up will be treated as part of a new holding under a company reconstruction (see **8.93** above) for capital gains tax purposes unless funds are provided to exercise the rights otherwise than under the tail-swallowing powers of the trustees under ITEPA 2003, Sch 2, para 77. In addition, if any rights are offered specifically to participants in the plan (or on special terms), the shares acquired will be outside the relief for company reconstructions and will be treated as a part disposal for capital gains tax purposes.

Relief from stamp duty

8.95   Where partnership or dividend shares are transferred by the trustees of a SIP to a participant, no stamp duty or stamp duty reserve tax is due on the stock transfer or in relation to the agreement to transfer (FA 2001, s 95). Stamp duty issues are not in point on the acquisition of shares for nil consideration, as with free and matching shares.

HMRC's power to require information

8.96   ITEPA 2003, Sch 2, para 93 enables HMRC to obtain such information as it may from time to time require for the performance of its functions from any person who may have the information (or can reasonably be expected to provide it). In particular, HMRC can obtain information to enable it:

(a)   to check anything contained in a notification of the SIP or any annual return; or

(b)   to determine the liability to tax (including capital gains tax) of any participant in the plan or any other person who may have such a liability in connection with the SIP.

It can also seek information about the administration of the plan and any proposed alteration. HMRC must give at least three months' notice of any information sought and there are penalties for non-compliance.

Plan returns

8.97   ITEPA 2003, Sch 2, para 81B provides that the company operating the SIP must file an annual return with HMRC by 6 July immediately following the end of the relevant tax year. This return must be in such form, and contain such information, as HMRC shall require and, under ITEPA 2003, Sch 2, para 81D must be filed electronically through the HMR online system. This return should also indicate whether, during the relevant tax year, any alterations to a 'key feature' of the plan have been made. Penalties may apply in the case of a late or missed filing.

8.98   If at any time HMRC has reason to believe that the requirements of ITEPA 2003, Sch 2 are not, or have not been, met, HMRC may open an enquiry into the SIP. Where, following such enquiry, HMRC consider that the legislative requirements have not been met, HMRC may require amendments to be made to the SIP terms, or may issue a closure notice specifying that the SIP shall not maintain tax-advantaged status from the date of the notice, or such earlier date as HMRC may specify. Such a determination will not affect the tax advantages enjoyed by participants, but may result in a penalty being imposed on the company operating the SIP calculated by reference to the tax savings being made by participants (see **4.55** above).

8.99   The company may appeal to the Tax Tribunal within 30 days against a decision of HMRC to:

(a)   impose penalties on the company;

(b)   withdraw corporation tax relief (see **9.21–9.23** and **10.19**); or

(c)   require amendments to a SIP.

Termination of plan

8.100   The plan may provide for the company by notice to terminate a plan early (ITEPA 2003, Sch 2, para 89(1)). The company may include in the plan such circumstances of early termination as it may determine. These may relate to the expiry of a specified period, a change of control of the company or at the exercise of a discretion on the part of the directors. Any plan termination notice must be served on the following without delay:

(a)   the trustees; and

(b)   all participants (including any individual who has entered into a partnership share agreement even though he may not yet have any shares).

8.101   The effect of service of a plan termination notice is that no further awards of shares can be made and the trustees must remove the shares from the plan as soon as practicable after the later of:

(a)   three months from service of notice; and

(b)   the first date on which shares may be removed from the plan without any income tax charge on the participants (which may, of course, be up to five years).

However, the shares may be removed with the consent of the participant at an earlier date. Partnership share money and any cash dividends which have not been reinvested must also be paid over to the participants.

HMRC does not object to the SIP trust deed providing for, or being amended to provide for, the distribution of surplus assets during the period between the service of a plan termination notice and the plan shares being removed from the trust.

Corporation tax deduction for the costs of setting up the plan

8.102   The costs of setting up a SIP are deductible for corporation tax purposes provided the scheme is not operated before approval (CTA 2009, s 987, previously ICTA 1988, Sch 4AA, para 7). In addition, the trustees' running expenses (including interest costs) in operating the plan are deductible for corporation tax purposes (CTA 2009, s 988, previously ICTA 1988, Sch 4AA, para 8).

OPERATING THE PLAN

8.103   There is nothing in the legislation which requires invitations to be issued at any particular time, although where the company operates the plan on a rolling monthly basis, new employees must be invited as soon as they satisfy any eligibility criteria. Listed companies offering free shares, or partnership shares on an annual basis, will generally follow the ABI Guidelines and provide for a participation 'window' following the announcement of results (see **3.28** above).

Model Code under the Listing Rules

8.104   The UKLA Model Code for Dealings in securities of listed companies generally restricts the acquisition of shares by persons discharging managerial responsibilities (PDMRs) during the period of 60 days prior to the preliminary announcement of annual results by a listed company, or during the shorter specified period in relation to the announcement of other periodic results. These restrictions do not apply, however, where shares are awarded or acquired under a SIP which is offered on similar terms to all or most employees of the participating companies (paragraph 2(i)).

Chapter 9

SIPs – Free Shares

INTRODUCTION

9.1   A Share Incentive Plan (SIP) can provide for the award of free shares. Income Tax (Earnings and Pensions) Act 2003 (ITEPA 2003), Sch 2 provides tax reliefs for the participant (see **9.14–9.20** below) and tax deductions for the company (see **9.21** and **9.22** below).

MAXIMUM ANNUAL AWARD

9.2   The maximum value of shares which can be awarded as free shares under a SIP each tax year is £3,600 (ITEPA 2003, Sch 2, para 35), increased from £3,000 from 6 April 2014. This is based on the market value of the shares on the date they are awarded. For this purpose, any restrictions (including forfeiture provisions) are disregarded in valuing the shares.

The market value of shares quoted on a recognised stock exchange will depend on whether those shares are acquired on the market, in which case HMRC will allow the market value to be determined by reference to the average acquisition costs of the shares over the period of up to five consecutive dealing days ending on the date of the award, or whether the shares are new issue (or already held in the trust), in which case HMRC will allow the market value to be determined by reference to the quoted price on the date of the award or on the previous dealing date, or as the average quoted prices over a period specified in the rules of up to five days immediately preceding the award. The market value of unquoted shares must be agreed with Shares and Assets Valuation at HMRC who have issued a form of application (Form VAL 230) for valuations which may be used by the employer company.

PERFORMANCE ALLOWANCES

9.3   It is possible for the plan to provide for free shares to be allocated on the basis of performance allowances (conditions). Performance allowances may determine whether or not free shares will be awarded to an individual and the number or value of the free shares to be awarded. It should be noted that this flexibility relates only to pre-allocation targets: the performance allowances cannot be imposed as conditions for the release of shares (i.e. once the trustee is holding shares for an employee those shares cannot be forfeited based on performance). This means that performance allowances will normally relate to one financial year and the awards will be made in the next financial year, thus effectively extending the plan term by the length of the performance period, as notifications of potential allocations will be sent to employees 12 months in advance of the allocation date). It remains open to companies, however, to operate group-wide targets which must be satisfied in order that the plan is operated in any year. In such cases the requirements in relation to performance allowances will not apply as employees need not be informed of the conditions for operating the plan in advance of the allocations being made.

9.4   ITEPA 2003, Sch 2, para 38 provides that if performance allowances are imposed in relation to an award, they must apply to all qualifying employees.

Performance allowances – measures and targets

9.5   ITEPA 2003, Sch 2, para 39 provides that any performance allowances used must:

(a)   be based on business results and other objective criteria; and

(b)   be fair and objective measures of the performance of the units to which they apply.

There is, therefore, no scope for the exercise of discretion in determining whether performance allowances are satisfied.

9.6   Performance allowances must be set by reference to performance units comprising one or more employees. In that case it will be easy to identify a performance unit – a group of companies, a company, a division or any business unit (even a single person) – provided objective (though not necessarily audited) information is available about the performance of that business unit. It is the policy of HMRC to rely largely on companies determining whether the business unit identified by the company satisfies the requirements and only intends to challenge unreasonable cases. However, an employee must not be a member of more than one business unit.

9.7   ITEPA 2003, Sch 2, para 40 requires each qualifying employee who has accepted an invitation to participate in an award of free shares to be notified of the performance measures and targets which will be used to determine the number and value of free shares to be awarded to him. In addition, a general description of the performance measures applying to employees generally must be given to all qualifying employees. It is necessary to give this information as soon as practicable. This does not necessarily mean the information must be provided before the start of the financial period to which the target applies; in many cases companies will only determine the performance target well after the financial year has started and it is only necessary in these cases to give the information as soon as reasonably practicable thereafter. The company is entitled to exclude from the notice information which the company reasonably considers commercially confidential (ITEPA 2003, Sch 2, para 40(3)).

Performance allowances – Methods 1 and 2

9.8   There are two methods of setting performance allowances. In practice, Method 2 gives greater flexibility and will usually be satisfied (even if Method 1 is also coincidentally satisfied).

Method 1

9.9   Under Method 1:

(a)   at least 20 per cent of the total number of shares to be awarded to employees must be awarded without reference to performance but on the 'same' terms. The shares awarded on non-performance terms under the award will be on the 'same' terms as required by ITEPA 2003, Sch 2, para 9 (see **8.40** and **8.41** above);

(b)   the remaining shares must be awarded by reference to performance; and

(c)   no individual may receive more than four times as many performance shares as any individual gets non-performance shares (some, of course, may not receive any performance shares). If more than one class of share is awarded, the performance allowance rules apply to each class of share separately. In practice, it would be unusual to award more than one class of share at a time (ITEPA 2003, Sch 2, para 41).

Method 2

9.10   Under Method 2:

(a)   some or all of the shares must be awarded by reference to performance; and

(b)   the awarding of shares to qualifying employees who are members of the same employment unit must be on the same terms (ITEPA 2003, Sch 2, para 42).

Many plans will satisfy both Method 1 and Method 2 but there are differences which may be important:

(a)   either method allows for an element of non-performance shares – in the case of Method 1 there must be a minimum of 20 per cent of the shares covered by the award but in the case of Method 2 the company has a discretion to award any proportion of non-performance shares (but not 100 per cent);

(b)   under Method 1, no individual may receive more than four times the number of performance shares than non-performance shares, but no such ratio applies under Method 2; and

(c)   under Method 2, which provides for allocations to different employment units, awards of performance shares must be on the same terms (equally or pro rata salary, length of service or hours worked) as between members of the same employment unit (but not as between members of different employment units).

THE HOLDING PERIOD FOR FREE (AND MATCHING) SHARES

9.11   ITEPA 2003, Sch 2, para 36 provides that the company may set a holding period for each award of free (and matching) shares, ie it does not need to be permanently fixed under the plan rules but will be contained in the free shares agreement (see **9.12** below). The period may be between three and five years and must apply to all participants in the same award. The company may from time to time vary the length of the holding period for future awards but only within these parameters. As it has been possible, as a result of changes made by FA 2013, for SIP shares to be subject to restrictions, it would be possible for the company to impose an additional 'no sale' period once the shares cease to be subject to the SIP, which would effectively replicate, or extend, any holding period imposed. This could be used, for example, in place of a holding period where participants leave employment and the SIP holding period comes to an end early (see **9.13** below), although where tax charges arise on shares leaving the SIP, a sale of shares to cover tax may need to be permitted.

9.12   During the holding period, the participant must permit his shares to remain in the hands of the trustees and must not assign, charge or otherwise dispose of the beneficial interest in the shares. The plan must provide for the participant to be bound in contract with the company. A form of undertaking (the free shares agreement) must be entered into before any award of free shares is made to a participant. HMRC accept that, in relation to awards of free shares, companies may, rather than asking employees to enter into 'Free Share Agreements', operate an opt-out process whereby employees receive invitations to participate in a free share award and will be deemed to have accepted the award unless they opt out within a period specified in the invitation. Whilst HMRC require only a 14-day period to be open to employees for the acceptance of invitations, if the opt out method is used a period of not less than 25 days is required.

9.13   The holding period will terminate early if the participant ceases to have relevant employment (see **8.47–8.52** above). The obligation on the participant to leave his shares with the trustees is subject to the power of the trustees:

(a)   to act on directions from the participant in respect of general offers affecting the shares;

(b)   to sell shares to meet its PAYE obligations under ITEPA 2003, Sch 2, para 79; and

(c)   to remove shares with the consent of the participant on early termination of the plan.

The trustee may act on directions from the participant under (a) above in respect of:

(a)   a share for share takeover or offer of non-qualifying corporate bonds on a takeover;

(b)   an offer of qualifying corporate bonds (with or without other assets or cash) on a takeover;

(c)   a cash offer (with or without other assets) on a takeover; and

(d)   a company reorganisation.

INCOME TAX CHARGE ON FREE (AND MATCHING) SHARES

Ceasing to be subject to the plan

9.14   ITEPA 2003, s 505 provides that when free (and matching) shares cease to be subject to the plan, income tax may be chargeable depending on the period that has elapsed between the date of award and the date on which the shares cease to be subject to the plan. There is no tax payable on shares withdrawn from the plan after five years.

9.15   If the period since the award is less than three years, the amount which counts as employment income, and therefore the amount on which the participant is charged income tax, is the market value of the shares when they cease to be subject to the plan.

9.16   If the period since the award is three or more years (but less than five years) then the amount which counts as employment income is the lesser of:

(a)   the market value of the shares on the date of award; and

(b)   the market value on the date they cease to be subject to the plan.

9.17   If there has been a capital receipt since the date of award then the amount of tax to be paid is reduced by the tax paid on the capital receipt.

9.18   Forfeited shares are not subject to income tax on forfeiture. Only free and matching shares can be forfeited.

No relief where the beneficial interest in shares is disposed of during the holding period

9.19   ITEPA 2003, s 507 provides that where the beneficial interest in free (and matching) shares is disposed of during the holding period (in breach of the participant's obligations) then the amount which counts as employment income, and so the amount on which the participant is subject to income tax, is the full market value of the shares when they cease to be subject to the plan, regardless of the period which has elapsed since award. The amount of tax payable is reduced by the tax paid on any earlier capital receipt in respect of these shares.

Exemption from tax for good leavers and on takeover

9.20   ITEPA 2003, s 498 provides that there will be no charge to income tax on shares ceasing to be subject to the plan where the participant ceases relevant employment (see **8.47–8.55** above) as a 'good leaver' on account of:

(a)   injury or disability;

(b)   dismissal by reason of statutory redundancy;

(c)   a TUPE transfer;

(d)   a change of control (or other circumstances ending the associated company status) of the employer company;

(e)   retirement (see **8.65** above); or

(f)   his death.

There will also be no charge to income tax on shares ceasing to be subject to the plan in connection with a scheme of arrangement, takeover by way of general offer or compulsory acquisition of shares under the provisions of the Companies Act 2006 provided that the participant receives, for the SIP shares, cash consideration (and no other asset) and the participant did not have the opportunity of accepting replacement assets which could have remained in the SIP trust. This exemption will also not be available in connection with SIP shares awarded where HMRC consider that the award would not have been made but for the ability to take advantage of the transaction-related tax exemption.

CORPORATION TAX DEDUCTIONS FOR FREE (AND MATCHING) SHARES

9.21   CTA 2009, s 994 (previously ICTA 1988, Sch 4AA, para 2) provides a deduction for corporation tax on an amount equal to the market value of any free (and matching) shares awarded to employees. The deduction is given for the period of account in which the shares are awarded to employees in accordance with the plan. It is to be noted that the deduction may be given in a later year to which the shares are acquired by the trustees. Shares are identified for this purpose strictly in the order of acquisition by the trustees. There is in fact nothing in the legislation which requires actual expenditure to be incurred and indeed any amounts for the actual cost of the shares are specifically disallowed.

Group plans – allocation of deductible amounts

9.22   Where shares are awarded under a group plan, the amount to be deducted for corporation tax purposes (ie the market value of the shares) must be allocated between the various group companies whose employees participate in the award. The allocation to different group companies should be made strictly in proportion to the number of shares awarded to its employees.

Non-employee taxpayers

9.23   No deduction is allowed in respect of shares awarded to an individual who is not chargeable to tax under ITEPA 2003, Pt 2, Chs 4 or 5 in respect of general earnings from his employment.

Chapter 10

SIPs – Partnership Shares

INTRODUCTION

10.1   A SIP can provide for a participant to purchase partnership shares out of his pre-tax earnings (so that he obtains income tax and National Insurance contributions relief on the amounts deducted). Unlike free and matching shares which are subject to holding periods, partnership shares may be withdrawn from the SIP at any time subject to any income tax charge under Income Tax (Earnings and Pensions) Act 2003 (ITEPA 2003), s 506 (see **10.30–10.32** below), although this would not prohibit sale restrictions attaching to such shares once they have ceased to be subject to the SIP.

PARTNERSHIP SHARE AGREEMENTS

10.2   ITEPA 2003, Sch 2, para 44 provides that qualifying employees must enter into a partnership share agreement under which:

(a)   the employee authorises the company to deduct partnership share monies from his salary; and

(b)   the company undertakes to award partnership shares.

Deduction from salary

10.3   ITEPA 2003, Sch 2, para 45 provides that the partnership share agreement must specify:

(a)   what amounts are to be deducted (which may be an amount or a percentage of salary); and

(b)   at what intervals.

The company and the employee can vary the amounts and intervals from time to time.

Maximum deductions

10.4   There are two limits on the maximum amount of partnership share money which may be deducted.

10.5   Deductions in any tax year may not exceed £1,800 (ITEPA 2003, Sch 2, para 46(1)), increased from £1,500 from 6 April 2014. Such deductions may be one-off amounts or may be made at regular intervals (for example, monthly).

10.6   Deductions may not exceed ten per cent of the employee's salary in any tax year (ITEPA 2003, Sch 2, para 46(2)).

10.7   The plan may specify lower limits than those in **10.5** and **10.6** above either by substituting a lower percentage or by disregarding aspects of an employee's salary (such as overtime or other variable pay). Different limits may be specified in different awards of partnership shares provided they are less than those in **10.5** and **10.6**. Any amount deducted in excess of the maximum limits must be paid over to the employee as soon as practicable.

Minimum deductions

10.8   ITEPA 2003, Sch 2, para 47 provides that the plan must include a minimum amount which must be deducted on any occasion. This may not be an amount greater than £10. HMRC consider that the requirement for this minimum to apply 'on any occasion' that deductions are taken, does not (for employees paid more frequently) equate to a monthly equivalent deduction. This means, for example, that employees who participate on a weekly basis will have this minimum applied to each weekly deduction, even though their monthly paid colleagues will have the same minimum applied only once per month.

Effect of partnership share agreement on statutory benefits

10.9   ITEPA 2003, Sch 2, para 48 provides that partnership share agreements must contain a statement in the form prescribed by Regulations (see Employee Share Ownership Plans (Partnership Shares – Notice of Effects on Benefits, Statutory Sick Pay and Statutory Maternity Pay) Regulations 2000 (SI 2000/2090)) explaining the effects of participation in the plan on statutory salary-related benefits such as statutory sick pay or statutory maternity pay. The Government believes that only a small minority of employees will be prejudiced but nevertheless considers it important that the effects of statutory benefits are explained.

Partnership share money held for the employee

10.10   ITEPA 2003, Sch 2, para 49 provides that partnership share money which has been deducted from salary under a partnership share agreement must be paid to the trustees as soon as practicable and held by them pending application in the purchase of partnership shares. However, any surplus partnership share money must be repaid to the employee unless he agrees it may be carried forward and added to the next salary deduction (ITEPA 2003, Sch 2, paras 50(5) and 52(6)).

Partnership share account

10.11   Under ITEPA 2003, Sch 2, para 49, the plan must provide for any partnership share money to be kept by the trustees in an account with a specified financial institution (for example, a bank, building society or authorised EEA firm) (it cannot therefore be held by the company). It is not necessary for the account to be interest bearing but if it is held in an interest-bearing account then the trustees must account to the employee for the interest. In practice, few companies provide for interest to be paid especially in view of the relatively short periods monies are held on account.

Plans with no accumulation period

10.12   ITEPA 2003, Sch 2, para 50 provides that if the plan does not include an accumulation period (basically, a savings period of up to one year) then partnership share money must be applied in acquiring partnership shares on a date set by the trustees (being within 30 days of the last deduction from salary). The participant will be treated as acquiring the shares on the acquisition date even if he ceases employment between the date the partnership share money is deducted and the acquisition date (in other words the participant will get the shares and then they will be withdrawn from the plan with the tax consequences set out at **10.31** and **10.32** below (ITEPA 2003, Sch 2, para 97(2)).

10.13   The number of shares awarded to an employee depends on the market value (see **9.2** above in relation to the determination of market value) of the shares on the acquisition date (see **10.12** above) subject to not exceeding the maximum limit quoted at **10.5** and **10.6** above. Surplus partnership share money is dealt with as explained at **10.10** above.

Plans with an accumulation period

10.14   ITEPA 2003, Sch 2, para 51 provides that a plan may include an accumulation period of up to one year (basically a savings period which is intended to reduce the number of occasions on which partnership shares are purchased).

10.15   Where an accumulation period is provided for by the plan then the partnership share agreement must specify when each accumulation period begins and ends (and the first period must not begin later than the date the first deduction is made). An accumulation period must be the same for all employees who enter into partnership share agreements at any time.

10.16   A partnership share agreement may specify that the accumulation period may terminate upon the occurrence of a specified event, e.g. a takeover. There is no scope for discretion. Although the legislation provides for this to be inserted in the partnership share agreement it would normally be better to include any termination provision in the plan rules since the provision must apply to all employees eligible to participate in the award (ITEPA 2003, Sch 2, para 51(3)(b)).

10.17   ITEPA 2003, Sch 2, para 51(5) provides that the plan may provide that on a company reorganisation, any partnership share agreement shall apply to the new holding in the same way as the original holding.

Monies deducted in an accumulation period

10.18   ITEPA 2003, Sch 2, para 52 provides that plans that include one or more accumulation periods must provide for the trustees to apply the partnership share money deducted in any period in acquiring partnership shares within 30 days of the end of the accumulation period.

10.19   The number of shares awarded to each individual must be based on a calculation method specified in the relevant partnership share agreement. The company has a choice of specifying one of three methods:

(a)   the market value of the shares at the beginning of the accumulation period (see **9.2** above in relation to the determination of market value);

(b)   the market value of the shares on the date the shares are acquired, ie following the end of the accumulation period; or

(c)   the lower of these two values.

Method (c) is clearly the most beneficial for the participant, but it does have the effect that the number of shares which might be acquired by the participant may vary significantly from the number which the trustees can acquire with the partnership share monies actually deducted (as would method (a) in the case of an increasing share price). Any shortfall may need to be made good by the trustees which in many cases may involve the employer company in additional expenses in providing the shares. However, the employer company (or any company in the group) is not entitled to a corporation tax deduction for the amount of any actual additional expenses (CTA 2009, s 995(4), previously ICTA 1988, Sch 4AA, para 3(3)). Instead, CTA 2009, s 995(1) (previously ICTA 1988, Sch 4AA, para 3(1)) provides for a deduction against corporation tax for the excess of the market value of the partnership shares awarded over the amount of partnership share monies available.

Where methods (a) or (c) are used, HMRC accept that market value at the beginning of the accumulation period may, for non-UK companies, be fixed either in local currency and converted into sterling on acquisition, or in sterling at the exchange rate at the beginning of the period.

10.20   Where the amount of partnership shares money deducted during the accumulation period exceeds the cost of acquiring the partnership shares. This must be returned to the employee as soon as practicable unless he agrees it may be carried forward to the next accumulation period (ITEPA 2003, Sch 2, para 52(6)).

10.21   Where a participant leaves relevant employment during an accumulation period then all the partnership share money deducted must be paid over to the employee as soon as practicable (ITEPA 2003, Sch 2, para 52(7)). However, if the employee ceases to be in relevant employment at any time between the last deduction under the accumulation period and the date the shares are to be awarded then he is only treated as ceasing relevant employment immediately following the date of the award. In other words the participant will get the shares and then they will be withdrawn from the plan with the tax consequences set out at **10.31** and **10.32** below (ITEPA 2003, Sch 2, para 97(2)).

10.22   Where the partnership share agreement provides for an accumulation period to end upon some specified event (see **10.16** above), it may also provide that all partnership share money deducted prior to that event is to be reimbursed to the employee as soon as practicable rather than being used to acquire shares (ITEPA 2003, Sch 2, para 52(8)).

Limits on the maximum number of partnership shares to be awarded

10.23   The plan may authorise the company to impose a maximum number of shares which may be included in any award (ITEPA 2003, Sch 2, para 53). If any limit bites, then each individual award must be reduced proportionately. Different limits may apply for each award. Where the company is so authorised, partnership share agreements must oblige the company to notify any limits to be included in an award. This notice must be given before the deduction of partnership share money (or before the beginning of any accumulation period).

Stopping and restarting deductions

10.24   Participants must be able to stop and restart deductions at any time under a partnership share agreement (ITEPA 2003, Sch 2, para 54(1)). Where deductions are restarted, missed deductions can be made up by increasing the amounts of future deductions (provided that this is allowed by the company and the £1,800 per tax year limit is not exceeded). Plans which provide for an accumulation period may prevent more than one restart during that period. Deductions must be stopped by the company within 30 days of receipt of a stop notice (or such longer period as may be specified in the notice). Deductions must be restarted by the first deduction date falling not more than 30 days after the restart notice is given.

Withdrawal from partnership share agreements

10.25   ITEPA 2003, Sch 2, para 55 provides that plans must allow employees to withdraw from partnership share agreements by 30 days' notice in writing to the company given at any time. If notice of withdrawal is served then all partnership share money must be returned.

Repayment of partnership share money on withdrawal of approval or termination

10.26   ITEPA 2003, Sch 2, para 56 requires plans to provide that partnership share money is repaid as soon as practicable where either a plan termination notice is served by the company (see **8.100** above) or HMRC issue a closure notice following an enquiry under which the SIP loses its tax-advantaged status as a 'Schedule 2 SIP' for the purposes of Schedule 2.

TAX RELIEF FOR PARTNERSHIP SHARE MONEY

10.27 The amounts deducted from salary (partnership share money) are not regarded as employment income of the employee chargeable to tax (or National Insurance contributions). The effect, therefore, is that the participant purchases the shares out of pre-tax income. It is, however, treated as income of the participant for the purposes of determining his salary for pension and annuity purposes.

TAX CHARGES ON PARTNERSHIP SHARE MONIES PAID OVER TO THE EMPLOYEE

10.28 By virtue of ITEPA 2003, s 503, the following amounts paid over to a participant count as employment income of the participant and so are charged to income tax:

(a)   deductions of partnership share money in excess of the maximum deductions (see **10.7** above);

(b)   surplus partnership share money remaining after the acquisition of shares (see **10.20** above);

(c)   partnership share money paid over on the employee leaving relevant employment (see **10.21** above, and note that the tax relief provisions set out at **10.32** below do not apply to the repayment of partnership share monies);

(d)   partnership share money paid over where the accumulation period is brought to an end by a specified event in the plan (see **10.22** above);

(e)   partnership share money paid over on a withdrawal from a partnership share agreement (see **10.25** above); and

(f)   partnership share money paid over ontermination or the SIP losing its tax-advantaged status (see **10.26** above).

TAX ON CANCELLATION PAYMENTS IN RESPECT OF PARTNERSHIP SHARE AGREEMENT

10.29 By virtue of ITEPA 2003, s 504, income tax is chargeable on the amount or value of any money or money's worth received by a participant in respect of the cancellation of a partnership share agreement.

PARTNERSHIP SHARES CEASING TO BE SUBJECT TO THE PLAN

10.30 Partnership shares cease to be subject to the plan either because the shares are voluntarily withdrawn on the instructions of the participant or because the participant ceases to be an employee.

10.31 Where partnership shares cease to be subject to the plan, income tax may be chargeable depending on the period they have been held in the plan:

(a) if the period is less than three years, the amount which counts as employment income, and therefore the amount on which the participant is charged to income tax is the market value of the shares when they cease to be subject to the plan;

(b) if the period is three years or more (but less than five years), the amount which counts as employment income is the lesser of the amount of partnership share money used to acquire the shares and the market value of the shares when they cease to be subject to the plan; and

(c) if the period is five years or more, no income tax is payable.

Any tax due is reduced by the amount of tax paid on any prior capital receipts.

10.32 ITEPA 2003, s 498 provides that there will be no charge to income tax on shares ceasing to be subject to the plan where the participant ceases relevant employment (see **8.47–8.53** above) as a 'good leaver' on account of:

(a) injury or disability;

(b) dismissal by reason of statutory redundancy;

(c) a TUPE transfer of the undertaking for which he works;

(d) a change of control (or other circumstances ending the associated company status) of the employer company;

(e) retirement on or after the specified age (see **8.63** above); or

(f) his death.

There will also be no charge to income tax on shares ceasing to be subject to the plan in connection with a scheme of arrangement, takeover by way of general offer or compulsory acquisition of shares under the provisions of the Companies Act 2006 provided that the participant receives, for the SIP shares, cash consideration (and no other asset) and the participant did not have the opportunity of accepting replacement assets which could have remained in the SIP trust. This exemption will also not be available in connection with SIP shares awarded where HMRC consider that the award would not have been made but for the ability to take advantage of the transaction-related tax exemption.

10.33 Where partnership shares are subject to compulsory sale provisions which result in those shares ceasing to be subject to the SIP, ITEPA 2003, s 506(2B) provides that the amount which is charged to tax, where the shares are sold within three years of award, will be the lower of the amount of partnership share money used in the acquisition of those shares and the market value of the shares at the time that they are offered for sale. This is the same calculation as for partnership shares ceasing to be subject to the SIP between three and five years from award.

10.34   Where partnership shares are subject to compulsory sale provisions following the date on which they have ceased to be subject to the SIP, for example where an participant leaves employment and is required to then offer the shares for sale, the tax consequences will follow the treatment set out at **10.31** and **10.32** above.

Chapter 11

SIPs – Matching Shares

INTRODUCTION

11.1   A Share Incentive Plan (SIP) can provide for participants to receive matching shares in respect of any partnership shares which are awarded to them. Unlike partnership shares, matching shares are subject to a holding period (see **9.11–9.13** above) and may be subject to restrictions (including forfeiture provisions) (see **8.59–8.65** above) in the same way as free shares.

GENERAL REQUIREMENTS FOR MATCHING SHARES

11.2   The plan must provide for the matching shares:

(a)   to be shares of the same class and carrying the same rights as the partnership shares to which they relate;

(b)   to be awarded on the same day as the partnership shares to which they relate are awarded; and

(c)   to be awarded to all employees who participate in the award on exactly the same basis (ITEPA 2003, Sch 2, para 59).

RATIO OF MATCHING SHARES TO PARTNERSHIP SHARES

11.3   The partnership share agreement must specify:

(a)   the ratio of matching shares to partnership shares for the time being offered by the company; and

(b)   the circumstances and manner in which the ratio may be changed by the company (ITEPA 2003, Sch 2, para 60).

11.4   The ratio of matching shares to partnership shares must not exceed 2:1 and, although the legislation requires the ratio to be applied by reference to the number of shares, HMRC has accepted that limits may also be based on values of matching shares awarded. There is nothing to prevent a ratio of 1:1 or one to any number of partnership shares, for instance, one matching share for every four partnership shares.

11.5   The matching ratio may also be stepped, for instance, two matching shares for each of the first ten shares and one matching share for each additional share thereafter (although it is not possible for the ratio to improve as shares are acquired, as this could favour higher-paid employees) or by reference to the achievement of group performance targets.

11.6   Where the ratio varies by reference to the number of partnership shares acquired, this ratio must apply to each award. The number of partnership shares acquired by the participant for these purposes cannot be aggregated across multiple awards.

11.7   Where the ratio results in a fraction of a matching share, any fraction may be carried forward to the next award.

11.8   The partnership share agreement must provide for the employee to be informed by the company if the ratio offered by the company changes before partnership shares are awarded to him under the agreement (ITEPA 2003, Sch 2, para 60(3)).

INCOME TAX, CAPITAL GAINS TAX AND CORPORATION TAX

11.9   The income tax, capital gains tax and corporation tax treatment of matching shares is identical to free shares (see **9.14** above for income tax treatment and **9.21** above for corporation tax deductions).

Share Incentive Plan

Set out below is a precedent for the trust deed and rules of a Share Incentive Plan providing for free, partnership, matching and dividend shares. It is intended to comply with the requirements of ITEPA 2003, Sch *2*. Certain provisions in the precedent (e.g. references to the London Stock Exchange, the scheme limits, and the alteration provisions) would not normally be included in the scheme of a private company.

Trust Deed of the [   ] Share Incentive Plan

THIS DEED is made the day of [ ]

BETWEEN:

(1) **[*COMPANY NAME* [LIMITED/PLC]]** whose registered office is at [*insert registered address*] registered in England and Wales under registration number [*insert registered number*] (the **'Company'**); and

(2) **[*TRUSTEE NAME*]** whose registered office is at [*insert registered address*] registered in England and Wales under registration number [*insert registered number*] (the **'Trustee'**).

NOW THIS DEED WITNESSES as follows:

1.   PURPOSE

The purpose of this Deed is to establish a trust for the share incentive plan known as the [*COMPANY NAME*] Share Incentive Plan (the **'Plan'**) which is a Schedule 2 SIP.

2.   STATUS

2.1   The Plan consists of this Deed and the attached Rules and all ancillary documents conforming to the terms of the Plan.

2.2   The definitions in the Rules apply to this Deed.

2.3   The Company may from time to time determine that Awards shall be made under any of Rules 6, 7, or 8 and that Rule 9 shall have effect. Where the Company determines that an Award shall be made under Rule 7 it shall also specify whether there is to be an Accumulation Period of up to 12 months, which shall apply equally to all Qualifying Employees in the Plan.

3.   DECLARATION OF TRUST

3.1   The Company and the Trustee have agreed that all the Shares and other assets which are issued to or transferred to the Trustee (or held on its behalf) are to be held on the trusts declared by this Deed, and subject to the terms of the Rules. When Shares or assets are transferred to the Trustee by the Company with the intention of being held as part of the Plan they shall be held upon the trusts and provisions of this Deed and the Rules.

3.2   The Trustee shall hold the Trust Fund upon the following trusts namely:

3.2.1   as to Shares which have not been awarded to Participants (**'Unawarded Shares'**), upon trust during the Trust Period to allocate those Shares in accordance with the terms of this Deed and the Rules;

3.2.2   as to Shares which have been awarded to a Participant (**'Plan Shares'**), upon trust for the benefit of that Participant on the terms and conditions set out in the Rules;

3.2.3   as to Partnership Share Money, upon trust to purchase Shares for the benefit of the contributing Qualifying Employee in accordance with the Rules; and

3.2.4   as to other assets (**'Surplus Assets'**), upon trust to use them to purchase further Shares to be held on the trusts declared in sub-clause 3.2.1 above, at such time during the Trust Period and on such terms as the Trustee in its absolute discretion thinks fit.

3.3   The income of Unawarded Shares and Surplus Assets shall be accumulated by the Trustee and added to, and held upon the trusts applying to, Surplus Assets.

3.4   The income of Plan Shares and Partnership Share Money shall be dealt with in accordance with the Rules.

3.5   The perpetuity period in respect of the trusts and powers declared by this Deed and the Rules shall be the period of 125 years from the date of this Deed.

3.6   The Trustee may purchase Shares by subscription (at par or any greater value), from treasury, by market purchase or by private treaty.

4.   NUMBER OF TRUSTEES

Unless the Trustee is a corporate trustee, there shall always be at least two trustees of the Trust Fund who together shall constitute the Trustee. Where there is no corporate trustee, and the number of trustees falls below two, the continuing trustee has the power to act only to achieve the appointment of a new trustee.

5.   INFORMATION

The trustees shall be entitled to rely without further enquiry on information supplied by any Participating Company for the purposes of the Plan and on any direction, notice or document purporting to be given or executed by or with the authority of any Participating Company or any Participant.

6.   RESIDENCE OF TRUSTEE

The Trustee shall be resident in the United Kingdom. The Company shall immediately remove a Trustee or any individual trustee that ceases to be so resident and, if necessary, appoint a replacement.

7.   CHANGE OF TRUSTEE

7.1   The Company has the power to appoint or remove any trustee for any reason. Any change of Trustee may be effected by written notice served upon the Trustee. Any Trustee or any individual trustee may resign on three months' notice given in writing to the Company, provided that there will be at least two trustees or a corporate trustee immediately after the retirement.

7.2   If the retiring Trustee is a sole corporate trustee the Trustee may appoint a successor as a Trustee if the Company does not itself do so before the date of such retirement. The Trustee shall not be responsible for any costs arising as a result of its retirement but will do all things necessary to give proper effect to its retirement.

8.   INVESTMENT AND DEALING WITH TRUST ASSETS

8.1   Save as otherwise provided for by the Plan the Trustee shall not sell or otherwise dispose of Plan Shares.

8.2   The Trustee shall obey any directions given by a Participant in accordance with the Rules in relation to his Plan Shares and any rights and income relating to those Shares. In the absence of any such direction, or provision by the Plan, the Trustee shall take no action.

8.3   The Company and the Participating Companies shall, as soon as practicable after deduction from Salary, pass any Partnership Share Money to the Trustee who will put the money into an account with:

8.3.1   a person falling within Section 991(2)(b) of the Income Tax Act 2007 (certain institutions permitted to accept deposits);

8.3.2   a building society; or

8.3.3   a firm falling within Section 991(2)(c) of the Income Tax Act 2007 (EEA firms permitted to accept deposits),

until it is either used to acquire Partnership Shares on the Acquisition Date, or, in accordance with the Plan, returned to the individual from whose Salary the Partnership Share Money has been deducted. There is no obligation on the Trustee to arrange for any Partnership Share Money to be deposited in an interest earning account or otherwise to account for interest, subject to the provisions of paragraph 49(4) of the Schedule.

8.4   The Trustee shall pass on any interest arising on invested Partnership Share Money to the individual from whose Salary the Partnership Share Money has been deducted.

8.5   The Trustee may either retain or sell Unawarded Shares at its absolute discretion. The proceeds of any sale of Unawarded Shares shall form part of Surplus Assets.

8.6   The Trustee shall have all the powers of investment of a beneficial owner in relation to Surplus Assets.

8.7   The Trustee shall not be under any liability to the Participating Companies or to current or former Qualifying Employees by reason of a failure to diversify investments, which results from the retention of Plan Shares or Unawarded Shares.

8.8   The Trustee may delegate powers, duties or discretions to any persons (including the Company, any Subsidiary or any directors or employees of the same) and on any terms including the execution of documents, cheques and other instruments. No delegation made under this clause 8.8 shall divest the Trustee of its responsibilities under this Deed or under the Schedule.

8.9 The Trustee may appoint any registrar, solicitor, accountant, banker, broker or other agent to transact all or any business and may act on the advice or opinion of such person and shall not be liable for any loss to the trust suffered in good faith in reliance upon such person.

8.10 The Trustee may allow any Shares to be registered in the name of an appointed nominee provided that such Shares shall be registered in a designated account. Such registration shall not divest the Trustee of its responsibilities under this Deed or the Schedule.

8.11 The Trustee may at any time, and shall if the Company so directs, revoke any delegation made under this clause or require any Plan assets held by another person to be returned to the Trustee, or both.

9. DIVIDENDS

The Trustee shall not demand or in any way enforce payment of any dividends which would otherwise be payable on any Unawarded Shares for the time being comprised within the Trust Fund but where dividends are received the Trustee shall retain such dividends on trust as an addition to Surplus Assets.

10. LOANS TO THE TRUSTEE

10.1 The Trustee shall have the power to borrow money (on such terms as the Trustee sees fit) for the purpose of:

10.1.1 acquiring Shares; and

10.1.2 paying any other expenses properly incurred by the Trustee in administering the Plan.

11. TRUSTEE'S OBLIGATIONS UNDER THE PLAN

Notice of Award of Free Shares and Matching Shares

11.1 As soon as practicable after Free Shares and Matching Shares have been awarded to a Participant (and at least once per year), the Trustee shall give the Participant a notice stating:

11.1.1 the number and description of those Shares;

11.1.2 the Initial Market Value of those Shares on the Award Date;

11.1.3 the Holding Period applicable to those Shares; and

11.1.4 if the Shares are subject to any Restriction, the details of that Restriction.

Notice of Award of Partnership Shares

11.2 As soon as practicable after any Partnership Shares have been acquired for a Participant (and at least once per year), the Trustee shall give the Participant a notice stating:

11.2.1 the number and description of those Shares;

11.2.2 the amount of money applied by the Trustee in acquiring those Shares on behalf of the Participant;

11.2.3   the Market Value of those Shares in accordance with which the number of Shares awarded to the Participant was determined; and

11.2.4   if the Shares are subject to any Restriction, the details of the Restriction.

Notice of acquisition of Dividend Shares

11.3   As soon as practicable after any Dividend Shares have been acquired on behalf of a Participant (and at least once per year) the Trustee shall give the Participant a notice stating:

11.3.1   the number and description of those Shares;

11.3.2   the Market Value of those Shares on the Acquisition Date;

11.3.3   the Holding Period applicable to those Shares;

11.3.4   any amount not reinvested and carried forward for the acquisition of further Dividend Shares; and

11.3.5   if the Shares are subject to any Restriction, the details of the Restriction.

Notice of any foreign tax deducted before dividend paid

11.4   Where any foreign cash dividend is received in respect of Plan Shares held on behalf of a Participant, the Trustee shall give the Participant notice of the amount of any foreign tax deducted from the dividend before it was paid.

Restrictions during the Holding Period

11.5   During the Holding Period the Trustee shall not dispose of any Free Shares, Matching Shares or Dividend Shares (whether by transfer to the employee or otherwise) except as allowed by the following paragraphs of the Schedule:

11.5.1   paragraph 37 (*power of the Trustee to accept general offers etc.*);

11.5.2   paragraph 77 (*power of the Trustee to raise funds to subscribe for rights issue*);

11.5.3   paragraph 79 (*meeting PAYE obligations*); and

11.5.4   paragraph 90(5) (*termination of plan: early removal of shares with participant's consent*).

PAYE Liability

11.6   The Trustee may dispose of a Participant's Shares (without the consent of the Participant) or accept a sum from the Participant in order to meet any PAYE liability in the circumstances provided in Sections 510 to 512 of ITEPA 2003 (*PAYE: shares ceasing to be subject to the plan*).

11.7   Where the Trustee receives a sum of money which constitutes a Capital Receipt which counts as employment income of the Participant, the Trustee shall pay to the employer a sum equal to that on which income tax is so payable.

11.8   The Trustee shall maintain the records necessary to enable it to carry out its PAYE obligations, and the PAYE obligations of the employer company so far as they relate to the Plan.

11.9   Where the Participant becomes liable to income tax under ITEPA 2003, Chapter 3 of Part 4 or Chapter 4 of Part 4 of the Income Tax (Trading and Other Income) Act 2005, the Trustee shall inform the Participant of any facts which are relevant to determining that liability.

Money's worth received by the Trustee

11.10 The Trustee shall pay over to the Participant as soon as is practicable, any money or money's worth received by it in respect of or by reference to any shares, other than new shares within paragraph 87 of the Schedule (*company reconstructions*) PROVIDED THAT the Trustee shall be under no obligation to distribute any Capital Receipt to a Participant if the amount of that Capital Receipt is less than £3.

11.11 Where the Trustee does not distribute a Capital Receipt pursuant to clause 11.10 above, such Capital Receipts shall be held as an addition to the trusts declared in clause 3.2.

11.12 Clause 11.10 shall be subject to:

11.12.1 the provisions of Part 8 of the Schedule (*dividend reinvestment*);

11.12.2 the Trustee's obligations under Sections 510 to 514 of ITEPA 2003 (*PAYE: obligations to make payments to employer etc.*); and

11.12.3 the Trustee's PAYE obligations.

General offers

11.13 If any offer, compromise, arrangement or scheme is made which affects the Free Shares or Matching Shares the Trustee shall notify Participants. Each Participant may direct how the Trustee shall act in relation to that Participant's Plan Shares. In the absence of any direction, the Trustee shall take no action. This provision shall also apply when there arises a right under section 983 of the Companies Act 2006 to require an offeror to acquire the Participant's Free Shares, Matching Shares or Dividend Shares, or such of them as are of a particular class.

Duty to monitor Participants in connected plans

11.14 The Trustee shall maintain a record of each Participant who has received, in addition to an Award under the Plan, an award under another Schedule 2 SIP established by the Company or a Connected Company.

12.   POWER OF THE TRUSTEE TO RAISE FUNDS TO SUBSCRIBE FOR A RIGHTS ISSUE

12.1 If instructed by Participants in respect of their Plan Shares the Trustee may dispose of some of the rights under a rights issue arising from those Shares to obtain enough funds to exercise the remaining rights.

12.2 The rights referred to are the rights to buy additional shares or rights in the same company.

13.   POWER TO AGREE MARKET VALUE OF SHARES

Where the Market Value of Shares falls to be determined for the purposes of the Schedule, the Trustee may agree with HM Revenue and Customs that it shall be determined by reference to such date or dates, or to an average of the values on a number of dates, as specified in the agreement.

14.   TRUSTEE NOT BOUND TO INTERFERE IN THE BUSINESS OF ANY COMPANY IN WHICH IT IS INTERESTED

14.1 The Trustee shall be under no obligation to:

14.1.1 become a director or other officer or interfere in the management or affairs of any company, any of the shares or stocks of which are for the time being comprised in the Plan or of any company associated with such company; or

14.1.2 seek information about the affairs of any such company but may leave the conduct of the affairs of any such company to its officers or other persons managing the company.

15. PERSONAL INTEREST OF THE TRUSTEE

15.1 The Trustee, any individual trustee, and directors, officers or employees of a corporate trustee, shall not be liable to account for any benefit accruing to them by virtue of their:

15.1.1 participation in the Plan as a Qualifying Employee;

15.1.2 ownership, in a beneficial or fiduciary capacity, of any shares or other securities in any Participating Company;

15.1.3 being a director or employee of any Participating Company; or

15.1.4 being a creditor, or being (or having another member of the group which is) in any other contractual relationship with any such Company including that of banker.

16. TRUSTEE'S MEETINGS

The Trustee shall hold meetings as often as is necessary for the administration of the Plan. There shall be at least two trustees present at a meeting except where the Trustee is a corporate trustee and due notice shall be given to all the trustees of such a meeting. Decisions made at such a meeting by a majority of the trustees present shall be binding on the trustees. A written resolution signed by the Trustee of all the trustees shall have the same effect as a resolution passed at a meeting held pursuant to this clause 16.

17. SUBSIDIARY COMPANIES

17.1 Any Subsidiary may with the agreement of the Company become a party to this Deed and the Plan by executing a deed of adherence agreeing to be bound by the Deed and Rules.

17.2 Any company which ceases to be a Subsidiary shall cease to be a Participating Company.

17.3 A company shall cease to be a Participating Company if notice is served by the Company that it shall cease to be a Participating Company.

18. EXPENSES OF THE PLAN

18.1 The Participating Companies shall meet the costs of:

18.1.1 the preparation; and

18.1.2 the administration and termination, of this Plan.

19. TRUSTEE'S LIABILITY AND INDEMNITY

19.1 The Participating Companies will pay to or reimburse the Trustee all charges and expenses properly incurred by it in connection with the Plan and agree jointly and severally to keep the Trustee (and any of the Trustee's employees or officers) fully indemnified against any claims, proceedings, losses or liability arising out of or in connection with the trust or the proper administration of the Plan. However the Trustee shall not be identified or exonerated in respect of any fraud, wilful default or negligence on their part or on the part of any of the Trustee's employees or officers, in breach of the terms of this Deed. This indemnity will similarly apply after the removal or retirement of a Trustee. The Trustee shall also have the benefit of any indemnities conferred upon trustees by law.

19.2   The Trustee may insure the Plan against any loss caused by the Trustee or any of the Trustee's employees, officers, agents or delegates. The Trustee may also insure itself and any of these persons against liability for breach of trust. Except in the case of a paid Trustee, the premiums may be paid from Plan assets.

19.3   A Trustee carrying on a profession or business may charge for services rendered on a basis agreed with the Company. A firm or company in which a Trustee is interested or, in the case of an individual trustee, by which he is employed, may also charge for services rendered on this basis.

20.   COVENANT BY THE PARTICIPATING COMPANIES

The Participating Companies hereby jointly and severally covenant with the Trustee that they shall pay to the Trustee all sums which they are required to pay under the Rules and shall at all times comply with the Rules.

21.   ACCEPTANCE OF GIFTS

The Trustee may accept gifts of Shares and other assets which shall be held upon the trusts declared by sub-clauses 3.2.1 or 3.2.4, as the case may be.

22.   TRUSTEE'S LIEN

22.1   The Trustee's lien over the Trust Fund in respect of liabilities incurred by it in the performance of its duties (including the repayment of borrowed money and tax liabilities) shall be enforceable subject to the following restrictions:

22.1.1   the Trustee shall not be entitled to resort to Partnership Share Money for the satisfaction of any of its liabilities; and

22.1.2   the Trustee shall not be entitled to resort to Plan Shares for the satisfaction of its liabilities except to the extent that this is permitted by the Plan.

23.   AMENDMENTS TO THE PLAN

23.1   The Company may, with the Trustee's written consent, from time to time, amend the Deed and/or the Plan by resolution of the Board provided that:

23.1.1   no amendment which would adversely prejudice to a material extent the rights attaching to any Plan Shares awarded to or acquired by Participants may be made nor may any alteration be made giving to Participating Companies a beneficial interest in Plan Shares; and

23.1.2   if the Plan is a Schedule 2 SIP at the time of an amendment or addition, any amendment or addition to a 'key feature' (as defined in paragraph 81B(8) of the Schedule) of the Plan shall not have effect unless after such amendment or addition the Plan shall remain a Schedule 2 SIP. Any such amendment shall be notified to HM Revenue and Customs in accordance with paragraph 81B of the Schedule.

23.2 no amendment to the advantage of present or future Participants or employees relating to eligibility, Plan limits, the price payable for the acquisition of Shares by Participants, the basis of individual entitlement and the provisions affecting any variations of share capital shall be made without the prior approval of the Company in general meeting unless the amendment is made so that the Plan qualifies, or continues to qualify, as a Schedule 2 SIP, or to take account of the provisions of any proposed or existing legislation, law or other regulatory requirements, or to take advantage of any changes to the legislation, law or other regulatory requirements, or to obtain or maintain favourable taxation, exchange control or regulatory treatment of the Company, any Subsidiary or any Participant or to make minor amendments to benefit the administration of the Plan.

24. POWER TO ESTABLISH OVERSEAS PLANS

The Company may establish one or more further plans for the benefit of employees overseas based on this Plan but subject to such modifications as the Board may consider necessary or desirable to take account of overseas securities laws, exchange controls and tax legislation, provided that any awards made under any such further plans shall count against the limits on individual participation under the Plan and any shares issued under any such further plans shall count against any limits on the issue of new shares under the Plan. Any such further plan, and any shares awarded under such plan, shall not form part of the Plan for the purposes of the Schedule.

25. VOTING RIGHTS

25.1 If required to do so by the Company the Trustee, on receipt of reasonable notice from the Company of any relevant meeting and of the full details of the resolutions proposed, will invite Participants to direct the Trustee on the exercise of any voting rights attaching to Plan Shares held by the Trustee on their behalf. The Trustee will not be obliged to attend any particular meeting and may exercise the voting rights either personally or by proxy.

25.2 The Trustee will only be entitled to vote on a show of hands if all the directions received from Participants who have given directions in respect of a particular resolution are identical.

25.3 The Trustee will not be under any obligation to call for a poll. In the event of a poll, the Trustee will follow the directions of Participants.

25.4 The Trustee will not vote in respect of (i) Plan Shares where no directions have been received; or (ii) Unawarded Shares.

25.5 Where Shares held under the Plan are registered in the name of a nominee for the Trustee, the Trustee will arrange for the directions of Participants received by it to be carried out by the nominee.

26. TERMINATION OF THE PLAN

26.1 The Plan shall terminate:

26.1.1 in accordance with a Plan Termination Notice issued by the Company to the Trustee under paragraph 89 of the Schedule; or

26.1.2   if earlier, on the expiry of the Trust Period.

26.2   The Company shall immediately upon executing a Plan Termination Notice provide a copy of the notice to the Trustee and each individual who has Plan Shares or who has entered into a Partnership Share Agreement which was in force immediately before the Plan Termination Notice was issued.

26.3   Upon the issue of a Plan Termination Notice or upon the expiry of the Trust Period paragraph 90 of the Schedule shall have effect.

26.4   Any Shares or other assets which remain undisposed of after the requirements of paragraph 90 of the Schedule have been complied with shall be held by the Trustee upon trust to pay or apply them to or for the benefit of the Participating Companies as at the termination date in such proportion, having regard to their respective contributions, as the Trustee shall in its absolute discretion think appropriate.

27.   COUNTERPARTS

27.1   This Deed may be executed in two counterparts, each of which shall be deemed an original and which shall together constitute one and the same document.

27.2   If this Deed is executed in more than one counterpart, it shall have effect when:

27.2.1   each party has signed a counterpart of this Deed; and

27.2.2   each of the counterparts has been dated.

27.3   If this Deed is not executed in more than one counterpart, it shall have effect when each party has signed it and it has been dated.

28.   GOVERNING LAW

28.1   The invalidity or non-enforceability of any provision or Rule of this Deed or the Plan shall not affect the validity or enforceability of the remaining provisions and Rules of this Deed and the Plan which shall continue in full force and effect.

28.2   This Deed and the Plan shall be governed by and construed in accordance with English Law and the English courts shall have exclusive jurisdiction to determine any dispute which may arise out of, or in connection with, this Deed or the Plan.

IN WITNESS whereof this Deed has been executed by the Company and the Trustee and is intended to be and is hereby delivered on the day and year first before written

Rules of the [   ] Share Incentive Plan

1.   DEFINITIONS

1.1   In these Rules and in the Deed, the following words and expressions have the following meanings:

'Accumulation Period' means, in relation to Partnership Shares, the period (not exceeding 12 months) during which the Trustee accumulates a Qualifying Employee's Partnership Share Money before acquiring Partnership Shares or repaying it to the employee;

'Acquisition Date' means:

(a)   in relation to Partnership Shares, where there is no Accumulation Period, the date set by the Trustee in relation to the Award of Partnership Shares, being a date within 30 days after the last date on which the Partnership Share Money to be applied in acquiring the Shares was deducted;

(b)   in relation to Partnership Shares, where there is an Accumulation Period, the date set by the Trustee in relation to the Award of Partnership Shares, being a date within 30 days after the end of the Accumulation Period which applies in relation to the Award; and

(c)   in relation to Dividend Shares, the date set by the Trustee in relation to the acquisition of Dividend Shares, being a date within 30 days after the dividend is received by them;

'Associated Company' has the same meaning as in paragraph 94 of the Schedule;

'Award Date' means, in relation to Free Shares or Matching Shares, the date on which such Shares are awarded;

'Award' means:

(a)   in relation to Free Shares and Matching Shares, the appropriation of Free Shares and Matching Shares in accordance with the Plan; and

(b)   in relation to Partnership Shares, the acquisition of Partnership Shares on behalf of Qualifying Employees in accordance with the Plan;

'Board' means the board of directors of the Company, or a duly authorised committee thereof or, following a change of Control of the Company, shall be the board of directors or duly authorised committee as constituted immediately prior to such event;

'Capital Receipt' has the same meaning as in Section 502 of ITEPA 2003;

'Company' means [COMPANY] [Limited/plc] (registered in England and Wales under No [NUMBER]);

'Connected Company' means:

(a)   a company which controls or is controlled by the Company or which is controlled by a company which also controls the Company; or

(b)   a company which is a member of a consortium owning the Company or which is owned in part by the Company as a member of a consortium;

'Control' has the meaning given by Section 719 of ITEPA 2003;

'Dealing Day' means a day on which the Stock Exchange is open for the transaction of business;

'Deed' means the Trust Deed of the [*COMPANY NAME*] Share Incentive Plan;

'Dividend Shares' means Shares acquired on behalf of a Participant on the reinvestment of dividends under Rule 9 of the Plan and which are subject to the Plan;

'Employees' Share Scheme' has the meaning given by Section 1166 of the Companies Act 2006;

'Free Share Agreement' has the meaning given in Rule 6.1;

'**Free Shares**' means Shares awarded under Rule 6 of the Plan which are subject to the Plan;

'**Group Plan**' means the Plan as established by the Company and extending to its Subsidiaries which are Participating Companies;

'**Holding Period**' means:

(a)   in relation to Free Shares, the period specified by the Company as mentioned in Rule 6.16;

(b)   in relation to Matching Shares, the period specified by the Company as mentioned in Rule 8.5; and

(c)   in relation to Dividend Shares, the period of three years from the Acquisition Date;

'**Initial Market Value**' means the Market Value of a Share on an Award Date;

'**ITEPA 2003**' means the Income Tax (Earnings and Pensions) Act 2003;

'**Market Value**' means, in relation to a Share on any day:

(a)   if and so long as the Shares are admitted to the Official List of the UK Listing Authority and admitted to trading on the Stock Exchange either:

(i)   where all Shares comprising an Award are purchased in the market by the Trustee over five or fewer consecutive Dealing Days ending either on the date on which the Award is made or on the immediately preceding Dealing Day, the average of the prices achieved by the Trustee in the purchase of such Shares; or

(ii)   the average of the middle market quotations of a Share as derived from the Daily Official List of the Stock Exchange for the [five or fewer] immediately preceding Dealing Days; or

(b)   subject to (a) above, its market value as determined in accordance with the provisions of Part VIII of the Taxation of Chargeable Gains Act 1992 (but when Shares are subject to a Restriction, determined on the basis that no such Restriction applies) and agreed for the purposes of the Plan with the Shares and Assets Valuation division at HM Revenue and Customs on or before that day;

'**Matching Shares**' means Shares awarded under Rule 8 of the Plan and which are subject to the Plan;

'**NICs**' means National Insurance contributions;

'**Participant**' means an individual who has received under the Plan an Award of Free Shares, Matching Shares or Partnership Shares, or on whose behalf Dividend Shares have been acquired;

'**Participating Company**' means the Company and such of its Subsidiaries to which the Plan is expressed to extend as have executed deeds of adherence to the Plan under clause 17 of the Deed;

'**Partnership Shares**' means Shares awarded under Rule 7 of the Plan and which are subject to the Plan;

'**Partnership Share Agreement**' has the meaning given in Rule 7.1;

'**Partnership Share Money**' means money deducted from a Qualifying Employee's Salary pursuant to a Partnership Share Agreement and held by the Trustee to acquire Partnership Shares or to be returned to such a person;

'Performance Allowances' means the criteria for an Award of Free Shares where:

(a)   whether Shares are awarded; or

(b)   the number or value of Shares awarded,

is conditional on performance targets being met;

'Plan' means this [*COMPANY NAME*] Share Incentive Plan;

'Plan Shares' means:

(a)   Free Shares, Matching Shares or Partnership Shares awarded to Participants;

(b)   Dividend Shares acquired on behalf of Participants, and

(c)   shares in relation to which paragraph 87(2) (*company reconstructions: new shares*) of the Schedule applies,

that remain subject to the Plan;

'Plan Termination Notice' means a notice issued under paragraph 89 of the Schedule;

'Qualifying Company' means:

(a)   except in the case of a Group Plan:

    (i)   the Company; or

    (ii)   a company that when the individual was employed by it was an Associated Company of:

        (A)   the Company; or

        (B)   another company being a Qualifying Company; and

(b)   in the case of a Group Plan:

    (i)   a company that is a Participating Company at the end of the Qualifying Period;

    (ii)   a company that when the individual was employed by it was a Participating Company; or

    (iii)   a company that when the individual was employed by it was an Associated Company of:

        (A)   a company qualifying under (b)(i) or (b)(ii) above; or

        (B)   another company being a Qualifying Company;

'Qualifying Corporate Bond' has the same meaning as in Section 117 of the Taxation of Chargeable Gains Act 1992;

'Qualifying Employee' means an employee who must be invited to participate in an award in accordance with Rule 4.4 and any employee that the Company has invited in accordance with Rule 4.5;

'Qualifying Period' means:

(a)   in the case of Free Shares, such number of months (not exceeding 18) before the Award is made as the Board shall determine from time to time;

(b)   in the case of Partnership Shares and Matching Shares, where there is an Accumulation Period, such number of months (not exceeding six) before the start of the Accumulation Period as the Board shall determine from time to time; and

(c)   in the case of Partnership Shares and Matching Shares, where there is no Accumulation Period, such number of months (not exceeding 18) before the deduction of Partnership Share Money relating to the Award as the Board shall determine from time to time;

'**Relevant Employment**' means employment by the Company or any Associated Company;

'**Restriction**' has the same meaning as in paragraph 99(4) of the Schedule;

'**Rule**' means a Rule of this Plan;

'**Salary**' has the same meaning as in paragraph 43(4) of the Schedule;

'**Schedule**' means Schedule 2 to ITEPA 2003;

'**Schedule 2 SIP**' has the meaning in paragraph 1 of the Schedule;

'**Shares**' means ordinary shares in the capital of the Company which comply with the conditions set out in paragraph 25 of the Schedule;

'**Stock Exchange**' means the London Stock Exchange plc;

'**Subsidiary**' means any company which is for the time being under the Control of the Company;

'**Tax Year**' means a year beginning on 6 April and ending on the following 5 April;

'**Treasury Shares**' means Shares to which Sections 724 to 732 of the Companies Act 2006 apply;

'**Trustee**' means the trustees or trustee from time to time of the Plan;

'**Trust Fund**' means all assets transferred to the Trustee to be held on the terms of the Deed and assets from time to time representing such assets, including any accumulations of income;

'**Trust Period**' means the period of 124 years beginning with the date of the Deed;

'**UK Listing Authority**' means the Financial Conduct Authority as the competent authority for listing in the United Kingdom under Part VI of the Financial Services and Markets Act 2000; and

'**UK Resident Taxpayer**' means an individual whose earnings from the employment by reference to which the individual meets the employment requirement in paragraph 15 of the Schedule are (or would be if there were any) general earnings to which section 15 of ITEPA 2003 applies (*earnings for a year when employee resident in the UK*).

1.2   References to any Act, or Part, Chapter or section (including ITEPA 2003) shall include any statutory modification, amendment or re-enactment of that Act, for the time being in force.

1.3   Words of the feminine gender shall include the masculine and vice versa and words in the singular shall include the plural and vice versa unless, in either case, the context otherwise requires or it is otherwise stated.

1.4   References to writing or written form shall include any legible format capable of being reproduced on paper irrespective of the medium used.

2. PURPOSE OF THE PLAN

The purpose of the Plan is to enable employees of Participating Companies to acquire Shares in the Company which give them a continuing stake in the Company.

3. PLAN LIMITS

10 per cent limit: Employees' Share Scheme

3.1   The maximum number of Shares which may be allocated under the Plan on any day shall not, when added to the aggregate of the number of Shares which have been allocated in the previous 10 years under the Plan and under any other Employees' Share Scheme adopted by the Company which may be satisfied by the issue of Shares, exceed such number as represents 10 per cent of the ordinary share capital of the Company in issue immediately prior to that day.

3.2   References in this Rule 3 to the 'allocation' of Shares shall mean:

3.2.1   in the case of any option, conditional share award or other similar award pursuant to which Shares may be acquired:

(A)   the grant (whether by the Company, the Trustee or otherwise) of the option, conditional share award or other similar award to acquire Shares, pursuant to which Shares may be issued; and

(B)   in so far as not previously taken into account under (A) above from the date of grant, any subscription for Shares which are issued for the purpose of satisfying any option, conditional share award or other similar award to acquire Shares; and

3.2.2   in relation to other types of Employees' Share Scheme, the issue and allotment of Shares,

and references to 'allocated' shall be construed accordingly.

3.3   In determining the above limits no account shall be taken of:

3.3.1   any allocation (or part thereof) where the option, conditional share award or other similar award to acquire Shares was released, lapsed or otherwise became incapable of vesting;

3.3.2   any allocation (or part thereof) in respect of which the Board or the Trustee has determined shall be satisfied otherwise than by the issue of Shares; and

3.3.3   such number of additional Shares as would otherwise have been issued on the exercise of an option for monetary consideration (*the exercise price*) but in respect of which the exercise price is not paid, in substitution for the issue of such lesser number of shares as have a market value equal only to the gain which the optionholder would have made on exercise (*equity-settled SAR alternative*).

3.4   References to the issue and allotment of Shares shall include the transfer of Treasury Shares, but only until such time as the guidelines issued by institutional investor bodies cease to provide that they need to be included.

4. ELIGIBILITY OF INDIVIDUALS

4.1   Subject to Rule 4.4, individuals are eligible to participate in an Award only if:

4.1.1 they are employees of a Participating Company;

4.1.2 they have been employees of a Qualifying Company at all times during the appropriate Qualifying Period;

4.1.3 in the case of Free Shares, they are eligible to participate in the Award at the time it is made;

4.1.4 in the case of Partnership Shares or Matching Shares:

(A) if there is no Accumulation Period, they are eligible to participate in the Award at the time the Partnership Share Money relating to the Award is deducted; and

(B) if there is an Accumulation Period, they are eligible to participate in the Award at the time of the first deduction of Partnership Share Money relating to the Award; and

4.1.5 they do not fail to be eligible under Rule 4.2.

4.2 Individuals are not eligible to participate in an Award in any Tax Year if they are, at the same time, to receive an Award under another Schedule 2 SIP established by the Company or a Connected Company, or if they would have received such an Award but for their failure to meet a performance target (see Rule 6.6).

4.3 If individuals are eligible to participate in an Award in any Tax Year in which they have received an Award under another Schedule 2 SIP established by the Company or a Connected Company, the following limits will apply as if the Plan and other plan or plans were a single plan:

4.3.1 the maximum annual award of Free Shares specified in Rule 6.5; and

4.3.2 the maximum amount of Partnership Share Money deductions specified in Rules 7.2 and 7.3.

Employees who must be invited to participate in Awards

4.4 Individuals shall be eligible to receive an Award of Shares under the Plan if they meet the requirements in Rule 4.1 and are UK Resident Taxpayers. In this case they shall be invited to participate in any Awards of Free Shares, Partnership Shares or Matching Shares, and acquisitions of Dividend Shares, as are set out in the Plan.

Employees who may be invited to participate in Awards

4.5 The Company may also invite any employee who meets the requirements in Rule 4.1 but who is not a UK Resident Taxpayer to participate in any Award of Free Shares, Partnership Shares or Matching Shares, and acquisitions of Dividend Shares, as are set out in the Plan.

5.   PARTICIPATION ON SAME TERMS

5.1 Every Qualifying Employee shall be invited to participate in an Award on the same terms. All who do participate in an Award shall do so on the same terms.

5.2 The Company may make an Award of Free Shares to Qualifying Employees by reference to their remuneration, length of service or hours worked.

5.3 The Company may make an Award of Free Shares to Qualifying Employees by reference to their performance as set out in Rules 6.6 to 6.15.

6.   FREE SHARES

6.1   The Company may at any time invite every Qualifying Employee to enter into an agreement with the Company (a 'Free Share Agreement') upon the terms of Rules 6.16 to 6.21.

6.2   Qualifying Employees may be invited to enter into a Free Share Agreement either by written acceptance or, where the Qualifying Employees are given reasonable notice of the proposed award of free Shares, by not having notified the Company, by a date to be specified by the Company, that they do not wish to receive the Award of Free Shares.

6.3   The Trustee, acting with the prior consent of the Company, may from time to time award Free Shares.

6.4   The number of Free Shares to be awarded by the Trustee to each Qualifying Employee on an Award Date shall be determined by the Company in accordance with this Rule 6.

Maximum annual Award

6.5   The Initial Market Value of the Shares awarded to a Qualifying Employee in any Tax Year shall not exceed £3,600 or such other sum as determined from time to time under paragraph 35(1) (*maximum annual award*) of the Schedule.

Allocation of Free Shares by reference to performance

6.6   The Company may stipulate that the number of Free Shares (if any) to be awarded to each Qualifying Employee on a given Award Date shall be determined by reference to Performance Allowances.

6.7   If Performance Allowances are used, they shall apply to all Qualifying Employees as follows:

6.7.1   Performance Allowances shall be determined by reference to fair and objective measures (performance targets) such as business results or other such objective criteria as the Company shall determine over such period as the Company shall specify;

6.7.2   performance targets must be set for performance units of one or more employees, the targets being broadly comparable in terms of the likelihood of each performance unit meeting them; and

6.7.3   for the purposes of an Award of Free Shares an employee must not be a member of more than one performance unit.

6.8   Where the Company decides to use Performance Allowances it shall, as soon as reasonably practicable:

6.8.1   notify each employee participating in the Award of the performance targets and measures which, under the Plan, shall be used to determine the number or value of Free Shares awarded to him; and

6.8.2   notify all Qualifying Employees of the Company or, in the case of a Group Plan, of all Participating Companies, in general terms, of the performance targets and measures to be used to determine the number or value of Free Shares to be awarded to each Participant in the Award **PROVIDED THAT** the Company may exclude from the notice given in accordance with this Rule 6.8.2 any information the disclosure of which the Company reasonably considers would prejudice commercial confidentiality.

6.9 Any Performance Allowance in respect of an Award of Free Shares may only be altered if events happen which mean that the Company considers that the original Performance Allowance is no longer appropriate and that an altered Performance Allowance reflects a fairer measure of the performance required.

6.10 Where one or more Performance Allowances are to be altered under Rule 6.9 the alterations may only be effected to the extent that the Company reasonably considers that it will subsequently be no more difficult for a Participant to satisfy a Performance Allowance as so altered than it was for him to achieve the Performance Allowance in its original form.

6.11 Where one or more Performance Allowances are to be altered under Rule 6.9 the provisions of Rule 6.8 shall apply to the altered Performance Allowances in the same manner as it applied to the Performance Allowances in their original form.

6.12 Where a Participant moves between performance units during the performance period the Performance Allowances which apply in respect of Awards to members of those performance units shall apply to the Award to that Participant pro rata according to the time the Participant remained in each of those performance units during the performance period.

6.13 The Company shall determine the number of Free Shares (if any) to be awarded to each Qualifying Employee by reference to performance using Method 1 (Rule 6.14) or Method 2 (Rule 6.15). The same method shall be used for all Qualifying Employees for each Award.

Performance Allowances: Method 1

6.14 By this method:

6.14.1 at least 20 per cent of Free Shares awarded in any performance period shall be awarded without reference to performance;

6.14.2 the remaining Free Shares shall be awarded by reference to performance; and

6.14.3 the highest Award made to an individual by reference to performance in any period shall be no more than four times the highest Award to an individual without reference to performance.

If this method is used:

- the Free Shares awarded without reference to performance (Rule 6.14.1 above) shall be awarded on the same terms mentioned in Rule 5; and

- the Free Shares awarded by reference to performance (Rule 6.14.2 above) need not be allocated on the same terms mentioned in Rule 5.

Performance Allowances: Method 2

6.15 By this method:

6.15.1 some or all Free Shares shall be awarded by reference to performance;

6.15.2 the Award of Free Shares to Qualifying Employees who are members of the same performance unit shall be made on the same terms, as mentioned in Rule 5; and

6.15.3 Free Shares awarded for each performance unit shall be treated as separate Awards.

Holding Period for Free Shares

6.16 The Company shall, in relation to each Award Date, specify a Holding Period throughout which a Participant shall be bound to permit his Free Shares to remain in the hands of the Trustee and not to assign, charge or otherwise dispose of his beneficial interest in the Free Shares.

6.17 The Holding Period shall, in relation to each Award, be a specified period of not less than three years or more than five years, beginning with the Award Date and shall be the same for all Participants who receive an Award at the same time. The Holding Period shall not be increased in respect of Free Shares already awarded under the Plan.

6.18 A Participant may, during the Holding Period, direct the Trustee:

6.18.1 to accept an offer for any of his Free Shares if the acceptance or agreement shall result in a new holding being equated with those shares for the purposes of capital gains tax;

6.18.2 to accept an offer of a Qualifying Corporate Bond (whether alone or with other assets or cash or both) for his Free Shares if the offer forms part of such a general offer as is mentioned in Rule 6.18.3;

6.18.3 to accept an offer of cash, with or without other assets, for his Free Shares if the offer forms part of a general offer which is made to holders of shares of the same class as their shares, or to holders of shares in the same company and which is made in the first instance on a condition such that if it is satisfied the person making the offer shall have control of that company, within the meaning of Sections 450 and 451 of the Corporation Tax Act 2010;

6.18.4 to agree to a transaction affecting his Free Shares or such of them as are of a particular class, if the transaction would be entered into pursuant to a compromise, arrangement or scheme applicable to or affecting:

(A) all of the ordinary share capital of the Company or, as the case may be, all the shares of the class in question; or

(B) all the shares, or all the shares of the class in question, which are held by a class of shareholders identified otherwise than by reference to their employment or their participation in a Schedule 2 SIP; or

6.18.5 where a right arises under Section 983 of the Companies Act 2006 to require an offeror to acquire their Free Shares, or such of them as are of a particular class to exercise that right.

6.19 The Participant's obligations with respect to the Holding Period:

6.19.1 come to an end if, during the Holding Period, he ceases to be in Relevant Employment; and

6.19.2 are subject to:

(A) paragraph 79 (*meeting PAYE obligations*) of the Schedule; and

(B) paragraph 90(5) (*termination of plan: early removal of shares with participant's consent*) of the Schedule.

Restrictions attaching to Free Shares

6.20   The Company may, in relation to each Award of Free Shares, specify any Restrictions which attach to such Free Shares (which may include forfeiture provisions).

Ceasing to be in Relevant Employment

6.21   Subject to Rule 6.20 above and Clause 11.6 of the Deed (which permits the Trustee to dispose of the Participant's Plan Shares in order to meet any PAYE liability), where a Participant ceases to be in Relevant Employment, all of that Participant's Free Shares shall be transferred to him as soon as practicable following such cessation of employment.

7.   PARTNERSHIP SHARES

7.1   The Company may at any time invite every Qualifying Employee to enter into an agreement with the Company (a 'Partnership Share Agreement') upon terms which conform to paragraph 44 (*partnership share agreements*) of the Schedule.

Maximum amount of deductions

7.2   The amount of Partnership Share Money deducted from an employee's Salary shall not exceed £1,800 (or such other sum as determined from time to time under paragraph 46(1) (*maximum amount of deductions*) of the Schedule) in any Tax Year.

7.3   The amount of Partnership Share Money deducted from an employee's Salary over any Tax Year shall not exceed 10 per cent (or such other percentage as determined from time to time under paragraph 46(2) of the Schedule (*maximum amount of deductions*) of the total of the payments of Salary made to such employee in that Tax Year.

7.4   Any amount deducted in excess of that allowed by Rule 7.2 or 7.3 shall be paid over to the employee, subject to both deduction of income tax under PAYE and NICs, as soon as practicable.

7.5   The Company may specify that the amount of Partnership Share Money deducted from an employee's Salary shall be lower than the limit specified in Rule 7.2 or 7.3 by:

7.5.1   substituting a percentage lower than that specified in Rule 7.3; or

7.5.2   excluding overtime and/or other variable pay from the calculation of an employee's Salary for the purposes of Rule 7.3.

Minimum amount of deductions

7.6   The minimum amount to be deducted under the Partnership Share Agreement on any occasion shall be the same in relation to all Partnership Share Agreements entered into in response to invitations issued on the same occasion. It shall not be greater than £10 (or such other sum as determined from time to time under paragraph 47(2) (*minimum amount of deductions*) of the Schedule).

Notice of possible effect of deductions on benefit entitlement

7.7   Every Partnership Share Agreement shall contain a notice under paragraph 48 of the Schedule.

Restriction imposed on number of Shares awarded

7.8   The Company may specify the maximum number of Shares to be included in an Award of Partnership Shares.

7.9   The Partnership Share Agreement shall contain an undertaking by the Company to notify each Qualifying Employee of any restriction on the number of Shares to be included in an Award.

7.10   The notification in Rule 7.9 above shall be given:

7.10.1 if there is no Accumulation Period, before the deduction of the Partnership Share Money relating to the Award; and

7.10.2 if there is an Accumulation Period, before the beginning of the Accumulation Period relating to the Award.

Awards with no Accumulation Period

7.11   The Trustee shall acquire Shares on behalf of the Qualifying Employee using the Partnership Share Money. They shall acquire the Shares on the Acquisition Date. The number of Shares awarded to each employee shall be determined in accordance with the Market Value of the Shares on that date.

Awards with Accumulation Period

7.12   If there is an Accumulation Period in respect of Awards made on any occasion, the Trustee shall acquire Shares on behalf of the Qualifying Employee, on the Acquisition Date, using the Partnership Share Money.

7.13   The number of Shares acquired on behalf of each Participant shall be determined by reference to one of:

7.13.1 the lower of:

(A)   the Market Value of the Shares at the beginning of the Accumulation Period but subject to any adjustment pursuant to Rule 7.14 below; and

(B)   the Market Value of the Shares on the Acquisition Date.

7.13.2 the Market Value of the Shares at the beginning of the Accumulation Period but subject to any adjustment pursuant to Rule 7.14 below; or

7.13.3 the Market Value of the Shares on the Acquisition Date,

And the Partnership Share Agreement shall specify which of Rules 7.13.1, 7.13.2. and 7.13.3 shall apply.

7.14   If a transaction occurs during an Accumulation Period which

7.14.1 results in a new holding of Shares being equated for the purposes of capital gains tax with any of the Shares to be acquired under the Partnership Share Agreement, the employee may agree that the Partnership Share Agreement shall have effect after the time of that transaction as if it were an agreement for the purchase of shares comprised in the new holding; and/or

7.14.2 results in a variation of share capital of the Company, then the Company may adjust the price to be used as the Market Value of the Shares at the beginning of the Accumulation Period in such manner as it may determine to take account of the variation of share capital, but subject to prior agreement of HM Revenue & Customs.

7.15 If a Qualifying Employee ceases to be in Relevant Employment during the Accumulation Period, any Partnership Share Money relating to an Award deducted during the Accumulation Period shall be repaid to him as soon as practicable, subject to deduction of income tax under PAYE and NICs.

7.16 The Board may determine that any subsisting Accumulation Period shall terminate upon the occurrence of:

7.16.1 any change of Control of the Company;

7.16.2 any reconstruction sanctioned by the Court under Part 26 of the Companies Act 2006;

7.16.3 the passing of a resolution for the voluntary winding-up of the Company; or

7.16.4 an event following which the Shares cease to comply with the conditions set out in paragraph 25 (*types of share that may be used*) of the Schedule.

Surplus Partnership Share Money

7.17 Any surplus Partnership Share Money remaining after the acquisition of Shares by the Trustee:

7.17.1 may, with the agreement of the Participant, be carried forward to the next Accumulation Period or, where there is no Accumulation Period, the next deduction; and

7.17.2 in any other case, shall be paid over to the Participant, subject to both deduction of income tax under PAYE and NICs, as soon as practicable,

save that where a Participant ceases to be in Relevant Employment, any Partnership Share Money held by the Trustee on behalf of the Participant shall be repaid to him as soon as practicable, subject to deduction of income tax under PAYE and NICs.

Scaling down

7.18 If the Company receives applications for Partnership Shares exceeding the Award maximum determined in accordance with Rule 7.8 then the following steps shall be taken in sequence until the excess is eliminated:

Step 1. the excess of the monthly deduction chosen by each applicant over the amount determined in accordance with Rule 7.6 shall be reduced pro rata;

Step 2. all monthly deductions shall be reduced to the amount determined in accordance with Rule 7.6; and

Step 3. applications shall be selected by lot, each based on a monthly deduction of the amount determined in accordance with Rule 7.6.

Each application shall be deemed to have been modified or withdrawn in accordance with the foregoing provisions, and each employee who has applied for Partnership Shares shall be notified of the change.

Variation of Deductions

7.19 The Participant may, with the prior agreement of the Company, vary the amount of the deductions and/or the interval at which the deductions are made.

Stopping and Restarting Deductions

7.20   The Participant may, at any time, give notice in writing to the Company to stop deductions in pursuance of a Partnership Share Agreement.

7.21   Subject to Rule 7.22, a Participant who has stopped deductions pursuant to Rule 7.20 may subsequently give notice in writing to the Company to re-start deductions in pursuance of the Partnership Share Agreement, but may not make up deductions which have been missed.

7.22   If there is an Accumulation Period in respect of an Award made on any occasion, the Participant may not re-start deductions more than once in any Accumulation Period.

7.23   Unless a later date is specified in the relevant notice:

7.23.1   the Company must, within 30 days of receiving a notice under Rule 7.20, ensure that no further deductions are made by it under the Partnership Share Agreement;

7.23.2   the Company must, on receiving a notice under Rule 7.21, re-start deductions under the Partnership Share Agreement not later than the date of the first deduction due under the Partnership Share Agreement more than 30 days after receipt of the notice under Rule 7.21.

Withdrawal from Partnership Share Agreement

7.24   An employee may withdraw from a Partnership Share Agreement at any time by notice in writing to the Company. Unless a later date is specified in the notice, such a notice shall take effect 30 days after the Company receives it. Any Partnership Share Money then held on behalf of an employee shall be paid over to that employee as soon as practicable. This payment shall be subject to income tax under PAYE and NICs.

Repayment of Partnership Share Money on the Plan ceasing to be a Schedule 2 SIP or Termination

7.25   Where the Plan is no longer a Schedule 2 SIP by virtue of paragraph 81H or paragraph 81I of the Schedule or a Plan Termination Notice is issued in respect of the Plan, any Partnership Share Money held on behalf of employees shall be repaid to them as soon as practicable after the relevant day (within the meaning of paragraph 56(2A) or (2B) of the Schedule) or after the Plan Termination Notice is notified to the Trustee, subject to deduction of income tax under PAYE and NICs.

Restrictions attaching to Partnership Shares

7.26   Subject to Rule 7.27, the Company may in relation to each Award of Partnership Shares specify any Restrictions which attach to such Shares.

7.27   Partnership Shares shall not be subject to any provision under which they may be forfeit.

7.28   Notwithstanding the provisions of Rule 7.27, Partnership Shares may be subject to a provision requiring such Partnership Shares to be offered for sale provided that the consideration at which the Partnership Shares may be required to be offered for sale must be at least equal to:

7.28.1   the amount of the Partnership Share Money applied in acquiring the Partnership Shares on behalf of the Participant; or

7.28.2 if lower, the Market Value of the Partnership Shares at the time they are offered for sale.

Ceasing to be in Relevant Employment

7.29 Subject to Rules 7.26 and 7.28 above and Clause 11.6 of the Deed (which permits the Trustee to dispose of the Participant's Plan Shares in order to meet any PAYE liability), where a Participant ceases to be in Relevant Employment, all of that Participant's Partnership Shares shall be transferred to him as soon as practicable following such cessation of employment.

Withdrawal of Partnership Shares

7.30 A Participant shall be entitled to withdraw from the Plan any Partnership Shares which have been awarded to him, at any time following the Acquisition Date.

8.   MATCHING SHARES

8.1 If the Company determines that Awards of Matching Shares are to be made, the Partnership Share Agreement shall set out the basis on which a Participant is entitled to Matching Shares in accordance with this Part of the Rules.

General requirements for Matching Shares

8.2 Matching Shares shall:

8.2.1 be Shares of the same class and carrying the same rights as the Partnership Shares to which they relate;

8.2.2 subject to Rule 8.4, be awarded on the same day as the Partnership Shares to which they relate are acquired on behalf of the Participant; and

8.2.3 in respect of an Award, be awarded to all Participants on exactly the same basis.

Ratio of Matching Shares to Partnership Shares

8.3 The Partnership Share Agreement shall specify the ratio of Matching Shares to Partnership Shares for the time being offered by the Company and that ratio shall not exceed 2:1 (or such other ratio determined from time to time under paragraph 60(2) (*ratio of matching shares to partnership shares*) of the Schedule). The Company may vary the ratio before Partnership Shares are acquired. Employees shall be notified of the terms of any such variation before the Partnership Shares are awarded under the Partnership Share Agreement.

8.4 If the Partnership Shares on that day are not sufficient to produce a Matching Share, the match shall be made when sufficient Partnership Shares have been acquired to allow at least one Matching Share to be appropriated.

Holding Period for Matching Shares

8.5 The Company shall, in relation to each Award Date, specify a Holding Period throughout which a Participant shall be bound to permit his Matching Shares to remain in the hands of the Trustee and not to assign, charge or otherwise dispose of his beneficial interest in the Matching Shares.

8.6 The Holding Period shall, in relation to each Award, be a specified period of not less than three years nor more than five years, beginning with the Award Date and shall be the same for all Participants who receive an Award at the same time. The Holding Period shall not be increased in respect of Matching Shares awarded under the Plan.

8.7   A Participant may, during the Holding Period, direct the Trustee:

8.7.1   to accept an offer for any of his Matching Shares if the acceptance or agreement shall result in a new holding being equated with those original Shares for the purposes of capital gains tax;

8.7.2   to accept an offer of a Qualifying Corporate Bond (whether alone or with other assets or cash or both) for his Matching Shares if the offer forms part of such a general offer as is mentioned in Rule 8.7.3;

8.7.3   to accept an offer of cash, with or without other assets, for his Matching Shares if the offer forms part of a general offer which is made to holders of shares of the same class as their Shares or to the holders of shares in the same company, and which is made in the first instance on a condition such that if it is satisfied the person making the offer shall have control of that company, within the meaning of Sections 450 and 451 of the Corporation Tax Act 2010; or

8.7.4   to agree to a transaction affecting his Matching Shares or such of them as are of a particular class, if the transaction would be entered into pursuant to a compromise, arrangement or scheme applicable to or affecting:

(A)   all of the ordinary share capital of the Company or, as the case may be, all the shares of the class in question; or

(B)   all the shares, or all the shares of the class in question, which are held by a class of shareholders identified otherwise than by reference to their employment or their participation in a Schedule 2 SIP; or

8.7.5   where a right arises under Section 983 of of the Companies Act 2006 to require an offeror to acquire his Matching Shares, or such of them as are of a particular class, to exercise that right.

8.8   The Participant's obligations with respect to the Holding Period:

8.8.1   come to an end if, during the Holding Period, he ceases to be in Relevant Employment; and

8.8.2   are subject to:

(A)   paragraph 79 (*meeting PAYE obligations*) of the Schedule; and

(B)   paragraph 90(5) (*termination of plan: early removal of shares with participant's consent*) of the Schedule.

Restrictions attaching to Matching Shares

8.9   The Company may, in relation to each Award of Matching Shares, specify any Restrictions which attach to such Matching Shares (which may include forfeiture provisions).

Ceasing to be in Relevant Employment

8.10   Subject to Rule 8.9 above and Clause 11.6 of the Deed (which permits the Trustee to dispose of the Participant's Plan Shares in order to meet any PAYE liability), where a Participant ceases to be in Relevant Employment, all that Participant's Matching Shares shall be transferred to him as soon as practicable following such cessation of employment.

9.   DIVIDEND SHARES

Reinvestment of cash dividends

9.1   The Free Share Agreement or Partnership Share Agreement, as appropriate, shall set out the rights and obligations of Participants receiving Dividend Shares under the Plan.

9.2   The Company may direct that some or all any cash dividend in respect of Plan Shares held on behalf of Participants may be applied in acquiring further Plan Shares on their behalf.

9.3   The Company's direction shall specify the amount of any cash dividend that shall be reinvested or how such amount shall be determined (the amount so specified or any amount determined in accordance with such direction being the "**Specified Amount**").

9.4   Dividend Shares shall be Shares of the same class and carrying the same rights as the Shares in respect of which the dividend is paid.

9.5   The Company may decide to:

9.5.1   apply the Specified Amount of all Participants' dividends to acquire Dividend Shares;

9.5.2   to pay all dividends in cash to Participants; or

9.5.3   to offer Participants the choice of either Rule 9.5.1 or 9.5.2 above.

9.6   The Company may modify or revoke any direction for reinvestment of cash dividends.

9.7   In exercising their powers in relation to the acquisition of Dividend Shares the Trustee must treat Participants fairly and equally.

9.8   Any amount of a dividend received in excess of the Specified Amount shall be paid to the Participant as soon as practicable.

9.9   The Trustee shall apply the Specified Amount of the cash dividend to acquire Shares on behalf of the Participant on the Acquisition Date. The number of Dividend Shares acquired on behalf of each Participant shall be determined by the Market Value of the Shares on the Acquisition Date.

Certain amounts not reinvested to be carried forward

9.10   Any amount of the Specified Amount of a dividend that is not reinvested because it is insufficient to acquire a Share may be retained by the Trustee and carried forward to be added to the amount of the next cash dividend to be reinvested.

9.11   If:

9.11.1   the Participant ceases to be in Relevant Employment; or

9.11.2   a Plan Termination Notice is issued,

any amount retained under Rule 9.10 that has not been reinvested shall be repaid to the Participant as soon as practicable. On the making of such a payment, the Participant shall be provided with the information specified in paragraph 80 (*repayment of excess cash dividend*) of the Schedule.

Holding Period for Dividend Shares

9.12   A Holding Period shall apply in relation to Dividend Shares throughout which a Participant shall be bound to permit his Dividend Shares to remain in the hands of the Trustee and not to assign, charge or otherwise dispose of his beneficial interest in the Dividend Shares.

9.13 The Holding Period in relation to Dividend Shares shall be a period of 3 years beginning with the Acquisition Date.

9.14 A Participant may, during the Holding Period, direct the Trustee:

9.14.1 to accept an offer for any of his Dividend Shares if the acceptance or agreement shall result in a new holding being equated with those shares for the purposes of capital gains tax;

9.14.2 to accept an offer of a Qualifying Corporate Bond (whether alone or with other assets or cash or both) for his Dividend Shares if the offer forms part of such a general offer as is mentioned in Rule 9.14.3;

9.14.3 to accept an offer of cash, with or without other assets, for their Dividend Shares if the offer forms part of a general offer which is made to holders of shares of the same class as their shares or to holders of shares in the same company, and which is made in the first instance on a condition such that if it is satisfied the person making the offer shall have control of that company, within the meaning of Sections 450 and 451 of the Corporation Tax Act 2010;

9.14.4 to agree to a transaction affecting his Dividend Shares or such of them as are of a particular class, if the transaction would be entered into pursuant to a compromise, arrangement or scheme applicable to or affecting:

(A) all of the ordinary share capital of the Company or, as the case may be, all the shares of the class in question; or

(B) all the shares, or all the shares of the class in question, which are held by a class of shareholders identified otherwise than by reference to their employment or their participation in a Schedule 2 SIP;

9.14.5 where a right arises under Section 983 of the Companies Act 2006 to require an offeror to acquire his Dividend Shares, or such of them as are of a particular class, to exercise that right.

9.15 The Participant's obligations with respect to the Holding Period:

9.15.1 come to an end if, during the Holding Period, he ceases to be in Relevant Employment; and

9.15.2 are subject to:

(A) paragraph 79 (meeting PAYE obligations) of the Schedule; and

(B) paragraph 90(5) (termination of plan: early removal of shares with participant's consent) of the Schedule.

Restrictions attaching to Dividend Shares

9.16 Subject to Rule 9.17, the Company may in relation to Dividend Shares specify any Restrictions which attach to the Dividend Shares.

9.17 Dividend Shares shall not be subject to any provision under which they may be forfeit.

9.18 Notwithstanding the provisions of Rule 9.17, Dividend Shares may be subject to a provision requiring such Dividend Shares to be offered for sale provided that the consideration at which the Dividend Shares may be required to be offered for sale must be at least equal to:

9.18.1 the amount of the cash dividend in respect of the Plan Shares applied in acquiring the Dividend Shares on behalf of the Participant; or

9.18.2 if lower, the Market Value of the Dividend Shares at the time they are offered for sale.

Ceasing to be in Relevant Employment

9.19 Subject to Rules 9.16 and 9.18, where a Participant ceases to be in Relevant Employment, all of that Participant's Dividend Shares shall be transferred to him as soon as practicable following such cessation of employment.

9.20 Where a Participant is charged to tax in the event of his Dividend Shares ceasing to be subject to the Plan, he shall be provided with the information specified in paragraph 80(4) (*charge on dividend shares ceasing to be subject to plan*) of the Schedule.

10. COMPANY RECONSTRUCTIONS

10.1 The following provisions of this Rule apply if there occurs in relation to any of a Participant's Plan Shares (referred to in this Rule as the **'Original Holding'**):

10.1.1 a transaction which results in a new holding (referred to in this Rule as the **'New Holding'**) being equated with the Original Holding for the purposes of capital gains tax; or

10.1.2 a transaction which would have that result but for the fact that what would be the new holding consists of or includes a Qualifying Corporate Bond.

10.2 If an issue of shares of any of the following description (in respect of which a charge to income tax arises) is made as part of a company reconstruction, those shares shall be treated for the purposes of this Rule as not forming part of the New Holding:

10.2.1 redeemable shares or securities issued as mentioned in paragraph C or D in Section 1000(1) of the Corporation Tax Act 2010;

10.2.2 share capital issued in circumstances such that Section 1022(3) of the Corporation Tax Act 2010 applies; or

10.2.3 share capital to which Section 410 of the Income Tax (Trading and Other Income) Act 2005 applies that is issued in a case where sub-section (2) or (3) of that section applies.

10.3 In this Rule 10:

10.3.1 **'Corresponding Shares'** in relation to any New Shares, means the Shares in respect of which the New Shares are issued or which the New Shares otherwise represent; and

10.3.2 **'New Shares'** means shares comprised in the New Holding which were issued in respect of, or otherwise represent, shares comprised in the Original Holding.

10.4 Subject to the following provisions of this Rule 10, references in this Plan to a Participant's Plan Shares shall be respectively construed, after the time of the company reconstruction, as being or, as the case may be, as including references to any New Shares.

10.5   For the purposes of the Plan:

10.5.1   a company reconstruction shall be treated as not involving a disposal of Shares comprised in the Original Holding; and

10.5.2   the date on which any New Shares are to be treated as having been appropriated to, or acquired on behalf of, the Participant shall be that on which Corresponding Shares were so appropriated or acquired.

10.6   In the context of a New Holding, any reference in this Rule to shares includes securities and rights of any description which form part of the New Holding for the purposes of Chapter II of Part IV of the Taxation of Chargeable Gains Act 1992.

11.   RIGHTS ISSUES

11.1   Any shares or securities allotted under clause 12 of the Deed shall be treated as Plan Shares identical to the Shares in respect of which the rights were conferred. They shall be treated as if they were awarded to or acquired on behalf of the Participant under the Plan in the same way and at the same time as those Shares.

11.2   Rule 11.1 does not apply:

11.2.1   to shares and securities allotted as the result of taking up a rights issue where the funds to exercise those rights were obtained otherwise than by virtue of the Trustee disposing of rights in accordance with this Rule 11; or

11.2.2   where the rights to a share issue attributed to Plan Shares are different from the rights attributed to other ordinary shares of the Company.

12.   GENERAL

12.1   The rights and obligations of any individual under the terms of his office or employment with the Company, any past or present Participating Company, Subsidiary, or Associated Company shall not be affected by his participation in the Plan and the Plan shall not form part of any contract of employment between the individual and any such company.

12.2   An individual who participates in the Plan shall waive all and any rights to compensation or damages in consequence of the termination of his office or employment with any such company mentioned in Rule 12.1 for any reason whatsoever, whether lawfully or otherwise, insofar as those rights arise or may arise from his ceasing to have rights under the Plan as a result of such termination, or from the loss or diminution in value of such rights or entitlements, including by reason of the operation of the terms of the Plan, any determination by the Board pursuant to a discretion contained in the Plan or the provisions of any statute or law relating to taxation.

12.3   Benefits under the Plan shall not form part of a Participant's remuneration for any purpose, except as required by law, and shall not be pensionable.

12.4   By participating in the Plan, the Participant consents to the collection, processing, transmission and storage by the Company, in any form whatsoever, of any data of a professional or personal nature which is necessary for the purposes of introducing and administering the Plan. The Company may share such information with any Participating Company or Associated Company, the Trustee, its registrars, brokers, other third party administrator or any person who obtains Control of the Company or acquires the company, undertaking or part-undertaking which employs the Participant, whether within or outside of the European Economic Area.

12.5 If as a result of an error or omission Free Shares, Partnership Shares, Matching Shares or Dividend Shares are not awarded to a Participant in accordance with the Plan, the applicable Trustee may, but without any obligation to do so, do all such acts or things as may be necessary to rectify the error or omission

Chapter 12

Savings-Related Share Option Schemes

INTRODUCTION

12.1 Under an approved savings-related share option scheme, 'Save-As-You-Earn' (SAYE) or 'sharesave' scheme, employees enter into a SAYE savings contract (referred to in the relevant legislation as 'savings arrangements') to save a fixed amount each month over three or five years. An option is granted at the outset over the maximum number of shares which may be acquired with the total savings and the bonus which is payable at the maturity of the savings contract. A tax-advantaged savings-related share option scheme has three features which it is generally thought makes it attractive. First, the options may be granted at up to a 20 per cent discount to the market value at the time of grant. Second, any gains on the exercise of the option will normally be free of income tax. Third, the bonuses (if any) payable under the SAYE savings contract are also tax-free.

12.2 Although the legislation was introduced with effect from 1 July 1981 under Finance Act (FA) 1980, it is substantially based on the previous approved savings-related share option scheme introduced in FA 1972 and repealed by FA 1974.

12.3 The latest HMRC figures show that there are approximately 940 live schemes in operation, with grants to over 1.7 million employees over a three-year period. On the assumption that the average scheme covers some seven subsidiaries, it would appear that there are about 6,500 companies currently covered by savings-related share option schemes. Certainly, a high proportion of the larger listed companies operate such schemes with only a few notable exceptions.

ELIGIBILITY CRITERIA

Legislative requirements

12.4 The scheme is specifically designed to encourage wide employee participation. Income Tax (Earnings and Pensions) Act 2003 (ITEPA 2003), Sch 3, para 6 provides that eligibility must be extended to every person who:

(a)   is an employee or a full-time director of the company which has established the scheme, or in the case of a group scheme, of a participating company;

(b)   has been such at all times during a qualifying period of not more than five years prior to the date of grant; and

(c)   is chargeable to income tax as UK resident in respect of his earnings.

12.5   A person will only be eligible to apply for an option if he is a director or employee of a participating company on the date of grant. If he leaves employment before the date of grant, then any application will become invalid. Although all eligible employees must receive invitations to participate, HMRC accepts that, as a practical matter, employees on notice of termination of their employment need not receive such an invitation.

Discretionary participation

12.6   ITEPA 2003, Sch 3, para 6(2) provides that whilst certain employees must be eligible to participate in any offers under the scheme, the scheme may extend participation to other directors and employees.

12.7   Generally speaking, companies usually extend their savings-related share option scheme to all employees who are in employment on a qualifying date shortly before the invitation of applications is sent out.

Overseas employees

12.8   In principle, there is nothing under ITEPA 2003, Sch 3 which excludes participation by employees outside the scope of UK tax on earnings, ie overseas employees.

ABI Guidelines

12.9   The ABI has not published guidelines relating to eligibility for a savings-related share option scheme but accepts participation by all employees.

12.10   ITEPA 2003, Sch 3 does not exclude participation by non-executive or part-time directors. However, the ABI's view is that non-executive directors should not participate in employees' share schemes and this view has prevailed at least amongst listed companies.

TIMING

12.11   There is nothing in the legislation which requires applications to be invited and options granted at any particular time. Generally, in accordance with ABI Guidelines, the schemes of listed companies provide for the grant of options in a 'window' following the announcement of results (see **3.28** above) or at other times there are exceptional circumstances which justify the grant of options at that time. Private companies usually provide for options to be granted at any time.

12.12   Schemes will generally provide for eligible employees to be invited to apply for the grant of options during the period of four weeks following establishment of the scheme, after each announcement of the annual or half-yearly results of the company or where changes to the approved savings contract are introduced. These periods for the invitation are merely indicative as there is nothing in the SAYE legislation which requires options to be granted at any particular time. Schemes will generally also provide that no options should be invited later than the 10th anniversary of the date of adoption of the scheme although, again, there is nothing in the SAYE legislation which restricts the life of a scheme to ten years.

ABI Guidelines

12.13   The provisions referred to above follow the ABI Guidelines, which provide for options to be granted within 42 days following the date of any announcement of results of the company, with no grant being made later than ten years after the establishment of the scheme.

Model Code under the Listing Rules

12.14   The UKLA Model Code for Dealings in securities of listed companies generally restricts the grant of options to persons discharging managerial responsibilities (PDMRs) during the period of 60 days prior to the preliminary announcement of annual results by a listed company, or during the shorter specified period in relation to the announcement of other periodic results. These restrictions do not apply, however, where options are granted under an SAYE scheme which is offered on similar terms to all or most employees of the participating companies (paragraph 2(i)).

PROCEDURE

12.15   The maximum amount which an optionholder may save under his savings contract each month is £500 (increased from £250 from 6 April 2014) including any amount he saves each month under any other corporate savings-related share option scheme (ITEPA 2003, Sch 3, para 25(3)(a)). A scheme may not provide for a minimum monthly savings amount higher than £10 per month (ITEPA 2003, Sch 3, para 25(3)(b)). The minimum monthly contribution under a savings contract is £5 per month.

12.16   HMRC requires that invitations must state the date by which any applications are to be made, the price per share and the maximum amount an applicant may save each month.

12.17   Invitations to apply for an option must be accompanied by a proposal for a savings contract which provides for the applicant to state the monthly savings contribution he wishes to make and (if given the opportunity) whether his option is to be granted on the basis of a three- or five-year bonus. Seven-year bonuses (i.e. five-year savings contracts with an additional two-year holding period) were phased out from 23 July 2013.

12.18   Under the form of application prescribed by HM Treasury, an optionholder is required to declare that the aggregate amount he is saving under all corporate savings-related share option schemes is not more than the maximum permitted under ITEPA 2003, Sch 3, para 25(3)(a), ie £500 a month. The Treasury's prescribed form of application also requires an applicant to declare that he or she is eligible to participate in the scheme and is at least 16 years of age. An employee under 18 years of age only has legal capacity to enter into contracts for 'necessaries' and therefore cannot be bound by the savings contract. Consequently, minors under 18 years of age cannot be bound by any corporate SAYE savings contract.

12.19   There is no obligation to supply applicants with a copy of the scheme rules, but companies which establish a scheme will normally prepare a guide for employees and this will be given to employees at the time of invitation.

Choice of three- or five-year options

12.20   ITEPA 2003, Sch 3, para 30 links the normal exercise date, or maturity, on any savings-related share option to the date a bonus is payable under the related savings contract. Under the current Building Society and Bank SAYE prospectuses (28 July 2014) bonuses are due at the end of a three- or five-year savings contract (although the current bonus rates only provide for a bonus under the five-year savings contract, with the three-year bonus currently being nil).

A company can operate an SAYE scheme by offering employees any of the following:

- a choice of a three- or five-;
- a choice of a three- and/or five-year option;
- a five-year option only; or
- a three-year option only.

12.21   The legislation also allows options to be granted on the basis that only the repayment of savings (ie not the bonus or interest) may be applied in the exercise of the option. However, there are very few companies which would consider offering options on this basis as most employees would expect to be able to use the full amount received in acquiring shares. Given the current bonus rates, however, this issue is of little relevance.

12.22   There is nothing to prevent an optionholder on any single occasion taking out two options, one under a three-year contract and one under a five-year contract. Indeed it may be prudent to do so if the optionholder is not sure he will be able to keep up the full amount of the payments. However, HMRC do not permit an SAYE scheme to provide for the optionholder to be granted parallel options of different periods over the same shares (although there is nothing objectionable to a single option linked to two or more savings contracts of different periods).

12.23   Most schemes are drafted on the basis of maximum flexibility so that the directors can determine the bonus or bonuses to be taken.

Weekly paid employees

12.24   Application forms may need to take account of whether employees are weekly or four-weekly paid. Since the savings contract is based on monthly contributions, the contributions of weekly (or four-weekly) paid employees may be deducted from their pay in consecutive periods and paid over to the savings authority and held in a 'feeder' account until the appropriate monthly amount is credited in the applicable month under the savings account.

Number of shares

12.25   Since the fundamental principle of any savings-related share option scheme is that the employee enters into a contract under which he agrees to save a fixed amount of his own choice each month, offers under the scheme are not expressed in terms of the number of shares for which an employee may apply, but in terms of the monthly amount he wishes to save. Application forms usually contain a table showing the total amount of savings and bonus at the maturity of the savings contract; it is rare for this to be shown in terms of the number of shares which will be available at the option price. An employee will, of course, know the option price and he can always calculate the number of shares if this is of concern to him.

12.26   Options under savings-related share option schemes are granted in consideration of the agreement of the optionholder entering into the savings contract with the savings body. It is not necessary for the optionholder to make any payment as consideration for the grant.

Period allowed for accepting invitations

12.27   HMRC generally require that optionholders must have a minimum of 14 days following the issue of invitations within which to make any application. It may be acceptable, however, for the scheme rules to provide for a shorter period where this is considered necessary, for example, where the invitation period is designed to coincide with the offer period in a flotation.

PRICE

12.28 ITEPA 2003, Sch 3, para 28 provides that the option price must be stated at the time the option is granted and must not be manifestly less than 80 per cent of the market value of the shares of the same class at that time. Where shares are subject to restrictions, market value is determined without reference to such restrictions, but the optionholder must be informed of the restrictions which apply to the shares (ITEPA 2003, Sch 3, para 28(5)).

12.29 For companies who feature on the Official List of the UKLA, market value has the same meaning as the capital gains tax legislation, currently being the lower of:

- half way between the highest and lowest prices at which bargains were recorded; and

- the 'quarter-up' figure (the lower of the two prices quoted for the shares on the Stock Exchange plus one-quarter of the difference).

At the time of writing, a draft regulation (The Market Value of Shares, Securities and Strips Regulations 2014) has been published for consultation which would result in a simplified calculation – see **4.81** above.

12.30 For unlisted companies, AIM shares, High Growth Market shares or shares listed on foreign stock exchanges, market value is the price those shares might reasonably be expected to fetch on a sale in the open market (TCGA 1992, s 272(1)). This will likely change, however, as a result of the proposed regulation referred to at **4.82** and **4.83** above. HMRC currently requires schemes to provide that the market value of the shares of such companies must be agreed in advance with Shares and Assets Valuation. HMRC will in practice usually agree that the relevant published price quoted in the Financial Times for AIM shares and the shares of companies listed on foreign stock exchanges may be taken as the market value although scheme rules may provide that the market value of the shares of companies listed on the New York Stock Exchange (but not NASDAQ) may be valued without reference to Shares and Assets Valuation.

12.31 Since offers must be made under savings-related share option schemes by invitation of applications, the exercise price will normally, in practice, be fixed by reference to the market value of the shares shortly before the invitations are made. Where the scheme rules provide for the price to be fixed by reference to the market value of the shares on the business day, or an average of the market values over one or more business days prior to the date of invitation, this will be treated as an 'agreement in writing' for the purposes of ITEPA 2003, Sch 3, para 28. If the scheme rules do not specify any particular day or days, HMRC will normally only agree the market value at the time of grant of the option. Following an announcement of results by the company, HMRC will not normally agree a market value fixed by reference to any day or days prior to such announcement.

12.32   HMRC's practice is that options should normally be granted within 30 days of any day by reference to which the price of the shares is determined. Where the price is fixed by reference to several days prior to the date of invitation, the earliest of those days must be treated as the first of the 30 days. HMRC do not normally allow the price to be fixed over more than five days.

12.33   Some schemes provide for the price to be fixed by reference to the market value on the date of grant. Under such arrangements, applications will be invited on the basis that the price will only be announced at the date of grant.

12.34   Companies with a large number of employees may find a period of 30 days between the fixing of the price and the date of grant as providing insufficient time for an offer under a savings-related share option scheme. Such companies may, therefore, issue invitations without details of the price which is only announced during the course of the offer period.

12.35   It was noted at **12.28** above that options must be granted at a price which is not manifestly less than 80 per cent of the market value of the shares at the relevant time. The scheme may provide for the price to be fixed at a higher price and a number of companies in fact give no discount. HMRC's interpretation of 'manifestly' is applied strictly. In calculating the price of shares, the company should always round up rather than round down the price. Most companies feel it is inelegant to express the share price in fractions of a pence, although there is no objection to this if it is required.

Foreign currency options

12.36   The exercise price may be stated in a currency other than sterling although under the savings contract any savings must be held in sterling. A scheme using the shares of a foreign parent may provide for the grant of options expressed in local currency over a variable number of shares depending on the amount of the proceeds of the savings contract after conversion from sterling. The number of shares under option cannot be determined, therefore, until exercise. Companies considering the grant of options with an exercise price payable in an overseas currency may be concerned that no cap can be placed on the total number of shares under option. Alternatively, the option price may be set in sterling, so that the savings and bonus match the number of shares under option, but this means that the company will bear the exchange rate risk on the conversion of the exercise monies.

SCALING DOWN

12.37   Most schemes contain limits on the number of new shares which may be issued under it and, even if such limits did not exist, most companies would still need to limit the number of shares which are made available under any offer. Schemes, therefore, need to contain provisions for scaling down applications where necessary.

12.38 HMRC will permit scheme rules to provide for the following successive steps to be taken to eliminate excess applications:

(a) each election for any bonus to be included in the repayment under the savings contract to be deemed to be an election for no bonus;

(b) each application for a five year contract to be deemed to be an application for a three year contract;

(c) the excess over any specified minimum monthly savings contributions (being not less than £5, and not more than £10, a month) chosen by each applicant to be reduced pro rata to the extent necessary (see **12.41** below);

(d) failing the above, applications to be selected by lot, each based on the minimum monthly savings contribution and the inclusion of no bonus in the repayment under the savings contract.

12.39 Where bonus rates are high it would clearly be wasteful and unfair to treat applications as not including any bonus. It would seem fairer in such circumstances to scale down monthly savings so that the full proceeds can be applied in the purchase of shares.

12.40 Where bonus rates are low, any scaling down would have minimal effect, or even no effect where the bonus rate is nil (as currently with three-year bonus rates).

12.41 Scaling down the excess of an application over a stated monthly contribution can be carried out on the basis of treating repayments as including either a five- or three-year bonus, although it is usually more convenient to carry out the calculations on the basis of only a five-year bonus. In particular, it is normally the excess over the minimum monthly contribution which is scaled down but there is no reason why a higher threshold cannot be adopted provided the scheme has the flexibility to permit the selection of any such threshold as the directors may determine from time to time. There is a certain merit in choosing, for instance, a threshold amount of £30 or £40 since it guarantees applications up to this amount.

12.42 A scaling down achieved through selecting by lot is undoubtedly a last resort. It would be very unfair to apply this method unless applications had first been scaled down by applying each of the other methods first. In such a case, it may well be better to consider withdrawing the offer altogether.

12.43 The scheme rules should give the directors the flexibility to apply any or all of the above methods as they consider appropriate, including agreeing with HMRC any other method of scaling down. HMRC's main concern is to ensure that all eligible employees participate on 'similar terms' as required by ITEPA 2003, Sch 3, para 7(1). It will not regard the following methods of scaling down as made on 'similar terms':

(a)   reducing all applications by the same amount, e.g. £50 off every application;

(b)   taking into account the savings already made in connection with other savings contracts (so as to favour new savers or current low savers);

(c)   refusing applications from optionholders who are already participating in the scheme, or who are already saving a certain amount under the scheme.

12.44   Surprisingly, it is acceptable to scale down applications pro rata to the remuneration of applicants or the length of their service since ITEPA 2003, Sch 3, para 7(2) provides that such factors would be 'similar terms'.

12.45   In order to assist any scaling down, each application form should authorise the directors to reduce the monthly savings contributions selected by the applicant.

BOARD RESOLUTION TO GRANT OPTIONS

12.46   Once the directors have resolved to invite applications, the procedure for the acceptance of applications and grant of options should follow automatically. If any scaling down is necessary because of excess applications, the procedures can be built into the resolution to grant the options. It is not necessary for the directors to meet twice, once in order to invite applications and then later in order to accept applications. The form of resolution to invite applications can provide for both the acceptance of all valid applications in full and the resulting grant of options. If applications exceed any limit on the number of shares to be made available, any one director may be authorised to approve the scaling down of applications in accordance with the prescribed steps.

12.47   An appropriate form of resolution for the grant of options is as follows:

Resolution

1.   IT WAS REPORTED to the Meeting that a proposal had been put forward for an invitation of applications to be made on [date] under the [ ] savings-related share option scheme and the following documents were produced to the Board accordingly:

(a)   proof letter of invitation;

(b)   proof application form;

(c)   proof employee guide.

2.   IT WAS PROPOSED that the following companies would participate in any offer:

[list participating companies]

3.   IT WAS RESOLVED THAT invitations to apply for the grant of options under the scheme be issued on [date] to all employees and directors of the Company and the participating companies referred to on the following terms:

   (i)   eligibility – all full-time directors and all employees who will have on [date] at least [ ] [months/years] continuous service with the Company and any participating company;

   (ii)   bonus offered – eligible employees shall be invited to apply for [three-year option only] [five-year option only] [for a three- [and/or] five--year option as they may choose];

   (iii) maximum monthly contribution – the maximum monthly contribution shall be £500;

   (iv)   option price – [ ]p being [80 per cent] of the middle market quotation of a share on the dealing day preceding [date of issue of invitation]/ [average of the middle market quotations of a share on the three dealing days preceding the date of issue of invitations] as derived from the Daily Official List of the London Stock Exchange for the relevant day;

   (v)   maximum number of shares – [ ] shares shall be available under this offer for the grant of options under the scheme; and

   (vi)   date of grant – options shall be granted on [date – not later than 30 days from the first price fixing date].

4.   IT WAS RESOLVED that all applications for the grant of options be accepted in full save to the extent such applications exceed the limit in which event all applications shall be scaled down by [a committee of the directors]/[any one or more of the directors] by means of any of the procedures which may be considered appropriate in Rule [ ] of the scheme rules.'

OPTION CERTIFICATE

12.48   Employees receiving an SAYE option grant should receive an option certificate setting out the relevant details of the option. Normally, HMRC will expect the following statements to be included in any option certificate:

(a)   the identity of the optionholder;

(b)   the name of the company;

(c)   the name of the scheme;

(d)   the maximum number of shares under option;

(e)   the date of grant;

(f)   the exercise price (per share); and

(g)   a statement that the shares are not transferable, and that the option rights will lapse upon the occasion of any assignment, charge, disposal or other dealing with the rights conveyed by it or in any other circumstances.

12.49   In addition, it may be helpful to include the following further information:

(a) the amount of the monthly contribution;

(b) the Bonus Date, ie the date on which the option will normally become exercisable;

(c) the date on which deductions from pay will commence;

(d) the maximum proceeds including the bonus on the savings account.

12.50 A recommended form of option certificate is as follows:

[Certificate No]

Share Option Certificate

[ ] plc/Limited

SAVINGS-RELATED SHARE OPTION SCHEME

Date of Grant	Monthly Savings Contribution (weekly- paid/ four- weekly paid employees – see note below)	Bonus Date (Date on which Option normally becomes exercisable)	Maximum Expected Repayment under the Savings Contract	Exercise Price per Share	Number of Shares under Option

This is to certify that: [ ] has been granted an Option to acquire the number of ordinary shares of [ ]p each fully paid in the Company at the exercise price per share shown above in accordance with and subject to the Rules of the [   ] Savings-Related Share Option Scheme

By Order of the Board

[Secretary of the Company]

NOTES

(1) Deductions from your pay in respect of your contributions will commence on the pay date [ ] 20 ... For weekly paid employees/four-weekly paid employees deductions will commence on the pay date [ ] 20 ... and will continue each week until contributions have been made and held in a 'feeder' account pending transfer to the savings account. Transfer will be made to the savings account each month at the monthly contributions rate shown above.

(2) The Option is not transferable, and will lapse upon any assignment, charge, disposal or other dealing.

(3) A copy of the scheme rules is available for inspection upon request to [ ].

THIS CERTIFICATE IS IMPORTANT AND SHOULD BE KEPT IN A SAFE PLACE.

EMPLOYEE COMMUNICATIONS

12.51 The key to effective employee communications in savings-related share option schemes is to focus on the limited number of decisions which an employee has to make when considering making an application to join the scheme. First, the employee needs to understand that the scheme involves entering into a three- or five-year savings contract to pay a fixed sum each month and so he needs to consider whether he is prepared to enter into such a contract and, if so, the amount he is prepared to save each month. In deciding whether to save, and the amount he wishes to save, he will need to take into account that:

(a)   he will be granted the right to buy shares (without any obligation to buy) at a fixed price which will represent a discount to the market value;

(b)   the rate of interest (if any) on any savings; and

(c)   the tax exemptions which are applicable in respect of any bonus and the option gains.

The employee needs to take account of the implications of his not remaining an employee until the bonus date, the third anniversary of grant (if earlier) or even the first anniversary of the commencement of the savings contract.

12.52 The second main decision which he may need to take into account is whether he wishes to elect for the a three- or five-year bonus. The longer the savings contract the higher the potential return.

12.53 In order to keep the communications sharply focused, it is appropriate initially to ensure information on certain areas is kept to a minimum, for instance, the suspension of monthly contributions and the rights of exercise or rollover of options on a takeover. Information about suspending payments and the exercise procedures are best supplied after the grant of options and can be enclosed with the option certificate or included in information packs with the annual sharesave account statements each year. In any event, the best time to supply detailed information about rights of exercise on a sale of a business or a takeover is as soon as any such event occurs or appears likely to occur. The right time to supply information about rights of exercise on any sale of the shares and any transfer of the shares into an individual savings account is at the time of exercise. Such information can be included in the statements usually sent out by savings bodies to remind savers of any forthcoming bonus date.

NON-TRANSFERABILITY OF OPTIONS

12.54 A savings-related share option scheme must exclude any right of voluntary transfer, assignment or charge in respect of option rights (ITEPA 2003, Sch 3, para 29). Sharesave contracts exclude any right of voluntary transfer and makes detailed provision for the actions to be taken by a savings body which becomes aware of a purported transfer of the benefit of the savings contract (see **12.71** below).

SAVINGS CONTRACT

12.55   Savings-related share option schemes are linked to a contractual savings scheme which is usually with a savings body nominated by the company, but in some cases may be selected by the employee from a panel of savings bodies nominated by the company. Only certified SAYE savings arrangements approved by the Treasury under ITTOIA 2005, s 703 and by HMRC (previously known as 'contractual savings schemes') may be used. These may only be provided by building societies, banks and European financial institutions.

12.56   The terms of the savings contracts offered by building societies and banks are broadly identical. The prospectuses have been changed with greater frequency in recent years and it is always essential to ensure that the current prospectus approved by HMRC is to be used in any offer. References in this section to 'paragraph numbers' are to paragraph numbers in the Building Society and Bank SAYE Prospectus dated 28 July 2014.

Eligibility

12.57   A person may only enter into a savings contract on the basis of a declaration to the savings body that:

(a)   he is not less than 16 years of age;

(b)   he is eligible to participate in a savings-related share option scheme operated by his current employer;

(c)   the aggregate of each monthly contribution under the proposed contract and all other approved savings contracts operated by banks, building societies and European financial institutions in connection with savings-related share option schemes do not exceed the lesser of:

    (i)   £500 (or such greater sum as HM Treasury may from time to time determine); or

    (ii)   the monthly contribution necessary to secure as nearly as may be repayment of an amount equal to the aggregate exercise price of the shares under the relevant savings-related share option scheme offer.

12.58   Under the terms of the prospectus, the savings body is precluded from accepting applications from persons under 16 years of age. However, in law persons under 18 years of age are not bound by the terms of the savings contract.

12.59   Paragraph 4 of the prospectus states that the savings body shall not be obliged to enter into a savings contract with an applicant although it is difficult to envisage the circumstances in which any savings body would exercise this discretion. This may, of course, result in the company which has granted the option being in breach of the terms of its own scheme if any employees with a statutory right to participate in any offer under the scheme were so excluded. In such circumstances, the company would need to appoint an alternative savings body for that employee.

Savings contributions

12.60   Savings contributions can only be credited to the savings account in 36 or 60 fixed monthly amounts of between £5 and £500 a month. The fixed monthly amount may be selected by the investor and must be in a multiple of £1.

Duration of the savings period

12.61   The savings contract starts when the first contribution is credited to the savings account. After the first month, each of the remaining 35/59 monthly contributions are due during each successive month. Since paragraph 18 of the prospectus provides that, where interest is paid in lieu of bonus, it is deemed to run from the first day of the month the relevant savings contribution is due, it follows that savings bodies normally require deductions from pay to be received by the end of the immediately preceding month. In this way savings bodies are in a position to credit the monthly contribution to the savings account on the first day of the month to which the contribution relates. There are provisions allowing investors temporarily to suspend or stop making payments (see **12.66** below).

Contributions from employees

12.62   Paragraph 6 of the prospectus states that employees' contributions shall be made through the employing company, as the agent of the employee, from deductions from pay authorised by the employee. This means that contributions cannot be made by direct debit or standing order direct from an employee's bank or building society account (although HMRC accepts that this may be the case in respect of former employees who continue to make savings, employees on maternity, parental or adoption leave, employees called up for military service, employees on long-term sick leave, employees seconded to another organisation and employees who are on sabbatical leave). The requirement for contributions to be deducted from pay also seems to exclude the participation of overseas employees under arrangements whereby a lump sum is placed in a 'feeder account' in sterling from which the regular monthly contributions are transferred although, again, this practice is widely adopted.

Weekly paid employees

12.63   Many employees are paid weekly or four-weekly and it can be difficult to synchronise the deductions from pay with the crediting of contributions to the savings contract on a monthly basis. The most common way of dealing with deductions from the pay of weekly paid employees is for the deductions to be made by the employee each successive week for 240 weeks and to be transferred each week (or each four weeks) into a feeder account with the saving body. Similarly, deductions from the pay of four-weekly paid employees are transferred into the savings body feeder account each four weeks. In both cases, this will mean the deductions from pay will be ahead of the due dates for crediting the monthly contributions. Indeed, the savings body feeder accounts will normally receive the final weekly deduction after approximately four years and seven months, some five months before the date on which the 60th monthly contribution is normally due. Savings bodies vary in their practice in relation to offering interest on feeder accounts; some offer interest automatically whilst most do not, although almost all will do so upon request. The average period of time sums are held in a feeder account is about two months and so the amounts of interest involved are relatively insignificant.

12.64   Where a company believes it is possible to cope with more frequent deductions from weekly paid employees then there is nothing to stop the company offering a 'deduction holiday' of four consecutive weeks at the end of each calendar year or waiving all fifth deductions in any month. In this way deductions from the pay of weekly paid employees can keep in step with the crediting of the monthly contributions to savings accounts.

12.65   A few companies even retain weekly deductions until the due date for the payment of the monthly contributions. Whenever an employer holds onto any deductions, it will, of course, be necessary for the employer to account for these deductions in the event the employee leaves employment before the transfer is made to the savings body.

Postponement and stopping contributions

12.66   The terms of savings contracts do not oblige an employee to make all 36 or 60 monthly contributions. An employee may postpone or stop making contributions. Up to six monthly contributions in total – not necessarily successive contributions – can be postponed. The effect of postponing any monthly contributions is that the period of the contract, including the bonus date, is set back by one month. If a seventh monthly contribution is postponed, the participant is treated as having given notice of an intention to stop paying contributions. Where such notice has been given, or is treated as having been given, no further contributions may be credited to the savings account and the investor is entitled to apply for repayment of his contributions in full with interest where applicable. The savings body is not automatically obliged to remit any balance on the account.

12.67   Interest is only applicable after the first anniversary of the start of the contract (or after 12 monthly contributions have been made, if later). Given that the contract only starts on the date in the first month on which the monthly contribution is 'received', care may need to be taken to ensure repayment is only obtained after that date in the month. Interest is calculated, in respect of each separate monthly contribution, from the first day of the month. Many schemes provide for options to lapse upon the optionholder giving notice of his intention to stop monthly payments although there is no statutory obligation to do so. If the scheme rules do not specifically provide for the lapse of options in such circumstances the option will only be exercisable to the extent the scheme rules allow, for instance, within six months of leaving employment on account of injury, disability or similar specified circumstances.

12.68   The current rate of interest on contributions which are withdrawn before completion of the savings contract is nil. Interest, if provided for under the savings contract, becomes payable once a full year has elapsed since the start of the savings contract and 12 monthly contributions have been made.

Bonuses

12.69   Bonuses are a lump sum paid in lieu of interest after the completion of the savings contract. They are payable upon the application of the investor to close his account. For contracts entered into from 28 July 2014, there continues to be no bonus payable under a three-year contract, but under a five-year contract upon completion of 60 monthly savings a bonus of 0.6 monthly contributions (equivalent to an annual equivalent rate of interest at 0.39 per cent). Bonus rates are adjusted automatically on an annual basis (taking effect generally from 1 September) by linking them to three- and five-year market swap rates (the market reference swap rates). There are, however, mechanisms for allowing bonus rates to be adjusted if the market reference swap rates move dramatically. This in itself can lead to problems where the mechanism results in a change of rates during the period between invitations being sent out and the employee returning the application as the previous bonus rates cannot automatically continue to apply following withdrawal. HMRC may, however, specify that certain SAYE contracts made after a withdrawal and variation are not to be affected by the change. Savings providers must be notified of the proposed variation or withdrawal of a savings prospectus at least 15 days prior to the variation or withdrawal taking effect.

Death

12.70   No more monthly contributions are payable or may be credited to the savings account after the death of an investor. Where the savings body has continued to receive any contributions after death, it is obliged to refund them and make any necessary adjustments to the savings contract. Personal representatives may withdraw the savings and any interest or bonus which is due. Where a savings contract has not been completed, no interest is payable where the account is closed before the first anniversary of the start of the contract and any interest thereafter is payable until the closure of the contract.

No transfer of the savings contract

12.71   A savings contract cannot be transferred to another person. Any purported transfer after completing the 36 or 60 monthly savings under the savings contract is treated as an application for repayment of the savings and the bonus and any interest to date which must be repaid to the investor, not his transferee. Any purported transfer before completion of the savings contract is treated as notice of intention to stop paying monthly contributions and accordingly all contributions are repaid together with any interest.

Tax relief

12.72 Any bonus or interest payable under a savings contract qualifies for exemption for tax purposes under ITTOIA 2005, s 702 and TCGA 1992, s 271(4). Such bonus or interest is exempt for all tax purposes which means that the taxpayer is not required to include it in his annual tax return.

SCHEME LIMITS

HMRC requirements

12.73 There are no limits under the legislation on the number of shares which may be allocated under a savings-related share option scheme or indeed any other type of approved scheme.

ABI guidelines

12.74 ABI Guidelines do not contain any specific limits on the number of shares issuable under savings-related share option schemes adopted by listed companies. An overall limit of ten per cent of the issued ordinary share capital over any ten-year period is the only scheme limit.

EXERCISE OF OPTIONS

12.75 The fundamental principle of a savings-related share option scheme is that the scheme shares are to be paid for out of the repayment and any bonus or interest payable under the linked certified savings contract.

12.76 However, the shares may only be acquired upon exercise of the options in fairly limited circumstances. The legislation sets out the circumstances in which options may be exercised.

Income tax on option gains

12.77 All gains on the exercise of an option in accordance with the rules of a savings-related share option scheme are exempt from income tax except where the right of exercise arises within three years of the date of grant in certain takeover situations. National Insurance contributions do not apply to options under savings-related share option schemes. Income tax which arises on options exercised within three years from grant is collected under self-assessment.

Exercise at the bonus date

12.78   Normally, options may only be exercised during the period of six months following the bonus date. For this purpose, the bonus date is the date on which the 36th or 60th monthly contribution is credited to the savings account.

12.79   Shortly before the time the bonus becomes payable most savings bodies automatically alert optionholders of their right to obtain repayment and exercise their options.

12.80   Once the three- or five-year bonus date is reached, there is no entitlement to interest during any further period in which the savings are left with the savings body.

Early exercise in the event of death

12.81   Under ITEPA 2003, Sch 3, para 32, a scheme must provide that, if an optionholder dies before the bonus date, any exercise of the option must normally be made within 12 months of his death. If he dies within the normal six-month period allowed for exercise after the bonus date, then the personal representatives are allowed, until 12 months after the bonus date, to exercise the option. These periods for exercise must be provided for irrespective of any other events (other than a winding up) affecting the company.

Early exercise upon leaving employment

12.82   A scheme must provide for a right of exercise during the period of six months following the date on which the employee leaves in certain involuntary circumstances which are set out in the legislation (although the period need not be the full six months). These circumstances are where the employee leaves on account of injury, disability, redundancy (within the meaning of the Employment Rights Act 1996), retirement, a transfer of employment under the Transfer of Undertakings (Protection of Employment) Regulations 2006 (TUPE), or the participant's employment being with a company which ceases to be an associated company of the company which established the scheme by reason of a change of control of that employing company. These events do not act to extend the period for exercise where an option has previously become exercisable.

12.83   Where employees leave employment before the bonus date, ITEPA 2003, Sch 3, para 34 provides that no right of exercise may be allowed before the third anniversary of the date of grant except on the personal grounds set out in **12.82** above, or, where the scheme permits, in the event of a takeover, scheme of arrangement, 'non-UK company reorganisation arrangement' voluntary winding-up or the disposal of the business for which the optionholder works in circumstances where TUPE does not apply. These events do not act to extend the period for exercise where an option has previously become exercisable.

12.84   ITEPA 2003, Sch 3, para 34 provides that where employees leave after the third anniversary of the date of grant, the scheme must state whether any right of exercise is to be permitted. The scheme must restrict any such rights after the third anniversary of grant to a period of six months after leaving employment.

12.85   The recent trend has been to allow all optionholders who leave employment after the third anniversary to exercise their options regardless of the reason for leaving. One reason for this is that undue restrictions in a scheme would undermine five-year contracts as those with three-year contracts would be able to exercise in any event. In some cases, an exception is made where the employee leaves on account of gross misconduct. HMRC will not approve a discretion on the part of the directors as to whether or not to allow exercise at the time of leaving employment.

Retirement

12.86   ITEPA 2003, Sch 3, para 31 provides that an optionholder may exercise his option if he ceases to hold the employment by virtue of which he is eligible to participate by reason of, amongst other things, retirement .

12.87   Although the inclusion of retirement in the plan is permitted, companies should be aware of the need to comply with the age discrimination rules in the Employment Equality (Age) Regulations 2006 (SI 2006/1031). In particular, the company must apply a definition of 'retirement' which complies with the legislation in not being age-related.

12.88   HMRC has not given guidance as to what may be an accept definition of retirement, save to provide that given the lack of a statutory definition, the term should be given its 'natural meaning'. Definitions used for other tax purposes may not be acceptable, and companies should develop their own retirement policies and practices. It will not, however, be acceptable for such policies to contain any element of discretion.

US participants

12.89   Tax issues may arise for participants in an SAYE who are, or become, US taxpayers. As an SAYE proivides for discounted options, the defered compensation plan rules of s 409A of the Internal Revenue Code (see **20.33** below) will apply to such individuals. In order for US taxpaying SAYE participants not to suffer a penal tax charge, HMRC permit SAYE rules to incorporate a provision which limits the right of exercise, however arising, to the period of two and a half calendar months following the end of the tax year in which the option first becomes exercisable. A US tax year is the same as a calendar year, so effectively exercise will be limited to 15 March in the next calendar year. As the exercise right is limited to this period, the SAYE option will be considered to be a short-term deferral and not subject to the s 409A penalty.

Exercise upon a takeover

12.90　Options under approved savings-related share option schemes may be exercised for up to six months after a takeover, scheme of arrangement, 'non-UK company reorganisation arrangement' or voluntary winding up (see Chapter 13). Any such exercise, even within three years of the date of grant, will be free from income tax on any gains which arise provided that the consideration for the shares acquired is cash (an no other assets) and there was no opportunity made available for the optionholder to effect a rollover of the option. In other circumstances, the exercise of such an option would be subject to income tax.

12.91　In the event of a change of control of the company whose shares are subject to SAYE options the shares of that company may cease to satisfy the provisions of ITEPA 2003, Sch 3, para 19 (see **4.59** above), in which case, absent anything provided for in the rules, the options could not be exercised from such date. HMRC has previously dealt with this in one of two ways: either the rules could provide for exercise in a non-tax advantaged manner, or the company could apply for withdrawal of approval following an amendment to the rules to remove references to the shares having to satisfy the para 19 requirement (in which case the legislation prior to 6 April 2014 allowed for exercise with tax reliefs). Since 6 April 2014, HMRC no longer approves SAYE rules, and cannot be asked, therefore, to withdraw approval. Instead, the legislation now provides, at ITEPA 2003, Sch 3, para 37(6B), that SAYE rules may permit exercise during a period of 20 days following the relevant event (essentially, being the event pursuant to which the shares no longer satisfy the legislative conditions) without this affecting the tax treatment on exercise. The rules, as an alternative, may provide for a conditional exercise in the period of 20 days prior to an anticipated change of control, with the exercise becoming ineffective if the change of control does not happen within that period (ITEPA 2003, Sch 3, para 37(6E)).

Number of shares which may be acquired on exercise

12.92　The fundamental principle of a savings-related share option scheme is the linkage between the amount of savings and any bonus and/or interest and the number of shares which may be acquired upon an early exercise. Any repayment under the savings contract will exclude the repayment of any contribution which falls due for payment more than one month after the date on which the repayment is made. This requirement was introduced to stop an abuse which was common upon takeovers and in other circumstances of early exercise of paying up savings contracts in advance, or at least up to the 59th monthly contribution, so as to increase the number of shares which may be acquired. Even apart from that abuse, this provision means that sums held in suspense accounts with the savings body by weekly paid employees cannot be used to acquire shares under the scheme until credited on the due date to the savings account as a monthly contribution.

Appendix 12A

Savings-Related Share Option Scheme

Set out below is a precedent for a savings-related share option scheme. It is intended to comply with the requirements of ITEPA 2003, Sch 3. The scheme may need to be amended in order to meet the needs of particular companies (for example, to take account of institutional investor guidelines and the UKLA Listing Rules for a listed company). Such provisions may not be necessary, however, for inclusion in the rules for a private company.

Rules of the [ ] Savings-Related Share Option Scheme

1. DEFINITIONS

1.1 In this Scheme, the following words and expressions shall bear, unless the context otherwise requires, the meanings set forth below:

'**Appropriate Period**' has the meaning given by Paragraph 38(3) of Schedule 3 to ITEPA;

'**Associated Company**' means an associated company of the Company within the meaning that expression bears in Paragraph 47 of Schedule 3 to ITEPA, save in respect of Rules 6.5.4 and 6.6 where the meaning given in Paragraph 35(4) of Schedule 3 to ITEPA shall apply;

'**the Board**' means the board of directors of the Company, or a duly authorised committee thereof or, following an event specified in Rule 7, shall be the board of directors or duly authorised committee as constituted immediately prior to such event;

'**Bonus Date**' means the earliest date on which the bonus due under the Savings Arrangements entered into in connection with an Option becomes payable;

'**Company**' means [COMPANY] [Limited/plc] (registered in England and Wales under No [NUMBER]);

'**Continuous Service**' has the meaning given to 'continuous employment' in the Employment Rights Act 1996;

'**Control**' has the meaning given by Section 995 of the Income Tax Act 2007;

'**Date of Grant**' means the date on which the Board grants an Option following acceptance of a duly completed form of application;

'**Date of Invitation**' means the date, being a date within the Invitation Period, on which the Board invites applications for Options;

'**Dealing Day**' means any day on which the London Stock Exchange is open for the transaction of business;

'Eligible Employee' means:

(A)   any individual:

   (1)   who is a full-time director (who is required to work at least 25 hours per week exclusive of meal breaks) or an employee of a Participating Company;

   (2)   whose earnings from the office or employment referred to in (1) meet (or would meet if there were any) the requirements set out in paragraphs 6(2)(c) and 6(2)(ca) of Schedule 3 to ITEPA; and

   (3)   who, on the immediately preceding Qualifying Date, had such minimum period of Continuous Service with any one or more Participating Companies (taken consecutively) as the Board may specify, provided that any period so specified shall not exceed five years prior to the Date of Grant; and

(B)   any other employee or category of employees whom the Board may approve;

'Employees' Share Scheme' has the meaning given by Section 1166 of the Companies Act 2006;

'Exercise Price' means the total amount payable in relation to the exercise of an Option, whether in whole or in part, being an amount equal to the relevant Option Price multiplied by the number of Shares in respect of which the Option is exercised;

'Invitation Period' means the period of 42 days commencing on any of the following:

(A)   the Dealing Day immediately following the day on which the Company makes an announcement of its results for the last financial year, half-year or other period;

(B)   the date on which the Board determines that exceptional circumstances exist which justify the grant of Options;

(C)   the date on which a change to the legislation affecting Schedule 3 SAYEs is proposed or takes effect; and

(D)   the date on which a new prospectus in relation to Savings Arrangements is announced or takes effect;

'ITEPA' means the Income Tax (Earnings and Pensions) Act 2003;

'Key Feature' has the meaning given by Paragraph 40(B)(8) of Schedule 3 to ITEPA;

'London Stock Exchange' means London Stock Exchange plc;

'Market Value' means, in relation to a Share on any day:

(A)   if and so long as the Shares are admitted to listing by the UK Listing Authority and traded on the London Stock Exchange, its middle market quotation (as derived from the Daily Official List of the London Stock Exchange); or

(B)   subject to (A) above, its market value, determined in accordance with Part VIII of the Taxation of Chargeable Gains Act 1992 (but when Shares are subject to a Restriction, determined on the basis that no such restriction applies) and agreed in advance with Shares and Assets Valuation at HM Revenue and Customs;

'**Maximum Contribution**' means, in relation to the relevant Savings Arrangements, the lesser of:

(A)   such maximum monthly contribution as may be permitted pursuant to Paragraph 25(3)(a) of Schedule 3 to ITEPA; and

(B)   such maximum monthly contribution as may be determined from time to time by the Board;

'**Minimum Contribution**' means, in relation to the relevant Savings Arrangements, the minimum Monthly Contribution allowed under the Savings Arrangements as may be determined from time to time by the Board but not to exceed the amount specified in Paragraph 25(3)(b) of Schedule 3 to ITEPA;

'**Monthly Contributions**' means monthly contributions agreed to be paid by a Participant under the Savings Arrangements entered into in connection with his Option;

'**Option**' means a right to acquire Shares under the Scheme which is either subsisting or (where the context so admits or requires) is proposed to be granted;

'**Option Price**' means the price per Share, as determined by the Board prior to the Date of Grant, at which an Eligible Employee may acquire Shares upon the exercise of an Option being not less than:

(A)   80 per cent of:

    (i)   the Market Value of a Share on the Dealing Day (which shall be a date within an Invitation Period) immediately preceding the Date of Invitation;

    (ii)   if the Board so determines, the average of the Market Values of a Share on the three Dealing Days (all of which shall be dates within an Invitation Period) immediately preceding the Date of Invitation; or

    (iii)   if the Board so determines, the Market Value of a Share at such other time as may be agreed in advance in writing with HM Revenue and Customs; and

(B)   if the Shares are to be subscribed, their nominal value,

but subject to any adjustment pursuant to Rule 10;

'**Participant**' means a director or employee, or former director or employee, to whom an Option has been granted, or (where the context so admits or requires) the personal representatives of any such person;

'**Participating Company**' means:

(A)   the Company; and

(B)   any other company which is under the Control of the Company, is a Subsidiary of the Company, and is for the time being designated by the Board as a Participating Company;

'**Qualifying Date**' means such date as the Board may determine in the 12-month period immediately preceding the commencement of the Invitation Period;

'**Repayment**' means in relation to Savings Arrangements, the aggregate of the

Monthly Contributions which the Participant has agreed to make and any bonus due at the Bonus Date;

'**Restriction**' has the meaning given by Paragraph 48(3) of schedule 3 to ITEPA;

'**Rule**' means a rule of this Scheme;

'**Savings Arrangement**' means a certified SAYE savings arrangement (within the meaning of Section 703 of the Income Tax (Trading and Other Income) Act 2005) approved by HM Revenue and Customs for the purpose of Schedule 3 to ITEPA;

'**Schedule 3 SAYE**' means any share option scheme that meets the requirements in force from time to time of Schedule 3 to ITEPA;

'**the Scheme**' means this [COMPANY] Sharesave Scheme in its present form or as from time to time amended in accordance with the provisions hereof;

'**Share**' means a fully paid ordinary share in the capital of the Company which satisfies the conditions specified in Paragraphs 18 to 20 and 22 of Schedule 3 to ITEPA unless the relevant Option is exercised within 20 days after the date on which the Option became exercisable pursuant to Rule 7.1, 7.3, 7.4 or 7.5;

'**Subsidiary**' has the meaning given by Section 1159 and Schedule 6 of the Companies Act 2006;

'**Treasury Shares**' means Shares to which Sections 724 to 732 of the Companies Act 2006 apply;

'**Trust**' means any employee benefit trust from time to time established by the Company; and

'**UK Listing Authority**' means the Financial Conduct Authority as the competent authority for listing in the United Kingdom under Part VI of the Financial Services and Markets Act 2000.

1.2   In the Scheme, unless the context requires otherwise:

1.2.1   the headings are inserted for convenience only and do not affect the interpretation of any Rule;

1.2.3   a reference to a statute or statutory provision includes a reference:

(A)   to that statute or statutory provision as from time to time consolidated, modified, re-enacted or replaced by any statute or statutory provision;

(B)   to any repealed statute or statutory provision which it re-enacts (with or without modification); and

(C)   to any subordinate legislation made under it;

1.2.4   words in the singular include the plural, and vice versa;

1.2.5   a reference to the masculine shall be treated as a reference to the feminine, and vice versa;

1.2.6   a reference to a person shall include a reference to a body corporate; and

1.2.7   any reference to writing or written form shall include any legible format capable of being reproduced on paper, irrespective of the medium used.

1.3   In this Scheme:

1.3.1   a reference to the "transfer of Shares" shall include both the issue and allotment of Shares and the transfer of Treasury Shares; and

1.3.2 a provision obliging, or permitting, any company to do anything shall be read as obliging, or permitting, such company to do that thing, or procure that thing to be done.

2. APPLICATION FOR OPTIONS

2.1 The Board may, during any Invitation Period, invite applications for Options from Eligible Employees. Invitations may be made by letter, poster, circular, advertisement, electronically, or by any other means or combination of means determined by the Board, and shall include details of:

2.1.1 eligibility;

2.1.2 the Option Price;

2.1.3 whether the Shares over which an Option is to be granted are subject to any Restriction and, if so, the details of such Restriction (or information as to where such details are set out in an accessible format);

2.1.4 the Maximum Contribution payable;

2.1.5 the Minimum Contribution payable;

2.1.6 whether, for the purpose of determining the number of Shares over which an Option is to be granted, the Repayment under the Savings Arrangements is to be taken:

(A) as including any specified bonus;

(B) as including any bonus selected by the Eligible Employee; or

(C) as not including a bonus;

2.1.7 the date by which applications made pursuant to Rule 2.3 must be received (being neither earlier than 14 days, nor later than 25 days after the Date of Invitation); and

2.1.8 if determined by the Board, details of the maximum number of Shares over which applications for Options are to be invited in that Invitation Period.

2.2. An application for an Option must incorporate or be accompanied by a proposal for Savings Arrangements.

2.3 An application for an Option shall be in such form as the Board may from time to time prescribe, save that it shall provide for the application to state:

2.3.1 the Monthly Contributions (being a multiple of £1 and not less than the Minimum Contribution) which the Eligible Employee wishes to make under the Savings Arrangements to be entered into in connection with the Option for which application is made;

2.3.2 that the Eligible Employee's proposed Monthly Contributions (when taken together with any Monthly Contributions he makes under any other Savings Arrangements) will not exceed the Maximum Contribution; and

2.3.3 if Eligible Employees may elect for the Repayment under the Savings Arrangements to be taken as including a bonus, the Eligible Employee's election in that respect.

2.4 Each application for an Option shall provide that, in the event of excess applications, each application shall be deemed to have been modified or withdrawn in accordance with the steps taken by the Board to scale down applications pursuant to Rule 3.

2.5   Proposals for Savings Arrangements shall be limited to such bank, building society or other person specified in Section 704 of the Income Tax (Trading and Other Income) Act 2005, as the Board may designate.

2.6   Each application shall be deemed to be for an Option over the largest whole number of Shares which can be acquired at the Option Price with the Repayment under the Savings Arrangements entered into in connection with the Option.

3.   SCALING DOWN

3.1   If valid applications are received for a total number of Shares in excess of any maximum number of Shares determined by the Board pursuant to Rule 2.1.8, or any limitation under Rule 5, the Board shall scale down applications in accordance with 3.1.1 to 3.1.4 below in such order and combinations as the Board may determine, save that the provisions set out in 3.1.3 and 3.1.4 shall not be applied before the provisions set out in 3.1.1 to 3.1.2, until the number of Shares available equals or exceeds such total number of Shares applied for:

3.1.1   by reducing, so far as necessary, the proposed Monthly Contributions pro rata to the excess over such amount as the Board shall determine for this purpose being not less than the amount of the Minimum Contribution;

3.1.2   by treating each election for a bonus as an election for no bonus;

3.1.3   by treating elections for five-year Savings Arrangements as elections for three-year Savings Arrangements; and

3.1.4   by selecting by lot.

3.2   If the number of Shares available is insufficient to enable an Option based on Monthly Contributions of the amount of the Minimum Contribution to be granted to each Eligible Employee making a valid application, the Board may, as an alternative to selecting by lot, determine in its absolute discretion that no Options shall be granted.

3.3   If the Board so determines, the provisions in Rule 3.1 may be modified or applied in any manner provided that any such modification or application does not breach any of the provisions of Schedule 3 to ITEPA.

3.4   If, in applying the scaling down provisions contained in this Rule 3, Options cannot be granted within the 30 day period referred to in Rule 4.2 below, the Board may extend that period by 12 days regardless of the expiration of the relevant Invitation Period.

4.   GRANT OF OPTIONS

4.1   No Option shall be granted to any person if, at the Date of Grant, that person has ceased to be an Eligible Employee.

4.2   Within 30 days of the Dealing Day by reference to which the Option Price was fixed (or where by reference to more than one Dealing Day, the first of such days) the Board may, subject to Rule 3 above, grant to each Eligible Employee who has submitted a valid application an Option in respect of the number of Shares for which application has been deemed to be made under Rule 2.6.

4.3   The Board shall issue to each Participant an option certificate in such form (not inconsistent with the provisions of the Scheme) as the Board may from time to time prescribe. Each such certificate shall specify:

4.3.1 the Date of Grant of the Option;

4.3.2 the number and class of Shares over which the Option is granted;

4.3.3 the Option Price;

4.3.4 whether the Shares over which the Option is granted are subject to any Restriction and, if so, the details of such Restriction (or information as to where such details are set out in an accessible format); and

4.3.5 the Bonus Date.

4.4   Except as otherwise provided in these Rules, every Option shall be personal to the Participant to whom it is granted and shall not be transferable.

4.5   No amount shall be paid in respect of the grant of an Option.

SCHEME ALLOCATION LIMITS

5.1   The maximum number of Shares which may be allocated under the Scheme on any day shall not, when added to the aggregate of the number of Shares which have been allocated in the previous 10 years under the Scheme and under any other Employees' Share Scheme adopted by the Company, exceed such number as represents 10 per cent of the ordinary share capital of the Company in issue immediately prior to that day.

5.2   References in this Rule 5 to the 'allocation' of Shares shall mean:

5.2.1 in the case of any option, conditional share award or other similar award pursuant to which Shares may be acquired:

(A)   the grant (whether by the Company, the Trustee or otherwise) of the option, conditional share award or other similar award to acquire Shares, pursuant to which Shares may be issued; and

(B)   in so far as not previously taken into account under (A) above from the date of grant, any subscription for Shares which are issued for the purpose of satisfying any option, conditional share award or other similar award to acquire Shares; and

5.2.2 in relation to other types of Employees' Share Scheme, the issue and allotment of Shares,

and references to 'allocated', in this Rule 5, shall be construed accordingly.

5.3   In determining the above limits no account shall be taken of:

5.3.1 any allocation (or part thereof) where the option, conditional share award or other similar award to acquire Shares was released, lapsed or otherwise became incapable of vesting;

5.3.2 any allocation (or part thereof) in respect of which the Board or the Trustee has determined shall be satisfied otherwise than by the issue of Shares; and

5.3.3 such number of additional Shares as would otherwise have been issued on the exercise of an option for monetary consideration (*the exercise price*) but in respect of which the exercise price is not paid, in substitution for the issue of such lesser number of shares as have a market value equal only to the gain which the optionholder would have made on exercise (*equity-settled SAR alternative*).

5.4   References to the issue and allotment of Shares shall include the transfer of Treasury Shares, but only until such time as the guidelines issued by institutional investor bodies cease to provide that they need to be so included.

6.   RIGHTS OF EXERCISE AND LAPSE OF OPTIONS

6.1   Save as provided in Rules 6.4, 6.5 and Rule 6.8, an Option shall not be exercised earlier than the Bonus Date under the Savings Arrangements entered into in connection therewith.

6.2   Save as provided in Rule 6.4, an Option shall not be exercised later than six months after the Bonus Date under the Savings Arrangements entered into in connection therewith.

6.3   Save as provided in Rules 6.4, 6.5 and 6.8 an Option may only be exercised by a Participant whilst he is a director or employee of a Participating Company.

6.4   An Option may be exercised by the personal representatives of a deceased Participant at any time:

6.4.1   within 12 months following the date of his death if such death occurs before the Bonus Date; and

6.4.2   within 12 months following the Bonus Date in the event of his death on, or within 6 months after the Bonus Date.

6.5   An Option may be exercised by a Participant within six months following his ceasing to hold office or employment with a Participating Company by reason of:

6.5.1   injury or disability;

6.5.2   redundancy within the meaning of the Employment Rights Act 1996;

6.5.3   retirement;

6.5.4   his office or employment being in a company which ceases to be an Associated Company by reason of a change of control within the meaning of sections 450 and 451 of the Corporation Tax Act 2010;

6.5.6   a relevant transfer within the meaning of the Transfer of Undertakings (Protection of Employment) regulations 2006;

6.5.7   the transfer of a business or part of a business to a person who is not an Associated Company where the transfer is not a relevant transfer within the meaning of the Transfer of Undertakings (Protection of Employment) Regulations 2006.

6.7   A Participant shall not be treated, for the purposes of Rule 6.4 or Rule 6.9.5, as ceasing to hold an office or employment with a Participating Company until he ceases to hold any office or employment with a Participating Company or an Associated Company.

6.8   An Option may be exercised within six months of the Bonus Date by a Participant who is a director or employee of a company which is not a Participating Company but which is an Associated Company;

6.9   An Option granted to a Participant shall lapse upon the occurrence of the earliest of the following:

6.9.1 six months after the Bonus Date under the Savings Arrangements entered into in connection with the Option, save where the Participant dies prior to the expiry of such period;

6.9.2 where the Participant dies before the Bonus Date, 12 months after the date of death; and where the Participant dies on, or in the period of six months after the Bonus Date, 12 months after the Bonus Date;

6.9.3 the expiry of any of the six-month periods specified in Rule 6.5, save where the Participant dies prior to the expiry of such period;

6.9.4 the expiry of any of the periods specified in Rules 7.3 or 7.4, (i) save where an Option is released in consideration of the grant of a New Option during one of the periods specified in Rules 7.3 and 7.4; pursuant to Rule 7.6; or (ii) where the Participant dies prior to the expiry of (including prior to the commencement of) such period;

6.9.5 the expiry of the period specified in Rule 7.5;

6.9.6 the Participant ceasing to hold any office or employment with a Participating Company for any reason other than those specified in Rule 6.5 or as a result of his death;

6.9.7 subject to Rule 7.5, the passing of an effective resolution, or the making of an order by the Court, for the winding-up of the Company;

6.9.8 the Participant being deprived (otherwise than on death) of the legal or beneficial ownership of the Option by operation of law, or doing anything or omitting to do anything which causes him to be so deprived, or becoming bankrupt; and

6.9.9 before an Option has become capable of being exercised, the Participant giving notice that he intends to stop paying Monthly Contributions, or being deemed under the terms of the Savings Arrangements to have given such notice, or making an application for repayment of the Monthly Contributions made.

7. TAKE-OVER, SCHEME OF ARRANGEMENT, AND LIQUIDATION

7.1 If any person obtains Control of the Company as a result of making a general offer to acquire Shares which is either unconditional or is made on a condition such that if it is satisfied the person making the offer will have Control of the Company, an Option may be exercised within six months of the time when the person making the offer has obtained Control of the Company and any condition subject to which the offer is made has been satisfied or waived.

7.2 For the purpose of Rule 7.1 a person shall be deemed to have obtained Control of the Company if he and others acting in concert with him have together obtained Control of it.

7.3 If any person becomes bound or entitled to acquire Shares under Sections 979 to 982 or 983 to 985 of the Companies Act 2006, an Option may be exercised within one month of the date on which that person first became so bound or entitled.

7.4 If, under Section 899 of the Companies Act 2006, the Court sanctions a compromise or arrangement applicable to or affecting:

7.4.1 all of the ordinary share capital of the Company or all of the shares of the same class as the Shares to which the Option relates; or

      7.4.2   all of the shares, or all of the shares of that same class, which are held by a class of shareholders otherwise than by reference to their employment or directorships or their participation in the Scheme or any other Schedule 3 SAYE,

an Option may be exercised within six months of the Court sanctioning the compromise or arrangement.

7.5   If notice is duly given of a resolution for the voluntary winding-up of the Company, an Option may be exercised within two months from the date of the resolution.

7.6   If any company (the 'Acquiring Company'):

      7.6.1   obtains Control of the Company as a result of making a general offer to acquire Shares;

      7.6.2   obtains Control of the Company in pursuance of a compromise or arrangement sanctioned by the Court under Section 899 of the Companies Act 2006; or

      7.6.3   becomes bound or entitled to acquire Shares under Sections 979 to 982 or Sections 983 to 985 of the Companies Act 2006,

any Participant may at any time within the Appropriate Period, by agreement with the Acquiring Company, release any Option granted under the Scheme which has not lapsed (the 'Old Option') in consideration of the grant to him of an option (the 'New Option') which (for the purposes of Paragraph 39 of Schedule 3 to ITEPA) is equivalent to the Old Option but relates to shares in a different company (whether the Acquiring Company itself or some other company falling within Paragraph 18(b) or (c) of Schedule 3 to ITEPA).

7.7   The New Option shall not be regarded for the purposes of Rule 7.6 as equivalent to the Old Option unless the conditions set out in Paragraph 39(4) of Schedule 3 to ITEPA are satisfied, but so that the provisions of the Scheme shall for this purpose be construed as if:

      7.7.1   the New Option were an option granted under the Scheme at the same time as the Old Option;

      7.7.2   except for the purposes of the definition of 'Participating Company' in Rule 1, the reference to '[COMPANY] [Limited/plc]' in the definition of 'Company' in Rule 1 were a reference to the different company mentioned in Rule 7.6 (provided that the scheme organiser (as defined in Schedule 3 of ITEPA) shall continue to be the Company); and

      7.7.3   Rule 12.2 were omitted.

8.   MANNER OF EXERCISE

8.1   An Option may only be exercised during the periods specified in Rules 6 and 7, and only with monies not exceeding the amount repaid (including any bonus or interest) under the Savings Arrangements entered into in connection therewith as at the date of such exercise. For this purpose, no account shall be taken of such part (if any) of the repayment of any Monthly Contribution, the due date for the payment of which under the Savings Arrangements arises after the date of the repayment.

8.2   Exercise shall be effected by the Participant (or by his duly authorised agent) in such manner as may be determined by the Board from time to time (including by electronic means).

8.3 Any notification of exercise pursuant to Rule 8.2 shall be accompanied by:

8.3.1 a remittance for the Exercise Price payable to the Company; or

8.3.2 an authority to the Company to withdraw and apply monies equal to the Exercise Price from the Savings Arrangements.

8.4 The effective date of exercise shall be the date of delivery of the notification of exercise.

9. ISSUE OR TRANSFER OF SHARES

9.1 The Company shall issue or transfer Shares, to the Participant pursuant to the exercise of an Option within 30 days following the effective date of exercise of the Option.

9.2 Shares issued and allotted pursuant to the Scheme will rank pari passu in all respects with the Shares then in issue at the date of such allotment, except that they will not rank for any rights attaching to Shares by reference to a record date preceding the date of allotment.

9.3 Shares to be transferred pursuant to the Scheme (including any Treasury Shares) will be transferred free of all liens, charges and encumbrances and together with all rights attaching thereto, except they will not rank for any rights attaching to Shares by reference to a record date preceding the date of transfer.

9.4 If and so long as the Shares are admitted to listing by the UK Listing Authority and traded on the London Stock Exchange or are admitted to trading on any stock exchange, stock market or other recognised exchange (the 'Relevant Exchange'), the Company shall apply for any Shares issued and allotted pursuant to the Scheme to be admitted to listing by the UK Listing Authority, or to be listed or traded on the Relevant Exchange, as soon as practicable after the allotment thereof.

9.5 Shares acquired pursuant to the exercise of an Option shall be subject to the Company's Articles of Association as amended from time to time.

10. ADJUSTMENTS

10.1 The number of Shares over which an Option has been granted and the Option Price thereof shall be adjusted in such manner as the Board shall determine following any capitalisation issue (other than a scrip dividend), rights issue, subdivision, consolidation, reduction of share capital or any other variation of share capital of the Company.

10.2 Any adjustment made pursuant to Rule 10.1 to take account of a variation in any share capital of the Company must secure that:

10.2.1 the total Market Value of the Shares which may be acquired by the exercise of the option is immediately after the variation substantially the same as it was immediately before the variation or variations; and

10.2.2 the total price at which those Shares may be acquired is immediately after the variation substantially the same as it was immediately before the variation or variations,

And that following any such variation the requirements of Schedule 3 to ITEPA continue to be met.

10.3 Subject to Rule 10.4, an adjustment may be made under Rule 10.1 which would have the effect of reducing the Option Price in relation to an Option to be satisfied by an issue of Shares to less than the nominal value of a Share, but only if, and to the extent that, the Board shall be authorised to capitalise from the reserves of the Company a sum equal to the amount by which the nominal value of the Shares in respect of which the Option is exercisable exceeds the adjusted Exercise Price, and so that on the exercise of any Option in respect of which the Option Price has been so reduced, the Board shall capitalise and apply such sum (if any) as is necessary to pay up the amount by which the aggregate nominal value of the Shares in respect of which the Option is exercised exceeds the Exercise Price for such Shares.

10.4 Where an Option subsists over both issued and unissued Shares, an adjustment permitted by Rule 10.3 may only be made if the reduction of the Option Price of both issued and unissued Shares can be made to the same extent.

10.5 The Board may take such steps as it may consider necessary to notify Participants of any adjustment made under this Rule 10 and to call in, cancel, endorse, issue or reissue any option certificate consequent upon such adjustment.

10.6 Any adjustment to an Option pursuant to this Rule 10 Shall be notified to HM revenue and Customs in accordance with Paragraph 40B(6) of Schedule 3 to ITEPA.

11. ADMINISTRATION

11.1 Any notice or other communication under, or in connection with, this Scheme may be given by the Company to a Participant personally, by email or by post, or by a Participant to the Company or any Group Company either personally or by post to the Secretary of the Company. Items sent by post shall be pre-paid and shall be deemed to have been received 48 hours after posting. Items sent by email shall be deemed to have been received immediately.

11.2 A Participant shall not be entitled to:

11.2.1 receive copies of accounts or notices sent to holders of Shares;

11.2.2 exercise voting rights; or

11.2.3 receive dividends,

in respect of Shares subject to an Option legal title to which has not been transferred to the Participant.

11.3 The Company shall at all times keep available for allotment unissued Shares at least sufficient to satisfy all Options under which Shares may be subscribed, or procure that sufficient Shares (which may include Treasury Shares) are available for transfer to satisfy all Options under which Shares may be acquired.

11.4 The decision of the Board in any dispute relating to an Option or the due exercise thereof or any other matter in respect of the Scheme shall be final and conclusive.

11.5 The costs of introducing and administering the Scheme shall be borne by the Company.

12. ALTERATIONS

12.1 Subject to Rule 12.2, the Board may at any time add to or alter the Scheme in any respect provided that the Scheme continues to qualify as a Schedule 3 SAYE.

12.2 Subject to Rule 12.3, no alteration or addition to the advantage of present or future Participants relating to eligibility, the limits on participation, the overall limits on the issue of Shares or the transfer of Treasury Shares, the basis for determining a Participant's entitlement to, or the terms of, Shares provided pursuant to the Scheme and the provisions for adjustments on a variation of share capital shall be made without the prior approval by ordinary resolution of the shareholders of the Company in general meeting.

12.3 Rule 12.2 shall not apply to any alteration or addition which is necessary or desirable in order to ensure that the Scheme continues to qualify as a Schedule 3 SAYE, or to comply with or take account of the provisions of any proposed or existing legislation, law or other regulatory requirements or to take advantage of any changes in legislation, law or other regulatory requirements, or to obtain or maintain favourable taxation, exchange control or regulatory treatment of the Company, any Subsidiary or any Participant or to make minor amendments to benefit the administration of the Scheme.

12.4 No alteration or addition shall be made under Rule 12.1 which would abrogate or adversely affect the subsisting rights of a Participant, unless it is made:

12.4.1 with the consent in writing of such number of Participants as hold Options under the Scheme to acquire not less than 75 per cent of the Shares subject to all Options under the Scheme;

12.4.2 by a resolution at a meeting of Participants passed by not less than 75 per cent of the Participants who attend and vote either in person or by proxy; or

12.4.3 pursuant to a decision of HM Revenue & Customs under paragraph 40I of Schedule 3 to ITEPA such that it is required in order that the Scheme qualifies or continues to qualify as a Schedule 3 SAYE,

and for the purpose of Rules 12.4.1 and 12.4.2 the Participants shall be treated as the holders of a separate class of share capital and the provisions of the Articles of Association of the Company relating to class meetings shall apply mutatis mutandis.

12.5 Any alteration to a Key Feature shall be notified to HM Revenue & Customs in accordance with Paragraph 40B(6) of Schedule 3 to ITEPA.

12.6 The Board may, in respect of Eligible Employees who are or who may become subject to taxation outside the United Kingdom on their remuneration, establish such schemes or sub-schemes (which shall not be Schedule 3 SAYEs) based on the Scheme but subject to such modifications as the Board determines to be necessary or desirable to take account of or to mitigate or to comply with relevant overseas taxation, securities or exchange control laws, provided that the terms of options granted under such schemes or sub-schemes are not overall more favourable than the terms of Options granted under the Scheme and provided that options granted, and shares issued, pursuant to such schemes or sub-schemes shall count towards the limits in Rule 5.

12.7 As soon as reasonably practicable after making any alteration or addition under Rule 12.1, the Board shall give written notice thereof to any Participant affected thereby.

13. GENERAL

13.1 The Scheme shall terminate on the 10th anniversary of its adoption or at any earlier time by resolution of the Board or an ordinary resolution of the shareholders in general meeting. Such termination shall be without prejudice to the subsisting rights of Participants.

13.2   The Company and any Subsidiary of the Company may provide money to the trustees of any trust or any other person to enable them or him to acquire Shares to be held for the purposes of the Scheme, or enter into any guarantee or indemnity for these purposes, to the extent that such is not prohibited by Chapter 2 of Part 2 of the Companies Act 2006, provided that any trust deed to be made for this purpose shall, at a time when the Scheme is approved by HM Revenue and Customs under Schedule 3 to ITEPA, have previously been submitted to HM Revenue and Customs.

13.3   Save as otherwise provided under the Plan:

13.3.1   Shares issued and allotted pursuant to the Plan will rank pari passu in all respects with the Shares then in issue at the date of such allotment, except that they will not rank for any rights attaching to Shares by reference to a record date preceding the date of allotment; and

13.3.2   Shares to be transferred pursuant to the Plan will be transferred free of all liens, charges and encumbrances and together with all rights attaching thereto, except they will not rank for any rights attaching to Shares by reference to a record date preceding the date of transfer.

13.4   If and so long as the Shares are admitted to listing and/or for trading on any stock exchange or market, the Company shall apply for any Shares issued and allotted pursuant to the Plan to be so admitted as soon as practicable.

13.5   Any transfer of Shares under the Plan is subject to such consent, if any, of any authorities in any jurisdiction as may be required, and the Participant shall be responsible for complying with the requirements to obtain or obviate the necessity for such consents.

13.6   The rights and obligations of any individual under the terms of his office or employment with the Company, any past or present Participating Company, Subsidiary, or Associated Company shall not be affected by his participation in the Scheme and the Scheme shall not form part of any contract of employment between the individual and any such company.

13.7   By participating in the Scheme, the Participant waives all and any rights to compensation or damages in consequence of the termination of his office or employment with any such company mentioned in Rule 13.5 for any reason whatsoever, whether lawfully or otherwise, insofar as those rights arise or may arise from his ceasing to have rights under or to be entitled to exercise any Option under the Scheme as a result of such termination, or from the loss or diminution in value of such rights or entitlements, including by reason of the operation of the terms of the Scheme, any determination by the Board pursuant to a discretion contained in the Scheme or the provisions of any statute or law relating to taxation.

13.8   Benefits under the Scheme shall not form part of a Participant's remuneration for any purpose and shall not be pensionable.

13.9   By participating in the Scheme, the Participant consents to the collection, processing, transmission and storage by the Company, in any form whatsoever, of any data of a professional or personal nature which is necessary for the purposes of introducing and administering the Scheme. The Company may share such information with any Participating Company or Associated Company, a nominee, the trustee of a Trust, its registrars, brokers, other third party administrator or any person who obtains Control of the Company or acquires the company, undertaking or part-undertaking which employs the Participant, whether within or outside of the European Economic Area.

13.10 The invalidity or non-enforceability of any provision or Rule of the Scheme shall not affect the validity or enforceability of the remaining provisions and Rules of the Scheme which shall continue in full force and effect.

13.11 These Rules shall be governed by and construed in accordance with English Law.

13.12 The English courts shall have exclusive jurisdiction to determine any dispute which may arise out of, or in connection with, the Scheme.

Chapter 13

Takeovers, Reconstructions, Demergers and Dividends

TAKEOVERS

13.1   Most employees' share schemes make some provision for the takeover of the company whose shares are used under the scheme. This is necessary to protect participants who might otherwise find that after a takeover they retain shares in a company which has become a dormant subsidiary and are therefore much less valuable. Where new shares may need to be issued, which is often the case in relation to a discretionary share option scheme or EMI, express provision needs to be made to protect the position of participants. On the other hand, under SIPs and many LTIPs, the trustees already hold sufficient shares and are, therefore, in a position to accept any offer which is made to shareholders generally.

Share purchase agreement v general offer

13.2   A takeover can be effected in one of a number of ways, the most common of which are:

(a)   by a share purchase agreement entered into by all the selling shareholders which is, therefore, normally only practicable where the offer is made for a private company with a limited number of shareholders;

(b)   a 'general offer' for the shares not already owned by the offeror (or its associates) and which will usually be expressed to be conditional upon (amongst other things) the acceptance of the offer by a majority of the ordinary shareholders such as to give the offeror control; and

(c)   a scheme of arrangement sanctioned by the Court pursuant to which all shares in the target company are transferred or cancelled in consideration of an issue of shares or a cash payment made by the offeror to the shareholders of the target company.

13.3   CSOP and SAYE scheme rules, even of private companies, will generally deal with the rights of optionholders on a 'general offer' rather than a share purchase agreement, mirroring the relevant legislative provisions. However, HMRC will in practice treat share purchase agreements as a 'general offer' provided identical terms are available to all shareholders of the same class. There is even a precedent for HMRC treating share purchase agreements as a 'general offer' even though the form, but not the value, of the consideration for each share to be acquired varied between different shareholders. Similarly, for non-UK companies, HMRC are willing to treat a wide range of arrangements which deal with takeovers or mergers under local law as being 'general offers' provided identical terms are available to all shareholders of the same class. Even if HMRC shows admirable flexibility in interpreting the term 'general offer', it is still preferable for the share option schemes of private companies to be drafted allowing for rights of exercise upon any 'change of control' rather than a general offer becoming unconditional.

Where a scheme provides for the vesting of options or awards on the sanction of a scheme of arrangement, care needs to be taken in considering the drafting of the scheme rules as, especially in older scheme rules which reflect legislative provisions now no longer in force, the schemes may provide for exercise or vesting only where the scheme of arrangement is for the purposes of a reconstruction of the company or its amalgamation with another company. A reconstruction or amalgamation will only occur where the shareholders of the target company receive share or partly share consideration for their shares in the target company, and so a right of exercise or vesting may not arise under the scheme of arrangement provision in the context of a cash-based offer. A practical solution to this issue is to invoke the rules relating to general offers, as a cash-based scheme of arrangement would also generally fall within this term. However, if the general offer provisions need to be relied on in such cases, it will be the scheme of arrangement going effective (ie the change of control) and not its sanction by the Court which will often be the exercise or vesting trigger. A further consideration is whether there are effective lapse provisions where a scheme of arrangement is treated as a general offer, as the compulsory acquisition provisions of CA 2006, ss 979–982 will not be applicable.

Public companies and the Takeover Code

13.4   The Takeover Code applies to offers for all listed companies. It also applies to offers for unlisted public companies considered by the Takeover Panel to be resident in the UK, the Channel Islands or the Isle of Man and to certain private companies considered to be so resident where for certain periods in the previous 10 years the company has been subject to public marketing arrangements. The Takeover Code lays down both principles and procedural rules relating to all takeover and merger transactions including full takeover offers, partial offers, schemes of arrangement, offers by a parent company for shares in a subsidiary and certain other transactions where control is to be obtained or consolidated.

13.5   Under General Principle 1 of the Takeover Code, all shareholders of the same class of an offeree company must be treated similarly by an offeror. There is, therefore, no scope for an offeror to treat the trustee of a Share

Incentive Plan (SIP), or for that matter, any other employee benefit trust, differently to other shareholders of the same class.

13.6   Under Rule 15 of the Takeover Code, where an offer is made for equity share capital and the offeree company has any options or other rights over shares, which would include employee share options, outstanding, the offeror must make 'an appropriate offer or proposal' to the holders of options to ensure that their interests are safeguarded (whether or not those options are exercisable). The Takeover Code requires 'equality of treatment' and the board of the offeree company must obtain competent advice on the offer or proposal and the substance of the advice must be made known to optionholders. In addition, details of the proposals being made in respect of options should be despatched to the holders at the same time as the offer is despatched to shareholders, but if this is not practicable then, after consultation with the Takeover Panel, the proposals should be despatched as soon as possible thereafter. A copy of the offer or proposal should be lodged with the Takeover Panel at the time of issue. The Takeover Panel has issued Practice Statement No 24 (Appropriate Offers and Proposals under Rule 15) which sets out further provisions which will apply in a takeover situation to employee options. The main provisions are:

(a)   *See-through value* – in order to be 'appropriate' the proposal to optionholders should be for no less than the 'see-through' value of the options calculated by reference to the offer consideration but taking into account any exercise price. The 'time value' of an option need not be recognised.

(b)   *No offer for underwater options* – where the see-through value is zero or negative (ie the option price is higher than the offer consideration), no Rule 15 offer or proposal will normally be required.

(c)   *Different offers* – provided that the see-through value of the offer made to optionholders is consistent with the value of the offer to shareholders, alternative offers, for example a different form of consideration which may include an option rollover, may be offered.

(d)   *Equality of treatment* – the principle of equality applies as between optionholders under the same scheme, but does not require the offeror to treat each share scheme in the same manner and so, for example, different offers may be made to the holders of options under different schemes.

(e)   *Offer period* – where an offer to optionholders may be accepted during the normal takeover period, this will be sufficient. However, where options may only be exercised after a change of control, the offer must remain open for acceptance for at least 21 days following the making of proposals to optionholders.

13.7   Rule 21 of the Takeover Code prohibits an offeree company, without the approval of its shareholders in general meeting, from (amongst other things) granting options in respect of any unissued shares either during the course of an offer, or even before the date of an offer, if the offeree has reason to believe that a bona fide offer may be imminent. Note 6 to Rule 21 provides that where the offeree company proposes to grant options over shares, the timing and level of which are in accordance with its normal practice under an established share scheme, the Takeover Panel will normally waive the need for shareholders' approval. Likewise, the Panel will normally give its consent to the issue of new shares or to the transfer of shares from treasury to satisfy the exercise of options under an established share option scheme.

Share and share option schemes

13.8   There are three ways in which the rights of participants can be dealt with on a takeover offer (although references below are to options, the same provisions may apply to share schemes where the participant has a conditional right to receive shares):

(a)   by exercise of the option so that the optionholder can accept the takeover offer;

(b)   by a rollover of options, ie release of the existing option in consideration of the grant of a replacement option of equivalent value over the shares of the offeror; and

(c)   by a release of the option for a cash consideration.

Where participants hold shares subject to restrictions, any takeover offer will extend to those shares and participants (or the trustee holding those shares, if appropriate) will be able to accept the offer subject to any terms set out in the governing plan rules or agreement.

Exercise and acceptance of the offer

13.9   The obligation under the Takeover Code which requires an offeror to make 'an appropriate offer or proposal' to optionholders (see **13.6** above) is invariably fulfilled by, amongst other things, allowing optionholders to exercise any rights of exercise they may have, and then accepting the takeover offer.

Savings-related share option schemes

13.10   Whether an optionholder under an SAYE scheme will be able to exercise his option and accept the takeover offer depends on the precise terms of the scheme rules. The legislation relating to SAYE schemes allows the scheme rules to provide for the exercise of options during (amongst other things):

(a)   the six months following a change of control as a result of a general offer becoming unconditional;

(b)   any period in which an offeror is bound or entitled to acquire shares in a company following the acquisition of 90 per cent of its shares under CA 2006, ss 979–982;

(c)   the six months following the sanction of a scheme of arrangement affecting all of the company's share capital, or all of the shares of the same class as those to be acquired under the SAYE scheme; and

(d)   since 6 April 2014, a 'non-UK copany reorganisation arrangement', being an arrangement under local laws which gives effect to a reorganisation of the company's share capital by consolidation and/or division, and which is approved by a majority of the company's shareholders.

The scheme rules may provide for a shorter period for the exercise of options following the takeover offer becoming unconditional, but in no circumstances may the scheme rules provide for a longer period of exercise nor may the right of exercise commence earlier (although it is possible for SAYE rules to provide that options may be exercised during the 20 day period prior to the anticipated date of any of the above events, with such exercise becoming ineffective if the change event does not happen within that 20 day window). As mentioned at **13.3** above, it appears to be HMRC practice to allow an exercise of options even if the takeover takes the form of a share purchase agreement rather than a general offer provided all shareholders are treated in the same manner and a cash scheme of arrangement will also trigger the 'general offer' provisions.

Where options under an approved savings-related share option scheme are exercised earlier than the normal bonus date under the linked savings arrangements, for example on the occurrence of a takeover, the optionholder will only be able to acquire such number of shares under option as may be purchased at the option exercise price with the accrued savings plus interest (if any). As a result, there is effectively a time apportionment applying to the options. Unless a rollover (see **13.16** below) is to be offered, the target company will often seek to agree with the offeror that employees are compensated for the inability to exercise in full (and/or for any unforeseen income tax liability), although the offeror is not obliged to agree to any such request.

Where, following a takeover, the shares under option no longer satisfy the legislative conditions, it would not be possible to exercise the option on tax-advantaged terms (and some schemes do not even provide for the right of exercise in such circumstances). ITEPA 2003, Sch 3, para 37(6B), introduced by FA 2014, now permits scheme rules to include a provision allowing options to be exercised within the period of 20 days following a takeover and still be treated as if exercised at a time when all the legislative conditions were met. Approved discretionary share option schemes

13.11   In the case of an approved discretionary share option scheme, there are no rules laid down in the legislation for the periods during which options are exercisable in the event of a takeover. In practice, however, most schemes allow for similar periods as under savings-related share option schemes. As with SAYE schemes, FA 2014 introduced the potential for options to be exercised within 20 days of a takeover where the legislative conditions cease to be met, and be treated as if all the legislative conditions were met at the time of exercise (ITEPA 2003, Sch 4, para 25A(7B)).

Income tax and National Insurance on CSOP and SAYE option gains

13.12   Gains arising on the exercise of CSOP and SAYE options following a takeover will be free of income tax where the option has been held for at least three years or the consideration under the offer is cash (without any other asset) and provided that the offeror does not offer a rollover. In all other cases, income tax will be due on the difference between the market value of the shares acquired, which will generally equate to the value of the consideration payable for those shares, and the exercise price (ITEPA 2003, ss 477, 519 and 524). For options other than SAYE options, income tax is payable under PAYE if the shares are listed or otherwise readily convertible assets (see **5.9** above); otherwise by self-assessment (which will also apply to any income tax on the exercise of SAYE options as a result of the shares not being treated as readily convertible assets). National Insurance contributions will also be due on the exercise of share options where the income tax is collected under PAYE. HMRC acknowledege the administrative difficulties which may arise where a significant number of individuals have to complete self-assessment returns solely on the basis of SAYE option gains. Consequently, it will be acceptable for employees to agree to have their tax liability accouted for through payroll – such an arrangement must be voluntary, as employees must have the opportunity of choosing to pay tax under self-assessment if they so wish. If this facility is to be offered, the company must seek permission from its PAYE tax district and tax amounts must be collected and paid to HMRC with the normal monthly remittance and fully accounted for in year end returns. HMRC Employee Shares and Securities Unit must also be notified of the arrangements.

Income tax and National Insurance on unapproved option gains

13.13   Income tax is chargeable on unapproved option gains. The income tax is payable through PAYE, and NICs are also payable, if the shares are listed or otherwise readily convertible assets.

13.14   An optionholder who accepts a takeover offer will normally be able to accept any of the choices of consideration open to shareholders whether this is cash, shares in the offeror, loan notes in the offeror or otherwise. This means that if a particular form of consideration – say any cash alternative – is only open to shareholders who accept the offer until a specified date which falls before the offer has become unconditional in all respects, the optionholders will be deprived of the opportunity to elect for that particular form of consideration. However, an optionholder may be able to obtain that particular form of consideration by exercising his option without accepting the offer. Assuming the shares arising on the exercise of the option are compulsorily acquired under the provisions of CA 2006, ss 979–982, the optionholder will be entitled to elect for any particular form of consideration which was originally available to shareholders under the offer (CA 2006, s 981(3)).

Rollovers of options – tax-advantaged options

13.15   A rollover of tax-advantaged (CSOP, SAYE and EMI) options involves an offer by an acquiring company to grant replacement options upon the release of the existing options in the target company. The replacement options must continue to satisfy the relevant legislation, including as to the type of share which may be used. Subject to this, repleacement options may be granted over shares in any company in the acquiring company's group (although, for EMI options, only shares in the acquirer may be used) and may be over issued or unissued share capital. It follows, of course, that unincorporated offerors cannot offer a rollover facility. An offeror which is under the control of a private company can only offer to replace the existing options by replacement options over its ultimate parent if the ultimate parent is so willing.

13.16   There are three principal reasons for a company offering a rollover facility. First, where a company with an SAYE scheme or CSOP is taken over by a private company then the scheme shares in that company will cease to satisfy the requirements of ITEPA 2003, Sch 3, para 19 (SAYE options) or ITEPA 2003, Sch 4, para 17 (CSOP options) upon the cessation of listing, with the result that, unless exercised within 20 days under a rule permitted by ITEPA 2003, Sch 3, para 37(6B), or Sch 4, para 25A(7B), income tax is chargeable on any option gains arising. The solution is to allow a rollover of options into the shares of a company in the acquiring group assuming those shares satisfy the provisions of ITEPA 2003, Sch 3, paras 18–20 and 22 or ITEPA 2003, Sch 4, paras 15–18 and 20, as appropriate. This is, therefore, the only way in which rights of exercise can be preserved with income tax relief in a takeover by a private company. The second reason for rollovers in SAYE and CSOP schemes is to avoid the premature income tax charge which may arise, depending on the consideration being offered on the takeover, where options are exercised within three years of the date of grant (see **5.25** above). The third reason for rollovers relates specifically to SAYE schemes. As noted above, in such schemes, optionholders are restricted on an early exercise of options to acquiring only such number of shares as may be purchased with their accumulated savings and interest at the date of exercise. An early exercise of options, therefore, has the effect that optionholders will lose the opportunity to realise the accrued gains on the shares to the extent the savings contract is incomplete (this may also be the case in relation to other share plans where time apportionment applies). The point of a rollover of options, therefore, is to allow the optionholder to continue saving until the bonus date and, therefore, eventually realise the gains on all the shares assuming, of course, that the shares under option retain their value between the date of the rollover and the eventual bonus date.

13.17   The facility for a rollover of tax-advantaged options only applies where:

(a)   the acquiring company obtains control of the company whose shares are held in the scheme as a result of making a general offer to acquire either all the issued ordinary share capital of the company which is made on a condition such that if it is satisfied the offeror will have control of all the shares of the same class as the shares used in the scheme;

(b)   the acquiring company obtains control of a company whose shares are scheme shares in pursuance of a compromise or arrangement sanctioned by the court under CA 2006, s 899;

(c)   the acquiring company becomes bound or entitled under CA 2006, ss 979–982 to acquire shares in a company whose shares are used under the scheme.

For EMI options, a rollover may also be offered where there is a 'qualifying exchange of shares', effectively where there is any other arrangement under which the consideration receivable by shareholders in the original company cosists wholly of the issue of shares in a new company.

13.18   The maximum period during which the offer to rollover tax-advantaged options may be made available by the offeror is:

(a)   where a general offer has become unconditional, six months;

(b)   where the court sanctions a scheme of arrangement under CA 2006, s 899, six months;

(c)   where the offeror's rights of acquisition under CA 2006, ss 979–982 are invoked, during the period the offeror is bound or entitled to acquire the shares of the dissenting shareholders.

13.19   The shares offered under the replacement option must satisfy the conditions of ITEPA 2003, Sch 3, paras 17–20 and 22 (SAYE options) or Sch 4, paras 15–18 and 20 (CSOP) and, for EMI options, the provisions of Sch 5, para 43 must be met. The replacement option is governed by the rules of the target company scheme – it is, therefore, immaterial whether the offeror has its own share option scheme. The replacement option must be 'equivalent' to the existing option. The total amount payable on exercise of the replacement option must be the same as the total amount payable under the existing option. The total market value of the shares under the replacement option must be equivalent to the total market value of the shares under the existing option immediately before the time of release. Where the shares in the offeror and the target company are both quoted on a recognised stock exchange and the offer is in the form of a share for share offer, then the basis of exchange of shares available to shareholders will be accepted by HMRC as 'equivalent' value and the offeror company need only notify HMRC of the exchange. In all other cases, the basis of exchange must be considered by Shares and Assets Valuation on the basis of the market values of the shares. An appropriate basis of exchange will be agreed for a limited period which will usually be a maximum of 21 days. When applying to HMRC for approval of any basis of exchange HMRC will normally require the following:

(a)   a copy of the proposed rollover calculation;

(b)   the offer documentation; and

(c)   a copy of the articles of association of the company whose shares will be used in the scheme, unless company is, or is to be, listed on a recognised stock exchange.

To avoid HMRC having to be approached on multiple occasions it may be possible to ensure that all options are rolled over on the same day.

Shares and Assets Valuation will agree that a rollover may be effected as follows: the original option price is adjusted by the market value of a share in the offeror on the day agreed with HMRC divided by the market value of share in the offeree on the same day; and the number of shares under individual options is adjusted by its reciprocal, ie the market value of a share in the offeree divided by the market value of share in the offeror.

Example 1

The optionholder has an option over 1,000 shares with an exercise price of 150p per share. An offer is made for the company at 500p per share. At the time that the rollover is made, a share in the offeror is worth 800p per share. The rollover calculation is as follows:

(a)   The exercise price of the replacement option is:

$$\frac{150p \times 800p}{500p} \quad \begin{array}{l}\text{(offeror share price)} \\ \text{(offeree share price)}\end{array}$$

$$= 240p$$

(b)   The number of shares under the replacement option is:

$$\frac{1,000 \times 500p}{800p} \quad \text{(the reciprocal of (a) above)}$$

$$= 625 \text{ shares}$$

The replacement option over 625 shares has an aggregate exercise price of £1,500 (240p × 625), being equal to the original aggregate exercise price (150p × 1,000). The aggregate gain on exercise of the new option is £3,500, calculated as 625 shares x (800 – 240), which is equal to the aggregate gain on the old option at the time of rollover, calculated as 1,000 shares × (500 – 150).

It is often the case that, where the rollover is to be effected immediately following the change of control, the market value of the two shares to be used in the calculation is taken on the last day of trading in the offeree's shares. Once the takeover has become effective, the offer consideration will likely be substituted for the market value of an offeree share as there will no longer be a readily ascertainable value for those shares, and the offer price will have been fixed.

13.20 The tax treatment of any rollover under a tax-advantaged share option scheme is as follows:

(a) Income tax – The replacement option is treated as granted at the same time as the old option was granted, with the result that income tax will only be payable on the exercise of the replacement option in the same circumstances as applied to the old option. In practical terms, this means that exercise rights and lapse provisions will be measured not from the date of the replacement option, but the date of the original option. Even if there were no express statutory provisions in ITEPA 2003, Sch 3, para 39(5) and Sch 4, para 27(5) about the effect of the SAYE and CSOP rollover provisions including overriding any income tax charges at the time of the rollover of options, ITEPA 2003, s 483 would still have the same effect.

(b) Capital gains tax – The release of the old option in consideration of the grant of a replacement option at a lower price is, in principle, a disposal of a chargeable asset (the old option) for the purposes of capital gains tax. This is because the surrender of rights is treated as a disposal for the purpose of TCGA 1992, s 22(1)(c). The proceeds of the disposal is the value which accrues to the optionholder as a result of his receiving an option to buy shares at a price which is less than their current market value. However, relief is provided in TCGA 1992, s 237A which provides for a rollover in respect of the option so that the replacement option is treated as the same asset as the old option.

There will be no National Insurance contributions liability on the rollover, and on the eventual exercise of the option National Insurance would only apply to the extent that it would have applied to the original option had that option been exercised at the same time.

Rollover of unapproved options and restricted share awards

13.21 The tax treatment of any rollover under an unapproved share option scheme (including an unapproved rollover of a tax-advantaged option, ie outside the scheme rules) is as follows:

(a) Income tax – the replacement option is treated as granted at the same time as the old option was granted with the result that income tax will be payable on exercise of the replacement option under ITEPA 2003, s 483. If the shares are readily convertible assets at the date of exercise then the income tax on any gains will be collected through PAYE (ITEPA 2003, s 700(2)).

(b) Capital gains tax – the capital gains tax treatment of the rollover of an unapproved option is identical to the treatment of the rollover of an approved option (TCGA 1992, s 237A): see **13.20** above.

(c) National Insurance contributions (NICs) – relief from NICs is available on the rollover of unapproved options where the total discount to the market value of the shares under the replacement option is not substantially greater than the total discount on the original option at the time of rollover (Social Security (Contributions) Regulations 2001, Sch 3, Pt IX, para 15).

The tax treatment of a rollover under a share scheme which provides for restricted (including forfeitable) shares is as follows:

(a)   Income tax – provided that the unrestricted market value of the replacement shares is no greater than that of the original shares immediately prior to the exchange, there will be no income tax in relation to the disposal of the original shares or the acquisition of the replacement shares, and the disposal is not a chargeable event (ITEPA 2003, s 430A(5)). Provided that the restrictions applying to the replacement shares mirror those attaching to the original shares, tax charges in relation to the replacement shares will follow those which would have applied to the original shares.

(b)   Capital gains tax – the capital gains tax treatment of a rollover of restricted shares will follow the normal rules for a share-for-share exchange under TCGA 1992, s 135.

(c)   National Insurance contributions (NICs) – relief from NICs is available on the acquisition of the replacement shares were no income tax charge arises (Social Security (Contributions) Regulations 2001, Sch 3, Pt IX, para 9). As there is no income tax charge on the disposal of the original shares, no NIC charge arises under Social Security (Contributions) Regulations 2001, reg 22(7).

Surrender of an option for a cash consideration

13.22   The offers made to optionholders on a takeover may include an offer to surrender their options in consideration of the payment of cash equal to any accrued gain.

13.23   The offer must be made by or on behalf of the offeror, not the target company, in respect of tax-advantaged options. The reason for this is that, where the payment is made by the target company, HMRC will regard this as a feature of the scheme which is not made available in accordance with ITEPA Sch 3 or Sch 4, as appropriate, and so would be contrary to ITEPA 2003, Sch 3, para 5 (SAYE) or ITEPA 2003, Sch 4, para 5 (CSOP).

13.24   In a letter to professional advisers dated 6 February 1991, HMRC accepted that a target company will often wish to advise and make recommendations to its optionholders about the various offers made by an offeror company and has indicated that it will not treat the provision of such advice and recommendations as unacceptable in connection with an SAYE or CSOP scheme. In practice, HMRC will normally accept the target company making the offers to its optionholders on behalf of the offeror. HMRC will treat any payments made by the trustees of an employee benefit trust which has a close relationship with the target company in the same way as if they were made by the company which established the scheme.

Taxation

13.25   Any sum received by an optionholder for the surrender of his option will be chargeable to income tax by virtue of ITEPA 2003, s 477(3)(b). The tax charge is based on the whole of the sum received less any sum paid for the grant of the option or for its surrender. The surrender of the option is also treated as a disposal of a chargeable asset (the option) for capital gains tax, but as the amount brought into charge to income tax will be taken into account in computing the amount of any chargeable gain, no gain will in practice arise. The surrender of an option for a cash payment will be subject to PAYE.

13.26   Following the introduction of the statutory corporation tax deduction in FA 2003 (now CTA 2009), the surrender of options for cash is likely to be unattractive as there will be a loss of the corporation tax deduction which would have been available had the options been exercised.
Private company offerors often propose a surrender for cash for administrative purposes as the statutory corporation tax deduction would, before changes introduced by FA 2014, have been lost in any event as a result of the shares which would otherwise have been acquired ceasing to satisfy the legislative consitions in CTA 2009, s 1016, namely that the shares acquired must either be in a company not under the control of another company, listed on a recognised stock exchange or in company under the control of a company listed on such an exchange. CTA 2009, s 1016(1A) now provides that where the shares are acquired within 90 days of the takeover, the legislative conditions will be deemed to still be met if they were met immediately prior to the takeover.

Share incentive plans

13.27   The basic point in relation to SIPs is that the plan shares are retained by trustees subject to certain restrictions on disposal. Where there is a takeover offer or reconstruction which is treated as a 'reorganisation' for capital gains tax purposes (ie the shareholders are entitled to a rollover) then the legislation treats the new holding as substituted for the original shares and held accordingly under the terms of the SIP. To the extent any such transaction is not treated as a reorganisation, it will usually be treated as a disposal of plan shares (for instance, a cash offer for the shares), or possibly a capital receipt if the original shares have been retained and the receipt represents a capital distribution not subject to income tax, e.g. an exempt demerger distribution of shares.

Takeover offers – relaxation of the trustees' obligations

13.28   In relation to free, matching and dividend shares under a SIP, ITEPA 2003, Sch 2, paras 36(1), 61 and 67 provide that each participant must agree that (amongst other things) during the relevant holding period, he will leave the shares with the trustees (para 36(1)(a)) and not assign, charge or otherwise dispose of the beneficial interest in the shares (para 36(1)(b)).

13.29 ITEPA 2003, Sch 2, para 37, provides that the above obligations shall not prevent the participant from directing the trustees in respect of his plan shares:

(a) to accept an offer of a new holding (shares or loan notes) provided the transaction is treated as a 'reorganisation' for capital gains tax purposes (para 37(2)) – see **13.32–13.39**;

(b) to direct the trustees to agree to a transaction affecting the shares pursuant to a scheme of arrangement (para 37(3));

(c) to accept a cash offer with or without any offer of shares, loan notes or other securities, if the offer forms part of a general offer which is made to the holders of the relevant class of share such that, if it is satisfied, the offeror will obtain control of the company (para 37(4)(a));

(d) to accept an offer of qualifying corporate bonds, whether alone or with cash or other assets or both, if the offer forms part of a general offer (para 37(4)(b)).

In relation to partnership shares under a SIP, the participant is free to direct the trustee in relation to those shares at any time as there is no applicable holding period.

Trustees' circular

13.30 As a matter of general trust law, the trustees should seek the directions of the participants in relation to any takeover offer or proposed scheme of arrangement and most trust deeds provide accordingly. This will normally involve the trustees sending copies of any offer or proposal document to shareholders or participants, together with an explanatory note, seeking their directions in writing by a date shortly before the closing date of the offer or proposal.

Cash offer

13.31 If the trustees accept a cash offer for the participant's plan shares under a SIP, the participant is treated as making a disposal of those shares. The participant may be chargeable to income tax if the shares are disposed of within five years of the appropriation. For further information on the income tax treatment of disposals of plan shares, see **13.9** above. No capital gains tax liability arises in relation to a disposal from a SIP.

Where forfeiture provisions apply to matching shares where the linked partnership shares are disposed of within the forfeiture period, the plan rules may not specifically deal with whether this would apply where the partnership shares are disposed of in connection with a takeover. HMRC accept that, if considered necessary, the plan may be amended to confirm the position. Where shares are acquired by the offeror as a result of a compulsory acquisition process (or through a scheme of arrangement – see **13.40** below), and the forfeiture provisions are drafted in terms of the participant 'withdrawing' partnership shares, then it would seem clear that in these circumstances there should not be a forfeiture of the matching shares (which would also be acquired under the compulsory acquisition process or scheme).

Share consideration

13.32   Where a takeover offer is made involving share consideration for the shares acquired, the transaction will be treated as a 'reorganisation' for capital gains tax purposes if the conditions of TCGA 1992, s 135 apply, namely:

(a)   the issuer holds, or in consequence of the exchange will hold, more than 25 per cent of the ordinary share capital of the target company; or

(b)   the issuer issues the shares pursuant to a general offer for the whole of the issued share capital of the company (or all the shares of the relevant class) which is made in the first instance on a condition that, if it were satisfied, the issuer would have control of the target company; or

(c)   the issuer holds, or will in consequence of the exchange hold, the greater part of the voting power in the target company. Given that any takeover offer will normally involve the acquisition of at least 51 per cent of the ordinary share capital of the company, there will not usually be any difficulty in establishing that any takeover offer will be treated as a 'reorganisation' for capital gains tax purposes.

13.33   Assuming the takeover offer is treated as a 'reorganisation' for capital gains tax purposes, the trustee of a SIP will be treated, after the time of such reorganisation, as holding the 'new holding' on the basis that:

(a)   there was no disposal of the original holding as a result of the exchange (ITEPA 2003, Sch 2, para 87(2)(a));

(b)   the new holding is treated as if it were appropriated under the scheme at the time of the original holding (ITEPA 2003, Sch 2, para 87(2)(b));

(c)   the conditions related to scheme shares under ITEPA 2003, Sch 2, Pt 4, are treated as satisfied with respect to the new shares as if they were (or were treated as) satisfied with respect to the original holding (ITEPA 2003, Sch 2, para 87(2)(c));

(d)   the provisions relating to the taxation of SIP shares apply to the new holding as they did to the original holding (ITEPA 2003, Sch 2, para 87(2)(d)).

13.34   Following any 'reorganisation' it is necessary, unless the new shares are a 'mirror image' of the old shares, to apportion the base value of the old holding amongst the new holding after the reconstruction.

Example 1

The old holding comprised 150 shares with an aggregate base value of £300 (£2 per share). After the reorganisation, the new holding comprises 200 shares: the aggregate base value continues to be £300, but each new share will have an apportioned base value of £1.50 per share. Where the new holding comprises two or more securities with different rights to the old shares (e.g. an offer of three ordinary shares and one preference share for every one old share) then the base value for each old share must be apportioned on the basis of the relative market values of the new shares immediately following the reorganisation.

Example 2

The old holding comprised 150 shares with an aggregate base value of £300 (£2 per share). After the reorganisation, the new holding comprises:

- 200 new ordinary shares in the offeror worth £2 each (£400 in aggregate);

- 100 new preference shares in the offeror worth 50p each (£50 in aggregate).

The base value will, therefore, be apportioned as follows:

200 new ordinary shares:

$$\frac{£300}{£200} \times \frac{£400}{£450} = 1.33 \text{ each}$$

50 new preference shares:

$$\frac{£300}{£50} \times \frac{£50}{£450} = 0.67 \text{ each}$$

13.35   If, as will usually be the case, there are shares comprised in the old holding with different base values (because they were appropriated at different times) then the apportionment of the base value must be made on each appropriation separately.

13.36   To the extent the participant takes both cash and shares for an original holding, the rules set out at **13.31** above will apply to the cash and the rules set out at **13.32–13.34** will apply to the shares.

Loan note consideration

13.37   Many takeover offers provide a loan note alternative to cash on the basis of £1 nominal of loan notes for every £1 cash available. In some cases

310

the loan notes may even be convertible into shares of the offeror. Almost any loan note denominated in sterling on normal commercial terms will be a 'qualifying corporate bond' (TCGA 1992, s 117).

13.38   Under ITEPA 2003, Sch 2, para 86(2)(b), the inclusion of a 'qualifying corporate bond' in the consideration for a takeover offer will not prevent the transaction being treated, so far as a participant in a SIP is concerned, as a 'reorganisation' for capital gains tax purposes with the result that the 'qualifying corporate bond' may be held as part of the participant's new holding.

13.39   As loan notes will have a final redemption date, and often may be redeemed by the issuer early in certain specified circumstances, the SIP participant may not always be in control of when the loan notes will be deemed to cease to be subject to the SIP (i.e. on redemption) and so may realise a tax charge where there is a redemption within five years of the award of the original shares. More problematic is where the participant leaves employment within that five-year period in circumstances where a tax charge arises, as this may not coincide with a redemption window for the loan notes, resulting in a tax charge for the participant which he may not be able to fund. In these circumstances, the company may offer to cover the PAYE until the next loan note redemption date which, provided that it is within 90 days following the end of the tax year, will allow the participant to reimburse the PAYE without a penalty charge arising under ITEPA 2003, s 222.

SCHEMES OF ARRANGEMENT

Share and share option schemes

13.40   Most share and share option schemes deal with the rights of participants on a scheme of arrangement sanctioned by the Court under CA 2006, s 899. Although references below are to options, the same provisions may apply to share schemes where the participant has a conditional right to receive shares. Where participants hold shares subject to restrictions, any scheme of arrangement will extend to those shares and participants (or the trustee holding those shares, if appropriate) will, subject to any terms set out in the governing plan rules or agreement, receive the consideration under the scheme of arrangement.

13.41   A scheme of arrangement which is to be sanctioned by the Court under CA 2006, s 899 involves at least three stages:

(a)   the approval of shareholders by means of a special resolution;

(b)   the sanctioning of the scheme by the Court; and

(c)   the filing of the scheme with the Companies Registration Office at which point the scheme becomes effective ('the effective date').

In addition to the above stages it is common for the scheme to have split hearings – the Court will first sanction the scheme of arrangement and then, at a second hearing held a few days later, will approve the reduction in share capital of the company. The benefit of the split hearing is that, where options are to be exercised upon the scheme sanction, those shares may be issued prior to the reduction hearing in order that the new shares become subject to the cancellation rather than having to be transferred to the new holding company for the same consideration as under the scheme of arrangement (and attracting stamp duty on such transfer).

Exercise of options

13.42   ITEPA 2003, Sch 3, para 37(4) allows optionholders under an SAYE scheme to exercise their options within six months of the sanctioning of the scheme of arrangement (provided that the scheme extends to all of the company's shares or all of the shares of the same class as those which are acquired on the exercise of the SAYE options) by the Court; CSOP and unapproved share option schemes will generally mirror these provisions.

13.43   Although the legislation specifically provides for a right of exercise under an SAYE scheme for up to six months after the scheme is sanctioned by the Court, the Court does not have any jurisdiction to make any order in respect of unissued shares which may arise on the exercise of options particularly if, as is usual, the scheme of arrangement involves the cancellation of shares (see *Re Tip Europe and Re Transfer Terminal (1987) 3 BCC 647*).

13.44   Unless the scheme of arrangement employs split hearings, it will not be practicable to allow optionholders to exercise their options before the record date for the scheme and, therefore, qualify to participate in the scheme of arrangement as shareholders. In addition, scheme rules usually allow up to six months after the date of the Court sanction within which to exercise and this will usually mean optionholders can exercise for a significant period after the effective date and, indeed, the record date. Companies normally deal with this problem by altering the articles of association, by special resolution at the shareholders meeting, so that any new shares issued after the effective date are automatically 'flipped up' either into shares of any company which will control the company as a result of the scheme of arrangement or for the same consideration as received by shareholders under the scheme of arrangement.

13.45   Companies prefer the administration to be dealt with expeditiously and will often encourage optionholders to give irrevocable instructions to exercise their options conditionally upon the scheme of arrangement being sanctioned. Although the rights of optionholders to exercise for the full period allowed by the rules cannot be excluded, this approach will normally ensure the bulk of the optionholders' administration is dealt with at the same time as the shareholders' administration. Having a right of exercise for such a period under an SAYE scheme will, however, allow participants to continue to make savings, potentially adding up to an additional five months' contributions before having to exercise. This is one of the main differences to a general offer, which is likely to be followed by an earlier lapse date as a result of the compulsory acquisition provisions of CA 2006, ss 979–982.

Rollover of options

13.46 Alternatively, if the scheme of arrangement involves a change of control then optionholders may exchange their existing options for replacement options over shares in the new corporate entity under a rollover (see **13.15– 13.20** above).

13.47 The tax treatment on a rollover following a scheme of arrangement is identical to that set out at **13.21** above.

Share incentive plans

13.48 A scheme of arrangement between a company and its members which is sanctioned by the Court under CA 2006, s 899 will, where the consideration comprises shares, be treated as a reorganisation for capital gains tax purposes (TCGA 1992, s 136). The scheme of arrangement will apply automatically to the shares held within the SIP in the same way as to shares held by any other shareholder once the scheme becomes effective. In any event, ITEPA 2003, Sch 2, para 37(3) provides that, notwithstanding the obligations on the participant to leave shares with the trustees during the period of retention, the participant may direct the trustees to accept a proposal affecting his scheme shares, if the proposal would be entered into pursuant to a compromise, arrangement or scheme applicable to or affecting (amongst other things) all the ordinary share capital of the company or all the shares of the relevant class. Where the scheme of arrangement consideration is cash, the position is as set out at **13.31** above.

VOLUNTARY WINDING-UP

Share and share option schemes

13.49 ITEPA 2003, Sch 3, para 37(5) permits a right of exercise by optionholders under a savings-related share option scheme within six months of the passing of a resolution for the voluntary winding-up of the company. CSOP and unapproved discretionary share option schemes are also usually drafted with a similar right of exercise. It is not clear whether any rights of exercise following a voluntary winding-up would bind a liquidator.

13.50 Share schemes providing for conditional allocations of shares will usually be drafted to include a vesting provision in the event of a voluntary winding up and where participants hold shares subject to restrictions, those shares will be subject to the winding-up and participants (or the trustee holding those shares, if appropriate) will, subject to any terms set out in the governing plan rules or agreement, receive the proceeds of the winding-up (ie a distribution of assets on the same basis as other shareholders).

Share incentive plans

13.51   On a voluntary winding-up of a company, participants are entitled to a distribution of assets on the same basis as other shareholders. Any distribution will be treated as a capital receipt and therefore subject to income tax for the tax year in which the distribution is declared ITEPA 2003, s 501.

DEMERGER

13.52   A demerger involves the distribution to the shareholders of a company of shares in a subsidiary. The intention is to give the shareholders of the distributing company a direct interest in the shares of the distributed business. Any such distribution must be made out of the distributing company's distributable profits unless it is made (amongst other things) in the course of a winding-up (CA 2006, s 829(2)(d)).

13.53   A demerger distribution will normally be made in either of the following ways:

(a)   a dividend in specie; or

(b)   a 'three cornered' distribution involving the transfer of a business or '75 per cent subsidiaries' to a new company which issues shares to the shareholders of the transferor pro rata.

Share and share option schemes

13.54   The holders of options (and participants granted conditional allocations over shares) are not entitled to receive dividends since they have not been entered on the register of members. For the same reason, they also have no right to any demerger distribution. Participants holding shares subject to restrictions (or the trustee holding those shares, if appropriate) may, if the terms of the governing plan rules or agreement so allow, receive the proceeds of the demerger on the same basis as other shareholders. In such cases, the governing plan rules or agreement may provide that the distribution is held on similar terms to the restricted shares to which the distribution relates.

13.55   Most share option schemes provide for employees of any company which is transferred outside the group to exercise their options usually for a period of six months after the transfer. A demerger involves a transfer of a company outside the group and so the employees of the demerged company may have a right of exercise at that time, although as the transfer of the employment will usually be to an 'associated company' there will be no right of exercise in respect of savings-related options unless the optionholder actually leaves employment or until the associated company status is lost. The employees of the distributing company will not usually have any rights of exercise as a result of the demerger, although the scheme rules will need to be reviewed to ensure that this is the case.

13.56 However, the value of the shares comprised in the option will depreciate as a result of the demerger perhaps rendering the options substantially less valuable.

13.57 In principle, the fairest way to deal with a demerger in an option scheme would be to provide for an adjustment of the options to reflect the effect of the distribution. Whilst this is possible in an unapproved share option scheme, HMRC will not permit any such power of adjustment in an SAYE or CSOP scheme on the basis that the only adjustments allowed under the legislation are in respect of 'variations in the share capital' within ITEPA 2003, Sch 3, para 28(3) and Sch 4, para 22(3).

13.58 There are various ways in which participants in employees' share schemes have been compensated for the effects of demergers:

(a) by effecting a consolidation of share capital (see Chapter 14) so as to preserve the price of a share – the consolidation effectively compensates for the fall in value upon the demerger;

(b) an alteration of the rights of optionholders either by incorporating early rights of exercise (so that optionholders can be entered on the register of members before the record date) or by providing for an adjustment of options after the demerger – each of these amendments would be to a 'key feature' of an SAYE or CSOP option scheme and would result in the loss of tax benefits (although HMRC has the ability to agree that the tax benefits of an SAYE are maintained in these circumstances);

(c) cash compensation; and

(d) the grant of compensatory unapproved option rights.

Share consolidation

13.59 This is probably now the most common way of compensating optionholders for the fall in value on a demerger. It preserves the share price and therefore the value of the options.

Loss of tax-advantaged status and the alteration of option rights

13.60 Since the alteration of subsisting rights of exercise is not permitted by the tax-advantaged scheme legislation, the company, in making such an alteration to SAYE or CSOP option rights to allow for their adjustment to reflect any demerger will have amended a 'key feature' of the SAYE or CSOP rules (ITEPA 2003, Sch 3, para 40B(8); Sch 4, para 28B(8)). This will need to be notified to HMRC but may also, under the terms of the scheme, require the prior approval of shareholders and optionholders as well.

13.61   Alternatively, the scheme may be altered with a view to conferring on the holders of options which have not matured new rights of exercise which will enable them to be entered on the register by the record date for the demerger.

13.62   Where a 'key feature' of a tax-advantaged plan is amended in a way which does not comply with the relevant legislation, HMRC may withdraw the tax-advantaged status of the scheme. Optionholders may consequently be disadvantaged in one of the following ways:

(a)   any premature exercise of options may precipitate an unexpected liability to income tax and NIC on any option gain and the consequential loss of the capital gains tax exemption benefits;

(b)   in the case of an SAYE scheme, any early closure of the scheme may result in the optionholder's loss of the accrued gains on those shares for which he has insufficient savings to buy at the time of an early exercise.

The loss of tax relief may be the specific subject of cash compensation. Employees may also be compensated for the loss of the ability to exercise in full.

Cash compensation

13.63   A sum may be paid by the company to optionholders as compensation for the depreciation in value of the shares as a result of a demerger distribution. Any payment received as compensation for the depreciation in the value of the shares comprised in the option as a result of the demerger is within the scope of ITEPA 2003, s 477(3)(c), and will be chargeable to income tax and NIC. As far as the company making the payment is concerned, it may be possible to seek a deduction in computing the profits of the company for corporation tax purposes provided that the payment is not seen to arise from dealings in the capital of the company rather than a payment in connection with employment.

Supplementary options

13.64   A distributing company, or the company the subject of the distribution, may grant parallel options at a reduced (or nil) price to reflect the value distributed in the demerger. For instance if the depreciation in value of the shares distributed is £3 a share, then the parallel option would be granted with an initial inherent value of £3.

13.65   The grant of the parallel option rights will normally be made under a specially established unapproved share option scheme providing for the grant of options at a price less than market value. The new scheme will normally need to be approved by shareholders if it may involve the issue of new shares and this can be obtained at the same time as the demerger approval. There is no liability to income tax and NIC on the grant of an unapproved option at a discount (ITEPA 2003, s 475(1)). The new options will normally be 'linked' to the old options so that the optionholder can only exercise the new option provided that he exercises the old option at the same time (whether in full or in part). This ensures that the optionholder does not benefit from a discounted option where the gain on exercise would have been lower under the old option.

Share incentive plans

13.66 Participants are entitled to receive any distributions on the same basis as other shareholders. A distribution of shares in a subsidiary which is not an exempt distribution for the purposes of CTA 2010, s 1075 will be subject to income tax in the normal way as for any dividend and may not be held within the SIP trust.

As noted at **13.55** above, a demerger gill generally involve employees of the demerged entity being transferred outside the group. Unlike under the SAYE legislation, the demerged entity may not be deemed to be an 'associated company', and HMRC has confirmed that this will be the case where both the existing and demerged companies are listed. The difference between the definition of 'associated company' for SIP and SAYE purposes is that the SAYE legislation will look back over a 12-month period to determine whether there has been common ownership, whereas the SIP definition looks only at the relevant time. As a result of this, employees leaving the group on a demerger will be required to remove their shares from the SIP, but will be able to take advantage of a tax-free release.

Distributions as part of a scheme of reconstruction

13.67 A demerger taking the form of a 'three cornered' distribution as described at **13.53** will normally qualify for a rollover for capital gains tax purposes and as an exempt distribution for income tax purposes.

13.68 A demerger distribution satisfying the conditions of CTA 2010, s 1075 and subsequent sections will be treated as an 'exempt distribution' so that no income tax will be payable on the value of the distribution received by shareholders. HMRC's advance clearance that the proposed distribution will be an exempt distribution must be obtained.

13.69 The capital gains tax rollover is available where there is an exchange of securities as part of an arrangement between a company and its members for the purposes of a scheme of reconstruction or amalgamation (TCGA 1992, s 136). If the receipt of the new shares qualifies as a company reconstruction for capital gains tax purposes, the value of the new shares will not be treated as a capital receipt (ITEPA 2003, Sch 2, para 86(2)(a)) and may continue to be held in the SIP trust and receive tax benefits on the same basis as the shares to which the new shares relate. Other than for tax purposes, the original shares and the new shares are not linked and may therefore be dealt with by the participant in isolation.

DIVIDENDS

Share and share option schemes

13.70   Distributions are only payable to members of a company (CA 2006, s 829(1)). Participants holding shares subject to restrictions (or the trustee holding those shares, if appropriate) may, if the terms of the governing plan rules or agreement so allow, receive dividends on the same basis as other shareholders.

13.71   The holders of options or conditional allocations over unissued shares are not entitled to any dividends during the period of the options except as specifically provided by the scheme rules. Share option schemes will often provide that optionholders are entitled to all dividends or other rights arising by reference to record dates since the date of exercise. If the scheme rules are silent, then an optionholder will only be entitled to receive dividends and other rights arising on or after the date of allotment. Schemes will often provide for the company to make a payment (a 'dividend equivalent') to the participant of a cash sum (or for the provision of shares of an equivalent value) equal to the dividends which would have been received in respect of shares acquired on exercise or vesting had the participant owned those shares throughout the vesting period.

13.72   In the case of options over existing shares, the entitlement to dividends or other rights belongs to the person who is the registered holder of the shares at the record date.

SHARE INCENTIVE PLANS

13.73   Any dividends received by the trustees in respect of or by reference to any plan shares must either be paid over to the participant or reinvested in further dividend shares. Further details in relation to dividend shares can be found at **8.71** above.

13.74   The trustees will need to split any dividend received between individual participating employees and, where the dividend is paid out, provide them with vouchers for the amounts to which they are individually entitled. Individual vouchers should be issued in the name of the trustees regardless of any arrangement to mandate dividends directly to employees.

SPECIAL DIVIDENDS

13.75   A special dividend is a large dividend intended to return value to shareholders and the position is explained at **13.70–13.74** above. One effect of a special dividend is that the value of the shares may fall. It is common for companies paying a special dividend to effect a share consolidation so as to preserve the price of each share and the value of the share options.

SCRIP DIVIDENDS

13.76   Scrip dividends are commonly offered by companies as an alternative to cash at the election of the shareholder. The company's articles of association will normally provide for scrip dividends to be offered by the directors with the sanction of a resolution of the company. Most scrip dividends are based on shares with an equivalent value to the cash dividend. However, a number of companies have offered so-called 'enhanced scrip dividends' under which the value of the shares significantly exceed the value of the cash dividend. Scrip dividends are paid-up out of a capitalisation of reserves.

Share and share option schemes

13.77   Optionholders (and participants holding conditional allocations over shares) will not normally be entitled to any scrip dividend since they are not members of the company. Participants holding shares subject to restrictions (or the trustee holding those shares, if appropriate) may, if the terms of the governing plan rules or agreement so allow, receive scrip dividends on the same basis as other shareholders. In such cases, the governing plan rules or agreement may provide that the shares received are held on similar terms to the restricted shares to which the scrip dividend relates.

13.78   Since scrip dividends are paid up out of a capitalisation of reserves, there is no obvious reason why in principle optionholders are not entitled to an adjustment of options to reflect the capitalisation of reserves. Although under an enhanced scrip dividend the interests of the non-electing shareholders (including the optionholders) are clearly prejudiced, it seems unlikely that HMRC would be prepared to accept that an adjustment of options may be made since the adverse effects on options arise from shareholders accepting the offer, rather than the terms of any variation of share capital.

Share incentive plans

13.79   Any scrip dividend paid by a UK company cannot form part of the SIP holding and will generally be paid over to the SIP participant (ITEPA 2003, Sch 2, para 86(4)(c)) and will be treated as income in the hands of UK recipients (CTA 2010, s 1049 and ITTOIA 2005, s 409). On the other hand, a scrip dividend paid by a foreign company will not be treated as income in the hands of the recipient since CTA 2010, s 1049 does not apply. Indeed, any scrip dividends paid by a foreign company will normally satisfy the requirements for a capital gains tax reorganisation and, accordingly, the scrip shares will be held within the SIP trust as 'new shares'.

Chapter 14

Variations of Share Capital

INTRODUCTION

14.1   Most employees' share schemes make provision for rights and capitalisation issues, sub-divisions, consolidations and reductions of share capital. Such transactions are commonly known in the context of employees' share schemes as 'variations of share capital' as a result of the use of this term in relation to share option schemes in the Income Tax (Earnings and Pensions) Act 2003 (ITEPA 2003), Sch 3, para 28(3) and Sch 4, para 22(3). There is, of course, a significant difference in the impact a variation of share capital has on a Share Incentive Plan (SIP) and other types of share or share option schemes: whilst the shares of a participant under a SIP are affected directly, the price (if any) and number of shares under options and awards need to be adjusted so as to keep the participant in the same relative position as before the variation of share capital.

LISTING RULES

14.2   The Listing Rules do not contain any specific requirements in relation to variations of share capital other than requiring shareholders' approval for any changes to the provisions of schemes relating to rights issues, capitalisation issues, consolidations, sub-divisions and reductions of share capital.

14.3   The ABI/IMA does not make any specific reference to the adjustment of options and awards on a variation of share capital. However, it is understood that any adjustments which can be justified as fair and reasonable will be acceptable to these bodies.

TAX-ADVANTAGED SCHEMES

14.4   In the case of tax-advantaged share option schemes, HMRC requires any proposed adjustment, which must satisfy the requirements of ITEPA 2003, Sch 3, para 28(3A) (SAYE) or Sch 4, para 22(3A) (CSOP), to be agreed in advance. HMRC has, historically, not required capitalisation (bonus) issues to be approved, although this exemption does not feature in recently redrafted guidance. The company should write to Shares and Assets Valuation for their approval of the proposed adjustment. The address of Shares and Assets Valuation is given at **4.87** above.

RIGHTS ISSUES

14.5   Rights issues are normally made at a discount to the market value of the shares immediately before the rights issue is announced. Participants in a SIP can usually obtain the benefit of this discount by taking up the rights issue in respect of their shares or by selling those rights (see **14.9** below).

Share schemes

14.6   On the other hand, option and award holders are not entitled to be entered on the register of members, but, if the scheme so allows, an adjustment may be made in respect of the price (if any) and number of shares under the option or award to compensate them. The adjustment which Shares and Assets Valuation will agree in relation to the tax-CSOP and SAYE schemes using listed shares is as follows: the option price is adjusted by the hypothetical 'ex rights' price divided by the last cum rights price; and the number of shares under individual options is adjusted by its reciprocal, ie the last cum rights price divided by the hypothetical ex rights price.

Example 1

The optionholder has an option over 1,000 shares with an exercise price of 150p per share. The company announces a rights issue of one rights share at 250p for every four existing shares. The last cum rights price is 320p. The calculation is as follows:

(a)   The hypothetical ex rights price is:

		pence
4 existing shares @ 320p	=	1280
1 new rights share @ 250p	=	250
		1530

Hypothetical ex rights price	=	$1530 \div 5$
	=	306p

(b)   The adjustments are as follows:

(i)   to the option price:

$$\frac{150p \times 306p}{320p} \quad \begin{array}{l} \text{(hypothetical ex rights price)} \\ \text{(last cum rights price)} \end{array}$$

$= 143p$

321

(ii)   to the number of shares:

$$\frac{1,000 \times 320p}{306p} \quad \text{(the reciprocal of (i) above)}$$

$= 1,045$ shares

14.7   The last cum rights price is the closing price for the last day before the rights issue becomes effective. In a listed or AIM company, this will be the last day before dealings commence in the nil paid rights shares. HMRC does not take the last dealing day before the announcement (unless it also happens to be the last cum rights price day). Any adjustment based on such a day would reflect the impact which the announcement of the rights issue had on market sentiment towards the shares rather than the actual impact of the variation of capital.

14.8   Any company seeking HMRC's approval to an adjustment to options in respect of a rights issue will need to submit a copy of the rights issue document together with a copy of the proposed adjustment calculation. In the case of an unlisted company, a copy of the last three years accounts, the scheme rules and the memorandum and articles of association would also need to be submitted.

Share Incentive Plans

14.9   A SIP trust deed must contain a provision requiring the trustees to deal only pursuant to a direction given by or on behalf of the participant with any right to be allotted additional shares, securities or rights of any description (ITEPA 2003, Sch 2, para 72(1)). There is no corresponding obligation on trustees to seek the direction of participants in relation to any rights issue. However, most trust deeds are drafted on the basis that the trustees will seek such directions and in practice an explanatory circular will normally be prepared by registrars to be sent out to scheme participants contemporaneously with the despatch of the rights issue document to shareholders.

14.10   The possible courses of action which can normally be taken by a shareholder in relation to any rights issue are as follows:

(a)   take up the rights, which involves payment at the rights issue price;

(b)   sell the rights nil paid;

(c)   'tail-swallow', ie sell such part of the rights as realises sufficient cash proceeds to take up the balance of the rights (see ITEPA 2003, Sch 2, para 77(1)); or

(d)   allow the rights to lapse, in which case, depending on the terms of the rights issue, the rights will usually be sold in the market at the expiry of the offer period and the net proceeds distributed to shareholders.

As best practice, participants should be given all the choices available to shareholders, although the SIP may provide for 'standing' instructions, generally set out in the partnership or free shares agreement, given by participants to 'tail-swallow' in the event of any rights issue. Any such agreement will, however, be subject to any contrary instructions of the participant at the relevant time.

Where a rights issue takes effect during an accumulation period, and the partnership shares acquisition price is to be determined by reference either to the share price at the beginning of the accumulation period or to the lower of the share price at the beginning and end of such period, HMRC will allow for an adjustment to be made to the price to be used in order that participants are not prejudiced by there having been a discounted rights issue.

Taking up the rights

14.11 The SIP trust deed will normally provide that the trustees are only bound to act on the directions of the participant to take up a rights issue if instructions and payment by the participant are received no later than a specified number of days before the last date for taking up the rights. This is normally no earlier than five days before the last date for shareholders.

14.12 Where the participant directs the SIP trustee to take up rights by providing additional funds, the shares acquired do not form part of the SIP holding by virtue of ITEPA 2003, Sch 2, para 88(5) and are treated as new shares acquired pursuant to a securities option. Although such shares will be acquired at a discount, which would generally be taxable (ITEPA 2003, s 476), the amount by which the SIP shares reduce in value is offset against such discount (ITEPA 2003, s 480(3)), which should result in no liability to tax at the point that the rights are taken up.

14.13 The effect of the rights issue will generally be to reduce the market value of the SIP shares held by the trustee, which is then reflected, on any disposal of the SIP shares in the amount which is liable to income tax (if any).

14.14 On a disposal of the new rights shares, capital gains tax will be calculated by reference to the rights issue price paid for those shares.

Sale of the rights nil paid

14.15 The sale of the rights nil paid is not a disposal of plan shares – the rights were never part of the participant's holding – but they are treated as a 'capital receipt' (ITEPA 2003, s 501). The trustees may sell the rights in the market for a price which broadly represents any premium in dealings over the rights issue price. The trustees cannot, therefore, guarantee any price for the rights, and for that matter, cannot guarantee any sale.

14.16 Capital receipts are chargeable to income tax as employment income under PAYE. NICs will also apply in respect of such amounts.

14.17 The SIP trustee will generally withhold from the capital receipt a sufficient amount in order to meet the PAYE liability.

'Tail-swallow'

14.18 A 'tail-swallow' involves the disposal of such part of the rights shares nil paid as realises sufficient cash to take up the balance of the rights. ITEPA 2003, s 502(5) provides that any proceeds of the disposal will not be a capital receipt for the purposes of ITEPA 2003, s 501. As a result no PAYE is deducted from such proceeds – the whole of the proceeds can be applied in taking up the balance of the shares.

14.19 The legislation (ITEPA 2003, Sch 2, para 88) provides that references to a participant's shares are treated after the rights issue as including the 'new shares'. In addition, the new shares are treated as being identical to, and having been acquired at the same time as, the original holding to which those new shares relate.

Allow the rights to lapse

14.20 Where the rights are allowed to lapse and no payment is received, no liability to income tax arises and there is no effect on the SIP shares. If the rights shares are disposed of and a cash payment is received, then the cash will be dealt with as a 'capital receipt' in the same way as set out above.

CAPITALISATION ISSUES

Share schemes

14.21 A capitalisation issue (or 'bonus' issue) is treated as a 'variation of share capital' for the purposes of ITEPA 2003, Sch 3, para 28(3) and Sch 4, para 22(3). Consequently, an adjustment of SAYE and CSOP options is permitted.

14.22 The adjustment for any capitalisation issue is normally arithmetically straightforward although current HMRC guidance provides that the prior approval of HMRC Shares and Assets Valuation should be sought for any proposed adjustment.

Share Incentive Plans

14.23 A capitalisation issue is a 'company reconstruction' within ITEPA 2003, Sch 2, para 86. Capitalisation shares are allotted without payment in proportion to existing holdings in the company. The legislation provides that, after the reconstruction, references to a participant's shares includes the 'new shares'. In addition, the capitalisation issue is treated as not involving any disposal of the original holding and the new shares are treated as having been appropriated at the time the original holding was appropriated (ITEPA 2003, Sch 2, para 87). See also **14.10** above in relation to share capital variations during an accumulation period.

SUB-DIVISIONS AND CONSOLIDATIONS

14.24   Although sub-divisions and consolidations are normally straightforward arithmetical adjustments, HMRC nevertheless requires the prior approval of HMRC Shares and Assets Valuation to any such adjustment to options. A sub-division or consolidation is a 'company reconstruction' within ITEPA 2003, Sch 2, para 86 as an alteration of share rights. The same tax consequences apply, therefore, as for a capitalisation issue (see **14.23** above).

REDUCTION OF SHARE CAPITAL

14.25   A reduction of share capital is provided for by the Companies Act 2006 (CA 2006), s 641. A reduction may take the form of:

(a)   the extinguishment or reduction of the liability to pay up shares;

(b)   the cancellation of any paid-up share capital which is lost;

(c)   repayment of share capital which is in excess of the company's requirements.

The reduction must be authorised by a special resolution of the company supported by a solvency statement (private companies) or otherwise with the confirmation of the Court.

Share schemes

14.26   A reduction of share capital often means a fall in the value of the shares. In such circumstances it is usual to consolidate the shares so as to preserve the share price and protect the value of share options and awards.

14.27   A reduction of shares involving the cancellation of paid-up share capital whether by Court order or by means of market purchases, will normally have no effect on the share price and there is therefore no need to adjust share options and awards.

Share Incentive Plans

14.28   A reduction of share capital is treated as a 'reorganisation' for capital gains tax purposes by ITEPA 2003, Sch 2, para 86. It follows, therefore, that a participant's newly reduced scheme shares will normally be held by the trustees under the scheme on the same terms as the shares prior to the reduction. However, where the reduction of share capital takes the form of the issue of redeemable share capital, those shares will not form part of the SIP holding. See also **14.10** above in relation to share capital variations during an accumulation period.

OTHER VARIATIONS OF SHARE CAPITAL

14.29   The term 'variation of share capital' in ITEPA 2003, Sch 3, para 28(3) and Sch 4, para 22(3) is not a legal term and its meaning will depend on the types of transaction HMRC is prepared to treat as a 'variation'.

In particular, arrangements which are accepted by HMRC as being similar to a rights issue, and which therefore lead to the same treatment for tax-advantaged options, include:

(a)   a vendor placing with clawback where, in connection with the acquisition of another company, shares are issued to the target's shareholders on the basis that those shares are then placed on behalf of the vendors – where 'clawback' applies the shares are offered to the issuer's existing shareholders on a pro rata basis;

(b)   a vendor rights offers, which is similar to a vendor placing save that the shares issued to the target's shareholders on will automatically be offered, through provisional allotment letters, rather than by application, to the issuer's existing shareholders; and

(c)   a cash open offer, which is similar to an underwritten rights issue save that there is no secondary market in the rights offered.

Where the shareholders are offered shares at a discount to the market value, an adjustment to options might be appropriate on a similar basis to the adjustment made for a rights issue (see **14.6–14.8**). Shares taken up in a vendor placing by the trustees of a SIP against payment from the participants will usually be dealt with within the scheme as a reorganisation for capital gains tax purposes provided the vendor placing involves an 'issue' of shares, otherwise there will be no new shares (see ITEPA 2003, Sch 2, para 86).

14.30   HMRC is not prepared to include exempt demerger distributions in the types of transaction which might be treated as variations of share capital.

Chapter 15

Accounting and the Statutory Corporation Tax Deduction

ACCOUNTING FOR SHARE AWARDS

15.1   All UK companies, both listed and unlisted, must provide for 'share-based payments' in their accounts in accordance with accounting standard FRS 20 (Share-based payments), which mirrors the international standard IFRS 2. FRS 20 has applied to the accounts of listed companies since 1 January 2005 and for those of unlisted companies since 1 January 2006.

FRS 20 (IFRS 2) share-based payments

15.2   Prior to FRS 20, companies which issued shares to satisfy awards under employee share schemes would not recognise an expense in their profit and loss account, as this would be treated as a share capital transaction. International standard setters, however, considered that the provision of shares to employees forms part of their remuneration and should therefore be recognised in the accounts as an expense to the company's profit and loss account. This principle was then extended to encompass other forms of share-based payment, such as the grant of share options.

Fair value

15.3   At the time that a company makes an award or grant to an employee which constitutes a share-based payment, it must record the 'fair value' of that payment as an expense in its profit and loss account, with a credit made of a corresponding amount in either a share account in shareholders' funds (where the liability is to be equity settled) or in the company's cash account (for cash-settled share-based payments). Although guidance has been given in relation to valuing options and awards in order to determine the 'fair value' there is no specific definition given in FRS 20. As the fair value of an option or award is measured at the time of its grant, it will not be clear at that stage whether the option will be exercised or the award will vest. As a result, the fair value attributed to the option or award will need to reflect this future uncertainty. The expense provided for in the company's accounts will be the fair value of the award less any amount payable by the employees for the grant of the option or award.

15.4 There are two ways in which the share-based payment expense which is recorded in the profit and loss account may be adjusted. The first is where fair value is reassessed in a subsequent accounting period. This may only happen where there is a cash settled share-based payment (see **15.8** below). Alternatively, there may be situations where an adjustment may be made to 'true up' the expense to reflect the number of shares likely to vest, although as noted at **15.5** below, there is no ability to make such an adjustment in relation to the extent to which market-based performance conditions are being met.

Performance targets

15.5 Where the exercise of an option or the vesting of a share award is subject to the achievement of performance targets, the calculation of the fair value will include an assessment of whether it is considered that those performance conditions will be met. However, this will only apply where the performance conditions are market-based (for example, share price targets and total shareholder return) in which case there will be no subsequent adjustment of the expense which has been recorded if the condition is not satisfied and awards do not vest (which is different to the position in relation to non-market based performance conditions, for example profit targets, earnings per share or return on capital).

Equity or cash settlement

15.6 There are different accounting treatments in relation to share-based payments which depend on whether the liability is equity settled (ie shares are transferred to the participants to satisfy the option or award); cash settled (for example, under a 'phantom' arrangement where the participant receives a cash amount calculated by reference to the share price, or growth in value of the share price); or where there is a choice between receiving equity or cash of equivalent value.

Equity-settled share-based payments

15.7 If an option or award is granted which is to be equity settled, and the fair value is expensed at grant, companies must then adjust (or 'true up') that expense in each subsequent accounting period. Essentially this means that the company must reassess the number of shares under the option or award that they consider are likely to vest (based on the initial fair value, but adjusted solely for the vesting proportion). The idea behind this adjustment is that when the vesting proportions are actually known, the total expense recorded will be equal to the number of shares which vest multiplied by the fair value per share at the date of grant. However, the exception to this is where there is a market-based performance target, where the likelihood of satisfying that target is not taken into account in any truing up calculation.

Cash-settled share-based payments

15.8 If an option or award is granted which is to be cash settled, and the fair value is expensed at grant, companies must then adjust that expense in each subsequent accounting period until the cash payment is actually made. For cash-settled options and awards, the fair value is adjusted in each accounting period as well as making an adjustment to reflect any changes in the proportion of the options or awards which is likely to vest.

Cash/equity alternative to settling a share-based payment

15.9 Where a scheme provides a choice as to how the share-based payment liability is to be settled (ie a share scheme with a cash alternative), the accounting treatment will depend on whether the choice as to settlement rests with the employer or the employee. In summary, if it is the employee's choice as to whether to receive cash or shares, cash-settled accounting treatment is followed with an annual reassessment of fair value; if the choice rests with the employer, then the equity-settled accounting treatment is followed. However, the company would be required to substitute the cash-settled accounting treatment if there is an established practice for paying cash or where there is little value in the shares such that there is no 'commercial substance' to making an equity payment.

Vesting and non-vesting conditions

15.10 The International Accounting Standards Board (IASB) has given guidance on how certain types of vesting conditions may affect the calculation of 'fair value'. Share schemes will normally provide that certain conditions need to be met before an option becomes exercisable or an award vests. The IASB has distinguished between 'vesting' and 'non-vesting' conditions and has confirmed that only vesting conditions, being performance or employment-related conditions, may affect the truing up of the fair value calculation. Non-vesting conditions, which may only affect the fair value calculation at the outset, relate to provisions extraneous to the employment or the actual option or award and include the requirement to maintain savings arrangements under a savings-related share option scheme or the need to retain certain shares for a period of time before other shares can be released under a deferred bonus scheme.

15.11 If options or awards are cancelled during the normal vesting period the company must immediately recognise in its accounts the full amount of the remaining expense. One result of this is that where an employee chooses to cancel an existing savings arrangement connected to an option under a savings-related share option scheme (ie a 'non-vesting' condition), the resulting lapse of the option must be expensed by the company even where a new option is granted in its place.

STATUTORY CORPORATION TAX DEDUCTION

15.12   The Corporation Tax Act 2009 CTA 2009 rewrote the provisions of FA 2003, s141 and Sch 23 and provides for a statutory corporation tax deduction to employing companies for employee share acquisitions. FA 2014 introduces, from 6 April 2015, an extension to the statutory corporation tax deduction for companies which 'host' employees who are employed overseas but working in the UK (effectively treating the employee as employed by the host employer for these purposes). From 6 April 2015, references to the 'employing company' will therefore include a host employer. A second extension relates to employees who are granted options whilst working outside the UK and who later take up UK employment; in such case, the UK employer will, from 6 April 2015, be able to take advantage of a statutory corporation tax deduction where the individual becomes liable for UK income tax on part of the option gain.

15.13   The deduction is available to the employing company (not the company issuing the shares) in respect of both share awards (such as under LTIPs) and the acquisition of shares pursuant to a share option. In either of those cases, the share award or share option must have been acquired by reason of the employment of the acquiring person or another person. It is to be noted that the statutory corporation tax relief is only available if shares are acquired. There is no relief, for instance, for a cash cancellation or where the employee realises a gain by assigning an option for valuable consideration. The requirement that shares are acquired has, in practice, discouraged cash cancellations in respect of share options on the takeover of companies.

15.14   The deduction for the employer basically matches the amount on which the employee is (or would have been, had the employee been UK tax resident) subject to income tax on earnings (or would be but for any available tax relief). It also matches the timing of the income tax liability of the employee.

Requirements for relief

15.15   The deduction is only available if the following requirements are met.

(a)   Business condition – the business (for the purposes of which the award was made) must be carried on by the employing company and be within the charge to UK corporation tax (in respect of the profits of the relevant business) (CTA 2009, s 1007). An option granted by a UK company to an employee of an overseas subsidiary for the purposes of that overseas subsidiary will not therefore obtain a deduction. On the other hand, an option granted to an employee of an overseas subsidiary in connection with his secondment to the UK company will satisfy this condition (CTA 2009, s 1007A).

(b)   Shares condition – the shares must satisfy the same conditions as apply to an SAYE scheme. They must be ordinary shares which are fully paid up and not redeemable. Further, they must be of a class listed on a recognised stock exchange, or in a company that is either not controlled by another company or is the subsidiary of a company with listed shares (CTA 2009, s 1008).

(c)   The company whose shares are acquired – the company whose shares are acquired must be:

(i)   the employing company; or

(ii)   the parent company of the employing company; or

(iii)   the company that, at the time of the award (or when the option is granted), is a member of a consortium that owns the employing company or the parent company; or

(iv)   where at the time of the award (or when the option is granted), the employing company is a member of a consortium that owns another company (C), a company that at that time is a member of the consortium or a parent company in relation to a member of the consortium, and, is also a member of the same commercial association of companies as C. In other words, it is possible to look upwards through the group or consortium structure to the company whose shares are subject to the award (CTA 2009, ss 1008 and 1016).

In the case of options where the shares are in a company which is taken over between grant or exercise, the test will be satisfied if the options are replaced by options over the shares in a qualifying acquiring company before the date of exercise. Consideration given for the grant or exercise of the new option is treated as given for the grant of the replaced option (CTA 2009, s 1022). The statutory deduction will also be available for a period of 90 days following the takeover, even if the statutory conditions are not met, providded that they were met immediately prior to the takeover.

(d)   Income tax position of the employee – in the case of share awards, the employee who acquires the shares must at all material times be subject to income tax on his earnings from the employment in respect of which the shares were awarded (or would be if he were resident and ordinarily resident in the UK) and the employment duties must be performed in the UK.

In the case of share options, he must at all material times be chargeable to income tax at the time he is granted or exercises the option (or would be if he were resident and ordinarily resident in the UK) and the duties by reason of which the option was granted must be performed in the UK (CTA 2009, ss 1009 and 1017).

Amount of relief

15.16   The amount of statutory corporation tax relief given on an award of shares (or shares acquired pursuant to an option) is the difference between:

(a) the market value of the shares when the shares are acquired; and

(b) the total money or money's worth given in respect of the acquisition of the shares (including the grant of any option).

Where an employer and employee have agreed or jointly elected that the employee will bear some or all of the employer's Class 1 National Insurance contributions on the share option gain, the consideration for the acquisition of the shares pursuant to an option does not include any of the liability so borne.

15.17   The statutory corporation tax relief takes priority over any common law tax deductions for the cost of providing the shares, e.g. payments to EBTs (see **16.29–16.34** below) or any common law 'tax symmetry' arrangements. Costs of providing shares include expenses directly related to the provision of shares or (in the case of employee share schemes) any cost paid by the employer in respect of the participation of the employee in the scheme. The statutory corporation tax relief does not give a deduction for the costs of establishing the employees' share scheme, administration costs, borrowing costs of the employer and any fees, commission, stamp duty or similar incidental expenses of acquiring the shares, but most of these costs will be deductible under general principles anyway.

15.18   However, the statutory corporation tax deduction is not available where any of the following statutory Share Incentive Plan (SIP) tax deductions are available under CTA 2009, Pt 11, ch 1 (previously ICTA 1988, Sch 4AA) (CTA 2009, s 1037):

(a) deductions for free and matching shares;

(b) deductions for expenses in providing partnership shares; and

(c) deductions for contributions to plan trusts.

15.19   The statutory corporation tax deduction is available where an option is exercised by personal representatives after the death of the employee.

How relief is given

15.20   The relief is given for the accounting period in which the beneficial interest in the shares is acquired. It is given as a deduction in computing trading profits of the business in respect of which the option was granted (or as an expense of management in the case of an investment company).

Restricted shares

15.21   'Restricted shares' are shares which are owned beneficially by the employee but are subject to a risk of forfeiture in specified circumstances (see **7.36–7.45** above). Except where an election is made under ITEPA 2003, s 425 for the restricted securities to be subject to income tax on acquisition on the unrestricted market value, income tax will normally be charged on the occurrence of any of the post-acquisition chargeable events specified in ITEPA 2003, s 427, including upon the securities ceasing to be restricted securities, or any variation of the restrictions or the disposal of the restricted securities. In line with the principle that the statutory corporation tax deduction should match the amount on which the employee is taxable in amount and timing, the statutory corporation tax deduction in respect of the acquisition of restricted securities will be given in the accounting period of the employing company in which the shares are acquired or there is a chargeable event under ITEPA 2003, s 426, or the employee dies. The amount of the deduction will match the amount of employment income which is taxed either as earnings of the employee, or as a result of the post-acquisition chargeable event, or on the death of the employee.

Convertible shares

15.22 'Convertible shares' are shares which are acquired subject to a right of conversion into other securities, which will usually be more valuable (see **7.46–7.50**). Where the recipient acquires convertible shares, the statutory corporation tax deduction is available on the acquisition of the shares (including pursuant to an option) and on any chargeable event in relation to the convertible shares as specified in ITEPA 2003, s 438, or on the death of the employee. The amount of relief under the statutory corporation tax deduction will match the amount of the employment income which will be taxable on the employee, and the timing of the deduction will also correspond.

Chapter 16

EBTs and Using Existing Shares

WHAT IS AN EBT?

16.1 An Employee Benefit Trust or 'EBT' (sometimes referred to as an Employee Share Ownership Plan or 'ESOP') – is a trust established by a company for the benefit of its employees (and former employees and certain relatives and dependants). As a separate legal entity to the company, it is in a position, subject to satisfying all relevant legal requirements, to acquire and hold shares in the company and transfer them to employees either under the company's established employees' share schemes or directly.

16.2 Whilst the purpose of a share scheme is to provide for the distribution of shares to employees, an EBT is principally a vehicle for the acquisition and holding of shares. The establishment of an EBT therefore involves consideration of the possible means by which it will finance its acquisition of shares (see **16.10** below). As the EBT is a separate entity to the company and its group, care will need to be taken in structuring the EBT arrangements in order that the trust does not 'earmark' shares for the employees participating in the share scheme, as to do so could lead to a tax charge under the 'disguised remuneration' provisions of ITEPA 2003, Part 7A (see **16.71–16.74** below).

EMPLOYEES' SHARE SCHEMES LINKED TO AN EBT

16.3 Many potential uses for an EBT have been put forward including making a market in the shares of a private company, and as a vehicle for an employee or management buy-out particularly where there is a wish to hold shares for future employee or management investors. However, the vast majority of EBTs have been established to hold shares for distribution under one or more share schemes adopted by the company establishing the EBT (see Chapter 7).

16.4 The number of EBTs reflects the wider use of existing shares in employees' share schemes. One reason for this is that an allocation of existing shares under an employees' share scheme does not count against the dilution limits, imposed by institutional investor bodies, on the number of new shares (and treasury shares) which may be made available under employees' share schemes (see **3.18–3.21** above) so, as companies have come up against these limits, they have turned to the use of existing shares supplied through an EBT. A number of companies have also found that in the longer term the use of existing shares can be cheaper than the issue of new equity. This is particularly the case if interest rates are relatively low and dividend yields have been maintained.

Example 1

A company lends £10m to an EBT interest-free which is used to buy two million shares at £5 per share for the purpose of a share option grant. As consideration for the interest-free loan, dividends are waived by the trustees. In the first year, the net dividend is 10.5p and is assumed to grow at five per cent per annum. Interest rates are assumed at three per cent throughout the period. It is assumed that the company borrows the money from the bank to lend to the EBT.

Loan period	Interest paid by the company to the bank	Tax relief @ 20% on interest paid on the bank loan	Dividends waived by the trustees	(Net annual cost) or net annual saving of EBT
	£	£	£	£
1st Year	(300,000)	60,000	210,000	(30,000)
2nd Year	(300,000)	60,000	220,500	(19,500)
3rd Year	(300,000)	60,000	231,525	(8,475)
4th Year	(300,000)	60,000	243,101	3,101
5th Year	(300,000)	60,000	255,256	15,256

Assuming that the interest costs of financing the acquisition of shares in the above example are fixed, any increase in dividends results in a reduction of the net cost of providing existing shares. Indeed, in the fourth year in the above example, there is a cross-over as a result of which there is a net saving, ie the dividends waived exceed the interest costs of financing the acquisition of shares. The main saving in using existing shares, however, is the avoidance of dilution: there is a permanent saving every year after the exercise of options of the amount of dividend which would otherwise be payable. The amount of dividend saved in later years is likely to far exceed the cost of financing the shares between grant and exercise even on any discounted basis for timing differences.

16.5   Another reason for satisfying options and awards under employees' share schemes using existing shares through an EBT is that it is not necessary to obtain shareholders' approval for the establishment of an all-employee share scheme under the Listing Rules, or other schemes in which directors do not participate where the scheme uses existing shares only.

Share option schemes

16.6   EBTs may conveniently be used in connection with share option schemes including tax-advantaged schemes. Bearing in mind that optionholders will pay for the shares on exercise of the options, the exercise monies can be used by the trustees to recoup any earlier outlay at the time of grant on acquiring the shares. If the options are granted at market value at the same time as the acquisition of the shares, the amount payable by the optionholders should exactly match the trustees' acquisition costs. Whilst an exact match between the cost of the shares to the trustees and the exercise price payable by the optionholders may be achieved in the case of share option schemes where options are granted at market value, this will rarely be the case under a savings-related share option scheme as options are usually granted at a discount to the market value. In such cases, the company may need to contribute the cost of any discounts which are given on the grant of the options. Where nil-cost options, or other free share awards, are granted, no monies will ever be received by the trustees from participants

Share Incentive Plans

16.7   EBTs may be a convenient 'warehouse' for shares which can later be used for appropriation under a SIP, although the SIP trust itself can be used in the same manner as any other EBT. The EBT trustees can acquire and hold the shares with loans provided by the company. At appropriation, SIP trustees will pay their contribution from the company to acquire the shares; the EBT trustees can then in turn repay their loans from the company. Where SIP trustees are themselves used to warehouse the shares, they are able to borrow and hold shares for up to five years free of capital gains tax (see **8.18** above).

LTIPs

16.8   Where an EBT is established to allocate shares to employees under an LTIP, the acquisition of the shares by the EBT trustees will also need to be financed by outright contributions. LTIPs usually confer substantial share benefits on a limited number of senior executives, often against specified performance targets. There are no statutory corporation tax deductions for payments to the EBT trustees and so the deductibility will depend on whether the qualifying conditions in CTA 2009, ss 1290–1297 are satisfied (see Chapter 15).

FINANCING OF EBTs

16.9   The EBT trustees' acquisition of shares will generally need to be financed by the company in one form or another. The form it takes will usually be governed by the purpose for which the EBT has been set up. Broadly speaking, if the shares acquired by the EBT trustees are to be distributed free to employees, then the company will need to make substantial gifts or loans which may need to be written off at a later stage. A contribution to the EBT trustees may be given in the form of dividends on the shares (the although trustees would suffer income tax on the receipt of such dividends), or from the sale of some of the shares at a profit (in which case, at least for a UK resident trustee, capital gains tax may be an issue), but substantially the whole of the finance will need to be provided directly by the company. On the other hand, if the shares are to be sold or transferred to employees on the exercise of market value share options, then the acquisition cost of the shares should be wholly or substantially recoverable by the EBT trustees from employees on exercise of the options. In these circumstances, the EBT trustees need only obtain interim finance until the shares are sold or transferred to the employees.

16.10   If EBTs are analysed on the basis of whether they are primarily established to give or to sell shares to employees, they fall within the two following categories:

Established to gift shares to employees	*Established to sell shares to employees*
1. Free and matching shares under SIPs (see Chapters 9 and 11)	1. EBTs established to hold shares for share option schemes
2. LTIPs (for senior executives) (see Chapter 7)	2. EBTs established to make a market in the shares in private companies
3. Long service award schemes involving free shares under ITEPA 2003, s 323	

The financing of EBTs established to gift shares

16.11   Banks and other financial institutions will have little or no part to play in the financing of an EBT which is established to provide gifts of shares for employees. This type of EBT will usually be funded by contributions or loans from the company.

16.12   A company which makes voluntary contributions to acquire existing shares will need to take into account that the contributions will, unless applied in subscribing for new shares, reduce the company's cash flow. The payment and any surplus which arises on termination of the trust are irrecoverable by the company (see **16.32** below). The deductibility of any payments for tax purposes will be of prime importance to most companies but, except for SIPs (see Chapters 8–11), deductibility will depend on satisfying the qualifying conditions in CTA 2009, ss 1290–1297 (see Chapter 15). As an alternative, in order to avoid surpluses arising in the trust on termination, the funds to be provided are often made under the terms of an interest-free loan which can be called in to recover any surplus or written off at a later date if no longer required.

The financing of EBTs established to sell shares

16.13   As indicated at **16.9** above, EBTs established to sell shares will recoup the costs of acquiring the shares. The main requirement for such EBTs is to obtain the most appropriate form of interim finance.

16.14   Any payment by the company under any guarantee of the EBT trustees' obligations to a third party financier, or under any indemnity of the trustees, will not be deductible for tax. In managing its risks in respect of any EBT, a company may need to consider a programme of voluntary payments to ensure that the EBT remains solvent over the long term.

Loan by the company

16.15   A loan from the company is often the most efficient form of finance for EBT trustees if only because the EBT trustees will be able to borrow the required amount of funds at the right time and on as many occasions as the EBT trustees require. There will be no need to provide security or give warranties and undertakings.

16.16   In principle, interest may be payable on any loan but as the interest would only be paid out of dividends received or any growth in value of surplus shares, the EBT trustees will probably not be in a position, initially at least, to meet the full amount of interest payable if this is charged at a commercial rate. In later years, if dividends grow or options or awards lapse such that there are surplus shares with growth value, there may be a cross-over point at which the amount of dividends received and growth on surplus shares exceeds the interest payments, but this will not usually happen for some time, if at all. In the meantime, any insufficiency to meet interest outgoings would need to be waived by the company.

Loans from a third party financier

16.17   The company may be unwilling to use its cash for loans to the EBT trustees. In these circumstances, the company may require EBT trustees to obtain loan finance from a third party lender. Any third party lender will expect dividends to be paid and will normally require the company to guarantee the EBT trustees' obligations in respect of the loan.

16.18   It is doubtful that any UK resident EBT trustees would be entitled to claim a deduction for interest payable on a loan to acquire shares since such expenditure would be to the benefit of the capital of the trust and, therefore, capital in nature (see *Carver v Duncan HL [1985] STC 356*).

Call options and UK banks

16.19   Some EBTs have been financed by call option arrangements with a bank. The bank buys the shares in its own name, but grants an option in favour of the EBT trustees who can call for the shares during an agreed period. This type of arrangement ensures that the EBT will always be able to call for sufficient shares at a set price without having to acquire those shares until they are needed in order to satisfy options and awards. The bank will determine the price payable by the EBT trustees, based on a model which calculates the bank's carrying costs plus a margin, after giving credit for all dividends and monies paid by the EBT trustees, and this will be the only outgoing of the EBT until the shares are required, thus giving certainty to the EBT in relation to the cost of providing shares to employees.

ESTABLISHMENT OF AN EBT

Power of the company to establish an EBT

16.20   No specific authority is required for the establishment and operation of an employee benefit trust by a company (subject to any listing rule requirements).

16.21   The directors must take care to ensure that any acts they take in relation to the establishment and operation of an EBT are in the best interests of the company, and that any exercise of their powers and discretions is for a proper purpose. In particular, the establishment of an EBT to prevent a bid being made for the company would not be carried out for a proper purpose (see *Hogg v Cramphorn [1967] Ch 254*). However, it would always be open to the members to pass a resolution approving or ratifying any act of the directors. Accordingly, the directors should carefully minute the reasons for establishing any EBT.

Shareholders' approval

16.22   Under the Listing Rules, an EBT is an 'employees' share scheme' and its establishment will normally require shareholders' prior approval. However, where the EBT is to be established by a listed company for the purpose of delivering shares under an existing employees' share scheme which has an appropriate power to establish an EBT or the EBT is limited to acquiring shares by market purchase (rather than through new issue or treasury shares), no specific approval will normally be necessary.

Identity of the trustees

16.23   The first decision which must normally be made in relation to the identity of any trustees to be appointed is whether they should be UK or non-UK resident. In most cases, non-UK resident trustees will be appointed for the capital gains tax advantages referred to at **16.46** below and to ensure the EBT trustees are outside the scope of the Financial Services and Markets Act 2000. However, UK resident trustees must be appointed for SIPs (see Chapter 8) and where an EBT is established to take a gift of shares from a transferor who seeks rollover relief under TCGA 1992, s 165. Rollover relief applies to certain gifts of shares in an unquoted company, the transferor's personal company or the transferor's trading company. The relief is denied where the transferee is neither resident nor ordinarily resident in the UK (TCGA 1992, s 166).

16.24 Although EBTs established in connection with LTIPs (see Chapter 7) will normally be established with non-UK resident trustees in order to ensure that the capital gains tax benefits are maintained in respect of any shares which remain unallocated, it would be possible to establish a UK resident EBT for an LTIP which has only UK resident participants as it is likely that the trustees would escape capital gains tax charges under TCGA 1992, s 239ZA (previously Extra-Statutory Concession D35). This concession applies where shares are transferred to UK resident employees for nil payment, but in circumstances where the receipt of the shares is chargeable to income tax on earnings (see **16.42** below). The charge to income tax on the employee recipient is offset against what would otherwise have given rise to a capital gains tax charge on the EBT trustees.

16.25 If UK resident trustees are appointed, the company may wish to appoint directors of the company as trustees. However, unless the EBT trustees are to be funded with outright gifts, the appointment of directors may involve difficulties under CA 2006, s 197 which prohibits the making by a company of loans and quasi-loans to its directors.

16.26 Where a non-UK resident trustee is to be appointed, usually the trustee will be selected from amongst the many banks and other businesses offering such services in the Channel Islands or the Isle of Man. Although the costs of appointing such trustees vary depending on the nature of the activities to be performed, there will normally be a minimum of £1,500 set up and £1,500 annual fees with additional transaction fees. In some cases, the cost may be significantly greater.

16.27 Any EBT which is to be non-UK resident should be established as a discretionary trust in order to ensure that the non-UK residence is not challenged by HMRC on the basis that the trust is controlled by the company establishing the EBT. However, the EBT trustees will need to obtain information from the company about the potential beneficiaries. It is usual, therefore, for a liaison committee of directors or other senior executives to be appointed as a point of contact for the EBT. In many cases, this will be a group of individuals, initially directors of the company, with the exclusive power to appoint their successors.

16.28 Where an EBT is established with non-UK resident trustees a notification must be made within three months to HMRC under IHTA 1984, s 218 setting out the details (name and address) of the company and the non-resident trustees. This notification may be made to IHT Compliance, Lifetime Transfers Team, Ferrers House, Castle Meadow Road, Nottingham NG2 1BB.

TAX ASPECTS

Tax considerations for the company

Employee benefit contributions

16.29   Payments of employee benefits contributions (or EBCs) which do not attract a statutory deduction (see **16.30** below) are subject to two tests in order to determine if and when a deduction for corporation tax purposes is available:

(a)   the payment must be deductible under general principles, that is to say, it must be wholly and exclusively incurred for the purposes of a trade and must be revenue in nature; and

(b)   the special restrictions in CTA 2009, ss 1290–1297 (previously FA 2003, Sch 24) (see **16.34** below) must also be satisfied.

EBCs are payments or asset transfers (not loans) to a third party (typically an employee benefit trust) who is entitled or required under the terms of the trust to hold or use such money or assets for the provision of benefits to employees of the employing company.

Statutory deductions for the costs of providing shares

16.30   In the context of employee share schemes, a statutory deduction is specifically allowed for:

(a)   shares or awards for which the statutory corporation tax deduction is available under CTA 2009, ss 1001–1038 (previously FA 2003, Sch 23) (see **15.12–15.22** above);

(b)   shares or awards under SIPs for which a deduction is allowed under CTA 2009, ss 983–998 (previously ICTA 1988, Sch 4AA) (see Chapter 8).

Since awards of shares by an EBT will, in most circumstances, qualify for the statutory corporation tax deduction under CTA 2009, ss 1001–1038 (which specifically prohibits the availability of any other deduction), the number of occasions on which it will be necessary to consider the availability of a tax deduction under general principles will be relatively few, at least so far as share awards are concerned. Other statutory deductions specified in CTA 2009, s 1290(4) include payments for goods or services, retirement benefits contributions and accident benefit scheme contributions.

Trading expenses deduction

16.31   A payment by a company to EBT trustees will be deductible in computing the company's trading profits under general principles if it is revenue in nature and made wholly and exclusively for the purposes of the company's trade. Expenditure which is intended to acquire or enhance a capital asset will, therefore, not be deductible. In particular, expenditure designed as a once and for all contribution to a fund will not be revenue (*Atherton v British*

Insulated and Helsby Cables Ltd (1925) 10 TC 155). The second condition that the payment is made wholly and exclusively for the purposes of its trade will usually be established where the nature of the payments is to reward employees for their efforts (*Heather v P-E Consulting Group Ltd (1972) 48 TC 293; Jeffs v Ringtons Ltd (1985) 58 TC 680; E Bott Ltd v Price (1988) 59 TC 437*). In practice, the approach which should be adopted by a company seeking a deduction is to make a series of voluntary payments of varying amounts from year to year and avoid any 'one-off' lump sums.

16.32 The company which establishes an EBT should not benefit under the trust, not even as an ultimate beneficiary, if it wishes to obtain a tax deduction for any contributions (*Rutter v Charles Sharpe & Co Ltd (1979) 53 TC 163*).

Special restrictions on the deductibility of EBCs

16.33 Where a payment to an EBT satisfies the 'general principles' test mentioned at **16.31** above, it will still need to satisfy the special restrictions in CTA 2009, ss 1290–1297 (previously FA 2003, Sch 24) as to:

(a)   the deductibility of the EBC; and

(b)   the timing of any deduction.

16.34 CTA 2009, s 1290(2) requires that any deduction for an EBC cannot be given unless the EBT uses the funds (ie the funds must be 'paid out') to provide a 'qualifying benefit' or to discharge 'qualifying expenses'. A qualifying benefit is defined as:

(a)   a benefit that gives rise to both an employment income tax charge and to an NICs charge (or would do so if the employee had a UK employment);

(b)   a benefit provided in connection with the termination of the recipient's employment; or

(c)   a benefit provided under an employer-financed retirement benefits scheme.

'Qualifying expenses' are expenses incidental to the cost of providing the assets provided which would be deductible for tax purposes if incurred by the employer.

CTA 2009, s 1290 also governs the timing of any deduction. EBCs provided in an accounting period which result in the provisions of benefits in (or within nine months after) the accounting period will be deductible in that accounting period. However, if there is a delay before the qualifying benefits are provided (shares or other assets transferred) then the tax deduction is deferred until the accounting period in which they are provided (CTA 2009, s 1290(3)).

Loans

16.35 If a close company advances money to the trustees of an EBT, the provisions of CTA 2010, s 455 will apply if the trustees are 'participators' in the close company. Even if the trustees are not 'participators', difficulties may arise under CTA 2010, s 459 depending on how loan monies are used. This provision applies where a close company makes a loan which does not give rise to a liability as a loan to a participator under CTA 2010, s 455, and a third party either 'makes a payment or transfers property to ... a relevant person who is a participator'. If this happens then the loan or advance to the third party is treated as if it were made to a participator. One example of this is where the EBT trustees make a payment to buy shares from a shareholder (who will inevitably be a participator); this payment will be treated as a payment within CTA 2010, s 459. CTA 2010, ss 455 and 459 apply to a 'relevant person' who is a participator, or to associates of a participator. The term 'relevant person' includes not only an individual but also extends to 'a company receiving the loan or advance in a fiduciary or representative capacity. Arguably, any subsidiary of a close company specially formed to act as the EBT trustee will be within this definition.

16.36 Where any loan (whether actual or deemed) is caught by CTA 2010, s 455 or 459, the company is obliged to make an interest-free deposit of tax with HMRC which is only refundable to the extent the loan is subsequently repaid.

16.37 The question arises whether any interest-free loan used to acquire shares will give rise to a charge to corporation tax under CTA 2010, s 779. This provides that where, under a loan transaction, a company agrees to transfer (which includes by waiver) 'income arising from property' then a charge to tax arises on the amount of income foregone. As noted above, trustees often waive dividends which may otherwise have been used to pay loan interest; where the provision of the interest-free loan is linked to the waiver of dividends, there is a risk that HMRC may apply the CTA 2010, s 779 provision. This risk is mitigated where the waiver arises under the EBT trust deed, rather than under any loan agreement entered into between the parties.

16.38 Where interest-free loans are made by the company to a subsidiary which acts as a corporate trustee there is also a risk of HMRC seeking to impose the transfer pricing provisions of Part 4 of the Taxation (International and Other Provisions) Act 2010 (previously ICTA 1988, Sch 28AA) so that, for tax purposes, the company is to be treated as making the loan on arm's-length terms with the effect that the subsidiary is treated as receiving a market rate of interest. However, HMRC does not appear to take such an approach in practice.

Tax considerations for the trustees

Income tax

16.39 Voluntary contributions to trustees are not income for tax purposes. On the other hand, regular payments made under a legal obligation will be treated as annual payments chargeable to income tax. The company is under an obligation to deduct tax at the basic rate from such payments (ITA 2007, s 901).

16.40　The income tax 'settlement' provisions of ITTOIA 2005, s 619 and subsequent sections deem income to be that of the settlor notwithstanding that it is payable to some other person where the settlor retains an interest. However, it is considered that these provisions only apply where the settlor is an individual and it is unlikely that the settlor company would retain an interest in an EBT.

16.41　Trustees pay income tax at 45 per cent on any income received (except for dividends where the tax rate is 37.5 per cent). An offshore trustee of a discretionary trust will be subject to UK income tax on UK source income as a trust within ITA 2007, s 479. By ITA 2007, s 496B (previously Extra-Statutory Concession A68), to avoid an effective double tax charge UK trustees may reclaim tax paid by them when payments made to employees are treated as earnings (which will normally be the case). In the case of an offshore discretionary trust, the UK resident beneficiary may be able to claim relief for any such double taxation (see **16.52** below).

16.42　Under ITTOIA 2005, s 752, the trustees are exempt from income tax on any interest payments received from employees under any scheme whereby the trustees borrow money from the company to lend to employees to buy shares in the company. The relief is only available to the extent the interest receivable by the trustees from employees matches the interest payable to the company.

Capital gains tax

16.43　UK resident trustees of a discretionary trust are chargeable to capital gains tax on their chargeable gains at the flat rate of 28 per cent.

16.44　Any distributions of shares by UK resident trustees to a beneficiary is a disposal for capital gains tax as far as the trustees are concerned even if it is a receipt of taxable earnings as far as the employees are concerned. The trustees disposal of the shares will be treated as made for a consideration equal to the market value of the assets transferred (TCGA 1992, s 17(1)). It follows, therefore, that any assets transferred at an undervalue would appear to be taxed in the hands of both the EBT trustees and the employee. However, there are a number of potential reliefs from tax:

(a)　by TCGA 1992, s 239ZA (previously Extra-Statutory Concession D35), the trustees will be relieved from any capital gains tax liability where the transfer of assets is made for no payment, the employee is liable to tax on earnings on the value of the assets received, the trust is an employee trust within IHTA 1984, s 86 (although it is not necessary for the trust property to be held for the benefit of 'all or most employees') and the beneficiaries do not own more than five per cent of the share capital of the company (see also **7.56** above); and

(b)   where TCGA 1992, s 239ZA does not apply, a joint 'holdover' election under TCGA 1992, s 165 and TCGA 1992, Sch 7 might be available if the asset transferred is shares in either an unquoted trading company or group or the transferor's personal holding company or his trading company or group. Generally, a company will qualify as a personal company if as little as five per cent of voting shares are held by the transferor and his associates.

16.45   Non-UK resident trustees are exempt from UK capital gains tax even if the shares are in a UK company.

16.46   TCGA 1992, s 87 provides for the attribution of certain trust gains accruing to non-UK resident trustees to UK beneficiaries. The trust's gains are only assessable on the UK beneficiaries to the extent these beneficiaries receive capital payments. However, the courts have indicated that commercial arrangements are unlikely to be settlements because they do not normally contain any element of bounty (see *IRC v Plummer [1979] STC 793*). It is understood that HMRC takes the view that employees' benefit trusts which represent normal commercial arrangements entered into to provide remuneration for employees are not 'settlements' and, therefore, any transfer of shares by such a trust is outside the scope of s 87.

16.47   TCGA 1992, s 86 provides for the attribution to the settlor of certain chargeable gains accruing to non-UK resident trustees where the settlor has an 'interest' in the trust. The company which established the EBT is potentially a settlor for these purposes if either it has a residual interest in the trust property in default of other beneficiaries or the company lends money to the EBT. However, where the EBT is part of a normal commercial arrangement for the remuneration of employees so that there is no element of 'bounty' involved, HMRC accepts that the provisions of the section are unlikely to apply.

Inheritance tax

16.48   Discretionary trusts are subject to inheritance tax on every 10th anniversary of the trust and on any distribution out of the trust at other times. Any distribution which is income in the hands of the recipient (or would be if he were UK resident) is exempt from inheritance tax (IHTA 1984, s 65(5)).

16.49   The 10th anniversary charge is based on the 'value of the property'. Where the trust property has been funded by loans and income has been distributed the trust will presumably have insubstantial net worth and any tax payable will be de minimis.

16.50   The 10th anniversary charge and the charge on distributions do not apply where the trust property is held for the purposes described in IHTA 1984, s 86. Property will be held for the purpose of IHTA 1984, s 86 if beneficiaries include 'all or most' employees and directors of (amongst other things) the particular employing company or the property is held on the trusts of an approved share incentive plan. HMRC does not regard the inclusion of either charitable trustees or the company's pension trustees as the ultimate beneficiary as prejudicing the 'all or most' employees test. See also **7.57** above.

16.51   Under IHTA 1984, s 72, an inheritance tax charge arises where property ceases to be held on employee trusts within IHTA 1984, s 86 unless it is distributed trust property. A particular instance where this section may apply is in connection with the grant of share options at a price which is less than the market value of the shares at the date of grant, although HMRC has indicated that the valuation of any depreciation on the granting of the option would be extremely difficult.

Tax considerations of employees

16.52   Any transfer of shares or payment of cash to employee beneficiaries will be employment income for tax purposes. Where shares are transferred at an undervalue, the amount of the undervalue is an emolument (*Weight v Salmon (1935) 19 TC 174*). A former employee will be within the scope of income tax on earned income (*Bray v Best [1989] STC 159*) but he is assessable for the last tax year of his employment (ITEPA 2003, s 30). UK resident trustees must deduct tax under PAYE for payments made to employees (*Clark v Oceanic Contractors Inc (1982) 56 TC 183*) and income tax will be payable through PAYE (and NICs will be payable) on a transfer of shares in a listed company or if the shares are readily convertible assets. A third party may also be liable to deduct tax through PAYE if it knows the exact quantum of the emoluments (*IRC v Herd [1993] STC 436*).

Where an employee receives a discretionary payment from an offshore trust comprising income which has been taxed in the hands of the trustee, he may be able to claim relief for some of the tax suffered by the trustee under Extra Statutory Concession B18.

ESC B18 will generally be of limited effect as it is only available where:

(a)   the trustees have made a trust returns for each tax year, giving details of all sources of trust income and payments made to beneficiaries;

(b)   the trustees have paid all tax due, and any interest, surcharges and penalties arising; and

(c)   the trustees keep available for inspection by HMRC any relevant tax certificates.

Any employee wishing to make a claim under ESC B18 should contact HMRC Trusts & Estates at the same address as set out at **16.28** above.

16.53   Where a person as an employee acquires a chargeable asset, for capital gains tax purposes, the acquisition will be by reason of his employment and consequently the cost will be equal to the market value at that time (TCGA 1992, s 17).

EBTs AND SHARE OPTIONS

16.54   EBT trustees need a specific power in the trust deed to grant options under the company's share option scheme. The EBT trustees will normally enter into an agreement with the company to transfer shares in satisfaction of the company's obligations under the share option scheme. Alternatively, the trustees may grant the options under the scheme, but there may be capital gains tax (for UK-resident EBTs) and inheritance tax difficulties where it grants options at less than market value (see **16.51**). Similarly, where the EBT trustees make the share option grant, there may be a risk of HMRC deeming the trustee to have 'earmarked' assets within the trust in order to settle such options, resulting in an income tax charge on the employee under the 'disguised remuneration' provisions of ITEPA 2003, Part 7A, unless an exemption applies (see **16.72** below).

Income tax

16.55   The tax rules applying on the grant and exercise of options are identical whether the option is granted over new or existing shares.

Capital gains tax

16.56   The grant of an option is a disposal by the EBT trustees for the purposes of capital gains tax (TCGA 1992, s 144). No chargeable gains arise, however, provided that the option constitutes an employment-related securities option within the meaning of ITEPA 2003, Ch 5, Pt 7 (TCGA 1992, s 149A).

16.57   On the exercise of an option, TCGA 1992, s 144ZA provides that the market value rule is disapplied where an asset is acquired or disposed of on the exercise of employment-related securities (TCGA 1992, s 144ZB(2)(a)). Where the EBT trustees' acquisition cost of the shares is not less than the option exercise price, no chargeable gain should arise.

Inheritance tax

16.58   The grant of options at open market value gives rise to no difficulties in respect of inheritance tax. However, where the option is granted at less than market value, a tax charge arises under IHTA 1984, s 72(2)(c) on the value of the property leaving the trust. This is because whilst distributions to employee beneficiaries are outside the scope of the tax charge, the grant of an option is not treated as an immediate distribution, but a transaction which causes a depreciation in the value of the trust (albeit that HMRC has indicated that the valuation of any depreciation on the granting of the option would be extremely difficult). The same tax consequences apply where the trustees agree with the company to transfer shares pursuant to any obligations of the company to transfer shares on the exercise of options. HMRC has indicated that the position may be different if the trustees were under an obligation to transfer shares imposed by the trust deed.

ACCOUNTING FOR EBTs

16.59 The accounting principles applying to EBTs will to some extent depend on whether the company establishing the EBT accounts under international accounting standards or UK GAAP.

At group level, EBTs are accounted for under IFRS 10 on a group consolidated basis. Essentially this means that, in respect of most assets held by the EBT, until those assets vest in employees, they should be treated as group assets. Shares in the sponsoring company, ie the company establishing the EBT, however, are not treated as assets but are treated in the same manner as treasury shares. The sponsoring company is treated as reacquiring its own shares (even though, from a legal perspective, these shares continue to be held by a third party shareholder and are eligible for voting and, save in respect of any waiver by the trustee, dividends) and should therefore present them as a deduction in arriving at shareholders' funds rather than as assets. Any loans of the EBT would be treated as loans of the sponsoring company.

In relation to accounting at an individual level, international and UK accounting standards differ in that the UK GAAP treatment (currently provided for under UITF 32 and 38) is effectively the same as the consolidated basis treatment under IFRS 10 in that the company looks through the trust and does a quasi-consolidation. UK GAAP rules are, however, changing from 1 January 2015 and will be more closely aligned with IFRS. Where the sponsoring company is reporting under IFRS, or new UK GAAP, at the individual company level, the EBT will be accounted for in the same way as any cost of investment in a subsidiary, as the trust will be treated as a separate entity.

LISTING RULES

16.60 Under the Listing Rules, EBTs are treated as employees' share schemes and therefore require the prior approval of shareholders before they are established (whether as a stand-alone resolution or as part of the approval of an employees' share scheme). However, no shareholders' approval is required where the trustees cannot acquire new shares in the company establishing the EBT.

16.61 Where the directors are discretionary beneficiaries of an EBT, any funding of the EBT may also be a related-party transaction, but it will not normally be necessary to obtain the prior approval of shareholders unless only directors can benefit under the EBT. However, in practice, EBTs will rarely require shareholders' approval under these provisions either because they are within the de minimis rules or because the UKLA will clear the transaction where employees as well as directors will benefit.

DISCLOSURE AND TRANSPARENCY RULES

16.62 The Disclosure and Transparency Rules impose certain disclosure requirements which may affect an EBT, particularly where the EBT holds voting rights of three per cent or more of the company's total voting rights (DTR 5.1.2). General dealings by the EBT will not be on the 'own account' of a PDMR and so will not be discloseable under DTR 3.1.2.

ABI GUIDELINES

16.63   The ABI Guidelines recommend that where an EBT proposes holding more than five per cent of a company's issued ordinary share capital, the arrangements should first be submitted to shareholders for their prior approval. This five per cent limit is applied in respect of shares held at any one time rather than in aggregate over the life of the EBT.

16.64   Informally, the ABI/IMA has made other recommendations in relation to the governance of EBTs. In particular:

(a)   the appointment of at least one independent trustee is encouraged – the ABI/IMA prefers the appointment of non-executive directors, but an independent professional trustee is acceptable;

(b)   the ABI/IMA recommends that purchases of shares by the EBT trustees are made through the market and not by a private sale, particularly if this is from a prominent founder member; and

(c)   the ABI/IMA recommends that dealings by EBTs are disclosed.

DIRECTORS' REPORT AND ACCOUNTS

16.65   Where the company lends money to EBT trustees under the authority given in CA 2006, s 682(2)(b), (c) or (d), then the aggregate amount of the loans included in the balance sheet must be disclosed under the Large and Medium-sized Companies and Groups (Accounts and Reports Regulations) 2008 (SI 2008/410, Sch 1, para 64(2)).

16.66   Where the company gives a guarantee of the EBT's obligations to a third party lender to repay any loan, or to the bank under any put and call option arrangements, then this will be a contingent liability which needs to be noted in the accounts assuming no provision is made in respect of the liability under the Large and Medium-sized Companies and Groups (Accounts and Reports) Regulations 2008 (SI 2008/410, Sch 1, para 63).

16.67   Information is also required in respect of the aggregate amount of the directors' emoluments. Emoluments include the estimated money value of any other benefits received by him otherwise than in cash. A directors' interest in an EBT as discretionary beneficiary does not appear to be a 'benefit' which can be received, but a distribution of free shares undoubtedly is such a benefit and will need to be disclosed (unless disclosed elsewhere in connection with subsisting awards under the company's employees' share schemes).

16.68   The Large and Medium-sized Companies and Groups (Accounts and Reports) Regulations 2008, as amended for accounting periods ending on or after 30 September 2013 (SI 2008/410, Sch 8, para 17) requires the directors' remuneration report, within the annual report, to list each director's (and their connected persons') interests in shares. These interests do not, however, include the interests of directors as discretionary beneficiaries under an EBT. Interests in shares under share option and share award schemes must be included as 'scheme interests' and disclosed separately distinguishing between share and share options, those with and without performance conditions attaching and those which are unvested, vested but not exercised, or exercised during the relevant financial year.

MODEL CODE

16.69   The trustee of an EBT is not caught by the Model Code, which prohibits dealings by PDMRs during a 'prohibited period' (essentially any close period or other time when there is inside information in relation to the company, irrespective of the knowledge of the PDMR).

The acquisition of shares by the trustee of an EBT during a prohibited period is not, therefore, restricted. However, the trustee will usually only acquire shares following a recommendation from the company to acquire shares. The making of such a recommendation during a prohibited period would potentially be restricted under the insider dealing and market abuse regimes. Where there is the likelihood of shares needing to be bought into the EBT during a prohibited period any recommendation to the trustee should be made in advance of the prohibited period, potentially by a standing instruction to purchase shares.

FATCA

16.70   The provisions of the US Foreign Account Tax Compliance Act (FATCA) and the equivalent enhanced automatic exchange of information agreements between the UK and its Crown Dependencies will be relevant to EBTs.

The trustee is under an obligation to identify UK and US taxpayers and provide relevant information in respect of transfers to those individuals to its local tax authorities, which then provide the information, as appropriate, to HMRC and the US Internal Revenue Service, as appropriate. The trustee is required to undertake due diligence on beneficiaries to make sure that it is providing the correct information, and will therefore require certain information to be provided by the company. As a minimum, in order to satisfy its due diligence obligations, the trustee will likely require the company to identify its UK and US taxpayers and then provide the individual's home address and tax number (US) or NI number (or date of birth if these numbers are unknown). The trustee will also have to provide, to its local tax authorities, certain information that it will already hold in relation to the relevant amounts distributed to the UK and US tax payers.

DISGUISED REMUNERATION

16.71   As the EBT is a separate entity to the sponsoring copany's group, care needs to be taken in structuring EBT arrangements in order that the trustee does not 'earmark' shares to specific employees participating in the company's share schemes. To do so could lead to a tax charge under the 'disguised remuneration' provisions of ITEPA 2003, Part 7A.

16.72   ITEPA 2003, Part 7A includes exemptions from the upfront tax charge for certain acts in connection with benefits, bonuses and employee share schemes:

(a)   Arrangements in connection with the acquisition, holding or provision of shares in connection with a tax-advantaged SIP, SAYE, CSOP or EMI provided that no more shares are involved than are expected to be needed for delivery under such arrangements within a ten-year period (ITEPA 2003, s 554E).

(b)   Arrangements which form part of a package of benefits which is available to a substantial proportion (being at least 50 per cent.) of the company's employees (ITEPA 2003, s 554G).

(c)   Deferred (forfeitable) remuneration which is due to vest no later than five years from the award date (ITEPA 2003, s 554H).

(d)   Arrangements in connection with the delivery of shares (or a cash equivalent) under a (forfeitable) award that is due to vest no later than ten years from the award date and provided that no more shares are involved than are expected to be needed for delivery under such arrangements (ITEPA 2003, s 554J).

(e)   Arrangements in connection with the delivery of shares (or a cash equivalent) under an award that is due to vest on an exit event, provided that the company is a trading company and no more shares are involved than are expected to be needed for delivery under such arrangements (ITEPA 2003, s 554K).

(f)   Arrangements in connection with (forfeitable) share options (or phantom options) that are due to vest no later than ten years from the grant date and provided that no more shares are involved than are expected to be needed for delivery under such arrangements (ITEPA 2003, s 554L).

(g)   Arrangements in connection with share options (or phantom options) that are due to vest on an exit event, provided that the company is a trading company and no more shares are involved than are expected to be needed for delivery under such arrangements (ITEPA 2003, s 554M).

Each of the above provisions sets out detailed conditions which must be met in order to take advantage from the exemption from the upfront tax charge.

16.73   Relying solely on one or more of the above exemptions creates a risk that a tax charge may arise if any one of the conditions of the relevant exemption is breached, even if unintentionally. Based on the published HMRC guidance, therefore, most companies operating an EBT in connection with their share plans have taken a more prudent course of action and moved away from the trustee granting share options and awards, and have put in place arrangements with the trustee under which the trustee agrees to satisfy options and awards granted by the company. By doing so, the company is seeking to ensure that no 'earmarking' of shares occurs.

16.74   HMRC has stated that, in general, there will be no earmarking where there is only a discretionary pool of shares held in the EBT, the trustee has not made the awards to the employees, and the trustee does not know the number of shares to be awarded to any particular employee. This can be achieved by the trustee being informed only of the aggregate number of shares under awards being made to a group of specified beneficiaries or by not providing details of the beneficiaries until the awards are due to vest.

Chapter 17

NISAs and Pension Plans

NISAs

17.1   New Individual Savings Accounts (NISAs) were introduced as a replacement for Individual Savings Accounts (ISAs) with effect from 1 July 2014. A UK resident individual may invest up to £15,000 (from 1 July 2014) in different types of financial products including cash and stocks and shares. Whereas, before 1 July 2014, an individual was only able to invest part of the annual ISA allowance in cash, the annual limit for investment into one or more NISAs is aggregated so that the investor is able to use the whole of the annual allowance either in cash or stocks and shares, or may divide the allowance between a cash NISA and stocks and shares NISA in whatever proportion he or she wishes. It is also possible to open a single NISA which is able to hold both cash and stocks and shares, if permitted by the NISA provider.

17.2   NISAs are exempt from income tax on any income received, including dividends, interest and bonuses. Any gains on the disposal of stocks and shares held in a NISA are exempt from capital gains tax. Individuals are able to redeem their investments, or withdraw money from a NISA, at any time without losing tax relief. In addition, no return of income or gains is made to HMRC in respect of NISAs, or indeed in relation to the establishment of a NISA.

REGISTERED PENSION SCHEMES AND SIPPs

17.3   The provisions in relation to pension schemes were simplified from 6 April 2006. Registered pension schemes provide a number of tax benefits, including employer and employee contributions being tax deductible, investment income rolling up on a tax-free basis with no capital gains tax charges arising and, on retirement, the availability of a tax-free lump sum. The contribution limits under such arrangements are set based on a lifetime limit (£1.25 million in the tax year 2014/15). An annual limit (£40,000 in the tax year 2014/15) also applies, although this may be increased by 'carrying forward' unused allowances from the previous three years.

An example of a flexible registered pension plan is the Self Invested Personal Pension (SIPP). SIPPs benefit from the same provisions relating to contributions, tax reliefs and, eligibility, but the difference relates to what type of investments the arrangements may comprise. Whereas a conventional personal pension generally involves the plan holder paying money to an insurance company for investment in an insurance policy, a SIPP allows the plan holder much greater freedom in what to invest in and for the plan to hold these investments directly. In particular, shares in an employing company may be held in a SIPP.

EMPLOYEE SHARE SCHEMES

17.4   Participants who receive shares on the exercise of an option granted under a tax-advantaged SAYE scheme or have shares released from a Share Incentive Plan (SIP) may transfer into a NISA up to £15,000 worth of shares (assuming no other NISA subscriptions are made in those years). The shares eligible to be transferred into a NISA include both quoted and unquoted shares. The investor has 90 days to transfer the shares into the NISA from the date of exercise in the case of an SAYE option and, in the case of a SIP, 90 days from the date the shares cease to be subject to the plan. The benefit of these arrangements is that, on sale of the shares, all future gains will be tax free. It would usually be disadvantageous for an employee participating in a SIP to direct that any shares are transferred into a NISA before the release date (generally the fifth anniversary of allocation) since this would involve a charge to income tax.

17.5   Where employees purchase 'Partnership Shares' under a SIP, although the provisions for a transfer into a NISA refer to shares being 'appropriated', HMRC accept that purchased shares are included in this definition.

17.6   Similarly, in relation to registered pension schemes, a participant's shares from a tax-advantaged SAYE scheme or SIP may be transferred into a registered pension scheme within 90 days from the date of exercise of the SAYE option or within 90 days from the date the shares cease to be subject to a SIP (FA 2004, s 195). The benefit of such a transfer is that income tax relief will be given on the market value of the shares transferred into the registered pension scheme, grossed up at the basic rate, with higher rate taxpayers also able claim further relief. Transfers must be limited to shares with a value not exceeding the registered pension scheme limits and employees must have UK earnings chargeable to income tax at least equal to the value of the shares transferred (FA 2004, s 190).

17.7   Where shares emerging from a tax-advantaged SAYE scheme or SIP are transferred into a NISA or registered pension scheme, it is necessary to value the shares for the purpose of the relevant limits in that tax year. In addition, the transfer into a NISA or registered pension scheme is deemed to be at market value, but the legislation does not confer relief from capital gains tax at that time. Where shares are transferred from a SIP there should be no CGT liability (as a result of the shares ceasing to be subject to the SIP at market value), but CGT on SAYE options is based on the market value of the shares on exercise. A potential CGT charge may, therefore, arise but this may be limited where employees are able to use the annual CGT exemption. All transfer valuations are based on the value at the date of transfer rather than the date of exercise or release. Quoted shares are valued by reference to the normal rules for the valuation of quoted shares in TCGA 1992, s 272. Unquoted shares are valued by agreement with Shares and Assets Valuation under the normal tax rules for valuing unquoted shares in TCGA 1992, s 273. Generally, a value will be agreed for a specified period although HMRC may adjust values in the light of circumstances which come to light at a later date.

Sponsored NISAs and SIPPs

17.8   It is not surprising that a number of listed companies have sponsored managers to offer NISAs and SIPPs, usually limited to the shares of the sponsoring company only, to their shareholders and employees. The object of the exercise is to reduce the manager's costs on the basis of the highest possible take-up. However, the interest in sponsored NISAs and SIPPs for shareholders has been lukewarm to say the least.

17.9   Given the large numbers of shares emerging from some all-employee share schemes, there is a much greater demand for sponsored NISAs and SIPPs from employees than from shareholders generally.

17.10   Cash subscriptions may, of course, be made by arranging for the plan manager to dispose of the investor's holding of shares, and then investing the sale proceeds in the plan. Unfortunately, the obligation on managers to allow a seven-day cooling-off period meant that the number of shares disposed of and the number acquired through the NISA rarely matches each other exactly.

Financial assistance – CA 2006, s 678

17.11   The Companies Act 2006 (CA 2006), s 678 prohibits the giving by a public company of financial assistance to a person directly or indirectly for the purposes of the acquisition of shares in that company. 'Financial assistance' means loans, indemnities and any other financial assistance given by a company if the net assets are thereby reduced to a material extent or if the company has no net assets.

17.12   In any sponsored NISA or SIPP, the company may incur part of the marketing and the ongoing management costs. Generally speaking, this will not be unlawful financial assistance even if the suppliers are paid direct rather than through the manager. The payments are unlikely to reduce the net assets of the company to any material extent. Moreover, if the sponsored NISA or SIPP is established to encourage or facilitate the acquisition of shares by employees, former employees and certain relatives, it may be possible to rely on the exemption for employees' share schemes in CA 2006, s 682(2)(b).

Regulated activities – FSMA 2000

17.13   Any sponsoring company must ensure its activities do not amount to 'regulated activities' within the meaning of the Financial Services and Markets

Act 2000 (FSMA 2000), s 19 unless the documentation is approved by the manager, who must be a person authorised under FSMA 2000. Arguably, the sponsoring company should do no more than appoint the manager perhaps in consideration for a one-off fee. Support of the plan manager by allowing advertising to be inserted in literature sent by the company to its shareholders has tended to be disregarded by regulatory authorities, but the companies may be exposing themselves to some risk on this. There is an exemption if the sponsored NISA or SIPP is an employees' share scheme.

Financial promotion – FSMA 2000

17.14   Usually the marketing material for any sponsored NISA or SIPP will be issued by the manager who will be an authorised person under FSMA 2000. Any reference in the director's report and accounts to the sponsored NISA or SIPP will be a financial promotion within the meaning of FSMA 2000, s 21. Such advertisements require the approval of an authorised person.

Chapter 18

Administration and Tax Returns

ADMINISTRATION

18.1   Before making an offer under a scheme, a company will need to consider the terms of its scheme rules to ensure that proposed grants are within the terms of the scheme. In particular, scheme rules normally provide for the timing of offers, the limits on the number of shares available individually and under the scheme, eligibility and the procedure for making the offers.

18.2   A form of board resolution for granting options is set out at **5.54** and **5.55** above (discretionary share option scheme), and at **12.47** above (SAYE scheme).

18.3   Forms of share option certificate are set out at **5.60** above (share option schemes) and at **12.50** above (SAYE schemes).

Maintaining registers

18.4   A register of options or interests under a SIP needs to be maintained. There are no statutory requirements relating to the information to be retained on the register although normally the information will be retained in a form suitable for completing the relevant annual scheme tax return. SIP trustees will also feature in the company's share register, usually maintained by the company's registrar.

18.5   In the case of an SAYE, most building societies and banks providing sharesave contracts will maintain an option register in addition to the details of sharesave contracts. Where SIP administration is outsourced, usually to the SIP trustee, the SIP trustee will maintain the register of interests in the SIP.

18.6   Any register is only as good as the systems established for providing relevant information. The company must always ensure details of employees who leave employment and the grounds of their leaving are passed to the relevant registrar or administrator as quickly as possible.

Dividends

18.7   In relation to SIPs, where cash dividends are payable, the registrar will need to ensure that the dividends and tax vouchers are mandated for payment to the SIP trustee on behalf of participants, and the SIP trustee will need to provide sufficient information to participants in order that any income tax liability may be accounted for (ITEPA 2003, Sch 2, para 80(3)).

Takeover offers, rights issues and other variations of share capital

18.8   The registrar will be involved in sending circulars to shareholders in the event of any takeover offer, reconstruction proposals, rights issue or other circular to shareholders. In the case of SIPs, the SIP trustee will be involved in distributing such circulars and will also need to seek directions from participants in relation to their shares.

Voting rights

18.9   In SIPs, there are a variety of ways in which the voting rights of participants, if any, may be dealt with, including taking instructions on how votes are cast on a poll or possibly appointing employees to attend and vote as proxy for the trustees.

ANNUAL RETURNS

Unapproved share schemes

Returns of share acquisitions

18.10   By virtue of ITEPA 2003, ss 421J and 421JA, each person who is a 'responsible person' is under a duty to provide HMRC with particulars of any 'reportable event' within 30 days of receiving from HMRC a notice requiring such information to be given, and in any event must submit an annual return to HMRC by 6 July in the tax year following that in which the reportable event takes place.

18.11   'Reportable events' (ITEPA 2003, s 421K) are:

(a)   the acquisition of:

    (i)   shares or securities;

    (ii)   an interest in shares or securities; or

    (iii)   a right to acquire shares or securities (ie grant of an option) available by reason of the employment of the acquirer or any other person;

(b)   a post-acquisition chargeable event under the restricted securities tax regime in ITEPA 2003, Pt 7, Ch 2;

(c)   a post-acquisition chargeable event under the convertible securities tax regime in ITEPA 2003, Pt 7, Ch 3;

(d) the doing of anything which gives rise to employment income under ITEPA 2003, s 446L (artificial enhancement of the market value of securities);

(e) an event which discharges a notional loan relating to securities under ITEPA 2003, s 446U (securities acquired for less than market value);

(f) a disposal of securities by virtue of which ITEPA 2003, Pt 7, Ch 3D applies (securities disposed of for more than market value);

(g) the receipt of a benefit which is taxable earnings under ITEPA 2003, s 447;

(h) the assignment or release of an option over securities acquired by reason of employment; and

(i) the receipt of any benefit in money or money's worth received in connection with an option over securities.

18.12 A 'responsible person' (ITEPA 2003, s 421L) in relation to a 'reportable event' is each of the following:

(a) the employer;

(b) any host employer of the employee (broadly any person who would normally be expected to operate PAYE on the earnings of the employer although not the employer);

(c) the person for whom the securities or option over securities were acquired (for instance, an EBT); and

(d) certain other intermediaries responsible for issuing the securities, e.g. a broker.

18.13 Each responsible person has an obligation to provide the relevant particulars until any one of the responsible persons has provided the particulars.

18.14 For tax years commencing 6 April 2014 and subsequently, HMRC will no longer issue a 'Form 42' to employers in relation to their filing obligations. Instead, the responsible person must register to use HMRC's online system (see **4.45** above). Although non-tax advantaged arrangements must be registered with HMRC, there is no requirement to register each plan or arrangement separately, and all information may be submitted to HMRC under the same reference.

18.15 The information to be returned to HMRC is prescribed by the format of the online annual returns, but includes details of all employees, the number and class of shares, the date of the option grant or acquisition price as the case may be and the prices and values involved. HMRC operates by reference to National Insurance numbers and these are best included wherever possible.

18.16 Where an overseas parent company grants options or awards over its own shares to an employee of its UK subsidiary, the overseas parent company is, strictly speaking, under an obligation to report the grant and to report the acquisition or transfer of the shares at the time of exercise or vesting as a 'responsible person' being the person from whom the securities were acquired. The UK subsidiary is also under an obligation to make a return in respect of the acquisition of the shares as a 'responsible person' being the employer in question.

18.17 In addition, a UK resident employee is liable to make a return of his option or share gains in the share schemes section of the 'Additional information' pages of the self-assessment tax return (supplementary pages SA101).

Returns of employee benefits

18.18 The employing company is under an obligation each year to make a return of all benefits provided for the employee. These returns are made on forms P9D and P11D by 6 July following the end of the tax year (Income Tax (Pay as You Earn) Regulations 2003 (SI 2003/2682), regulation 85).

18.19 None of the above obligations on the company whose shares are used, or the employing company, discharge the employee from his own responsibility to make a return of any income arising from shares and options on which he is chargeable to income tax.

Tax-advantaged schemes

Annual returns

18.20 For tax years commencing 6 April 2014 and subsequently, HMRC will no longer issue annual returns in respect of each of the tax-advantaged schemes (previously Form 39 for SIP, Form 34 for SAYE and Form 35 for CSOP). Instead, all annual returns must now be filed electronically through a process via the same online system used for the initial self-certification of the relevant arrangements on the establishment of the scheme (see **4.47–4.50** above). HMRC expect that most annual returns will be submitted by uploading an attachment to the online service which contains all of the required information.

18.21 Where a company has been taken over and options rolled over, HMRC will normally accept a return submitted by the acquiring company. In some cases this may be the only company available to make the return as the company which established the scheme may have been wound up.

Power to obtain further information

18.22 ITEPA 2003, s 421J(4) contains powers under which HMRC may by notice require any responsible person to give such information about a reportable event as it may specify in the notice. If there was no reportable event then the responsible person is required to state to that effect.

Online filing

18.23   In order to file electronically, users must be registered for the PAYE online service (see **4.49** above). Where users experience problems registering or submitting the necessary information online HMRC's online services helpdesk can be contacted on 0300 200 3600.

Chapter 19

Internationally Mobile Employees

INTRODUCTION

19.1   It is now common for multinational companies to extend their incentive arrangements to selected employees globally. Such companies may also seek to extend their all-employee schemes on a similar basis to employees wherever they are situated. Where grants or awards are made to such employees, the local tax and securities laws issues will need to be considered (see Chapter 20). However, consideration will also need to be given to how the participants in those schemes are taxed if they are to move between different jurisdictions once the grant or award has been made. As the UK is currently out of line with the recommendations of the OECD on the interpretation of double tax treaties, particularly in connection with share options, FA 2014 provides for changes to the way in which share options and awards held by internationally mobile employees are taxed, which will come into force from 6 April 2015. These changes follow the proposals set out in the Office of Tax Simplification's report on unapproved share schemes.

GENERAL TAXING PROVISIONS IN THE UK

19.2   Earnings from an employment are taxed by reference to rules set out in the Income Tax (Earnings and Pensions) Act 2003 (ITEPA 2003), Pt 2. 'Taxable earnings' includes general earnings in money or money's worth as well as specific employment income (which includes amounts treated as earnings in respect of services and securities options and restricted securities under ITEPA 2003, Pt 7).

Shares as general earnings

19.3   The acquisition of shares by an individual as part of his earnings as a director or employee is chargeable to tax as general earnings on any undervalue or benefit received (*Weight v Salmon (1935) 19 TC 174*). If, however, the employee is not subject to UK tax when the shares are acquired (even if the share award had been made whilst resident in the UK) then the local jurisdiction's taxing provisions are likely to apply.

19.4   Where shares are acquired under a long term incentive plan, HMRC may seek to tax all or a portion of the value of shares received on the basis

362

that HMRC is able to attribute a portion of the value of those shares to being 'for' a tax year in which the employee was resident in the UK. This is because the provisions of ITEPA 2003, s 16, which follows the decision in *Bray v Best [1989] STC 159*, provide that general earnings for a particular period, even if received in a later period, will be taxable in the earlier period. HMRC takes the view that a long term incentive award is earned across the tax years comprised in the vesting period.

19.5 There are also exceptions to this general rule on the taxation share acquisitions in relation to share options and other acquisitions of securities where the provisions of ITEPA 2003, Pt 7 apply.

Share options

19.6 ITEPA 2003, Pt 7, Ch 5, which deals with the taxation of securities options, does not currently apply to an option over securities if, at the time of grant, the earnings from the employment were not general earnings to which ITEPA 2003, s 15 applies, that is to say, earnings for a year in which the optionholder was resident in the UK for tax purposes (ITEPA 2003, s 474). This means that the acquisition of shares or securities pursuant to any option will, at least in part, be taxed under Chapter 5 if the employee is resident in the UK in the year of grant of the option, even if the employee leaves the UK following grant.

19.7 From 6 April 2015, ITEPA 2003, s 474 will be revoked, both for new and also existing options. This means that the exemption from UK income tax on option gains where the individual was not UK resident at grant will be removed. Instead, in circumstances where the optionholder is either not resident in the UK throughout the period from grant to vesting (or, if earlier, the date of any chargeable event) or is, in any tax year, subject to the remittance basis for taxation, the tax treatment will be governed by ITEPA 2003, Pt 2, Ch 5A.

Restricted securities

19.8 ITEPA 2003, Pt 7, Ch 2, which applies to tax restricted securities at the time that restrictions are lifted, does not currently apply to restricted securities acquired by an employee who, at the time of acquisition, was not resident in the UK for tax purposes (ITEPA 2003, s 421E).

19.9 Currently, whether or not the acquisition of the securities was subject to tax on acquisition, provided that the employee was resident in the UK at that time, there are potential income tax charges in the UK on the lifting of restrictions even if the employee has left the UK following acquisition. Conversely, where an employee holding restricted securities moves to the UK, the benefit of the lifting of restrictions on those securities is currently not subject to UK tax.

19.10   From 6 April 2015, ITEPA 2003, s 421E will be revoked both for new and also existing restricted securities. This means that the exemption from UK income tax on the benefit of the lifting of restrictions where the individual was not UK resident at the time the securities were acquired will be removed. Instead, in circumstances where the individual is either not resident in the UK throughout the period from the date on which the shares were acquired to the date of the lifting of restrictions (or, if earlier, the date of any other chargeable event) or was, in any tax year, subject to the remittance basis for taxation, the tax treatment will be governed by ITEPA 2003, Pt 2, Ch 5A

RESIDENCE AND DOMICILE

19.11   An employee's liability to UK tax is, and will continue to be, based on two key concepts, that of residence and domicile.

19.12   Since 6 April 2013, there has been a series of statutory tests to determine whether an individual is resident in the UK in any one tax year (from 6 April to 5 April) for tax purposes (FA 2013, s 218 and Sch 45). In order to be treated as UK resident, the individual must meet at least one of the 'automatic UK tests' and none of the 'automatic overseas tests'. The tests are complex, although the test most individuals will meet in being treated as UK resident is likely to continue to be that of being present in the UK for 183 days or more in that tax year.

19.13   The rules relating to residence are complex and further guidance can be found in HMRC booklet RDR1 which can be downloaded from the HMRC website.

19.14   Domicile is a general law concept which is distinct from residency and nationality. An employee's domicile will generally have derived from his or her parentage, although it is possible for the employee to have chosen a domicile if he or she can show that there is an intention to reside permanently or indefinitely in a particular jurisdiction.

SHARE OPTIONS

Tax treatment to 5 April 2015

19.15   Where an employee receives the grant of a share option there are no income tax consequences as a result of ITEPA 2003, Pt 7, Ch 5. On the exercise of that option, or other 'chargeable event', until 5 April 2015, the full gain is subject to income tax under ITEPA 2003, s 476 where the optionholder was UK resident at grant (and this will generally be the case irrespective of the employee's residency status at the time of exercise), but is not subject to tax in the UK if the optionholder was not UK resident at grant.

19.16   If an employee who was UK resident at grant is no longer resident in the UK when a chargeable event occurs and the employee is resident in a jurisdiction with which a double taxation treaty is in place, the employee will be able to make a claim that the UK tax charge is restricted to the amount which relates to the UK employment. This is referred to as 'time apportionment' and essentially apportions the taxable amount based on the period of time that the employee was working in the UK between the date of grant and, generally, the date on which the option vests (although in relation to the UK/US double taxation treaty, apportionment is based on the time period between grant and exercise).

19.17   If the employee is no longer resident in the UK when a chargeable event occurs and the employee is resident in a jurisdiction with which a double taxation treaty is *not* in place, the UK tax charge will not be restricted by time apportionment and the employee's claim for relief from double taxation will be limited to approaching the taxing authorities in the jurisdiction of residence.

Tax treatment from 6 April 2015

19.18   From 6 April 2015, the position outlined at **19.14–19.16** will change, both for new and existing share options.

19.19   The provisions of ITEPA 2003, Pt 2, Ch 5B will apply if, during the 'relevant period' (for share options, the period from the date of grant to the date on which the option first becomes exercisable):

(a)   the optionholder is taxable on the remittance basis (see **19.28** below) at any time;

(b)   the optionholder is not resident in the UK for the whole of a tax year; or

(c)   there is a split year in relation to the individual in respect of which any part of the relevant period falls within the overseas part of that split year.

19.20   ITEPA 2003, Pt 2, Ch 5B provides for the apportionment of the optionholder's gain on exercise, as calculated under ITEPA 2003, ss 478–479 into:

(a)   taxable specific income, which is subject to UK tax, and relates to the period during which the individual is UK tax resident (other than where the individual is taxed on a remittance basis);

(b)   chargeable foreign securities income, which is taxable in the UK on a remittance basis (see **19.34–19.37** below); and

(c)   unchargeable foreign securities income, which is outside the scope of UK taxation, and relates to the period during which the individual is not UK tax resident and has no UK duties.

19.21   Apportionment of the optionholder's gain on exercise, is done based on the number of days within the relevant period that fall within each of these categories as a proportion of the number of days within the relevant period.

RESTRICTED SECURITIES

Tax treatment to 5 April 2015

19.22   ITEPA 2003, Pt 7, Ch 2 applies where the employee is resident in the UK on the acquisition of the restricted securities. Where such an employee receives securities subject to restrictions there may be no, or a reduced, income tax charge. On the lifting of those restrictions, or other 'chargeable event', an income tax charge may then apply. As with share options, this will generally be the case irrespective of the employee's residency status at that time. Where the employee was not resident in the UK on grant, there will be no tax in the UK where restrictions on shares are lifted, even if the individual has become resident in the UK since acquisition.

19.23   If, at the time that restrictions are lifted or there is an alternative chargeable event, the employee, who was resident in the UK on acquisition, has become resident outside of the UK, then the tax treatment will currently depend on whether the jurisdiction in question is one with which the UK has entered into a double taxation treaty.

19.24   If the employee is no longer resident in the UK when restrictions are lifted or there is an alternative chargeable event and the employee is resident in a jurisdiction with which a double taxation treaty is in place, the employee will be able to make a claim that the UK tax charge is restricted to the amount which relates to the UK employment. Prior to 6 April 2008, HMRC did not accept that time apportionment would apply to restricted securities, as the view was taken that the securities were 'earned' by the time of acquisition. Following the changes to the rules on residency in FA 2008, however, HMRC accept that time apportionment may apply to the 'untaxed proportion' of the restricted securities between the date of acquisition and the date of the lifting of restrictions or other chargeable event.

19.25   If the employee is no longer resident in the UK when restrictions are lifted or there is an alternative chargeable event and the employee is resident in a jurisdiction with which a double taxation treaty is *not* in place, the UK tax charge will not be restricted by time apportionment and the employee's claim for relief from double taxation will be limited to approaching the taxing authorities in the jurisdiction of residence.

Tax treatment from 6 April 2015

19.26   From 6 April 2015, the position outlined at **19.22–19.25** will change, both for new and existing restricted securities.

19.27   The provisions of ITEPA 2003, Pt 2, Ch 5B will apply in the same way as set out at **19.19–19.21** with the benefit of the lifting of restrictions, as calculated under ITEPA 2003, s 428, apportioned based on a 'relevant period' which, for restricted securities, runs from date on which the restricted securities are acquired to the date of the relevant chargeable event.

DOMICILE AND REMITTANCE

19.28 Individuals who are non-domiciled in the UK are able to choose whether they wish to be taxed on their overseas income and gains on an 'arising' basis (ie all income and gains to be subject to UK tax when the amounts arise) or on a 'remittance' basis (ie subject to UK tax only when remitted to the UK).

Tax treatment to 5 April 2015

19.29 ITEPA 2003, Pt 2, Ch 5A currently deals with the taxation of employment-related securities on a remittance basis. Where an employee receives overseas income which counts as employment income under ITEPA 2003, Pt 7, Chs 2, 3 or 3C to 5 (excluding ITEPA 2003, s 446UA), and the employee is taxed on a remittance basis during any part of the 'relevant period' (essentially the period from the grant of the option/acquisition of restricted securities to the date of the chargeable event), then the provisions of ITEPA 2003, s 41A will apply such that, instead of the whole amount of the employment income being taxable in the UK at that time, only that part which relates to UK duties is so taxable and the remainder will be subject to the remittance basis. This untaxed amount is referred to as 'foreign securities income'.

19.30 The assessment of the amount of foreign securities income will be important from the perspective of the operation of PAYE where the securities are readily convertible assets as PAYE will apply to the amount of the employment income received, less the amount assessed to be foreign securities income.

19.31 The provisions relating to foreign securities income are limited in scope as they will only apply to employees who are non-UK domiciled, have duties which are performed outside the UK and who receive securities which are not themselves received or used in the UK. HMRC considers that all shares in UK companies are 'used' in the UK and so would be immediately remitted on acquisition.

Tax treatment from 6 April 2015

19.32 From 6 April 2015, the provisions of ITEPA 2003, Pt 2, Ch 5A will be replaced by the new ITEPA 2003, Pt 2, Ch 5B outlined at **19.19–19.21**.

19.33 ITEPA 2003, s 41H sets out how to determine the proportion of an individual's foreign securities income which is chargeable to tax in the UK if it is remitted.

19.34   Foreign securities income may be 'chargeable' if:

(a)   the individual is taxed on the remittance basis (see **19.28** above);

(b)   the individual does not meet the requirement of ITEPA 2003, s 26A (see **19.36** below);

(c)   the relevant employment is with a foreign employer; and

(d)   the duties of the relevant employment are performed wholly outside the UK.

19.35   Foreign securities income may also be 'chargeable' if:

(a)   the individual is taxed on the remittance basis (see **19.28** above);

(b)   the individual does meet the requirement of ITEPA 2003, s 26A (see **19.36** below);

(c)   some or all of the duties of the relevant employment are performed outside the UK.

If any of the duties of the relevant employment are performed in the UK, then there is an apportionment on a 'just and reasonable' basis such that only the proportion that relates to duties performed outside the UK will be classed as chargeable foreign securities income and the balance will be taxable specific income and taxed in the UK.

19.36   ITEPA 2003, s 26A sets out a three-year test to apply to UK resident taxpayers who are taxed on a remittance basis. The test will be met if:

(a)   the individual was not resident in the UK for tax purposes throughout the three previous tax years;

(b)   the individual was UK resident in the previous tax year, but not during the three tax years prior to that;

(c)   the individual was UK resident in the previous two tax years, but not during the three tax years prior to that; or

(d)   the individual was not UK resident in the previous tax year, was UK resident in the year before that, but was not UK resident during the three tax years prior to that.

TAX-ADVANTAGED SHARE PLANS

19.37   The legislation governing SAYE schemes and SIPs requires that all UK resident eligible employees must be invited to participate in those schemes. The legislation also provides that other categories of eligible employee may also be invited to participate, and so it is often the most simple route for companies offering such schemes to invite all employees on the UK payroll to participate without having to assess the residency status of those employees.

Chapter 20

Cross-border Share Plans

INTRODUCTION

20.1   Many multinational groups extend their long-term incentive plans and share option schemes to selected employees in their overseas subsidiaries, and it is now common for such companies to look to increase employee participation by extending their all-employee share schemes cross-border. Companies considering extending their share plans cross-border will need to address a number of issues, including the tax position of employees and local subsidiaries, securities laws, exchange control, employment laws and consultation, data protection and translation. In relation to the UK tax-advantaged schemes, there are also particular issues to be aware of in relation to extending such schemes to overseas employees and where a non-UK company seeks to establish a scheme under ITEPA 2003, Schs 2, 3 or 4.

EXTENDING UK TAX-ADVANTAGED PLANS TO OVERSEAS EMPLOYEES

20.2   ITEPA 2003, Pt 7 does not exclude participation by overseas employees in either of the two types of tax-advantaged option scheme or the SIP.

Company share option plans

20.3   There are few limitations to extending a CSOP to non-UK employees, save that the limit on the value of the shares available is identical for both UK and non-UK participants, namely, £30,000 worth of shares. There may be tax benefits for employees who are granted such options in connection with UK duties, although there are unlikely to be any other benefits for employees who are not UK resident at grant (or, from 6 April 2015, who do not become UK resident during the vesting period). Most discretionary share options for non-UK employees will therefore be granted under an unapproved scheme or under an addendum designed to take into account local legal requirements, which may also provide tax benefits to such employees under local lawand removes the restrictions which are only necessary for approval under ITEPA 2003, Sch 4.

Savings-related share option schemes

20.4   A UK SAYE scheme has three attractive features for UK employees:

(a)   a tax-free discount in the option price;

(b)   a tax-free bonus under the savings contract; and

(c)   tax-free gains on the exercise of options.

In virtually all overseas jurisdictions the bonus under UK sharesave contracts and any gains accruing on the exercise of an option (as distinct from the sale of the shares) will be subject to income tax. Although certain jurisdictions impose a tax charge on the discount on the grant of an option, this is not generally the case.

Exchange rate risk

20.5   Overseas employees who participate in a UK SAYE scheme are exposed to an exchange risk. Savings must be paid into a UK sterling savings account. If the exchange rate rises before the exercise of the option, it may be more attractive to take the bonus rather than the shares. Alternatively, if the exchange rate has fallen, it may wipe out any benefits to the employee in that, after conversion into local currency, the realised proceeds may be less than the savings. These are extreme examples, but clearly the eventual gain made by overseas employees may be substantially distorted by currency fluctuations.

UK savings accounts

20.6   Strictly speaking, savings contributions in connection ith a UK SAYE scheme must be deducted from pay each month or week and paid into a sharesave account with a UK bank, building society or a European financial institution. Where overseas employees, in particular ex-pats, are paid in UK sterling this does not cause any great difficulty but obviously the deduction may need to vary from month to month where salary is paid in foreign currency.

Overseas savings legislation

20.7   There are no equivalent schemes to the UK SAYE scheme overseas except the Irish savings-related share option scheme and, arguably, the US stock purchase plan under s 423 of the Internal Revenue Code, but even that does not offer any beneficial savings medium.

Common overseas scheme modifications

20.8   Many of the companies which have extended their sharesave schemes overseas have done so by establishing unapproved share option schemes which provide for regular monthly savings to be made by deduction from local currency pay and held in appropriate investment media (but not necessarily a UK sharesave account) or in a choice of currencies. This removes the difficulty for companies in requiring employees to save in an inappropriate investment media or in a particular currency which may result in the erosion of benefits due to adverse exchange movements.

Expats

20.9   As far as expats are concerned, they will usually have UK bank accounts and it should be possible for them to make arrangements for deductions to be made each month by direct debit into the sharesave account.

Share incentive plans

20.10   Non-UK resident employees may participate in a SIP on the same terms as UK residents, although they need not be included if the company so wishes. Generally, the lack of tax benefits in relation to non-UK resident employees makes participation unattractive, although where free and/or matching shares are made available this could be a factor in extending participation. Often companies will establish an unapproved addendum to the SIP in order to allow overseas employees the ability to participate whilst removing the restrictions which are only necessary under ITEPA 2003, Sch 2.

Similar advantages to UK employees

20.11   A UK SIP has one major tax advantage for UK employees, namely, the avoidance of any tax on the value of the shares received where the employee leaves the shares with the plan trustees for the full five years. Tax benefits for all-employee schemes are growing in popularity around the globe. There are schemes offering similar tax advantages in a number of jurisdictions including the Republic of Ireland (profit sharing scheme), France (free shares scheme, requiring a four-year restricted period from grant, often a two-year vesting period followed by a two-year holding period), Germany (although the limit on free shares is relatively low) and, to a certain extent, in the US under s 401 of the Internal Revenue Code.

Employer contributions

20.12   Employers running overseas schemes will normally be entitled to a similar tax deduction for the cost of any contributions to the trustees to purchase shares for its own employees as under a UK SIP.

Separate offshore trusts

20.13   The normal solution to extending SIPs to overseas employees is to arrange for an unapproved SIP trust to be established, usually offshore, so as to avoid falling within the UK tax net. An unapproved SIP gives greater flexibility in the determination of the distributable pool, the identification of the eligible employees for any particular offer (nomination may even be restricted to individual employees) and greater flexibility in the determination of the restrictions on sale of the shares and avoidance of the complications of operating PAYE. A single trust may be established to cover a number of schemes although some companies have established a separate trust or sub-trust for each participating company. The trust will normally be established as a discretionary trust under which the employees have no entitlement to the shares until their release so as to avoid the premature tax charge in some countries on the appropriation, rather than release, of the shares. Under most overseas employees' share schemes, the period of restriction on sales is normally two or three years, to tie in with local tax treatment.

UK TAX-ADVANTAGED ADDENDA TO OVERSEAS SCHEMES

20.14   Any participation by a UK resident employee in an employees' share scheme established by an overseas parent will normally be on 'unapproved' terms so far as UK tax is concerned. However, an overseas parent may be prepared to adapt its scheme so that the conditions for tax-advantaged status of the scheme are satisfied, or it may be prepared to establish a separate UK tax-advantaged scheme. A separate scheme largely based on an existing scheme of the parent is commonly described as a 'sub-scheme' if only to acknowledge that it is a modification of the existing scheme. In practice, the most common types of sub-scheme have been UK CSOPs based on US share option plans and UK matching offers (under a SIP) based on matching offer arrangements which are common in US multinational share plans.

20.15   Many US share plans contain a power to establish appropriate arrangements for overseas employees. This will normally be accepted as giving sufficient power to establish a separate UK sub-plan. A certified resolution of the Remuneration Committee of the overseas company will normally be treated as satisfactory evidence of the establishment of the sub-scheme.

20.16   HMRC normally prefers dealing with an appropriate UK resident. A UK subsidiary of an overseas parent which establishes a tax-advantaged scheme will therefore often be asked to act as its agent for dealing with HMRC.

ESTABLISHMENT OF SCHEMES FOR
OVERSEAS EMPLOYEES

20.17   Where a UK company proposes the establishment of an employees' share scheme for overseas employees, account must still be taken of all the normal requirements which apply to the establishment of a scheme for UK employees, in particular the requirements of the Listing Rules and the ABI

Guidelines. In addition, a UK company will need to take account of the local regulations on securities laws, exchange control and tax in making any offer.

20.18   The Listing Rules require all schemes of UK domestic companies (including overseas major subsidiaries) involving the issue of new shares to be approved by shareholders of the UK company. However, where a UK company proposes the establishment of a series of schemes for overseas subsidiaries substantially based on an existing UK scheme but modified to take account of local tax, exchange control and securities law requirements, then the directors of the UK company may obtain a general authority to establish such overseas schemes without specific shareholders' approval in each case (Listing Rules, rule 13.8.13).

20.19   The ABI Guidelines are intended to apply to all companies in which their members hold shares and, therefore, shares quoted on overseas stock exchanges are in theory covered, although in practice only UK listed companies will comply with the ABI Guidelines. The ABI expects any new shares which are allocated under any overseas scheme to be counted against the scheme limits in the UK.

20.20   An appropriate form of shareholders' resolution authorising directors to establish overseas schemes similar to any UK scheme is as follows:

'The Directors be hereby authorised to establish arrangements for non-UK employees to acquire shares in the Company which, although substantially based on any existing scheme of the Company, are modified to meet any relevant local securities law, tax and exchange control requirements provided that any such arrangements which are established for overseas employees will not be materially more favourable for such employees than the corresponding arrangements for UK employees, and any shares allocated under such arrangements will be counted against the limits in the existing schemes on the maximum number of shares which may be newly issued. In addition, no such arrangements will be established using the shares in a subsidiary of the Company'.

20.21   An overseas all-employee share scheme which uses only existing shares supplied through an EBT will not normally need to be submitted for shareholders' approval.

OVERSEAS LAWS AND THE MAKING OF SHARE OFFERS TO OVERSEAS EMPLOYEES

20.22   Overseas laws need to be taken into account in any share offer made to overseas employees. Any company proposing an offer of shares to overseas employees should seek specific local advice before making any offer. The main points to be considered are:

(a)   securities laws:

- whether there is an obligation to file any prospectus or listing document with the local regulatory authorities before making any share offer and, if so, the nature of the information to be filed;

- whether there is an obligation to supply any particular information to employees at the time of making any share offer;

(b)   taxation and social security contributions:

- whether there are liabilities to tax or social security which arise for the employee or employer in respect of participation in the scheme;

- whether any local subsidiary is liable to withhold tax or social security in any circumstances;

- whether any local subsidiary is obliged to report any taxable income or gains to the regulatory authorities;

(c)   exchange control/central bank requirements:

- whether there are any restrictions on the holding of foreign securities or on the remittance abroad of funds for the purchase of foreign securities;

- whether the share certificates of foreign securities must be deposited with any bank or other person;

- whether there are any obligations on the repatriation of gains from investments in foreign securities;

(d)   employment law: whether there are any employment law requirements (such as an obligation to obtain the local works council approval or for employee consultation); and

(e)   data protection law: whether there are any restrictions on the passing of personal details, particularly computer data, to a non-employer, in connection with any share offer.

Securities laws

20.23   Within the EU, securities laws are to a greater extent aligned as a result of the implementation of the EU Prospectus Directive, although local regulators may adopt different interpretations of the requirements. A number of overseas countries outside of the EU also now accept the view that an offer of shares to employees should not require the filing of any document with the regulatory authorities, although this is not always the case. There are those who, like the EU, have introduced specific relaxations, particularly where the number of employees is limited. An example is offers into the US which, under Rule 701 of the Securities Act of 1933, are allowed each year within certain limits.

Taxation

20.24   Generally speaking, earnings derived from shares and share options will be subject to income tax in most countries, although there are still some jurisdictions which impose corporate taxes or capital taxes in relation to share benefits. There are certain countries which provide comparable tax benefits to those offered under the UK tax-advantaged schemes, but this needs to be considered on a country-by-country basis. The main issue for a local employer will be whether there are any withholding obligations which arise as a result of their employees' participation in share plans, to ensure that there is sufficient information available in order to deal with such withholdings, and a mechanism in place to allow for a sale of shares on behalf of the employee if pay is insufficient to deduct the full amount of the tax due.

Exchange control/central bank requirements

20.25 Exchange controls have been dismantled in many countries over the past two decades and are now rarely a hindrance to the operation of schemes. There are, however, some notable exceptions including South Africa, India and China.

OTHER ADMINISTRATIVE MATTERS TO BE TAKEN INTO ACCOUNT

Support of local management

20.26 Any UK group which makes a share or share option offer to employees of an overseas subsidiary will need the support of local management to communicate and handle the operation of the scheme locally. It is usually sensible to appoint a 'local coordinator' as a point of contact for the UK company in handling the offer.

Communications

20.27 Where an offer is made available to local employees, it may be necessary to translate all employee communication materials and application forms into the local language. This is usually best done by providing a UK template of the material and leaving it for local management to translate and print locally.

Pricing of offers

20.28 Local employees will rarely have UK sterling bank accounts and any remittances to the UK will need to be converted. Normally, the parent company will prescribe an appropriate rate of exchange for any offer and the local coordinator will arrange for local currency payments to be converted into UK sterling before they are remitted electronically to the designated branch of the UK parent company's bankers. Any currency risk may be borne by either the local company or the UK parent as may be agreed.

Offshore currency funds

20.29   A number of companies with share option schemes have established arrangements whereby employees can save the monies to exercise the option in any one of a number of possible currencies. This enables employees to switch between currencies as they consider appropriate during the option period.

Option schemes

20.30   The exercise of an option will involve the completion of notices of exercise and the remittance of the relevant funds to the UK company. Again, the local subsidiary may be able to assist in these arrangements.

Rights of shareholders

20.31   The articles of association of many companies provide that there is no obligation on a UK company to send notices of meeting to overseas members, although in practice most public companies do so. As far as dividends are concerned, these will be paid in the normal way.

US EMPLOYEES

Option schemes

20.32   Many UK public companies have established share option schemes for US employees. These usually provide for non-qualifying options in respect of which the optionholder is chargeable to US taxes on the exercise of the option, but the local employing company may be entitled to a deduction for the option gains. Other schemes for US employees may provide for the grant of incentive stock options which confer relief from income tax on certain option gains, but no deduction for the employing company. The favourable tax treatment of US incentive stock options is only available where the following conditions are satisfied:

(a)   the plan is approved at a meeting of the parent company shareholders;

(b)   the total number of shares that may be issued under the plan is specified;

(c)   eligibility to participate in the plan is specified;

(d)   certain alterations must be approved by shareholders;

(e)   options are granted within ten years of the earlier of the date of the plan and shareholders' approval of the plan;

(f)   options are not capable of exercise more than ten years after grant;

(g)   the exercise price is not less than the market value of a share at the time of grant;

(h)   the value of the shares in respect of which the option first becomes exercisable in a calendar year is no more than US$100,000.

It will be noted that as shareholders' approval is needed for the grant of incentive stock options, the establishment of such a scheme under a general directors' authority to establish schemes for overseas employees may rule out this type of arrangement.

Section 409A

20.33   Section 409A of the Internal Revenue Code was introduced under the American Jobs Creation Act and governs the taxation of non-qualified deferred compensation plans. The provisions significantly limit how and when participants are able to defer compensation under non-qualified deferred compensation plans, which include share and share option plans. If a share plan does not comply with the provisions of s 409A (and is not exempt) then tax charges will be imposed earlier than anticipated and will also be increased by 20 per cent. If this tax is late or underpaid because s 409A applies, interest will also be charged.

20.34   Section 409A will also affect US taxpayers participating in UK share plans due to the application of US taxes to US citizens irrespective of tax residency. As a result, it is important to ensure that the rules of all share plans in which any US citizen (wherever situate) participates or may participate comply with the provisions of s 409A.

20.35   Unlike US tax-favoured plans, there is no exemption for UK tax-advantaged share plans which may, therefore, be classified as deferred compensation under s 409A.

Company share option plans

20.36   Share options with an exercise price equal to at least 'fair market value' at grant are exempted from s 409A. Fair market value is defined in s 409A for these purposes. CSOP options are likely, therefore, to be exempt from s 409A, as ITEPA 2003, Sch 4 requires that these options must be granted with an exercise price at least equal to market value at grant (as determined in accordance with TCGA 1992 and HMRC practice). Although this will generally be the case, plan rules which provide for an average of quoted values over a period before grant may not comply with the provisions of s 409A.

Enterprise Management Incentives

20.37   EMI options may be exempt from s 409A unless they have an exercise price at below the market value on grant.

Savings-related share options

20.38   Sharesave options will generally have an exercise price below market value and so will not be exempt from s 409A. However, provided that the exercise rights under the SAYE scheme are limited, no penalty should arise under s 409A. HMRC accept that the SAYE rules may provide that an SAYE option may only be exercised by a US taxpayer within the normal exercise period specified in the rules or, if shorter, the period of two and a half months after the end of the year in which the option first becomes exercisable. It may, alternatively, be possible to operate a US stock purchase plan under s 423 of the Internal Revenue Code in place of a sharesave scheme and this would be automatically exempt from the deferred compensation provisions.

Share incentive plans

20.39   SIP awards could be affected if there is an offer of free or matching shares, although there may not be a deferral of tax for US purposes in relation to such offers to which s 409A would apply.

Unapproved share plans

20.40   Provided that there is a 'substantial risk of forfeiture' which applies to share awards, the arrangements are unlikely to be caught by s 409A provided that the plan does not provide for the delivery of shares later than the end of the period of two and a half months following the end of the taxable year in which the right is no longer subject to the substantial risk of forfeiture.

Offshore trusts

20.41   If an offshore EBT is to be used in connection with share awards to a US taxpayer, the trust's assets may be subject to s 409A and treated as being transferred to the US taxpayer at an earlier stage than anticipated. This is not the case if the employee is working in the jurisdiction in which the trust is located, but this is unlikely to be the case for most EBTs.

EMPLOYEE BENEFIT TRUSTS

20.42   There are also a number of other jurisdictions which impose tax charges on employee benefit trusts used to deliver shares to employees, and so part of the due diligence exercise for a company extending its share schemes globally is to ensure that the company's arrangements for delivering shares to employees comply with local laws.

20.43   In France, trusts which have a French tax-resident settlor or which include French tax-resident employees as potential beneficiaries, or which hold assets located in France (which would include French company shares), are subject to reporting requirements, and potentially wealth tax charges. The French tax authorities have confirmed, however, that trusts established for the management of employee savings plans or employee shareholding schemes are exempt as trusts created by a company 'for their own account'. Most standard EBTs will, therefore, be outside the reporting and wealth tax provisions, but more broad-based trusts may need to be assessed on a case-by-case basis.

20.44   Canadian non-resident trust rules may result in filing obligations and potential tax liabilities for non-Canadian trusts under which Canadian tax-residents benefit. These rules deem the trust to be resident in Canada for tax purposes and charge to tax the proportion of the trust's world-wide income and gains that relates, provided that the necessary election is filed, to benefits provided to Canadian tax-residents. It is also possible for the trust to elect for the tax charge to arise on the Canadian employer in order to take advantage of lower corporation tax rates.

Index

[References are to paragraph number and appendices]